California
Rivers and Streams

California Rivers and Streams

The Conflict between Fluvial Process and Land Use

Jeffrey F. Mount

ILLUSTRATIONS BY
Janice C. Fong

UNIVERSITY OF CALIFORNIA PRESS
Berkeley   Los Angeles   London

University of California Press
Berkeley and Los Angeles, California

University of California Press
London, England

Copyright © 1995 by
The Regents of the University of California

Library of Congress Cataloging-in-Publication Data
Mount, Jeffrey F., 1954–
    California rivers and streams: the conflict between fluvial
process and land use / Jeffrey F. Mount: illustrations by Janice C.
Fong.
        p.   cm.
    Includes bibliographical references (p.   –   ) and index.
    ISBN 0–520–20192–2 (cloth: alk. paper). — ISBN 0–520–20250–3
(paper: alk. paper)
    1. Rivers—California.   2. Land use—California.   I. Title.
GB1225.C3M68   1995
333.91′62′09794—dc20   95–10822
                                                                          CIP

Printed in the United States of America

1 2 3 4 5 6 7 8 9

The paper used in this publication meets the minimum
requirements of American National Standard for Information
Sciences—Permanence of Paper for Printed Library Materials,
ANSI Z39.48–1984 ⊗

Dedicated to the memory of Ethel Daugherty and Barbara Sylvain,
who opened the doors so that I might step through

CONTENTS

PREFACE

The rivers of California transport the state's most valuable and hotly contested natural resource, water. While they do this, they periodically inundate our homes, erode our property, and deposit sediment in our backyards, forming one of the state's most pernicious natural hazards. Rivers also act as the state's great septic system, carrying away the effluent of our agricultural and urban areas. For the past one hundred fifty years the state of California has been damming, diverting, polluting, and reshaping its rivers to supply the needs of an exploding population and economy. This forceful reconfiguration and redistribution has, at the close of the twentieth century, brought the state to an important crossroads. Business as usual with our number one resource will no longer be acceptable; major changes are in the offing, and we have to alter the way we manage water and our rivers.

Despite the fact that the lives of all Californians are affected in some way by rivers, as a population we remain largely uninformed about, or simply uninterested in, river processes and their interactions with various land uses. To illustrate, between large flooding events, we tend to view rivers as static channels that simply convey water and house fish. When floods come and the rivers go about the business of transporting runoff and sediment and sculpting the landscape, we seem to be genuinely surprised at the results. During the copyediting stage of this book, the floods of January 1995 were leaving their mark across the entire state of California. Widespread flooding in *both* northern and southern California (an unusual occurrence) led to millions of dollars in property damage, the displacement of thousands of families, and the seemingly annual westward migration of the Federal Emergency Management Agency. What seemed lost in all the discussion of human suffering and the efforts to clean up from the floods was the fact that we Californians are, quite simply, asking for it. We deliberately choose to build our businesses and homes on this state's floodplains, despite overwhelming evidence that eventually we are going to be flooded. We log, mine, farm, and pave our landscape in a way that often increases the magnitude and frequency of floods. And once flooded, we demand expensive engineering solutions that ultimately cannot prevent future flooding or, in some cases, actually exacerbates the problem. Moreover, here in California we have become perennial mendicants, waiting for federal largess to save us from our myriad disasters and allowing us to rebuild directly in harm's way. Worse still, as an inherently litigious society, we are quick to point the finger of blame at others for our own poor choices. In all of this, were we simply to have paid more attention to rivers as dynamic geomorphic systems that are easier to work with, rather than against, we might have spared ourselves much of the calamity that marks the beginning of 1995. It is folly, but it is indicative of the way we view this state's rivers.

This book examines the way rivers work in California and the manner in which our land use practices interact with dynamic river processes. At the outset, it should be noted that this book does *not* attempt to solve the problems that face California's rivers. This is a nearly impossible task better left to the real experts in the field. Rather, in an act of literary cowardice, this book attempts to achieve two more modest, but closely related, goals. First, for those interested in rivers simply as geomorphic "systems," Part I provides an overview of the physical and biological processes that shape the rivers and watersheds of California. The basic principles of hydraulics and fluvial geomorphology along with the driving forces of climate and plate tectonics are reviewed and applied directly to the understanding of California's diverse and dynamic river systems. Part II builds on this foundation by evaluating selected land use practices that affect, or are affected by, California's rivers. These examples are used to reinforce the understanding of river processes and demonstrate the consequences of not paying attention to basic principles when making land use decisions. In this regard, the book is a case study. It is not an exhaustive look at all of the problems facing California's rivers today. Rather, it is a vehicle for understanding how these rivers worked prior to the arrival of Europeans as compared to how they are working now. Most important, this is *not* a how-to book for land use planners and engineers. There are no recipes for solving land use problems, no designs for mitigating impacts. This book is intended to educate, not to dictate, and, through education, to build appreciation of the state's rivers and provide a vehicle for participating in the debate about their future.

The benchmark audience for this book are the students who populate my Rivers of California: Geology and Land Use class taught at the University of California, Davis. This is a General Education class intended to appeal to sophomores and juniors with only basic backgrounds in the physical sciences. Beyond this benchmark audience, it is anticipated that this book will appeal to those who, for a variety of reasons, are interested in how rivers work and how we interact with them. Natural historians who may have wondered why rivers seem to behave in such chaotic, but seemingly predictable, fashion will find answers here. The same goes for fishermen, rafters, kayakers, and anyone who is interested in how a river functions on all scales. Those intrigued by the ongoing evolution of the physiography of California and the origin of the considerable differences in landscapes will get something out of the book. This book will also serve as a primer for understanding the daily barrage of river-related land use planning issues confronting Californians at the state and local levels. It provides some simple background information that allows an informed public (or legislator) to question the methods and assumptions presented by experts who make decisions about the fate of the rivers and to be intellectually involved in the related decision-making processes. But, again, this book is not intended to provide an answer to the problems that face California's rivers. It explains why there are problems, not necessarily what to do about them.

It should be clearly understood that this book is written by an opinionated geologist, not a wildlife biologist, water quality specialist, hydrologist, or engineer. Because our backgrounds shape our views, this book is slanted toward rivers as long-lived geomorphic systems that evolve over thousands of years in response to the geologic and climatic forces that influence them. Fiddling with the variables that control rivers will inevitably produce changes in river behavior that can result in land use problems. This is a point of view significantly different from that held by most hydrologists and engineers, who see a river as a natural resource *and* hazard whose seemingly capricious behavior needs to be controlled by bigger and better engineering solutions. Problems created by altering the variables will be corrected by yet more engineering solutions. The geologist sees these solutions as ultimately "temporary" and doomed to eventual failure. Water quality, fisheries, and wildlife experts also take a different point of view. Their emphasis is on habitat or places for organisms to live as well as the chemical characteristics of a river. Although these issues are mentioned frequently in Part II, they are viewed primarily as "output," or the net result of the physical processes that dominate a river. Finally, although I do cite failures of planning and politics, I specifically steer away from a summary of the overall political theater surrounding the development of rivers of California. This is an unwieldy subject that is covered in a number of other University of California Press books and the well-known books by Marc Reisner and other experts. Of course, being an *opinionated* geologist, I have been unable to resist the opportunity to point out some of the more glaring abuses of the state's rivers along with some outright failures to pay attention to basic principles.

JFM
January 1995

ACKNOWLEDGMENTS

I am especially indebted to Don Erman and the University of California Water and Wildland Resources Center who generously supplied funding to offset some of the costs of preparing the text and figures.

The idea for this book stemmed from conversations with Elizabeth Knoll, formerly of UC Press. Her encouragement, enthusiasm, and humor made this onerous task enjoyable. Robert Matthews (UC Davis) helped get the rivers course started and offered advice about environmental issues. I received abundant editorial assistance from Katherine Laddish (UC Davis) and Sheila Berg (UC Press), who scrutinized every inch of text and saved me from innumerable literary blunders. Janice Fong (UC Davis) developed all of the line drawings in this book, miraculously turning the illegible into fine scientific graphics. Mary Graziose (UC Davis) patiently assembled all of the plates. Dr. Rand Schaal (UC Davis), obsessed pilot, graciously provided all of the oblique aerial photographs. Matilda Evoy-Mount assisted with fieldwork.

I received abundant technical advice and editorial comments from a wide range of experts. Peter Sadler (UC Riverside) and G. Mathias Kondolf (UC Berkeley) conducted a thorough and invaluable review of the text, catching innumerable boneheaded mistakes and recommending revisions that helped immensely. I benefited from the river insights and peculiar perspectives of Mitchell Swanson (Swanson and Associates). I received excellent technical advice and encouragement from Barbara Evoy (California State Water Resources Control Board), Carl Hauge (California Department of Water Resources), Rick Humphreys (California State Water Resources Control Board), Troy Nicolini (U.S. Army Corps of Engineers), Gary Griggs (UC Santa Cruz), Darryl Davis (U.S. Army Corps of Engineers),

Archie Matthews (California State Water Resources Control Board), Bob
Collins (U.S. Army Corps of Engineers), Ross Johnson (California Department of Forestry and Fire Protection), and Koll Buer, Ralph Scott, and
Howard Mann (California Department of Water Resources). All errors of
omission or commission, however, are my own.

Finally, I am indebted to many friends and colleagues for their help
in discovering the remarkable beauty of the rivers of California. Dennis
Johnson and the staff of Outdoor Adventures UC Davis started this whole
thing by showing me and the Department of Geology at UC Davis the
virtues of running geologic field trips by whitewater raft. For more than a
decade, Outdoor Adventures UC Davis has been shepherding my students
safely down California's rivers while I blather on endlessly about the rocks,
geomorphology, bureaucrats, and the way rivers work. In particular, Dennis and his river friends, Matt Perry, Steve Grove, Barb Cartwright, Randy
Boid, and Barry Brown (along with others), foolishly trained me as a whitewater guide and then sat back to enjoy (and videotape) the results. Tony
Finnerty, Jim McClain, John Bric, Karla Thomas, Katie McDonald, Ray
Beiersdorfer, Marty Giaramita, Pete Osmolovsky, Tim Fagan, Laura Ben-
ninger, and other adrenaline junkies spent hours with me exploring the
rivers of California, developing new and exciting field trips, collecting information, and fishing me out of the water when I flipped, wrapped, or
ripped my boat. Steve Glass introduced me to the Grand Canyon and en-
thusiastically encouraged my use of rivers as the ultimate outdoor class-
room. Gerald Weber and Sue Holt spent weeks with me on Grand Canyon
trips helping me merge science and politics into a coherent understanding of rivers. But most of all, my long-suffering wife, Barbara Evoy, by
virtue of her patience, understanding, and professional devotion to water
issues, promoted the development of my passion for rivers that ultimately
led to the writing of this book. Thanks to all; apologies to those I forgot.

PART I

How Rivers Work

ONE

Introduction to
the Rivers of California

The First 4 Billion Years

INTRODUCTION

More than 4 billion years ago (give or take a few hundred million), condensation within the earth's atmosphere formed the first primitive rain. Although it is likely that the first rains contained some pretty nasty stuff, their physical interaction with the earth's surface was probably no different from what we see today. Rainfall that was not immediately vaporized back into the atmosphere was probably absorbed by a fairly porous earth. Eventually, however, the ability of the earth to absorb this moisture was exceeded by the rate of rainfall, leading to the first surface runoff. Driven by gravity, this runoff flowed across the earth's surface, eroding and sculpting as it went. Differential rates of erosion and irregularities in the earth's topography allowed water to concentrate in rivulets, which, in turn, collected into gullies and eventually into the very first rivers. Wherever runoff and rivers occurred, gravity drove fluids relentlessly toward and into topographic depressions or basins, until the world was dotted with large "lakes" that ultimately coalesced to form the first oceans.

The oldest rocks known on the earth today are the streaks of highly metamorphosed sediments that occur within the 3,824-million-year-old Amîtsoq gneisses of western Greenland. The importance of these rocks to the geologic and biologic scientific community is considerable. For geologists, these rocks provide insight into the makeup of the earth's early crust. For biologists, the big news is that the metamorphosed sediments may contain evidence of early life. This in itself is remarkable considering the antiquity of these rocks and the preconceived notions about how long it must have taken for life to begin on earth. These rocks also hold important clues for those of us searching for the earliest evidence of rivers. Most researchers agree that these sediments were probably deposited in one of the earth's early oceans or lakes adjacent to or within an active volcanic terrain. However, the deposits contain conglomerates composed of rounded cobbles. By analogy with the processes that deposit these kinds of sediments today, the metamorphic rocks of the Amîtsoq gneisses represent the first evidence for the erosive processes of the earth's early rivers.

For all of their 4-billion-year history, rivers have been doing the primary job of carting off discharge and the weathering products of the terrestrial portions of the earth and delivering them to the oceans. For the most part, rivers have been performing this job in the same basic way for all this time. Here in California, which lies at the western edge of the North American continent and is therefore a relatively young piece of real estate, the rock record tells us that rivers have been flowing across our landscape for a bit more than a billion years—a relatively short period of time in the overall scheme of things. Changes in climate, physiography, and sea level have produced regional differences in the nature of California's rivers, but in general, the same fundamental physical processes have been controlling their dynamics for all this time—with two notable exceptions.

The first change in the "rules" that govern the behavior of rivers took place relatively recently. In the Late Silurian, around 400 million years ago, vascular plants colonized the terrestrial surface of the earth. Although the earliest plants occurred in swamp- and marshlike environments, their initial expansion into better-drained, more upland environments probably took place in the riparian corridor along ancient rivers. Prior to the advent of land plants, rivers carved their channels across a landscape largely devoid of stabilizing vegetation. Although there may have been lichen and bacterial mats before land plants evolved, it is doubtful that they made much of a difference. As will be shown later, the vegetation that makes up the riparian corridor influences the shape, stability, and dynamics of river channels. Therefore, in the Late Silurian the physical processes of rivers became inseparable from the biological processes and have continued that way through today.

The second change in the rules was that crowning accident of evolution: humankind. After 400 million years of unencumbered river meandering, braiding, aggrading, eroding, and flooding, Kingdom Animalia introduced an organism that would profoundly change the way rivers work in California and much of the rest of the world. The earliest human immigrants to California came from the north more than ten thousand years ago. By the time they arrived, the present configuration of California's landscape was well established and broadly similar to that of today, albeit a bit wetter and cooler (fig. 1.1). These early settlers colonized the floodplains of California, with the largest populations concentrated along the resource-rich rivers of the northern half of the state. The arrival of Native

Fig. 1.1. Map of California depicting the major rivers discussed in the text. (Modified from California Department of Water Resources maps.)

Americans in California did little to disturb the rivers. Most of these populations were hunter-gatherers whose passive occupation of the landscape did not change it dramatically. Unlike those who would follow, Native Americans did little to resist the natural processes of rivers. When the rivers flooded, Native Americans just picked up or abandoned their dwellings and got out of the way, returning to the floodplains and riparian corridors when the waters had receded. Limited water diversions were built for agriculture, each to be washed away in the next year's floods. For all but a small fraction of the ten-thousand-year history of human occupation in California, the rivers operated pretty much under the same constraints that they had since the Silurian. The rules were not really changed until the arrival of Europeans.

Because of their small populations, the early European and Russian colonists of California had little impact on the rivers. It was not until the industrial revolution spilled into California via the gold rush that the state's rivers were transformed. Within one hundred fifty years, the dynamics, character, and even location of all but a few of California's rivers would be completely altered. The few hundred thousand people that called California home in the early nineteenth century would blossom to over 34 million by the end of the twentieth century, with most of that growth occurring in the last fifty years. From an eighteenth-century perspective, the impacts that this future explosion in population and technology would produce would have been unimaginable. In order to capture, control, and redistribute more than 60 percent of the water that runs off of the surface of California, the state's engineers, our own highly evolved breed of beavers, have built more than 1,400 dams and thousands of miles of levees, canals, and aqueducts that channelize surface water throughout the state, shepherding it from the water-rich to the water-poor, protecting us from flooding, and supplying us with electrical power. The domestication of California's rivers, which has fueled this country's largest state economy, has left few rivers in their natural state. Beyond the complete reorganization of most of California's rivers, a variety of land uses have fundamentally changed their behavior. To supply the urbanization of California with lumber, we log more than 400,000 acres of our watersheds every year, increasing the runoff and sediment supply to many of the state's rivers. More than 100,000 tons of gravel and sand are extracted from the state's riverbeds and floodplains each year, altering the critical balance between sediment supply and discharge. In pursuit of small amounts of gold trapped in modern and ancient placer deposits, we have washed whole mountainsides of debris into some rivers, choking them with sediment. Today, beef cattle and sheep graze over 70,000 square miles of the state's watersheds, almost half of the total area of the state, and trample thousands of miles of riparian corridor, changing runoff characteristics, sediment supply, and the stability of river channels. In addition to the physical changes, we discharge the runoff from our urban streets and our used agricultural water directly into our rivers, degrading overall water quality and straining our drinking water supplies. In just 2 percent of the history of human occupation of California and 0.0002 percent of the state's total river history, a blink of the eye by geologic standards, the rules by which the rivers of California operate have been fundamentally changed. With these changes have come a plethora of wildlife and fisheries management, land use planning, and engineering headaches that make up the focus of a monumental political tug-of-war.

Part I of this book covers how rivers work and how their behavior reflects not only their own internal feedback mechanisms but also their relationship to the forces that shape their overall watersheds. This, in a way, represents a summary of rivers as they have operated over the last 400 million years in California up until the arrival of Europeans. Part II examines some of the land uses of the last one hundred fifty years that have dramatically changed California's rivers, with an emphasis on those uses that have produced the most problems for those who manage rivers.

HOW A RIVER WORKS

Landslides, floods, and earthquakes remind us on a yearly basis that the irregular, sometimes craggy landscape that we call California is an active, constantly evolving geomorphic surface that records the competing processes of mountain building and mountain destruction. The interaction of tectonic crustal plates sliding and colliding along the western margin of North America is responsible for the formation of the six major mountain ranges and innumerable smaller ranges that dominate the landscape. From the geological perspective, the tectonic uplift of these mountain ranges is occurring at a staggering rate. The Sierra Nevada range, the most critical for the well-being of California's water users, is currently rising at a rate of approximately 0.1 inch per year. In human terms this appears minuscule and insignificant, but on a geologic time scale this rate is capable of producing extraordinary edifices. At this rate, the state's highest mountain, Mount Whitney, would double in height in just a few million years, moving rapidly past Mount Everest's current height. Moreover, the high rate of uplift in the Sierra Nevada is nothing new. It has been rising at this rate for much of the last 5 million years. Thus it logically should be twice as high as it presently is.

Two processes act to diminish the actual growth of mountain ranges. First, the semiplastic interior of the earth adjusts to the formation of large heavy features on and in the crust by allowing them to sink. In a manner analogous to adding heavy cargo containers to the deck of a ship, large mountain ranges built by tectonic collisions are compensated to some extent by an increase in their draft. That is, their keels ride a bit deeper than the rest of the land. Thus every incremental increase in the thickness of the crust that makes up a mountain range leads to partial adjustment by subsidence or sinking.

The second and perhaps most important process that prevents mountains from quite literally scraping the sky is the work that our atmosphere does to erode them as they rise. Our oxygen- and water-rich atmosphere,

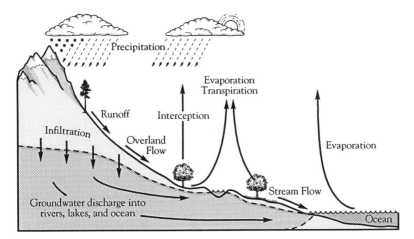

Fig. 1.2. Hydrologic cycle in California. (Modified from Dunne and Leopold 1978.)

as well as the plant life that supports it, physically and chemically attacks the rock that makes up the mountain ranges, dislodging, dissolving, or altering minerals to form clays and soil. The intensity of this attack is governed principally by the amount of water moving through the hydrologic cycle (fig. 1.2). Rainfall, which drives the hydrologic cycle in California, is derived primarily from the Pacific Ocean. Solar heating and evaporation of this immense reservoir of water supplies the moisture and the energy for the storms that water California. A seemingly arbitrary and capricious jet stream sweeps this moisture eastward into California (we would be a desert if the air masses moved from east to west), where it falls as rain and snow. When precipitation falls as rain with sufficient intensity and duration, it flows rapidly downhill, coalescing and gathering energy as gravity pulls it along. The ability of this water to move the weathered material is immense and more than capable of carrying away the mass of most mountains over a relatively short period.

The rivers of California are the by-product of this earth-atmosphere contest. On average, around 2 feet of precipitation falls on the surface of California, although, as most Californians will gloomily point out, this is the average of extremes rather than some useful indicator of "normal" rainfall. Of this 2 feet, only one-third eventually runs off. A variety of processes conspire to reduce the amount of runoff that occurs (see fig. 1.2). A great deal of the moisture is intercepted by vegetation and evaporated back to the atmosphere before it makes it to the ground. In addition, much of the moisture that makes it to the ground infiltrates and forms soil moisture near the surface or groundwater below the surface. The transpiration of plants and further evaporation then returns most of the soil moisture to the atmosphere. That moisture which is not intercepted, evapo-transpirated, or infiltrated is driven to the sea by gravity, collecting into overland flow and scouring and sculpting the ever-changing surface of California.

While rainfall and direct runoff from the slopes do most of the work of eroding California's watersheds, it is the rivers that complete the process by carving the river valleys and shipping the products of erosion and run-off to the Pacific Ocean or other "sinks." The ability of rivers to shape val-leys and move sediment is both immense and routinely underestimated by land use planners and engineers. As an example of the power of these forces, during the spectacular Christmas floods of 1964 in northern Cali-fornia, the Eel River carried discharges that were the highest in the re-corded history of California. Near the town of Scotia, south of Eureka, the flow rate of the Eel River exceeded 752,000 cubic feet per second (cfs) on December 23, 1964 (based on U.S. Geologic Survey stream-gauging rec-ords). This is a flow rate comparable to the peak discharges recorded north of Saint Louis, Missouri, during the Mississippi River floods of 1993—but all from a watershed of only 3,000 square miles! To put this in perspective, if each cubic foot of water weighs approximately 63 pounds, then more than 47 million pounds of water passed through the river channel *every second.* The mass of water would have been roughly equivalent to a herd of 15,000 Ford Country Squire station wagons thundering down the river canyon every second. Moreover, to move this herd through some of the narrower portions of the Eel River channel at 10 miles per hour, they would have to be arranged in waves 100 cars across and 150 cars high! It seems unlikely that engineers and land use planners would, if given a choice, ignore the power of a flow of 15,000 Country Squires per second (a new unit: css?). Yet, as is demonstrated elsewhere in this book, they have, they *have* to, and they will.

There is a dynamic, shifting balance in California between the pro-cesses that are generating uplift of the mountains and the rainfall, gravity, and atmosphere that are attempting to dismantle them. As the height and ruggedness of many of our mountain ranges attest, the forces of uplift are dominating our landscape at present. This has not always been the case, and it is a virtual certainty that this balance will change, but for the dura-tion of the human species, California will be a very mountainous place.

GRADE AND EQUILIBRIUM

The rivers that do the work of draining California come in all shapes, sizes, and compositions. Despite the remarkable variability of California's rivers, they are each the predictable product of the interaction between identifiable physical and, to a lesser degree, chemical and biological processes. From the high-discharge rivers that drain the dense forests of the north coast to the flash flood–prone rivers that drain the chaparral and scrub of the south coast, the differences in morphology and behavior can be ascribed to variation in a definable suite of parameters.

During the early and middle part of this century, a concerted effort was made by geologists, geomorphologists, and hydrologists to quantify the variables that control or record the behavior and morphology of rivers. Like my mother, who vacuumed anything that stood still and washed anything that moved, these scientists indiscriminately measured every conceivable geomorphic feature they could, without concern about how or why they might be related to rivers. Then, stirring this alphabet soup of variables together through mathematical regression techniques, they began to sort out their relative impact and interrelatedness. From this questionable approach emerged an understanding of the remarkably complex nature of rivers as part of geomorphic "systems."

One prominent school of thought about rivers is based, in part, on the concept of grade or equilibrium. Grade assumes that the present morphology and behavior of a river reflects a balance of the forces that operate through it and upon it. In natural systems that move energy and matter, there is a tendency for the system to arrange itself in a manner that both reduces the amount of work and distributes that work as evenly as possible. These two tendencies are often in conflict with each other in rivers. The energy and matter that flows into and through a river system is the discharge and sediment load provided to it by its watershed. Intuitively, the most efficient means for a river to route this energy and matter to the sea would seem to be to develop a perfectly straight channel of uniform slope. However, because water accelerates under the influence of gravity, energy expenditures (work) would not be equally distributed along the entire straight channel. In addition, since tributaries add water to a river, the amount of energy and matter in the system progressively increases downslope. Rivers deal with this tendency for nonuniform distribution of work by adjustments in profile, channel cross section, and channel pattern (chaps. 4, 7). The concave-up longitudinal profiles of rivers and their alluvial floodplains with meandering channels and associated riffles and pools are all the product of the rivers' attempts to minimize the amount of work performed and to spread that work out as evenly as possible. In this manner rivers are self-regulating, evolving just the right pattern and profile to handle the amount of discharge and sediment delivered to them. This balance is termed *grade* (not to be confused with slope or gradient) and records a state of *equilibrium* within a river system.

As anyone who lives on the floodplain of a river will note, the physical features of a river are hardly static. Channel morphology, location, gradi-

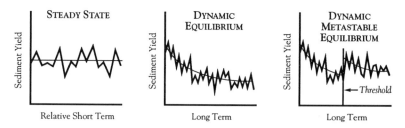

Fig. 1.3. Illustration of various time scales of equilibrium in river systems. *Sediment Yield* refers to total amount of sediment derived from a river basin per year, usually expressed as tons/acre.

ent, sediment load, and discharge all appear to be changing in space and time. For this reason, grade or equilibrium within a river is based on the time frame being considered. Figure 1.3 presents an example of the temporal differences in equilibrium in a river system. Over relatively short periods of time (tens of years), rivers may appear to fluctuate dramatically, seeming to render the concept of equilibrium meaningless. However, over intermediate periods of time, such as tens to hundreds of years, fluctuations appear to occur within some limited range. This variation around some mean condition reflects an overall balance of the fluctuating variables of the river system and defines what Stanley Schumm called the "steady state" condition.

Over the long term the mean condition of a river is unlikely to remain static. Rather, processes like regional incision or downcutting by a river or subtle shifts in climate and mountain building are likely to produce gradual changes in the amount of energy and matter supplied to a river system. Short- and medium-term variations will continue to take place, but they will shift around some slowly changing mean condition (fig. 1.3). Called *dynamic equilibrium* by Schumm, this is a long-term condition of virtually all rivers in California and, for that matter, the world.

Although dynamic equilibrium is a useful concept, long-term change in river systems rarely occurs as an inexorable, steady shift in mean conditions. As many studies have shown, significant change appears to be accomplished by dramatic shifts over relatively short periods with long periods of gradual change in between. Burdened with the unwieldy term *dynamic metastable equilibrium,* this process may be the nature of long-term change in fluvial systems.

Dramatic change in rivers can often be tied to shifts in external influences like climate, tectonics, or the cumulative impacts of certain land use practices. In most cases the shifts in these external influences are incremental rather than sudden. The translation of these gradualistic shifts in external variables into abrupt change in river morphology and behavior is not well understood. Schumm has suggested that during long-term change, thresholds within fluvial systems are reached which create short-lived episodes of readjustment followed by development of a new dynamic equilibrium (fig. 1.3). In many ways, this process is analogous to a soldier's life: 98 percent boredom and 2 percent terror, with most of the significant work being accomplished during moments of terror. Regardless of their origin, episodes of terror in fluvial systems are the most difficult to predict yet may be the most important.

A MODEL RIVER SYSTEM

Whether steady state, dynamic, or dynamic metastable, equilibrium within a river system is the result of complex interactions between the geometric properties of a river, the landscape over which it flows, and the forces that act on it and within it. It is well established that adjustments in a river system and their upstream or downstream translation are the result of "negative feedback" whereby changes in one river characteristic influence changes in other characteristics, which, in turn, eventually influence and restore that which was originally altered (fig. 1.4). Negative feedback is, in an obscure way, analogous to the way some dogs chase their tails. Having bitten its own tail for reasons too opaque for human understanding, a dog (well, at least my dog) will leap to the fray, chasing and biting that which caused it pain, thereby causing more pain, stimulating it to run even faster. As the dog tires and the pain becomes more bothersome, it can't chase its tail as effectively. This leads to fewer bites, decreased running, and eventually a winding down to the state of repose that previously occupied most of the dog's faculties. Taken to its unwarranted extreme, this analogy illustrates that tail-chasing dogs have achieved some kind of dynamic metastable equilibrium through negative feedback. (The nature of feedback within fluvial systems and its role in maintaining grade and equilibrium are discussed in detail in chaps. 2 through 9.)

Figure 1.5, a generalized deterministic river model, provides a summary of the relationship between the various processes and geomorphic features of fluvial systems. The "variables" of the model, which include both forces that act on and in a river and the physical features of the river that respond to these forces, are grouped into hierarchical nodes or function boxes. These groupings are based on two criteria: (1) the mutual interdependency or intensity of negative feedback of the variables and (2) the global influence of the variables on the river system. It should be noted that because of the complex feedback that occurs within a river system, figure 1.5 is, by necessity, hopelessly oversimplified. An accurate summary would involve construction of a Rube Goldberg contraption with innumerable arrows, boxes, and strings coupled with a mind-numbing,

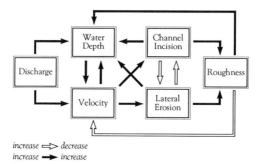

increase ⇨ *decrease*
increase ➡ *increase*

Fig. 1.4. Feedback loops within a fluvial channel in response to increases in discharge. Arrows indicate nature of influences on variables within the channel. Relationships are discussed in chaps. 3 and 4.

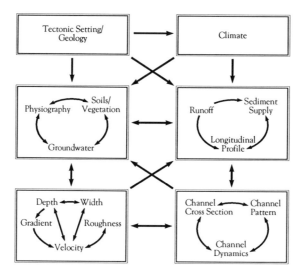

Fig. 1.5. Generalized model illustrating hierarchical process and geomorphic variables in river systems. Arrows indicate direction of influence between variables.

endless discussion of the physical relationships. Those seeking a deeper discussion of river models are referred to the readings listed at the end of this chapter.

The variables that are grouped at the top of the river model, tectonic setting/geology and climate, represent the ultimate driving forces that dictate the occurrence, character, and behavior of rivers in California. In essence, the establishment of a least-work design that balances energy expenditures occurs in response to these forces. These *independent variables* have virtually no feedback from the river system itself. Foremost of these is tectonic setting. By controlling the location and magnitude of uplift of mountains, the tectonic activity directly controls development of rivers. Indeed, without mountains, the rivers of California would be, at best, insignificant. Like plate tectonics, the geology and climate of the state also control many aspects of the rivers and receive little to no feedback or influence from the rivers. However, both geology and climate are themselves influenced by plate tectonics. For example, the composition and structure of rocks in any region are a product of tectonic activity in the past as well as the present. In addition, tectonic processes influence precipitation patterns. As Pacific air masses reach California, the major mountain ranges intercept the moisture, turning it to voluminous mixtures of rain and snow. The nature and distribution of the state's surface runoff is intimately tied to the state's volatile tectonic setting.

Outside of tectonics, climate, and geology, all of the variables within the river model of figure 1.5 are involved in feedback, either direct or indirect, and are thus *dependent variables*. Of these, physiography (the size, shape, and elevation of the watershed), soils, vegetation, and groundwater are the most "independent," receiving only minimal direct feedback from the river. Each of these variables, in turn, directly controls the discharge and sediment supply that are delivered to the rivers of a watershed and the shape of the longitudinal profile. Because discharge and sediment supply represent the energy and matter that move through a river system and because the profile determines how energy is expended, much of the behavior and geometry of a river can be tied directly to variations in these key variables.

A river's attempt to establish equilibrium is often viewed holistically or on a watershedwide basis. However, all adjustments within a river system are the aggregate product of innumerable changes at the local scale. Most of these changes are accomplished through incremental shifts in five key variables or conditions: velocity, channel width, channel depth, gradient, and bed "roughness" or the resistance of a bed to flow. The negative feedback within this group of dependent variables is well developed and almost immediate; adjustment in any one variable is accommodated immediately by the other four (see fig. 1.4). Changes in these five key variables inevitably involve interaction between the flow of a river and the bank material that encases it, changing the shape of the channel cross section, the pattern of the channel, and its evolution over the long and short term. As discussed in chapter 4, the processes of self-regulation and energy balance within a river system produce dynamic, rather than static, channels. As farmers and ranchers who live along rivers without levees will certainly attest (or complain), natural river channels are in a state of perpetual adjustment involving reconfiguration of channel morphology, lateral migration, and channel switching.

SUMMARY

Rivers have been conducting the primary task of transferring runoff and weathering products away from the terrestrial portions of the earth for more than 4 billion years. During most of this time rivers have acted in broadly similar fashion, changing in response to the climatic, geologic, and tectonic conditions of their watersheds. Two events changed the way in which rivers operate. First, the appearance of vascular land plants approximately 400 million years ago changed the erosional resistance of riverbanks and significantly changed the way rivers work. Second, and most important, humans have shown a remarkable capacity for altering or even eliminating the natural functions of a river. In California, these changes have been most profound during the last one hundred fifty years.

The contest between the processes that build mountains and the processes that tear them down dictates the location, character, and size of California's rivers. Driven principally by interaction between tectonic plates, the major mountain ranges in California are rising at a geologically rapid pace. Working against this process is the hydrologic cycle, which routes water into and across California's landscapes. Rivers carve the canyons that collect the effluent of the interaction between tectonics and the hydrologic cycle, shipping them to the lakes and valleys of California or eventually to the ocean. The shape and behavior of these rivers reflect a least-work adjustment to the supply of this effluent and a balance of energy expenditures, where grade or equilibrium is achieved through constant change.

Although rivers appear to be constantly changing, even on a yearly basis, they develop, over the medium term, a steady state condition whereby variation occurs around some mean condition within some finite, limited range. In contrast, long-term changes in the independent variables translate throughout the river system, adjusting all of the dependent variables to some degree. This change may be accommodated by gradual shifts in some mean condition, reflecting maintenance of dynamic equilibrium. However, thresholds within the river model may lead to dramatic, short-lived bursts of change followed by a resumption of dynamic equilibrium conditions. This dynamic metastable equilibrium is probably the long-term condition of all rivers in California.

RELEVANT READINGS

Calow, P., and G. E. Petts, eds. 1992. *The Rivers Handbook: Hydrological and Ecological Principles,* 2 vols. Oxford: Blackwell Scientific Publications.

Chorley, R. J., S. A. Schumm, and D. E. Sugden. 1985. *Geomorphology.* London: Methuen.

Dunne, T., and L. B. Leopold. 1978. *Water in Environmental Planning.* San Francisco: W. H. Freeman.

Leopold, L. B. 1984. *Water: A Primer.* San Francisco: W. H. Freeman.

———. 1994. *A View of the River.* Cambridge: Harvard University Press.

Leopold, L. B., M. G. Wolman, and J. P. Miller. 1964. *Fluvial Processes in Geomorphology.* San Francisco: W. H. Freeman.

Morisawa, M. 1968. *Streams: Their Dynamics and Morphology.* New York: McGraw-Hill.

———. 1985. *Rivers.* New York: Longman.

Newson, M. D. 1994. *Hydrology and the River Environment.* Oxford: Oxford University Press.

Richards, K. S. 1982. *Rivers: Form and Process in Alluvial Channels.* New York: Methuen.

Ritter, Dale F. 1986. *Process Geomorphology.* 2d ed. Dubuque: W. C. Brown.

Schumm, S. A. 1977. *The Fluvial System.* New York: Wiley.

Wolman, M. G., and H. C. Riggs, eds. 1990. *Surface Water Hydrology.* Vol. O-1 of *The Geology of North America.* Boulder: Geological Society of America.

TWO

Water in Motion

INTRODUCTION

Water, as it moves across the slopes and tributaries of a watershed, is the energy that runs the engines of any river system. And gravity is the driving force behind water, accelerating it at a rate of 32.2 feet per second^2 toward the center of the earth. Given this acceleration, one could envision that a river should be constantly increasing its velocity as it flows downhill. Moreover, once something with significant mass (like 15,000 Ford Country Squire station wagons) gets moving, it has momentum and is difficult to stop. Yet in any given reach of river over any short period of time, current velocity varies little. The fact that water does not continuously accelerate reflects the balance between the forces that drive water (gravity), keep it in motion (momentum), and try to stop it from moving (friction). The balance achieved by these forces dictates the physical behavior of a river at all scales and is a reflection of the way in which a river expends its energy.

During the past century there have been great advances in the development of theoretical models for the movement of water in streams and rivers. All of these models are based on well-established physical principles and are supported by laboratory experiments. However, the complexity of flow within most natural systems greatly exceeds our ability to mimic it in the laboratory or even in our most advanced computer simulations. Most of our "understanding" of flow within rivers is based on gross assumptions and generalizations coupled with voluminous empirical observations. In this chapter, some of these assumptions and observations are described and applied to water moving through a river.

UNSTEADY, NONUNIFORM FLOW

In the laboratories (and minds) of most hydraulic engineers, water passes through channels as *steady, uniform flow*. In their flume experiments, the engineers usually control the flow velocity so that it stays constant in time (*steady*) and does not vary along the length of the flume (*uniform*). But while creating steady, uniform flows allows a numerical analysis of the variables that control flow behavior, it hardly mimics the conditions found in natural systems. As five minutes of observation of any given stretch of river will show, velocity does not remain constant in either time or space. Channel constrictions or obstructions lead to significant changes in the speed of the water (see discussion below). Moreover, unless controlled by a dam, changes in discharge will undoubtedly lead to temporal changes in velocity. Thus, rather than occurring as the scientifically convenient steady, uniform flow, virtually all natural systems contain *unsteady, nonuniform flow*.

The variations in velocity that define unsteady, nonuniform flow in natural systems are tied directly to the *continuity of flow equation*. This equation relates the discharge (Q) to the product of the cross-sectional area of the channel that is occupied by the flow (A) and the mean velocity of the flow through that cross section (v), where

$$Q = vA. \tag{2.1}$$

This simple equation explains unsteadiness (changes in Q over time in one place) and nonuniformity (change in A with position). In unsteady flow, changes in discharge (usually expressed in cfs or in cubic meters per second, *cms*) must be accompanied by changes in depth and velocity. For example, increases in discharge during flooding translate directly to local increases in the velocity (v) of the river along with its depth and width. The increase in depth and width translates to an increase in the overall cross-sectional area of the flow (A). The systematic response of the depth of a river to increases and decreases in discharge is the basis for the numerous river gauges that are seen all over California (fig. 2.1.).

Within any given channel reach, there is considerable variation in the channel profile or cross section. The occurrence of large boulders or erosionally resistant outcrops can act to constrict a channel, allowing less space for the water to pass through. As the continuity equation (eq. 2.1) indicates, if a given discharge has to pass through less cross-sectional area, the reduction in area must be offset in part by an increase in velocity in order to balance the discharge-velocity-channel area relationships. Conversely, a variety of parameters that are independent of channel cross section, such as slope or roughness, can lead directly to changes in the velocity of a flow (reviewed below). If discharge remains constant, then these changes in velocity must be accompanied by opposing changes in cross-

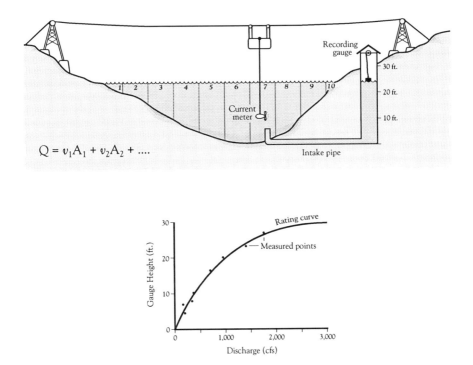

$$Q = v_1A_1 + v_2A_2 + \ldots.$$

Fig. 2.1. The *stage* of a river is the measured elevation of the water surface above some datum, often sea level. The stage can be measured visually using a large ruled gauge or, more commonly, with a floating gauge similar to the design shown above. Hydrologists estimate the discharge associated with any given river stage by summing the product of velocity × area measured in equal increments across a channel. Discharge and stage are measured for a variety of flows and are plotted on a graph. A line fit to these measured points is called a *rating curve*. These curves allow hydrologists to continuously monitor discharge of a given river. Note that the slope of the rating curve decreases with increasing discharge. Because of the trapezoidal shape of most channels, increases in discharge are accommodated by more rapid increases in width of the flow, rather than depth. In addition, as the cross-sectional area of the flow increases, proportionately less flow is in contact with the bed, reducing the impact of frictional resistance of the channel bed. This allows higher velocities to pass through the channel, decreasing the area occupied by the flow and reducing increases in stage. The U.S. Geological Survey maintains more than 600 river gauging stations throughout California and supplies information directly to the State Flood Operations Center.

sectional area of the flow. In essence, faster flows take up less space and slower flows take up more.

MOVING WATER: HOW FAST, HOW DEEP?

The continuity of flow equation is fundamental to river engineering, flood-plain management, and the innumerable structures that we build to handle surface runoff. From the engineering perspective, the faster we can make discharge move through a channel, the smaller the structure we will have to build to handle it simply because high-velocity flows require smaller cross-sectional areas. The goal of *most* flood control channels built in California during the past one hundred years has been (1) to shorten the distance that water has to travel by straightening channels and (2) to make the water flow as fast as possible by smoothing the channels. As discussed in chapters 15 and 16, the result of this approach has been a great deal of money spent with erratic success.

Of course, for any water engineering structure to succeed, the velocity of the flows that will be moving through it must be estimated with great precision and accuracy. Herein lies the rub. The equations used most commonly to calculate velocity of a flow, the Manning equation (used principally in American engineering) and the Chezy velocity formula (used in the rest of the world), are empirically derived. This means that scientific "fudge factors" or coefficients are built into these equations. Coefficients are an essential part of most engineering equations for two reasons: they make the units balance, and they make the calculations based on these equations match the laboratory or field experiments. The Chezy velocity formula and the Manning equation illustrate this perhaps best of all.

The Chezy and Manning equations are based on two key assumptions expressed by Chezy in the late 1700s. First, as outlined in the introduction to this chapter, in uniform flow where velocity remains constant, the forces driving the flow must be exactly balanced by the total force of bed resistance. These forces are

Driving force = Total weight of water × sine of the bed slope

Resisting force = Total bed area exposed to flow × bed shear stress.

The effectiveness of the driving force is dependent on the amount of water (thus the weight) and the steepness of the slope. Obviously, the greater the slope, the more effective gravity is at driving water quickly downhill. The resisting force is primarily the drag exerted by the flow on the bed. Termed *mean bed shear stress* and labeled τ_0, this essentially represents the frictional resistance that the bed offers to the flow. In this case, the greater the total bed area exposed to the flow (e.g., shallow broad channels), the greater the resisting force. In addition, the greater the friction between bed and flow, the greater the total resisting force (fig. 2.2). It is at this point that the second assumption and the major fudge factor enters into the construction of the Chezy and Manning equations.

Chezy assumed that the force resisting the flow varies with the square of the velocity, according to

$$\tau_0 = kv^2. \tag{2.2}$$

That is, as the velocity of a flow (v) increases, the forces that are acting to slow it down (τ_0) increase at a much greater rate. This assumption has been borne out by numerous laboratory and field experiments and is perfectly valid. But of course, the amount of bed shear stress exerted by a flow on the bed is going to depend on the nature of the bed itself. This is where the important fudge factor (k) appears. Known as the *roughness coefficient,* k is a number that makes velocity and bed shear stress balance for different bed conditions. A smooth concrete-lined channel is going to exert much less resistance to a flow than an irregular boulder-lined or vegetation-covered channel. Because of this, equal discharges are likely to flow much faster through a smooth channel than a rough channel. It is this roughness coefficient that makes the relationship between bed shear stress and velocity work for different bed conditions.

Based on the important assumptions about the balance of forces and the relationship between bed shear stress, roughness, and velocity, Chezy developed the following relationship:

$$v = C(Rs)^{1/2}, \tag{2.3}$$

where C is the "Chezy coefficient" that decreases in value with increasing bed roughness, R is the hydraulic radius, or hydraulic mean depth expressed as the ratio of A/p, where A is the cross-sectional area of the channel and p is the wetted perimeter, and s is the slope of the channel (fig. 2.3).

The alternative formula, the Manning equation, was developed in the late 1800s. This formula is

$$v = (1.49R^{2/3}s^{1/2})/n, \tag{2.4}$$

where v, R, s are the same as defined for equation 2.3 and n is the Manning roughness coefficient, which, unlike the Chezy coefficient, increases with increasing roughness. An example of the range of values of n is shown in table 2.1.

The Manning roughness coefficient has been studied for more than a century in flumes and in the field. Engineers have simply measured the values of v (velocity), R (hydraulic radius), and s (slope) in any given flume or channel and solved for the value of n (roughness). What has

Fig. 2.2. Examples of variations in bed roughness. *Top*: Pine Creek north of Bishop in the Owens Valley. Coarse material deposited by debris flow processes on Pine Creek fan has very high bed roughness. *Bottom*: Channel deposits of Middle Fork of the Eel River. Better-sorted, finer-grained gravels reduce bed roughness, allowing higher-velocity flows through a channel.

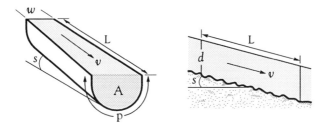

Fig. 2.3. Definition diagram for Chezy and Manning
equations. See text for discussion of variables.

TABLE 2.1   Manning Roughness Coefficients of Natural Streams

Description of Stream	Range of n	Normal n
Small Streams (< 100-ft. width)		
Clean, straight, bankfull, no riffles or deep pools	0.025–0.033	0.030
Straight, no riffles or pools, no stones or vegetation	0.030–0.040	0.035
Clean, sinuous, some pools and riffles	0.033–0.045	0.040
Sinuous, some pools and riffles, some stones and vegetation	0.035–0.050	0.045
Sinuous, lower stages, more stones	0.045–0.060	0.050
Sluggish reaches, weedy, deep pools	0.050–0.080	0.070
Deep pools, very weedy, floodway with timber and brush	0.075–0.150	0.100
Major Streams (> 100-ft. width)		
No boulders or brush	0.025–0.060	
Irregular and rough reach	0.035–0.100	
Mountain Streams		
Clean channel, steep banks with vegetation on banks submerged at high flow, bed of gravel and cobbles	0.030–0.050	0.040
Same as above but with bed of cobbles and large boulders	0.040–0.070	0.050
Floodplains		
Pasture, no brush, short grass	0.025–0.035	0.030
Pasture, no brush, high grass	0.030–0.050	0.035
Scattered brush, many weeds	0.035–0.070	0.050
Medium to dense brush	0.045–0.160	0.070
Heavy stand of timber, little undergrowth, flood below branches	0.080–0.120	0.100
Heavy stand of timber, little undergrowth, flood reaching branches	0.100–0.160	0.120

SOURCE: Modified from Chow 1959.

developed is table after table of roughness coefficients that have qualitative, adjective descriptors attached to them. Descriptors like *mountain streams with rocky beds and rivers with variable sections and some vegetation along bank* (see fig. 2.2A) are used to establish a roughness coefficient of .040 to .050. Although seemingly precise, this is hardly accurate or even objective and has led to considerable errors in calculation. Moreover, two things happen to bed roughness during significant flows. First, as flows deepen, the value of n tends to decrease, regardless of the condition of the bed material. Second, and perhaps most important, the tendency of rivers to erode, transport, and deposit sediment distorts the actual roughness values. This is primarily because a mobile sediment bed tends to absorb shear exerted on the bed by the flow. This built-in error has led to some spectacular flood control failures in California when engineers have failed to recognize the impact of sediment in their flood control channels.

Regardless of the inadequacies of the flow formulas used to estimate current velocities, they do offer a useful resource for evaluating the influence of changes in channels on the conditions of flow. In particular, in nonuniform flow where differences in bed conditions, channel shape, and slope occur along any given reach, the Chezy and Manning equations allow estimations of the nature of changes in current velocity. The equations not only quantify the importance of bed roughness but also illustrate that changes in hydraulic radius, slope, and velocity of flow are nonlinear. Narrow, deep channels typically have a greater hydraulic radius than broad, shallow channels of equivalent cross-sectional area. In this case, since the cross-sectional areas are equal, it is the wetted perimeter, p, that exerts considerable influence on the flow velocities. The relatively small wetted perimeter of the narrow, deep channel places less of the bed in contact with the flow at any given time. This reduces the influence of bed roughness, allowing faster flow velocities.

Of course, as any rafter, kayaker, or canoeist knows, increases in slope have a profound influence on the velocity of water within a channel. The Manning equation, which is based on the presumed balance between bed shear stress and velocity, shows that velocity is proportional to the square root of the slope. For example, although velocity increases with increasing slope, it does so at a much slower rate. Thus a fourfold increase in slope may only lead to a doubling of velocity.

The continuity of flow equation coupled with the Manning and Chezy equations form the underpinnings of understanding the nature of nonuniform flow conditions in virtually all natural river systems. Subtle changes in bed conditions, shape of the channel, and slope all induce changes in the average velocity of a flow. Along any given reach, these velocity changes will greatly influence the depth and width of the river by controlling the total cross-sectional area occupied by the river. All of these relationships can be viewed directly in any mountain stream.

REYNOLDS NUMBER:
TURBULENT VERSUS LAMINAR FLOW

As the velocity of a flow within a channel is slowly increased from zero, the structure of the flow, or, rather, the aggregate behavior of the water molecules, changes dramatically. As Osborne Reynolds demonstrated in his laboratory experiments with flow in pipes, two general types of internal structure can be recognized within moving fluids. Reynolds introduced dye streaks into moving fluids in clear pipes. At low velocities the dye streaks showed that water is moving as a series of coherent slabs sliding past each other with little mixing between layers. He termed this slablike motion *laminar flow.* As flow velocities were increased, a threshold was crossed where the slabs broke up and chaotic, vertical mixing of the water occurred through the formation of eddies. Reynolds termed this fully mixed flow structure *turbulent flow.*

Reynolds recognized that the change in behavior from laminar to turbulent flow is tied to changes in diameter of the pipe and velocity of the flow. Since the velocity and diameter are important, the mass of the water passing through the pipe over any given interval of time is key to its behavior. Thus the *inertia* of water, a measure of the difficulty in either changing or initiating motion, appears to be key to predicting the behavior of flow.

Reynolds's injection of dyes into a fluid not only showed the difference in structure between laminar and turbulent flow but also demonstrated that there is a velocity gradient within a pipe. The highest velocities are located near the middle and the lowest velocities occur at the margins of the pipe. This gradient reflects the forces of friction between the pipe wall and the flowing water. In addition, Reynolds noted that changes in the hydraulic radius appear to influence fluid behavior. As noted above, the hydraulic radius is a measure of the effectiveness of bed roughness: the greater the hydraulic radius, the less fluid is in contact with the bed. The ability of frictional resistance or bed roughness to slow down a flow is directly dependent on the *viscosity,* or internal properties, of a fluid that offers resistance to flow (e.g., honey is highly viscous; water is not). The greater the viscosity of a fluid, the more effective the bed roughness. Because of this, Reynolds recognized that viscous forces as well as inertial forces must be predictors of fluid behavior.

From Reynolds's experiments came one of the most widely used nondimensional numbers in fluid mechanics: the *Reynolds number.* This number has no units (thus the term *nondimensional*) and merely reflects the ratio of inertial to viscous forces. In its most basic form it is defined as

$$R_e = (\rho_w vR)/\mu, \qquad (2.5)$$

where ρ_w is the density of the flowing water, v is the velocity, R is the hydraulic radius of the pipe, and μ is the dynamic viscosity. For wide, shallow channels, the hydraulic radius is approximately equal to the mean depth of the channel. Thus for many natural river systems, R is often referred to as the *hydraulic mean depth.*

At very low average flow velocities and extremely shallow depths, R_e values are low (<500), reflecting the predominance of viscous forces over inertial forces. At these values, flow will inevitably be laminar, with little vertical mixing, and the direction of flow will be consistent with the average flow direction. If you are a bug or a fish, laminar flow is likely to offer little resistance to your efforts to get around. When $R_e > 2,000$, the flows become fully turbulent with chaotic movement of water masses. Because of the development of random eddies, the flow velocity and direction in turbulent flows are actually the average of innumerable variations. As discussed in chapter 3, the eddies that develop in turbulent flow are key to the suspension and transport of sediment. Flow with R_e values between 500 and 2,000 are considered transitional and often behave in both laminar and turbulent fashion.

The R_e value of most natural rivers is $\gg 2,000$. For example, at a temperature of approximately 10°C the Reynolds number of a 50-centimeter-deep channel flowing at 25 centimeters per second is $R_e = 95,420$. Clearly, turbulent flow is the predominant type in open channels. Yet even within turbulent flows with high flow velocities there are likely to be microenvironments that contain laminar flow. These can be grouped into two types. The first is generated by local variations in channel morphology or roughness. For example, where water becomes very shallow across smooth surfaces (e.g., water pouring slowly over a smooth rock) or gathers in very shallow, virtually still pools, local R_e values can reach <500. The second and most common type of laminar flow occurs at the base of the bed where flow velocities are reduced to near zero by frictional resistance (fig. 2.4). Termed the *laminar sublayer,* this is restricted to and associated with *boundary layer* processes (discussed below).

FROUDE NUMBER:
SUBCRITICAL VERSUS SUPERCRITICAL FLOW

The second nondimensional number that is often cited in fluid dynamics is the *Froude number.* Like the Reynolds number, the Froude number is a ratio of forces that predicts the behavior of flow. In this case, the ratio is

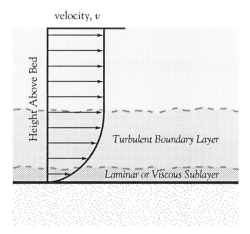

Fig. 2.4. Velocity profile of a flow illustrating the laminar sublayer and turbulent portion of the boundary layer. Length of arrows illustrates relative velocity measured at a given height above the bed.

between inertial forces and the forces of gravity that act on a flow. Unlike the Reynolds number, inertia in open channel flow is represented by v^2/D, where D = depth of the flow and v = average velocity; the gravity force is merely the acceleration due to gravity, g. The Froude number is defined by most engineers as the square root of the relationship of inertial to gravity forces:

$$F_r = v/\sqrt{gD}. \qquad (2.6)$$

Where $F_r > 1$, the inertial forces exceed the gravitational forces and the flow is referred to as *supercritical flow*. Where $F_r < 1$, the gravitational forces dominate the flow behavior and it is referred to as *subcritical flow*. In the unlikely instance where $F_r = 1$, the flow is referred to as *critical* or *transitional.*

Based on the Reynolds number and the Froude number, virtually all flows fall into four major categories (summarized in fig. 2.5):

1. *Subcritical-laminar* ($F_r < 1$; $R_e < 500$), where inertial forces are less than gravitational and viscous forces. Although common in slow-moving groundwater, this flow condition is rare within rivers and is typically associated only with viscous sublayers or very slowly moving, deep water.

2. *Supercritical-laminar* ($F_r > 1$; $R_e < 1$), where inertial forces are sufficient to dominate gravitational forces but are not sufficient to overcome the viscous forces. This type of flow is exceptionally rare in

rivers. It usually occurs where fast-moving water pours in a thin layer over the top of smooth rocks. Outside of rivers, supercritical-laminar flow presumably occurs during the formation of sheetwash during overland flow (see chap. 6).

3. *Subcritical-turbulent* ($F_r < 1$; $R_e > 2,000$), where inertial forces exceed viscous forces but are dominated by gravitational forces. This flow condition is by far the most common flow condition of rivers, regardless of flood level.

4. *Supercritical-turbulent* ($F_r > 1$; $R_e > 2,000$), where inertial forces dominate both viscous and gravitational forces. These flows are rare in large, low-gradient rivers like the lower Sacramento or Klamath. However, in high-gradient, shallow or narrow rivers where velocities are high and relative depths are much lower, supercritical-turbulent conditions are common, although spatially limited.

Reading the Rapids or Designing Flood Control Channels:
Subcritical-Turbulent versus Supercritical-Turbulent Flow

Of the four general flow types that can be recognized within rivers, only two, subcritical-turbulent and supercritical-turbulent, are widespread and common. In general, the difference between these two flows is manifested through dramatic changes in velocity and/or depth. The transition back and forth between subcritical-turbulent flow and supercritical-turbulent flow is the easiest to recognize on the surface of a river. This relationship is probably best illustrated by the occurrence of "holes" or "hydraulics" at the entrance to rapids on high-gradient rivers.

The occurrence of most rapids is associated with abrupt changes in gradient. The natural causes of these changes are numerous and can include accumulation of debris from side creeks or landslides, changes in the erosional resistance of bedrock types, the occurrence of faults or zones of structural weakness (see chap. 7). The gradient changes that create rapids worthy of fearsome names like Satan's Cesspool (South Fork of the American River), Maytag (Yuba River), and Bogus Thunder (North Fork of the American River) typically involve an abrupt steepening of gradient or slope followed by an equally abrupt decrease in gradient.

To a rafter, canoeist, or kayaker, there is a stretch of water above most rapids that belies the terror that awaits immediately below. The relatively low gradient and associated large channel cross-sectional area ensure a low flow velocity (Manning and continuity of flow equations). The gently swirling, roiling surface that makes up the stretch above most rapids reflects fully turbulent ($R_e \gg 2,000$), subcritical ($F_r < 1$) flow. In this flow condition, eddies or "bursts" form near the bed and around obstacles. The bursts mix and deflect the water mass as they grow upward, disrupting the gen-

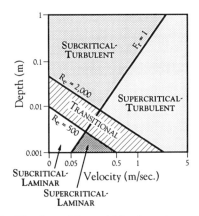

Fig. 2.5. Classification of flow within river channels and pipes based on nondimensional Reynolds and Froude numbers.

eral downstream flow direction. The inertia of these bursts carries them to the surface, where they create chaotic but gentle roils.

As whitewater enthusiasts will attest, at the head of most rapids is a "tongue" or "V" (fig. 2.6) that is often the point of entry for boats and kayaks. The tongue contains a number of unique features that illustrate well the role that changing inertial and gravitational forces have on the behavior of a river. The tongue coincides with a sharp increase in slope, which translates directly into an increase in velocity (eq. 2.4) and an associated decrease in the depth of the flow (eq. 2.1). As discussed above, increases in velocity and/or decreases in depth lead to an increase in the ratio of inertial to gravitational forces and Froude numbers greater than one.

Unlike the subcritical-turbulent flow characteristic of the low-gradient stretch immediately above the rapid, the supercritical-turbulent flow in the tongue does not have large, slow-moving eddies. Instead, the water moves more efficiently through the river, with less intense vertical mixing and smaller deviations from the average flow direction. Thus the roiling and swirling of the water surface that appears to dominate the upstream stretch of river gives way to a relatively smooth surface indicating that water is flowing rapidly in a somewhat more orderly fashion.

The transition from subcritical-turbulent to supercritical-turbulent conditions is referred to as a *hydraulic drop* due to a decrease in depth. In contrast, the abrupt transition from supercritical-turbulent to subcritical-turbulent flow that takes place at the base of the tongue is termed a *hydraulic jump,* or "hole," because it involves a rapid increase in depth of the flow. The transition from supercritical-turbulent to subcritical-turbulent conditions is one of the most prominent features on high-gradient rivers

Fig. 2.6. Raft entering turbulent-supercritical tongue of Warp II Rapid on the upper Kings River. Note smooth, shallow water ramp at entry to rapid and sharp transition to turbulent-subcritical conditions at base. John Lane, guide. Photo courtesy of Alan Webster.

and is a characteristic both revered and feared by whitewater rafters, kayakers, and canoeists. (See figs. 2.7, 2.8.)

The dramatic change in flow conditions that occur at a hydraulic jump or hole is associated with a decrease in slope and associated decrease in velocity of the flow (eqs. 2.1, 2.4). The return to subcritical-turbulent flow involves the abrupt formation of intense vertical mixing of the water and a sharp increase in depth. Because of the increase in depth, an upstream-breaking, solitary wave often forms at the transition point (fig. 2.7). The high-velocity, supercritical-turbulent water flowing into the hydraulic jump has considerable momentum and inertia. This causes the water to be carried downstream some distance along the bottom before being pulled back upstream near the surface and into the solitary breaking wave. The shear between the downstream-moving water and the upstream-moving water acts to enhance the steepness and intensity of the breaking wave. And, as any whitewater boater knows, this upstream-flowing water is what pulls boats back into holes where the high-velocity downstream flow against the upstream side of the boat is opposed by the wave breaking on the

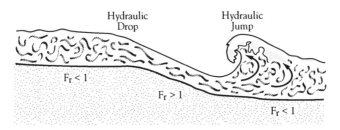

Fig. 2.7. Longitudinal profile of river illustrating hydraulic drop and hydraulic jump associated with changes in Froude number, gradient, velocity, and depth.

Fig. 2.8. Hydraulic jump associated with transition from supercritical-turbulent to subcritical-turbulent flow. Abrupt increase in depth and decrease in flow velocity at transition creates stationary wave capable of turning over rafts or sending paddlers for a swim. "Hole" developed at abrupt change in gradient. Increased gradient leads to development of high velocity, shallow depth, and supercritical flow conditions. Resumption of lower gradient leads to reduction in velocity, increase in depth, and conversion of flow back to subcritical, creating the dreaded hydraulic jump. Clavey Hole, Tuolumne River. Photograph by author.

downstream side of the boat. As I have repeatedly demonstrated to colleagues, the opposing forces cause the boat to flip, eject its contents, and
generate pandemonium, loss of pride, and an impromptu downstream yard
sale involving paddles, bags, and other unsecured goodies. Indeed, the intensity of the interaction between the breaking wave and the supercritical-
turbulent water flowing into the hole can cause logs, kayaks, paddles, and
even swimmers to tumble and spin around like a sock in a clothes dryer.

BOUNDARY LAYERS AND FLOW SEPARATION: LIFE IN THE FAST LANE

As noted above, there is a velocity gradient within pipes that reflects some
minimum velocity value near the wall of the pipe and a maximum velocity
near the center. The same applies to any flow in an open channel. At the
bed of the channel, the flow is retarded by the friction between the bed
and the flow. In principle, a very thin layer of water adjacent to the bed is
slowed to a stop by this frictional resistance (fig. 2.4). The effectiveness of
this flow retardation diminishes with increasing distance from the bed
until the velocity of the flow reaches a peak. The interval that contains this
velocity gradient is known as a *boundary layer* and exists in all open channel
flow.

The velocity gradient set up by frictional resistance between the bed
and the flow produces the transfer of momentum within a channel's flow.
Water that is flowing some distance from the bed has a greater momentum (mass × velocity) than water flowing adjacent to the bed. In low R_e
value flows where layers or slabs of fluid glide past each other, the momentum is transferred between slower and faster layers at the molecular level
along the contacts between slabs. Because this exchange of momentum is
relatively inefficient, therefore, the thickness of the boundary layer, or the
height above the bed where peak velocity is reached, is disproportionately
large (fig. 2.4). In contrast, in turbulent flow with high R_e values, momentum exchange is achieved by the vertical movement of eddies: water of low
momentum is carried upward and water of high momentum is carried
downward. This produces a very steep velocity gradient near the bed and a
relatively thin boundary layer. As discussed in chapter 3, this velocity gradient, which is tied directly to bed shear stress, leads to the erosion, suspension, and transport of sediment.

The *viscous sublayer,* also known as the *laminar sublayer,* is a relatively thin
layer of fluid that exists at the base of the boundary layer. In this layer, the
viscous forces dominate the flow, leading to very low R_e values. Where the
bed roughness is low (low *n* values), such as in riverbeds covered by fine
sand and silt, and overall turbulence within the flow is low, the viscous sub-

layer achieves its greatest thickness. However, where the bed is rough, such as in coarse sand and gravel beds, the grains protrude through the viscous sublayer, locally disrupting it and allowing turbulent eddies to directly affect the bed. The intrusion of these eddies into the viscous sublayer increases the bed shear stress and enhances the ability of a flow to erode and transport coarse sediment.

Why worry about boundary layers and viscous sublayers? Who cares? After all, water flowing through these layers only makes up a few percent of the total water flowing through a channel. The reason to belabor the boundary layer concept is at least threefold: (1) most turbulence and flow disruptions are initiated within or involve detachments of the boundary layer; (2) most of the work involved in eroding banks and channels, transporting coarse-grained sediment and depositing it, takes place within the boundary layer (chap. 3); and (3) most of the aquatic animals, insects, and plants live or work within the boundary layer.

The fluid moving near the channel bed and within the boundary layer has relatively little kinetic energy compared to the rest of the fluid. Thus if an adverse or upstream pressure gradient develops at any point, the fluid within the boundary layer will easily come to rest. The significance of this is that moving boundary-layer fluid that is immediately upstream collides with this stopped fluid and is displaced outward, separating it from the bed. This is the phenomenon known as *flow separation.* Each flow separation has a *separation point* where the boundary layer pulls away from the bed and an *attachment point* where the flow reattaches. Between the separation and attachment points there is a *separation bubble* or eddy involving a low-velocity, upstream flow of some of the separated fluid. (See fig. 2.9.)

Flow separation takes place on many scales, from separations around small disruptions in a bed (fig. 2.9) to separations formed by changes in channel geometry (figs. 2.10, 2.11). The significance of these separations is their formation of low-velocity turbulent-subcritical zones within otherwise fast-moving water. One aspect of flow separation that is easily visible is the formation of vortices. Where a boundary layer detaches from the bed, it enters the main current as a free shear layer in which water is going in opposite directions on either side. Known as an "eddy line" or "eddy fence" by whitewater boaters and fishermen alike, the shear along this contact produces intense *vortices,* or small, vertically oriented spiraling motions of water that typically form near the separation point, rise to the surface as they drift downstream, and ultimately dissipate before the reattachment point. Areas where vorticelike motion remains stationary are called *rollers.* The axis of rotation of these rollers is variable, depending on whether they are bank rollers or bottom rollers. Rollers typically occur immediately downstream of the separation point and can greatly influence erosion and sedimentation behind obstacles and at changes in channel cross section.

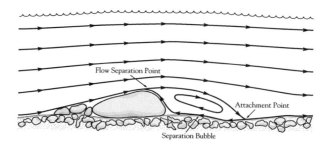

Fig. 2.9. Cross section depicting flow separation around an obstruction within a natural river. Displacement of the boundary layer causes an eddy or separation bubble to form immediately downstream or beneath detachment point.

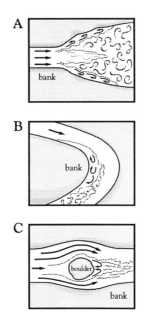

Fig. 2.10. Flow separation and the formation of vortices. *A*, Flow separation at channel widening. *B*, Separation of flow at bend or point bar. *C*, Separation of flow around obstacles in channel. (Redrawn from Morisawa 1985.)

Fig. 2.11. Examples of flow separation. *Top*: Staircase Rapid, North Fork of the American River. Note flow separation and eddy formation around large boulder in foreground and at margins of entry chute for rapid. *Bottom*: Obstruction in middle of river produces flow separation and separation eddy immediately downstream. Note development of hydraulic jump on either side of obstruction and supercritical flow across top. Indian Creek, Tuolumne River. Photographs by author.

Although essential for the generation of turbulence and sediment transport, boundary layers and flow separation make it possible for a variety of insects, plants, and animals to colonize river channels. If you rummage around the rocks in a mountain stream, you will uncover a host of insects that are exceptionally well adapted for making a living in fast-moving water. To save energy, these insects seek low-velocity separation bubbles behind or on irregular objects, although their food typically lies on rocks or in crevices within the high-velocity currents.

A variety of clever adaptations have appeared to allow these insects to feed. The dorsoventral flattening seen in most aquatic insects that forage in high-velocity streams is designed, in part, to reduce their exposure to currents by allowing them to hunker down within the boundary layer. Additional adaptations are small size, which allows them to fit within the boundary layer, streamlining, which reduces current drag, and development of claws, hooks, suckers, and friction pads for simply hanging on. The success of all these adaptations depends on the insects' remaining within the boundary layer.

Fish and some plants have adapted to microhabitats in or near boundary layers and flow separations. With their small size, fingerlings are able to reside completely within the boundary layer, allowing them to navigate and feed in currents that would normally wash them away. In the presence of moderate to high current velocities, most aquatic microphites develop strategies for surviving that involve firm attachments to some substrates and flexibility to allow them to lay flat within the low-velocity boundary layer. As all anglers know, a wide variety of game fish are particularly dependent on flow separations for survival in fast-flowing rivers. The low-velocity separation eddies and bubbles are ideal resting and feeding spots.

SUMMARY

Flow within rivers is typically unsteady and nonuniform, involving changes in velocity in both time and space. Within a given channel, the continuity of flow equation tells us that changes in discharge generate shifts in average velocity and cross-sectional area of channels. For a given discharge, the velocity of a flow can be estimated using the Manning equation, which is based on the relationship between average velocity, slope, hydraulic radius, and bed roughness. Several key dimensionless numbers predict the behavior of flows. The Reynolds number, which is the ratio of inertial to viscous forces, predicts the occurrence of laminar versus turbulent flow. The Froude number, which is the ratio of inertial to gravitational forces, determines if a flow is subcritical or supercritical. The Reynolds and Froude equations can be used to describe and classify most natural flows. Subcritical-turbulent flow is the most common flow in natural rivers;

supercritical-turbulent flow is less common. Changes between supercritical and subcritical flow regimes are accompanied often by dramatic changes in depth and velocity of flows, producing the hydraulic jumps and drops characteristic of rapids. Viscous forces predominate within the boundary layer of most flows, allowing the occurrence of laminar flow conditions immediately adjacent to smooth beds. Flow separation and the formation of separation eddies occur where a channel widens or where objects disrupt flow. Aquatic life, which seeks to reduce energy expenditures while resting or feeding, has developed a range of adaptations that exploit boundary layer and flow separation phenomena.

RELEVANT READINGS

Allen, John R. L. 1985. *Principles of Physical Sedimentology.* Boston: G. Allen and Unwin.

Chadwick, A. J. 1993. *Hydraulics in Civil and Environmental Engineering.* 2d ed. New York: Morfet.

Chow, V. T. 1959. *Open Channel Hydraulics.* New York: McGraw-Hill.

Dingman, S. L. 1984. *Fluvial Hydrology.* New York: W. H. Freeman.

Gregory, K. J., ed. 1977. *River Channel Changes.* Chichester, U.K.: John Wiley and Sons.

Manning, J. C. 1992. *Applied Principles of Hydrology.* New York: Maxwell Macmillan International.

Morisawa, M. 1985. *Rivers.* New York: Longman.

Raghunath, H. M. 1985. *Hydrology: Principles, Analysis, and Design.* New York: John Wiley and Sons.

Simon, A. L. 1986. *Hydraulics.* 3d ed. New York: John Wiley and Sons.

Vogel, S. 1981. *Life in Moving Fluids: The Physical Biology of Flow.* Princeton: Princeton University Press.

Ward, R. C., and M. Robinson. 1990. *Principles of Hydrology.* 3d ed. New York: McGraw-Hill.

Yalin, M. S. 1992. *River Mechanics.* Oxford: Pergamon Press.

THREE

A River at Work

Sediment Entrainment, Transport, and Deposition

INTRODUCTION

With the exception of those channel reaches that are composed entirely of bare rock, rivers line their channels with sediment. If you slosh your way around any mountain stream or shallow river, you can see the complex variation in the size and composition of this channel lining. During high water or flood conditions, you can hear the collisions of pebbles and cobbles as they roll or slide along the riverbed. Sediment, from Ford Country Squire–sized boulders typical of high-gradient rivers like the upper Kern and Tuolumne to the fine sand, silt, and clay of low-gradient rivers like the lower Sacramento and San Joaquin, is an essential ingredient of a river system.

As noted in chapter 1, the role that sediment plays in the shape and behavior of a river cannot be overstated. The river profile, the channel patterns, the loci of deposition and erosion—all reflect a river's attempts to balance energy expenditures, develop a least-work design, and process the discharge and sediment supplied to it by its watershed. Significant variations in sediment supply, whether through land use changes (like dams), climatic and tectonic events, or simply crossing thresholds in dynamic equilibrium (chap. 1), will lead to readjustments in the behavior and form of a river. To understand the impact that changes in sediment supply have on a river, it is necessary to understand the what-when-where-how of sediment *entrainment* (a fancy term for initiating motion of sedimentary particles), transport, and deposition. This chapter reviews those physical processes that influence sedimentation within river systems and the way in which rivers move their sediment load.

STREAM POWER, COMPETENCE, AND CAPACITY

The ability of a river to shuffle around sediment at any given time is not dependent so much on the amount of water that moves through it as on the stream power, or the ability of that water to do work. There are two principal types of energy associated with river flow: *potential energy*, or that energy which is gained by water when it is raised above some datum, and *kinetic energy*, or that energy formed by conversion of potential energy as water flows downhill. Kinetic energy does the job of eroding and transporting sediment and generating heat through friction with the bed. For any segment of a river, there is a continuous energy expenditure that can be measured as the loss of potential energy per unit length of channel. This energy loss is the rate of doing work, otherwise known as the *stream power*.

The relationship between stream power of a river and sediment transport can be evaluated in two ways: flow competence and flow capacity. For any given flow condition within a river, there is a maximum grain size that can be transported. This largest grain defines the *competence* of a given flow and can be used as a measure of overall stream power. For any given flow, there is also a maximum amount of sediment that the flow can transport. If sediment is added to that flow above the maximum, the river will deposit sediment on its bed until it again reaches the maximum amount it can transport. This maximum amount is known as the *capacity* of a flow. Most of the time, rivers transport less than their capacity, simply because less sediment is supplied to the river from its watershed. The rate of sediment that is transported by a river, or *sediment load,* is commonly expressed in tons per day. Along any river, variations in capacity and competence of a flow dictate the areas where erosion and deposition are going to take place. The causes of these variations are outlined below.

Sediment Entrainment (Competence)

When you look through the clear waters of a mountain stream, you will usually see that the riverbed is lined with coarse gravel and cobbles. This bed material is stationary in most conditions, refusing the day-to-day effort of the currents to move it along. Logically, most movement of the bed material takes place during high discharge events—those moments of terror described in chapter 1. When moving, coarse material will slide, roll, and occasionally bounce along the bottom of the channel. The material that moves along the bottom of the channel is called the *bedload* of a river. The coarsest sediment of a river flow, which defines its competence, is always moved as bedload.

The initiation of transport, or the entrainment of sediment on a bed, has been the subject of intense interest on the part of geologists, engineers, and, to a lesser extent, fisheries biologists. Innumerable flume experiments have documented critical thresholds for transport of different grain sizes in varying bed, depth, and velocity conditions. What has emerged from these experiments is the recognition that initiation of movement for a given grain size is not a simple process and that accurately predicting it in natural conditions is often difficult. Yet, as shown in Part II below, knowledge about entrainment thresholds of flows is key to a variety of land use planning and engineering problems. For example, the California Department of Fish and Game is actively attempting to restore salmon spawning habitats in the reaches of the Sacramento River immediately below Shasta Dam. One approach has been to mine coarse sand and gravel from tributaries and to simply dump it into the Sacramento to form spawning gravels. Of course, it is vital to know if this gravel is going to wash away during the winter releases from Shasta Dam, wasting these efforts (regrettably, it did). Alternatively, when the California Department of Transportation (CalTrans) builds bridges across rivers, they will often put the footings of their bridges directly in the sediment. Most bridge abutments and concrete piers constrict the cross section of a river, leading to an increase in the river's velocity (eq. 2.1). Will this increase in velocity lead to entrainment and scouring of the river sediment at that locality and possible failure of the bridge? Indeed, it has. The seemingly dull subject of sediment entrainment turns out to be important to all who manage or maintain our rivers.

The tractive forces of fluid drag and fluid lift, which are a function of the bed shear stress of a flow, are responsible for the entrainment of sedimentary particles. When a velocity gradient develops across a particle, fluid drag acts to slide or roll a grain over those surrounding it, while fluid lift tends to lift a grain up vertically, projecting it into the higher-flow velocities away from the bed. The factors that keep a grain from moving are its submerged weight (gravity) and the fact that it is usually wedged between adjacent grains. Wedging against the downstream grain acts like a fulcrum around which the grain must pivot before becoming fully entrained. The greater the angle formed by this fulcrum, the more difficult it is to entrain the grain. Thus in poorly sorted beds (those with a wide range of particle sizes), the relatively finer grain sizes can have higher entrainment thresholds as a result of wedging against other grains.

It is convenient to relate the initiation of particle motion to easily measured or averaged properties of the entire flow. Two commonly used approaches are to relate the maximum grain size moved to either the average velocity of the flow or the mean bed shear stress (chap. 2). Most hydraulic engineers use the more complicated but accurate latter approach, developed by A. Shields, which relates bed shear stress (as a function of

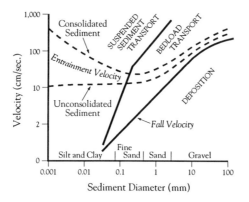

Fig. 3.1. Modified Hjulström diagram depicting threshold velocities for the entrainment and transport of sediment (dashed
lines) and fields indicating suspended versus bedload transport
for different grain sizes (solid lines). See text for discussion.

velocity), thickness of the laminar sublayer, and bed roughness to the maximum grain size entrained. The former approach, put forward by F. Hjulström, is the easiest to use and illustrate, although it is perhaps the most
deceptive. It is important to keep in mind that it is not velocity that en-
trains sediment but bed shear stress. The two, while related, are not syn-
onymous. The well-known Hjulström diagram, depicted in modified form
in figure 3.1, relates the critical (read: necessary) velocity for movement
of particles of a given diameter on a flat or plane bed.

The Hjulström diagram illustrates the intuitively obvious and some not-
so-obvious aspects of sediment entrainment. For sediment ranging from
fine sand (approximately 0.01 mm) to larger grains, the critical velocity is
proportional to grain size. A tenfold increase in grain size translates to a
two-and-one-half-fold increase in the velocity necessary for entrainment.
This is the "obvious" aspect of the diagram. Increasing grain sizes, by virtue of their greater submerged weight, require increasingly larger velocities or bed shear stresses for entrainment. As shown in the diagram, however, this relationship breaks down for grain sizes smaller than fine sand. A
variety of processes are responsible for the disruption in this trend. Particles less than 0.1 millimeter in size reside wholly within the laminar sublayer in most flows (R_e < 500). Like aquatic organisms, grains that lie
within the laminar sublayer experience reduced velocity gradients and less
lift force. In addition, the electrostatically charged surfaces of clay minerals make them stick together and become cohesive (a process known as
flocculation). The stickiness of clay-rich muds can make them more difficult to entrain than sands, even though their grain size is much smaller.

Fig. 3.2. Confluence of the Salmon and Klamath rivers. The Salmon River is a bedload-dominated stream that transports little sediment during moderate flows. The Klamath River transports large amounts of suspended load and is typically turbid during moderate flows. Photograph by author.

Sediment Transport (Capacity): Suspended Load and Bedload

If you were to stand adjacent to a small Sierran or Coast Range river that is in flood, you would hear the collisions of pebbles and cobbles as they move along the bed. From the frequency and intensity of these collisions it is easy to envision that the bedload of the river is moving as a layer of closely packed, randomly colliding particles sliding and rolling along the bed. However, the fact that you are unable to see this bedload indicates that sediment that is being carried by the river does not move solely along the bed. The turbidity of the river is an indication that finer particles (*fines*) are dispersed throughout the water column (fig. 3.2). In contrast to the bedload of a river, the fines that are transported above the zone of bed-load transport are called the *suspended load*. The total sediment load of a river is the combination of the coarse material that makes up the bedload and the finer material that makes up the suspended load (fig. 3.3). The physical processes that dictate whether a grain will be transported as bed-load or suspended load depend on the forces that cause a grain to settle to the bottom (gravity) and the forces that act to suspend the grain (turbulence and viscosity).

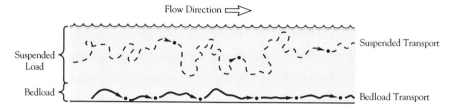

Fig. 3.3. Sediment transport within rivers can be broken up into suspended load (particles moving in suspension) and bedload (particles rolling or bouncing along the bottom).

Bedload transport.   The bedload transport system is a naturally compli-cated, negative feedback system. Ideally, it might be envisioned that bed-load material should tumble or roll continuously along with the currents until it eventually comes to rest somewhere. Instead, grains transported as bedload move along in a herky-jerky motion involving short bursts of transport interspersed with periods of no motion. In this manner the aver-age transport velocity of bedload grains falls behind that of the main cur-rent. This irregular motion of grains stems from the tendency of a current to mold and shape its bed into *equilibrium bedforms*. These bedforms are the ripples, dunes, sand waves, scours, and other surfaces that form on the bed of a river. They are dynamic, migrating either downstream or upstream, and appear to reflect some balance of forces or an equilibrium with flow conditions. For flows that contain a mobile sediment bed, the formation of bedforms appears to increase the Manning roughness coefficient, n (eq. 2.4). This is because the bedforms themselves increase the turbulence of the water as it flows over them and the movement of sediment uses or ab-sorbs kinetic energy, helping to reduce the overall flow velocity.

Where relatively clear water flows across shallow sandbars you can ob-serve the formation and migration of equilibrium bedforms. In subcritical flows, the downstream migration of bedforms is a function of erosion on the upstream, or *stoss,* side of the bedform coupled with deposition on the downstream, or *lee,* side (fig. 3.4). As water flows up the lee face of the bedform, it reaches a brink point where flow separation occurs. The flow separation leads to the formation of a separation eddy or bubble with flow reattachment immediately downstream of the migrating bedform. Bed-load and suspended load carried over and eroded from the stoss side of the bedform segregate at the point of flow separation. The coarse material accumulates at the brink point, increasing the overall slope of the lee face. At some point, the overall slope of the lee face becomes so steep that sedi-ment avalanches into the trough, effectively shifting the lee face of the ripple downstream. The coarser-grained suspended load that was carried

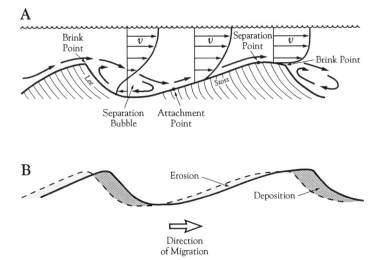

Fig. 3.4. Migration and morphology of ripple or dune formed by bed-load transport of sand. *A:* General form features illustrating formation of flow separation at brinkpoint and reattachment in trough and irregular velocity profiles formed over ripple surface. Note foresets formed by avalanching down face of dune. *B:* Downstream migration of ripples through erosion of the upstream, or stoss, side of the ripple and accumulation on the downstream, or lee, surface of the ripple.

past the separation point settles down through the low-velocity separation bubble, augmenting the avalanched bedload and adding to the apparent downstream migration of the ripple.

The episodic avalanching of the lee face of ripples and dunes followed by suspension deposition of fines produces steeply inclined, thin layers of contrasting grain size. These steeply inclined laminae, or *foresets,* are easily recognized within riverbank and channel deposits composed principally of sand-sized material and are a useful mechanism for evaluating ancient flow regime conditions and current directions.

Suspended load transport. If you drop a pebble into a lake or other body of perfectly still water, gravity will cause it to settle quickly to the bottom. If the water is deep enough, the pebble will accelerate to its terminal fall velocity and then maintain its speed until it strikes the bottom. The magnitude of this fall velocity must reflect a balance between the forces acting to settle the grain and those resisting its fall. Gravity is the downward-acting force that accelerates the grain. The effectiveness of this acceleration is a function of the submerged weight of the grain or the difference between the weight of the grain and the weight of water of equivalent volume. The greater the difference, the more effective gravitational acceleration will be (i.e., it sinks faster). The opposing forces are all associated with the viscosity of the water through which the grain falls. The greater the surface/volume ratio of the grain, the greater the viscous effects that slow it down. The greater the dynamic viscosity of the water, the slower the particle will fall.

From this relationship between gravitational and viscous forces emerged *Stokes's law*, in which the terminal fall velocity, ω_o, of a grain is

$$\omega_o = .0555D^2(\rho_s - \rho_w)g/\mu, \qquad (3.1)$$

where D is the diameter of the grain, ρ_s and ρ_w the density of the grain and the water, respectively, g the acceleration due to gravity, and μ the dynamic viscosity of the water.

So why bother about the terminal settling velocity of a particle? In reality, the Stokes equation only applies to grains that are less than 2 mm in diameter and, worse yet, are falling through virtually still water. The applicability lies in determining whether or not grains will remain in suspension in turbulent flow. As noted in chapter 3, the velocity of a flow with high R_e values really reflects the sum of the effects of numerous deviations from the primary flow direction. These flow deviations, which are a product of the formation of turbulent eddies and the exchange of momentum within the water column, have their own inertia. By exerting drag on the surface of grains in suspension, the flow deviations act to disperse particles in a variety of directions. Most important, where the velocity of the upward-oriented instantaneous flow deviation exceeds the terminal settling velocity of a grain, that grain will be pushed upward, keeping it in suspension in the water column. If the deviations are less than the settling velocity, the particle will settle out and, if there is sufficient bed shear stress, be transported as bedload.

The actual mechanics of particle suspension are much more complicated than a simple difference between settling velocity and velocity of flow deviations. A suspended particle will typically be kept in suspension by periodic, intense flow deviations associated with short-lived, high-velocity eddies. The more intense and frequent the turbulence, the larger the grain size that can be transported as suspended load and the greater the amount of material that will reside in suspension. Factors that enhance the intensity of turbulence act to increase the R_e value (eq. 2.5). These include the velocity of the flow, its hydraulic mean depth, and the bed roughness. Thus, fast-flowing deep rivers are capable of moving extraordinary volumes of material as suspended sediment.

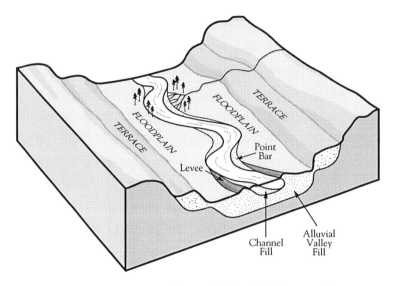

Fig. 3.5. Sites of storage of sediment within a fluvial system. Storage typically associated with sharp declines in capacity and competence of flow, whether on floodplains or within the channel.

Deposition: The Decline of Flow Capacity and Competence

Although rivers adjust to accommodate the sediment load and discharge supplied to them by their watersheds, these adjustments, which involve innumerable changes in channel morphology, do not occur immediately or during one single flow. For this reason, rivers deal with their sediment load by adjusting the hydraulic variables *and* by temporarily or even permanently storing sediment in a variety of sites. Temporary storage sites include channel bars, point bars, levees, and floodplains; long-term or even permanent storage sites include terraces and deltas. These sediment storage facilities all share one thing in common: they form where and when the competence and capacity of a river decrease. The loss of competence and capacity is usually associated with significant declines in velocity. Abrupt decreases in velocity are associated with increases in channel cross-sectional area ($Q = vA$), flow separations, declines in channel gradient and hydraulic radius, or significant changes in bed roughness.

Figure 3.5 summarizes the storage sites for sediment within an overall river system. Although coarse sediment is often stored within a channel in the form of bars and bed material (fig. 3.6), the most volumetrically significant storage sites are the floodplains and terraces. The floodplain of most natural rivers contains a mixture of colluvium, or coarse material, derived

Fig. 3.6. Temporary storage of sediment in point bars and gravel bars in the Eel River, Del Norte County, California. *Top*: Extensive coarse-grained point bars, main stem Eel River. *Bottom*: Note large, incised gravel bar formed at flow separation near railroad bridge, confluence of South and Middle Fork of the Eel River. These bars only form during exceptionally large and rare flows. Photographs by author.

from the valley walls, river channel deposits that occur as channels migrate back and forth across the valley, and fine-grained sediments deposited in areas outside of a channel during flooding events.

Grain Size Segregation

Because particles of differing size respond differently to flows, there is a natural segregation of grain sizes within depositional sites. For example, if you dump a mixture of clay, silt, and sand into a bucket of water, the difference in settling velocity will cause the mixture to segregate quickly: the coarsest material will reach the bottom of the bucket first, and the finer material will arrive later. The resulting deposit will therefore be *graded*, with the coarsest material on the bottom and the finer material on top. If you do this experiment repeatedly but agitate the water so that the finer material remains in suspension, then only the coarse sediment will accumulate at the bottom.

Rivers hydraulically segregate their sediment in a manner that is analogous to the bucket experiment. There are maximum grain sizes that can be moved as bedload and suspended load for any given flow condition. Any decrease in competence or capacity of the flow is going to affect these maximum grain sizes first: at about two-thirds of its entrainment velocity, the coarsest bedload ceases to move and the coarsest suspended load reverts to bedload transport (fig. 3.1). This process ensures that the deposits that are produced by small changes in competence and capacity are likely to be around the same grain size. If you take a shovel and dig through a sand or gravel bar, you will typically find very little overall variation in grain size. These well-sorted deposits indicate that a relatively small decline in competence and capacity leads to deposition of sediment of a limited range in size.

The process of leaving the coarsest sediment behind at each successive decline in competence causes hydraulic grain segregation on a regional or riverwide scale. For example, in the lowermost reaches of the larger rivers of California, like the Sacramento, San Joaquin, Feather, and Kings, you will rarely find sediment that exceeds 1 centimeter in diameter. Although it is logical to blame the state's innumerable dams for the dearth of coarse material (see chap. 16), these low-gradient lower reaches have been fine-grained for thousands of years. Rather, it appears that much of the coarsest sediment is stored in depositional sites in upland areas. This is perhaps best illustrated by the extensive gravel deposits that occur along the eastern edge of the Sacramento Valley. These deposits, which have been dredged repeatedly for gold, occur where the rivers that emerge from the Sierran foothills undergo a sharp decline in gradient as they hit the valley floor. This loss of gradient translates directly to a loss of competence and the concentrated dumping of the coarse load of these rivers.

Capacity can occasionally be decoupled from competence in its effects on a river. For example, even if a river is competent enough to transport coarse sand-sized material, the river will deposit it rather than transport it if the supply of that size material is excessive. Numerous California rivers provide ample illustrations of this process. Intense clear-cut logging in the north coast mountains has led to extraordinary runoff of sediment into creeks and rivers (see chap. 12). Redwood Creek, where it traverses Redwood National Park, has been overwhelmed by this influx of sediment. Although the competence of the creek has not been exceeded by this sediment, the capacity has been exceeded. Thus the river has been unable to handle its excess load and has deposited it directly within the channel, causing the channel to aggrade and migrate laterally, destroying old-growth stands of redwoods as it erodes its banks.

Perhaps no event in the history of California illustrates the decoupling of competence and capacity better than the hydraulic mining of the late 1800s. The impacts of this event, which are explored in detail in chapter 11, are unparalleled. Thousands of acre-feet of sediment were washed into the middle reaches of rivers that drain the central Sierra Nevada. The magnitude and abrupt nature of this sediment influx prevented the rivers from adjusting themselves to their new load. Their capacity exceeded, these rivers dumped their excess load within channels and on floodplains. The aggradation, or vertical accumulation, of channel sediments associated with these events is unprecedented: the base of the American River channel rose 40 feet, and the Yuba River channel near Yuba City rose 90 feet. These river changes, all a product of overwhelming the capacity but not the competence, changed the landscape of central and northern California.

In the absence of sufficient sediment supply, excess or unused stream power and associated excess competence of flows can also produce grain size segregation. The impacts of the state's innumerable dams and gravel extraction operations are reviewed in Part II. One of the more significant but unheralded impacts of these operations is the complete removal of coarse sediment sources for many of the state's rivers. The water released from dams is relatively clear, with almost all of the coarse sediment being trapped behind the dam. Since the clear water that is released from these dams has no sediment to transport, it has excessive stream power (referred to as "hungry water" by some). Thus during high flows the excess stream power will entrain coarse material without replenishing it. In a relatively short period, this process can produce considerable channel erosion as the river cannibalizes its sediment storage facilities such as floodplains and terraces.

Fig. 3.7. Coarse grained, armored bar on the Tuolumne River near Indian Creek. Hetch Hetchy and Cherry Lake reservoirs upstream trap bulk of coarse and intermediate material previously supplied to river. Excess stream power of flows released from dam winnow finer material from bars. Lack of replenishment leads to formation of layer of coarse material that exceeds competence of largest flows released from dams. Photograph by author.

Since maximum dam releases are inevitably less than the peak natural flows that shaped the river, there is a decline in the maximum competence following dam construction. The result of this excess stream power but lessened maximum competence is a winnowing of sediment stored in bars, channels, and floodplains, where bed shear stress is sufficient for entraining fine gravels and sands but is incapable of moving the coarsest material that accumulated prior to dam construction. This selective removal of the finer-grained material leads to *armoring* of channels, a process whereby coarse material, commonly cobble size or larger, eventually lines channels, locally inhibiting further erosion (fig. 3.7). Armoring has a number of negative side effects, especially for maintenance of spawning habitats.

SUMMARY

Rivers adjust their profile and pattern to accommodate their discharge and their sediment load. Sediment moves through rivers irregularly, either temporarily or permanently residing in a variety of depositional sites. Erosion, transportation, and deposition of sediment is primarily a function of variations in the competence and capacity of a river. The maximum grain size that a flow can transport is its competence; the total amount of sediment that can be transported is a river's capacity. Entrainment of sediment is a function of the drag and lift forces exerted on sedimentary particles and the resistance of that grain to entrainment. The greater the velocity and bed shear stress, the greater the grain size that can be entrained. Once entrained, most coarse-grained material will move as bedload, rolling or sliding along the riverbed. A mobile bed will create bedforms that are in equilibrium with the current. Grains fine enough to remain in suspension within a flow make up the suspended load of rivers. The size and amount of material transported in suspension is dependent on the settling velocities of grains and the magnitude of flow turbulence. Deep, high-velocity flows, which have the highest Reynolds numbers, are most effective at transporting material in suspension.

Rather than routing all sediment through quickly, rivers will typically store sediment within a variety of depositional sites. Short-term storage occurs in channel bars and in the channel bed. Intermediate storage occurs within the floodplain. Long-term storage occurs within elevated alluvial terraces. Declines in capacity and competence lead to deposition within all of these sites. Excessive stream power or declines in sediment supply can cause a river to selectively erode material in these sites. Where dams remove coarse sediment supply, reduced competence coupled with excessive stream power leads to winnowing of channel sediments and eventual armoring of the channels.

RELEVANT READINGS

Allen, John R. L. 1985. *Principles of Physical Sedimentology*. Boston: G. Allen and Unwin.

Friedman, G. M., J. E. Sanders, and D. C. Kopsaka-Merkel. 1992. *Principles of Sedimentary Deposits*. New York: Macmillan.

Graf, W. H. 1984. *Hydraulics of Sediment Transport*. Littleton, Colo.: Water Resources Publications.

Middleton, G. V., and J. B. Southard. 1978. *Mechanics of Sediment Transport*. Society of Economic Paleontologists and Mineralogists Short Course no. 3. Binghamton, N.Y.

Pye, K., ed. 1994. *Sediment Transport and Depositional Processes*. Cambridge: Blackwell Scientific Publications.

Reineck, H.-E., and I. B. Singh. 1980. *Depositional Sedimentary Environments, with Reference to Terrigenous Clastics*. 2d ed. New York: Springer Verlag.

FOUR

The Shape of a River

INTRODUCTION

Most of the business of a river is conducted through its channel. The day-to-day task of handling discharge, the year-to-year task of eroding, transporting, and depositing sediment, and the long-term adjustments toward some equilibrium are all dependent on processes that occur within or immediately adjacent to a river's main channel. The morphology and behavior of channels has long been considered a sensitive indicator of the "state" of any river as well as a record of processes acting within a watershed. For much of this century geomorphologists have been measuring and analyzing river channels in order to tie them in some predictable way to aspects of the hydrology and geology of their watersheds. For every study conducted, it seems there is a new set of equations (with fudge factors) that quantify these relationships. The scatter in the data is immense, the usefulness of the results suspect. What has emerged from these studies is the recognition that there are broadly applicable principles that govern the response of river channels to change within, or differences between, watersheds. Although it is difficult to predict the precise extent of the change, the *nature* of change can be estimated. The qualitative associations between river morphology and hydrology are explored in this chapter, with an emphasis on the response of rivers to changes in watershed conditions.

CHANNEL CROSS SECTIONS

A river balances and minimizes its energy expenditures through adjustment of its channel cross section. Along the entire length of a river the shape and size of an infinite number of cross sections are in constant variation, adapting to the discharge and sediment load that is delivered to it by the channel reach that lies immediately upstream. In aggregate these adjustments produce the distinctive channel patterns that record the establishment of dynamic equilibrium within the overall river system.

Bankfull Discharge and Channel Geometry

Rivers construct channel cross sections that are best adapted for the wide range of discharges delivered by their watersheds. It is clear from the all-too-common flooding of some regions in California that rivers do not form channels capable of containing the entire range of flows. This is somewhat counterintuitive, since most of the work that a river does takes place during infrequent runoff events. It seems logical to assume that these highly competent, rare large flows should scour large channels that are capable of accommodating all of the discharge without creating any flooding. Conversely, most of the time it appears that channels are, in fact, overdesigned for their discharge. During the major part of any given year, the flows that move through rivers do not come close to taxing even half the channel capacity. These common flows have such low overall stream power that they are incapable of eroding and transporting much sediment. Thus they exert little influence on the configuration of the channel.

A number of workers have noted that although unusually large discharge events are capable of greatly affecting river channels and river geomorphology, their occurrence is so rare that, when viewed in the long term, their effects are usually masked by intermediate, more frequent discharges. The ability of intermediate flows to erode, transport, and deposit sediment allows them to eventually undo the effects of the larger events and to control the equilibrium configuration of the channels. The intermediate discharge that appears to exert the greatest influence on the shape and size of channel cross sections and thus on the overall geomorphology of the river is generally known as *bankfull stage* or *bankfull discharge*. For most rivers, bankfull stage occurs when discharge fills the entire channel cross section without significant inundation of the adjacent floodplain.

Bankfull stage or bankfull discharge, Q_b, usually occurs with a frequency of 1.5 to 2 years for natural, undammed rivers. This does not mean that these flows will occur like clockwork every two years. Rather, over very long periods, bankfull discharge will occur *on average* every 1.5 to 2 years (see discussion of flood frequency, chap. 14). Apparently, bankfull discharges meet two key criteria for shaping channel cross sections: (1) the flows contain sufficient stream power to erode bank materials and to transport and deposit large volumes of sediment; and (2) they occur often enough that their effects are not muted by the weaker, but higher-frequency, smaller-discharge events.

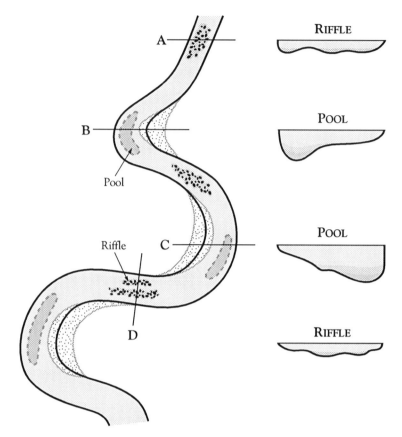

Fig. 4.1. Cross-sectional profiles of riffle and pools within a meandering
river. Note the asymmetric profile of pools located in meander bends and
symmetrical profiles of riffle sections within straight channel reaches.
(Modified from Morisawa 1985.)

The interaction between bankfull discharge and its channel produces a
wide range of channel cross sections. The causes of these variations are
numerous but are usually tied directly to interaction between the flow and
the bank materials. Within any given channel reach, the cross-sectional
profile of the river varies from symmetric to asymmetric (fig. 4.1). This
variation is due primarily to the tendency of a river to develop meanders
rather than a perfectly straight channel (discussed below). Within meander bends that are tightly curved, the cross-section profile becomes
strongly asymmetric. In the relatively straight stretches between meander bends, the profiles are more symmetric. Disruptions in the overall pro-

file shape are typically associated with obstructions or the development of channel bars.

The shape of a channel controls the structure of the flow that travels through it (and vice versa). Bed shear stress, the necessary ingredient for entrainment of sediment, is proportional to the velocity gradient (change in velocity with distance from the bed). In symmetric channels, the highest flow velocities and highest velocity gradients are located near the center of the channel, with the lowest gradients occurring near the margins. In contrast, in asymmetric channels, the velocities and gradients are always located adjacent to the steep-walled cut banks. During bankfull stage, the differences in distribution of bed shear stresses within symmetric and asymmetric channels control the style and magnitude of channel cross-section modification. The concentration of bed shear stress along the cut bank margin of asymmetric channels will cause them to erode the channel wall and expand laterally, whereas the concentration of bed shear stress in the center of symmetric channels will cause them to incise or deepen. To maintain continuity of flow during bankfull discharge ($Q = vA$), increases in channel cross section associated with erosion must be balanced by either a decrease in the velocity of the flow or by compensating deposition and reduction in cross-sectional area elsewhere in the channel. In symmetric channels, this deposition usually takes place in channel bars or along the margins. In asymmetric channels, deposition is usually restricted to the low-velocity margin of the channel opposite the most intense erosion. The balance between erosion on one side of a channel and deposition on the opposite side is the driving force behind lateral migration of channels (see discussion below).

Where channel reaches inundate their floodplains with a frequency greater than the 1.5 to 2 years typical of bankfull stage, depositional processes, rather than erosional processes, can act to expand the channel capacity. Discharge that is fully confined to a channel maintains high competence. When discharge exceeds channel capacity, there is a dramatic increase in cross-sectional area associated with expansion onto the floodplain (fig. 4.2). The velocity and depth of water flowing outside of the channel declines rapidly with distance away from the channel. The decline in depth and velocity, which produces sharp drops in R_e and F_r values, produces a rapid loss in stream power and competence. This decline acts to hydraulically segregate and deposit material that was formerly in suspension within the channel. The coarsest sediment (usually fine sand and silt) undergoes rapid deposition immediately adjacent to the channel, while the finest sediment is deposited away from the channel out on the floodplain. This is why Californians are always scraping mud, rather than sand, out of their homes after floods. Multiple flooding constructs a berm

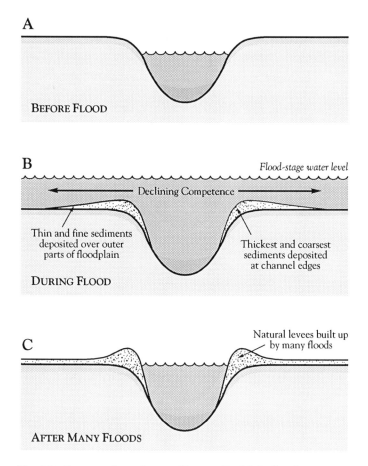

A

BEFORE FLOOD

B

Flood-stage water level

← Declining Competence →

Thin and fine sediments
deposited over outer
parts of floodplain

Thickest and coarsest
sediments deposited
at channel edges

DURING FLOOD

C

Natural levees built up
by many floods

AFTER MANY FLOODS

Fig. 4.2. Construction of natural levees. Rapid decline in competence of flows that occur outside of channel causes localized deposition of coarse material immediately adjacent to river. Multiple flooding episodes cause the levees to grow, increasing the overall channel capacity.

or levee adjacent to the active channel. As these levees increase in height the channel capacity increases, allowing the channel to contain larger and larger discharges.

Since a river adjusts to handle its load and discharge, it is logical to assume that the geometry and size of a channel cross section are controlled solely by these factors. However, another important control on channel morphology is the nature of bed and bank materials in which a river establishes itself. Where rivers traverse valleys filled with alluvium, the cohesive-ness of the sediment and its resistance to erosion will greatly influence the shape of a channel and, ultimately, the behavior of flow within it. Where bank materials are soft and easily erodible, scour of the banks causes chan-nels to expand laterally, forming cross sections that are wide and shallow. Where channel margins are resistant to erosion, there is a tendency for cross sections to become narrower, with steeper banks. The resistance of alluvial bank materials is dependent on a variety of factors. Finer-grained materials, like clays and muds, tend to be more cohesive and resistant to erosion. In addition, the degree of cementation and consolidation of sedi-ments will dictate their resistance. However, one of the most important factors controlling cross-section geometry in alluvial rivers is the presence and type of bank-stabilizing vegetation. The role of riparian vegetation in shaping channel cross sections is usually underappreciated. The mesh-work of roots from trees and the diverse riparian vegetation that are di-rectly dependent on river water can, in many cases, be as effective in stabi-lizing riverbanks as the scenic concrete and riprap liners that are the preferred fare of the U.S. Army Corps of Engineers (chap. 15).

As channels migrate laterally within alluvial valleys, they erode their own floodplain as well as channel deposits left behind by previous lateral migrations. In this way, they usually erode material that is compositionally similar to the load being supplied by the watershed. At the same time, the channel and overbank deposits that are accumulating at present in a river will be the bank materials of the near future as the channel migrates back and forth. For this reason, rivers with high suspended load/bedload ratios tend to have erosionally resistant banks composed of silt and clay. This re-sistance typically leads to the development of steep-sided, narrow channels that are, in an illustration of the complex circularity of feedback within these systems, ideal for transporting high suspended sediment loads. Riv-ers that are dominated by bedload tend to have less-resistant banks com-posed of sand and, to a lesser extent, gravels. These channels are more likely to be broad and shallow as well as highly unstable. The increase in wetted perimeter of these channels makes them ideal for transporting coarse bedload.

In upland regions where rivers are actively cutting into bedrock, the bank materials are an independent influence on channel geometry. The erosional resistance of the bedrock and the regional rates of uplift will typically dictate the channel geometry. Where the channel is fully con-tained within a resistant bedrock unit, the shape will be narrow and deep, whereas erodible bedrock will typically produce broad, shallow channels. Where incising channels encounter an erosionally resistant layer of bed-rock, they will initially expand laterally faster than they incise. When they are fully contained within the underlying resistant bedrock, they will re-establish a narrow, deep channel. In areas where uplift rates are high, steep-walled narrow channel cross sections will typically reflect rapid rates of incision, regardless of bedrock type.

CHANNEL PATTERN

Like a two-year-old child, a river cannot hold still. The innumerable and incessant adjustments that occur in a channel cross section translate to constant change in channel pattern and character. Since most unregulated rivers achieve dynamic equilibrium, this change can occur at various scales, ranging from incremental lateral migration to dramatic channel abandonment and switching. The reasons behind this incessant motion are among the more puzzling aspects of rivers and have given rise to numerous innovative and clever hypotheses and some enjoyable philosophical arguments. Regardless of the causes of this mobility (explored below), it is fundamental to all rivers and is the root of most morphologic classification schemes.

River and stream channel patterns can be grouped into two general classes: single channel and multichannel. The flow in single channel rivers is restricted to a discrete, sinuous channel. The larger rivers of California, like the San Joaquin, Sacramento (fig. 4.3), and Klamath, all occupy one relatively stable main channel surrounded by an extensive floodplain. Multichannel rivers, like the Santa Ana, Santa Clara, and Santa Maria and many of the small rivers and creeks that emerge from dry, steep mountain ranges (fig. 4.4), consist of numerous, unstable channels that bifurcate and join across a relatively broad wash. The differences between single and multichannel rivers reflect contrasting watershed conditions.

Single Channel Rivers

When examining single channel rivers in map view (fig. 4.5), the greatest variation appears to be in the way they snake across the landscape. This snakelike property is termed channel *sinuosity*. The sinuosity of a river is variably defined but is generally a reflection of the channel length required to cover a given point-to-point or straight-line distance. As shown in figure 4.6, the irregular course of a river usually occupies a portion of a valley, termed the *meander belt*. A line drawn down the center of this meander belt is referred to as the *meander belt axis*. In large valleys like the Sacramento, the meander belt axis does not always parallel the valley walls and thus tends to be longer than the valley itself. There are two possible axial measurements within the river channel: the *thalweg*, which is the deepest portion of the channel, and the *channel axis*, which is equidistant

Fig. 4.3. 1952 aerial photograph of Sacramento River in Glenn County, north of Sacramento. Note meandering single channel pattern of river. Also note extensive point bar development and heavily vegetated riparian corridor.

from the channel walls. Since the channel cross section of most meander bends is asymmetrical, the thalweg rarely coincides with the channel axis. Based on these features a *sinuosity index* (SI) can be defined for channels where

$$SI = \text{thalweg length/valley length} \qquad (4.1)$$

or

$$SI = \text{length of channel axis/length of meander belt axis.} \qquad (4.2)$$

Fig. 4.4. 1953 USDA aerial photograph of lower Cache Creek, Yolo County, California. This steep-gradient, bedload-dominated river occupies multiple, actively migrating channels during bankfull discharge events, forming an extensive braid plain. Intense aggregate mining has greatly disrupted the sediment budget for this river, creating a number of land use issues.

The latter sinuosity index has been used to separate single channel rivers into three general classes: *straight* (SI < 1.05), *sinuous* (SI 1.05–1.5), and *meandering* (SI > 1.5) (fig. 4.7).

Origin and Significance of Meandering

The scarcity of perfectly "straight" channels is widely believed to indicate that meandering is the more preferred state of single channel rivers. Why rivers prefer to meander is subject to debate. In general, the arguments revolve around the view that meandering is a response to either external forcing mechanisms, such as discharge and sediment supply, or internal mechanisms, such as flow separation and the development of vortices. The "extrinsic" view of meandering proposes that the sinuosity reflects the efforts of a river to maintain energy efficiency while balancing energy or power expenditures throughout its length. The "intrinsic" view

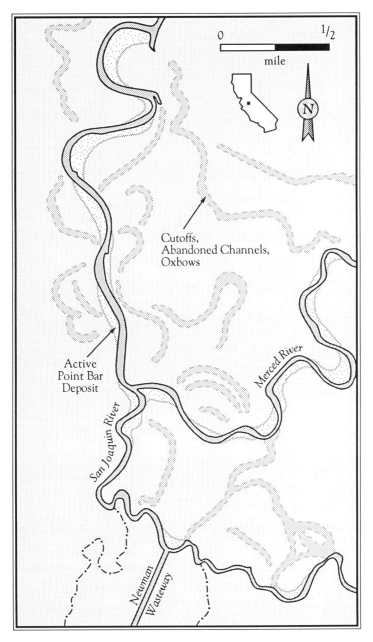

Fig. 4.5. Confluence of the Merced and San Joaquin rivers illustrating meander and point bar development. Note numerous abandoned channels and meander cutoffs on floodplain. Also note difference in meander wavelength and amplitude of the San Joaquin above and below confluence. Change in meandering is probably associated with addition of discharge from the Merced River.

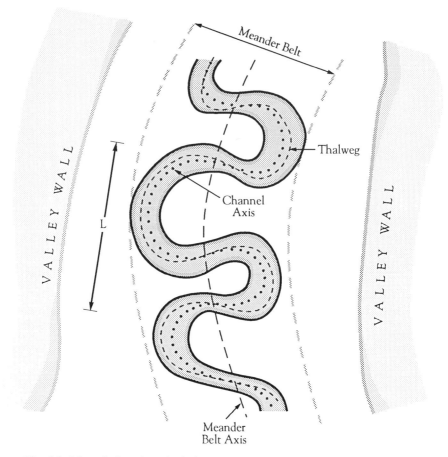

Fig. 4.6. Meandering river depicting some of the main physiographic features used for describing sinuosity in single channel rivers. *L* refers to the meander wavelength.

argues that meandering occurs whenever local perturbations in erosional resistance of bed or bank materials occur. These differences cause a deviation in the flow path that is self-accelerating and translated downstream. In essence, single channel rivers cannot help it; they *have* to meander.

The meandering of single channel rivers probably reflects both intrinsic and extrinsic processes. The wavelength and amplitude of meanders within rivers are clearly nonrandom. They can be correlated with aspects of the overall load, discharge, and gradient with which any stretch of a river has to work. Thus meandering must be associated with a river's attempt to handle its load and balance its energy expenditures. However, all of these adjustments in energy expenditures and load transport are ini-

STRAIGHT

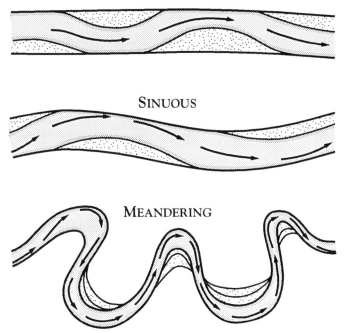

SINUOUS

MEANDERING

Fig. 4.7. Three general classes of single channel rivers based on their sinuosity index. Arrows indicate location of highest-velocity flows within each channel. Stippled area indicates development of lateral and point bars within channel. (Modified from Miall 1977.)

tiated by the natural tendency of flow to be deflected or diverted by in-homogeneities in bank and bed materials. That is, channels actively seek to develop an asymmetric profile, which, in turn, forces a river to develop meanders. In this manner, extrinsic and intrinsic processes work in concert to produce meandering rivers.

The intrinsic causes of meandering are the most extensively studied and the most easily recognized along any river. The "urge" to meander involves interaction between sediments that make up the bed and bank material and the oscillatory nature of flow within a channel. The longitudinal bed profile of most rivers and streams is broken into a series of alternating segments of high and low gradient. These segments form the *riffles* and *pools*, respectively, that are evident at low water levels (fig. 4.1). Riffles are the topographic high points on a bed profile. They are typically spaced five to seven channel widths apart and are composed of the coarsest bed-load that is being transported by the river. Pools, the haven of most river fish, are deep-water areas between the riffles. During high flow events, the pools are usually scoured, leaving a coarse gravel lag or channel armor and depositing material on the riffles.

Riffles and pools are a product of secondary circulation within channels. Turbulence induced by boundary roughness and interaction of the flow with any irregularities within channels sets up multiple *secondary flow cells,* or flow that moves downstream in a cylindrical, spiral motion. When secondary flow cells converge in the middle of a channel, there is a tendency for the flow to scour and form pools. Where the flow cells diverge, there is a tendency for the stream to erode its banks and build bars or riffles in the middle of the channel.

Once established in a channel, riffles and pools create even further disruptions in the uniformity of river flow. In low-gradient, low-sinuosity rivers (SI < 1.05) the overall stream power is usually low. Thus, although the riffles and pools create further flow disruptions, there is little erosion of the banks and the channel remains relatively static (an unusual case). Where stream power is great enough to erode bank materials, deflection of secondary flow cells will induce bank erosion and initiate the formation of meander bends (fig. 4.8). Once begun, the growth of meander bends is self-driven. As most rafters, canoeists, and kayakers know, as water runs into a tight meander bend it appears to pile up against the cut bank. Termed *superelevation,* this water creates a hydraulic head that sets up a strong secondary flow cell within the meander bend. Water within the flow cell plunges downward along the outside of the meander bend, crossing along the bottom and then upward into the other bank before flowing back toward the cut bank. The intense secondary flow cell created by superelevation acts to accelerate erosion of the bank and the bed on the outside of the meander. This, in conjunction with the high-velocity gradients that naturally occur on the steep sides of asymmetric channels (fig. 4.1), hastens the lateral growth of the meander bend.

The growth of a meander is not restricted to erosion along the outside of the meander bend. Left uncompensated, this increased widening of the channel would lead to a decline in velocity and a cessation of erosion. The rate of lateral migration of the outside wall of a meander is usually matched by deposition of material on the opposite bank, allowing the channel width to remain relatively constant during lateral movement. This deposition forms the prominent sedimentary feature of all meandering rivers: the *point bar* (figs. 4.3, 4.9).

Bed shear stress on a point bar varies depending on the water level. Overall, the sediments of a point bar indicate a gradual decline in velocity and bed shear stress from the base of the point bar to the top. The secondary flow cell that scours the cut bank and channel base moves sediment from the scour channel up the face of the point bar. As these

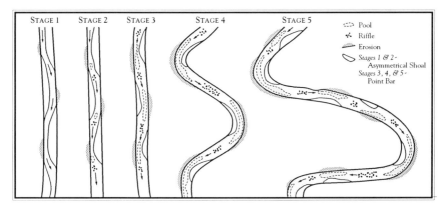

Fig. 4.8. Development of a meandering river, based on flume experiments. Establishment of asymmetric shoals along walls of straight channel deflects secondary flow cells and initiates bank erosion. Accelerated erosion along cut banks of meander bends leads to expansion of meander amplitude. (Based on experiments of Keller [1972].)

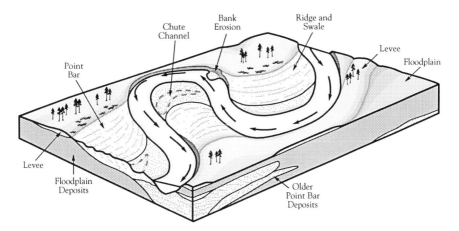

Fig. 4.9. Diagram illustrating the major geomorphic and sedimentary features of a meandering, single channel river. All of these features can be seen in aerial photographs shown in figs. 4.3 and 4.11. Note lateral growth or accretion of point bar deposits. Growth of point bar compensates erosion along cut bank, maintaining overall channel cross section and flow competence.

currents move up the bar and lose velocity, they lose competence. Thus at any given time there is a segregation of grain sizes on the point bar, with the coarsest material moving near the base of the bar and the finer material moving near the top.

As meander bends migrate, compensatory lateral growth of the point bar deposit occurs through accretion or deposition of sediment. The grain segregation that occurs on the face of the bar is reflected in the sediments that accumulate. When excavated, point bar deposits will typically be graded, consisting of coarse gravel deposits at the base (scour channel) overlain by stratified coarse sand (lower point bar) that grade into laminated fine sands (upper point bar). The point bar is typically capped by organic-rich silt and clay of overbank or floodplain deposits.

Although meander growth seems like a unidirectional process that should lead to ever-increasing meander amplitudes, it clearly is not. First, meanders can only expand to the width of their valleys before encountering more resistant bedrock. Second, meander growth is often disrupted by channel abandonment. A variety of factors can conspire to lead to the abandonment of meander bends or even wholesale abandonment of meander belts.

Downstream as well as lateral expansion of meanders will eventually cause meander channels to intersect, temporarily reestablishing a shorter and straighter channel and cutting off the channel that originally made up the large meander bend (figs. 4.10, 4.11A, B). Where both ends of these abandoned meander channels are cut off from the newly established channels, they form horseshoe-shaped lakes, known as *oxbow lakes*. These lakes become the sites of accumulation of fine overbank sediments and vast quantities of organic material such as peat. When the lakes fill with sediment, they commonly become swamps or wetlands. If one end of the abandoned meander continues to receive flow directly from the channel, *sloughs* are formed. These, too, eventually fill with sediment but are less likely to accumulate large quantities of peat. A second and perhaps more common cause of abandonment of meanders is associated with the development of cutoffs. During flooding events, flow across the inside of the point bar can establish chutes or channels. Intense scouring of these chutes can lead to the establishment of a new channel across the point bar and abandonment of the meander.

The tendency for deposition during overbank flooding events to be concentrated near the river can, in the long term, lead to a buildup of the meander belt itself. In portions of the Sacramento Valley, the meander belt axis actually sits at a higher elevation than the surrounding floodplain. During very large floods, a river will occasionally abandon its meander belt entirely and establish a new channel in the surrounding lower-lying areas of the valley. Termed *avulsion,* large-scale channel abandonment is a com-

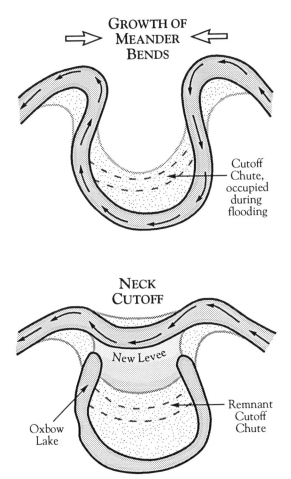

Fig. 4.10. Development of meander cutoffs. Lateral expansion of meanders can lead to development of neck cutoffs. Development of point bar chutes during flooding can also lead to cutoff (see fig. 4.11).

mon feature of most large and intermediate river systems (fig. 4.12). Avulsion is unlikely to occur in the near future in the Sacramento Valley because of the extensive network of levees and bypass systems that control flooding.

Given the complex process of development, growth, and abandonment of meanders, it is reasonable to wonder if their geometry has anything to do with watershed conditions at all. Legions of geomorphologists have measured the physical features of meanders and find that, when considered

Fig. 4.11A. 1952 USDA aerial photographs used for crop surveys illustrating channel evolution of Sacramento River, Glenn and Colusa counties. *Above*: Flow across surface of point bar leading to development of cutoff in meander bend during moderate discharge event.

Fig. 4.11B. *Above*: Recent episode of channel straightening through neck cutoff has led to development of multiple oxbow lakes. Channel straightening may be associated with flow regulation due to Shasta Dam.

Fig. 4.12. Avulsion of Owens River below Owens River Gorge. Sharp decline in gradient of Owens River as it enters Owens Valley has led to multiple episodes of avulsion. Note complete abandonment of channel and meander belt axis and establishment of new meander belt. Photograph by author.

over a large area, they appear to directly reflect a dynamic equilibrium condition. The most useful comparisons come from analysis of the radius of curvature and wavelength of meanders (fig. 4.6). Bankfull discharge, Q_b, has been equated to meander wavelength (L) by

$$L = 54.3 \sqrt{Q_b},$$ (4.3)

and average channel width (w) is tied to wavelength by

$$L = 12.34w.$$ (4.4)

This strong correlation of width to meander wavelength reflects the role of secondary circulation cells in negative feedback with channel size. As shown above, channel size and shape are primarily a function of the interaction of discharge, sediment load, and bank material properties. By controlling channel width and depth, these features influence the formation and wavelength of secondary flow cells. Convergence and divergence of these cells leads to the formation of riffle-pool sequences. In rivers with sufficient stream power, these riffle-pool sequences initiate bank erosion and the development of meander bends. Again, the feedback within these systems cannot be overstated; changes in one characteristic translate quickly to numerous others, which, in turn, affect the original character.

Multichannel Rivers

When asked to define a river, most people describe a single channel that meanders across the landscape. Yet many of the world's great rivers and a significant portion of California's rivers do not occupy a single, sinuous channel. During moderate to high discharge events, these *braided* rivers establish multiple channels that repeatedly diverge and join (figs. 4.4, 4.13).

To an engineer, the braided river must appear to be the utmost in inefficiency. By creating multiple channels instead of one single channel, the river increases the effectiveness of bed roughness by increasing the total wetted perimeter. To exacerbate this apparent error in design, braided river channel cross sections are typically broad and shallow with numerous sand and gravel bars that further increase bed roughness. The extrinsic view of meandering rivers argues that meander development reflects a river's attempt to maintain energy efficiency while balancing energy expenditures throughout. Ideally, the blatant inefficiency of a braided river might also be viewed in a similar manner. The creation of multiple, shallow channels with coarse sediment load acts to increase energy expenditures, effectively dissipating excess energy. It should be no surprise, therefore, that braided rivers are generally favored in settings with steep gradients, highly variable discharges, and abundant coarse load.

An important characteristic of braided rivers is the instability of their channels. Channel abandonment can occur on time scales varying from hours to months and can involve either gradual or sudden changes. The reason for the dynamic nature of braided river channels is rooted in their varying discharge, overall coarse sediment load, and unstable bank materials. During rapidly rising river stage, secondary circulation cells that form within channels quickly increase in intensity. As shown above, divergent flow cells cause the coarsest material being transported to accumulate within the center of the channel. In coarse bedload systems, these accumulations initiate the formation, growth, and downstream migration of channel bars. As a channel bar grows, it deforms or splits the flow, increasing bed shear stresses in channels or chutes on either side of the bar. Because the river is bedload dominated, the bank materials tend to be relatively coarse-grained and erosionally nonresistant. In addition, most braided rivers in California are formed in semiarid settings where little riparian vegetation protects banks. The nonresistant banks of braided rivers allow rapid lateral expansion of channel bars and erosion of the banks as bars grow and propagate downstream. The growth of these bars during

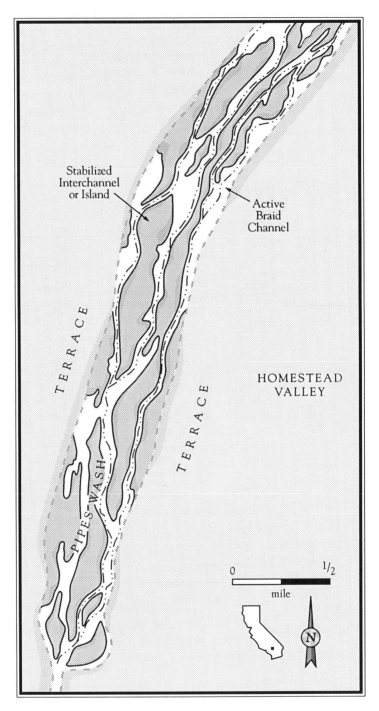

Fig. 4.13. Pipes Wash in Homestead Valley, southern California, illustrating multiple active and inactive channels and interchannel bars or islands of a typical semiarid, braided, multichannel river.

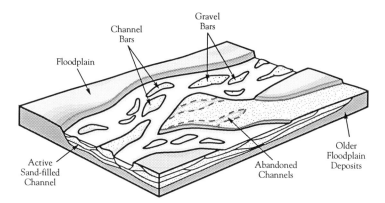

Fig. 4.14. Model braided river system illustrating principal geomorphic and depositional features. Note development of intrachannel bars and islands. Growth of bars promotes development of multiple channels during rising flood stage.

floods leads to the establishment of numerous islands that split the channel into multiple individual channels that branch and rejoin frequently (figs. 4.13, 4.14).

The shape and size of the bars that form in braided rivers is highly variable. In coarse-grained bedload rivers, the bars will typically align their long axis parallel to the current. Known as *longitudinal bars,* they migrate by erosion on the upstream side and accretion on the top and downstream sides in a manner analogous to the growth of ripples. Indeed, many have argued that the active channel bars of rivers are nothing more than large-scale equilibrium bedforms. Longitudinal bars are usually formed during rising stage when bedload transport is greatest and the river's competence is highest. However, the ultimate shape of the bar is, in part, dictated by falling stage flows when the bar is dissected and modified.

In braided rivers dominated by sand-sized bedload, the longitudinal bars give way to transverse or linguoid bars. These bars are tabular in shape, with their long axis perpendicular to the dominant current and sediment transport direction. Composed entirely of sand, transverse bars migrate by accumulation of sediment on the lee face and on the sides, causing them to expand laterally as well as in the downstream direction.

Straight versus Meandering versus Braided Rivers

Numerous studies have shown that there is a general continuum of river channel morphologies from straight to meandering to braided. With acknowledged scatter in the data, most workers recognize that the pattern is dependent primarily on differences in discharge, channel slope, and sediment load (table 4.1). As noted above, bankfull discharge appears to be the discharge level most responsible for the shape of channel cross sections. The same appears to apply to braiding versus meandering behavior. A comparison of channel slope to bankfull discharge differentiates meandering from braided rivers (fig. 4.15A): braided rivers dominate high bankfull discharge/high slope settings; meandering rivers dominate low slope/low bankfull discharge settings. Since channel cross section and both meandering and braided river behavior are also dependent on the transport and deposition of bed material, it is logical to assume that the patterns should be related to the amount and size of the bedload material as well. As shown in figure 4.15B, the relationship between total sediment load of a river and its slope defines the changes from straight to meandering to braided morphologies. Intriguingly, researchers have been able to mimic the development of straight, meandering, and braided channels in flume experiments. Their research shows that the transition between these channel types is not gradual. Rather, thresholds appear to be reached which cause a rapid realignment of the river channel to its new morphology.

California's rivers exhibit virtually all types of channel morphology and pattern. Rivers with high gradients and highly variable discharge carrying exceptionally coarse bedloads are common in southern California and the desert areas. Where not confined by bedrock canyons, these rivers have braided channel patterns. Of course, most of these rivers (like the Los Angeles River) are now polluted concrete-lined ditches. At the time of the first settlements, however, the river channels were braided and contained numerous active and inactive channels that ran primarily during the winter. Other prominent examples include rivers like the Santa Ana and the Santa Clara. Both have highly braided channels where they have not been channelized by public works projects. Meandering is the norm in northern California, where runoff conditions are somewhat more stable and the major rivers are dominated by a finer-grained sediment load. The Sacramento and San Joaquin rivers are the prime examples of meandering rivers. Again, channeling has greatly altered the original pattern of these rivers, but major portions still retain the very high sinuosity that dominates the lower reaches of these types of rivers.

Bedrock Rivers

All of this discussion about the controls on the formation of straight versus meandering versus braided rivers assumes that the river establishes itself within an alluvial valley that is large in comparison to the actual river channel. In areas that are undergoing rapid rates of uplift, rivers like the

TABLE 4.1 Geomorphic and Watershed Conditions of Straight and Multichannel Rivers

Type	Morphology	Sinuosity	Load	Width/ Depth Ratio	Erosive Behavior	Depositional Behavior
Straight	Single channel with pools and riffles, meandering thalweg	< 1.05	Suspension, mixed, or bedload	< 40	Minor channel widening and incision	Channel shoals
Sinuous	Single channel, pools and riffles, meandering thalweg	> 1.05, < 1.5	Mixed	< 40	Increased channel widening and incision	Channel shoals
Meandering	Single meandering channels; possible cutoff channels	> 1.5	Suspension or mixed	< 40	Channel incision, meander migration through bank erosion	Point bar formation, lateral accretion
Braided	Two or more active channels with numerous interchannel bars, small islands, abandoned channels	> 1.3	Bedload	> 40	Channel widening through bank erosion	Channel aggradation, channel bar formation

SOURCE: Modified from Morisawa 1985.

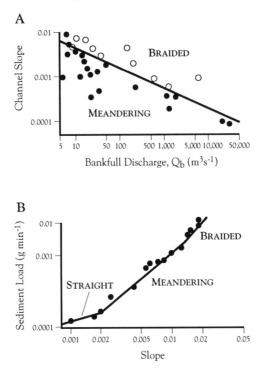

Fig. 4.15. Relationship of straight, meandering, and braided
rivers to sediment load, slope, and bankfull discharge.
(Adapted from Schumm and Khan 1972.)

upper reaches of the Kern, Kings, and Tuolumne will typically incise deep
canyons. Because of the rapid downcutting of these canyons, the rivers
establish relatively narrow and localized alluvial plains separated by long
stretches where the river is confined primarily to a gorge. Thus in plan
view, major portions of the rivers may actually be classified as "straight" or
"sinuous" even though they have very high slopes, high bankfull discharge
levels, and high total sediment loads. The overall channel pattern of these
upland rivers should be considered separately from their lowland counter-
parts in that the pattern is strongly influenced by the geology, rate of
uplift, and associated rate of incision.

CHANNEL PATTERNS IN DELTAS

With the exception of the Tulare Lake basin and other enclosed basins,
most of the runoff of California's rivers makes it to the Pacific Ocean. In
the absence of sediment traps like dams, the sediment should also have

the sea as its ultimate destination. Where the rivers meet the sea (or any lake, for that matter) and lose almost all of their competence and capacity, they rapidly dump their sediment, forming a localized accumulation of material right at the ocean/river join. The contiguous mass of sediment deposited at the mouth of a river is referred to as a *delta,* a term first used by Herodotus, who noted that the accumulation of sediment at the mouth of the Nile broadly resembled the symbol delta (Δ) in plan view. Because much of the oil and gas of the United States comes from ancient deltaic deposits, there is a vast literature on the accumulation of sediments and the flow of currents within deltas. Most of the work focuses on deltas like the Mississippi, where high sediment influxes and weak oceanic currents allow the accumulation of vast quantities of sediment that rapidly extend the delta seaward. Because the oceanic currents that sweep the coast of California are so vigorous, they are capable of eroding and transporting most of the sediment delivered by the rivers. This is why rivers like the Eel, Mad, and Klamath, which have exceptionally high sediment loads, have not built extensive deltas. The only places where typical deltas like the Mississippi's are able to establish are where ocean currents are relatively weak, which allows sediment to accumulate.

The only significant "delta" in California occurs at the confluence of the Sacramento and San Joaquin rivers (figs. 4.16, 4.17). Since it is fully 50 miles from what we would normally call the coast of California, by most standards the Sacramento/San Joaquin Delta cannot be considered a true delta. It is really an accumulation of sediment at the headwaters of a very large estuary. The San Francisco Bay/Delta estuary was formed by the rapid Holocene rise in sea level and the drowning of the river that once flowed through what is now San Francisco Bay. The shape and location of the present delta, which is controlled largely by uplift of the Coast Ranges near San Francisco, has little in common with deltas seen elsewhere in the world. Although it looks little like a true delta, the behavior and morphology of the river channels that transport sediment and water through the Sacramento/San Joaquin Delta are, at least on a local scale, very similar to deltas worldwide. As the meandering, single channel Sacramento and San Joaquin rivers enter the delta region, the sharp decline in gradient or slope causes the channels to bifurcate, forming a complex meshwork of channels or distributaries that split and merge repeatedly (fig. 4.16). This distributary channel network is created by three general processes. First, channel bifurcations can take place where channels essentially clog due to accumulation of material, such as at channel mouths. Second, bifurcations can form when distributary channels flood, breaching their own natural levees and eventually establishing a new channel. Termed *crevassing,* this process is the most common mechanism of channel bifurcation in deltas. Finally, flow within the delta is not entirely downhill. Large tidal fluctuations

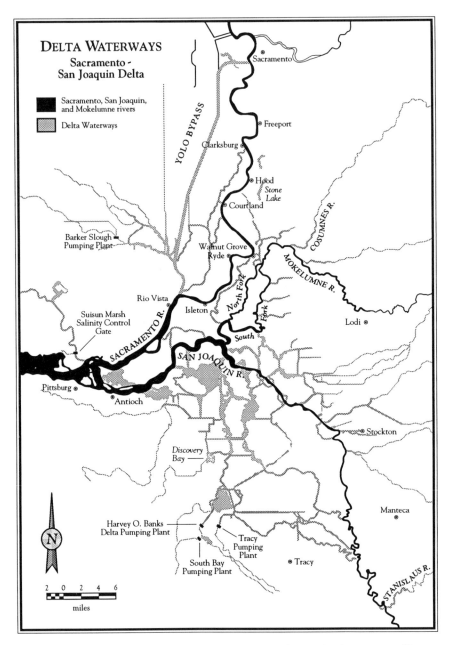

Fig. 4.16. A generalized map of the channels that make up the Sacramento/San Joaquin Delta/Estuary. Virtually all channels have been realigned through the construction of levees and the draining of large tracts of land. (Based on California Department of Water Resources maps.)

Fig. 4.17. 1972 aerial photograph of delta near confluence of Sacramento River (above) and San Joaquin River (below) illustrating anastomosing channel network. Photograph from W. L. Kahrl, *The California Water Atlas* (Sacramento: Governor's Office of Planning and Research, 1979).

cause water to literally back up in the channels closest to the bay, increasing overbank flooding and overall channel instability. The net result of these processes is the production of a lacework of *anastomosing* channels that split and join around organic-rich islands.

In the absence of human interference, the channels of the delta would be highly ephemeral, switching constantly, eroding islands and forming new ones, flooding and depositing fine sediment in large tracts between channels, and supporting what is widely recognized as the richest eco-system in the state. The man-made levees that line virtually all of the channels within the delta have "frozen" channel migration within it. In addition, farming practices that promote the oxidation of peat-rich soils within the delta have caused widespread deflation and lowering of the islands. Today, many of the islands lie well below sea level. These changes, coupled with the extensive pumping associated with the Central Valley Project (CVP) and the State Water Project (SWP), have altered and severely damaged the delta's overall plumbing system, forming a political and land use headache for all of California (chap. 16).

SUMMARY

Most of the work that a river does is conducted within its channel. The channel cross section and the plan view pattern of channels reflect the balance of energy expenditures by a river as it handles its load and discharge. The overall shape of channel cross sections is presumed by many geomorphologists to be controlled by the relatively frequent bankfull stage events coupled with the nature of the bank materials. Suspended load-dominated rivers tend to have fine-grained, erosionally resistant banks, which lead to the formation of steep-walled, narrow channels that are more efficient at moving material in suspension. Bedload-dominated rivers have bank materials that are primarily made up of coarse-grained, less cohesive sediment. Channels established in these materials tend to be wider and shallower.

The plan view pattern of river channels reflects a river's attempt to maximize energy efficiency while balancing energy expenditures over its length. Two general types of river patterns occur: single channel and multichannel. Single channel rivers occupy a relatively stable main channel. The morphology of single channel rivers varies from straight to sinuous to meandering. The development of sinuosity in a river takes place as secondary circulation cells develop within a channel. These cells create localized scouring (pools) and deposition (riffles), depending on whether flow cells converge or diverge within the channel. Once established, riffles and pools accelerate the lateral migration of channels by enhancing lateral scour. In particular, meander bends develop adjacent to pools due to intense scouring of the channel wall. Point bars develop on the inside portion of meander bends where helical flow allows accumulation of sediments. Meanders are commonly abandoned as channels migrate, creating oxbow lakes and sloughs. The sinuosity of a single channel river and the wavelength of the meanders appear to reflect the magnitude of bankfull stage conditions.

Multichannel rivers develop numerous shallow, broad channels that bifurcate and join repeatedly, thereby forming islands. The development of numerous channels appears to reflect a river's efforts to dissipate excess energy and transport an exceptionally coarse load. The braided river channels are highly unstable due to the growth and migration of longitudinal and transverse bars. The bars grow to eventually form islands, which deflect flow, forming new channels. In addition, coarse-grained bank materials are less resistant to erosion, which promotes channel instability.

The type of channel pattern and sinuosity is generally dependent on the slope, discharge, and sediment load of a watershed. Meandering rivers are favored in settings characterized by steady discharge, low slope, and low, fine-grained sediment loads. In contrast, multichannel rivers are common in watersheds with highly variable discharge, high slopes, and coarse, voluminous loads.

The Sacramento/San Joaquin Delta is the interface between two meandering rivers and the San Francisco Bay estuary. The delta contains a meshwork of channels that wrap around low-lying islands. The loss of stream power within the delta causes channels to aggrade, promoting channel bifurcation. Crevassing during flood stage also causes channels to bifurcate and join neighboring channels. Channel instability is enhanced by the effect of tides that reverse flows in some channels and increase the elevation of flows within others.

RELEVANT READINGS

Best, J. L., and C. S. Bristow, eds. 1993. *Braided Rivers.* Geological Society Special Publication no. 75. London: Geological Society.

Elliott, C. M. 1984. *River Meandering.* Proceedings of the ASCE Conference on Rivers 1983, New Orleans, 24–26 October 1983. New York: American Society of Civil Engineers.

Gregory, K. J., ed. 1977. *River Channel Changes.* New York: John Wiley and Sons.

Ikeda, S., and G. Parker, eds. 1989. *River Meandering.* Water Resources Monograph no. 12. Washington, D.C.: American Geophysical Union.

Keller, E. A. 1972. "Development of Alluvial Stream Channels: A Five-Stage Model." *Geological Society of America Bulletin* 82: 753–756.

Keller, E. A., and W. N. Melhorn. 1974. *Form and Fluvial Processes in Alluvial Stream Channels.* West Lafayette: Purdue University Water Resources Research Center.

Knighton, D. 1984. *Fluvial Forms and Processes.* Baltimore: E. Arnold.

Leopold, L. B. 1994. *A View of the River.* Cambridge: Harvard University Press.

Leopold, L., and M. G. Wolman. 1957. *River Channel Patterns: Braided, Meandering, and Straight.* U.S. Geological Survey Professional Paper no. 282–B.

Mangelsdor, J., K. Schuermann, and F.-H. Weiß. 1990. *River Morphology: A Guide for Geoscientists and Engineers.* Berlin: Springer Verlag.

Miall, A. D. 1977. *Fluvial Sedimentology.* Calgary: Canadian Society of Petroleum Geologists.

Morisawa, M. 1985. *Rivers*. New York: Longman.

Richards, K. S. 1982. *Rivers: Form and Process in Alluvial Channels*. New York: Methuen.

————, ed. 1987. *River Channels: Environment and Process*. New York: Blackwell Scientific Publications.

Schumm, S. A., and H. R. Kahn. 1972. "Experimental Study of Channel Pattern." *Geological Society of America Bulletin* 83: 1755–1770.

Thorne, C. R., J. C. Bathurst, and R. D. Hey, eds. 1987. *Gravel Bed Rivers*. New York: John Wiley and Sons.

Warner, R. E., and K. Hendrix, eds. 1984. *California Riparian Systems*. Berkeley, Los Angeles, and London: University of California Press.

FIVE

Origins of River Discharge

INTRODUCTION

The previous chapters have belabored the point that the overall behavior and morphology of a river is a function of its least-work adjustment to the runoff and sediment load that is delivered by its watershed. As the January 1995 floods attest, runoff is highly variable in space and time. Although most of this state's major rivers contain measurable discharges during the entire year, the vast majority of runoff occurs during the winter and spring months when warm Pacific winter storms deliver rain and snow to the watersheds. As outlined in chapter 2, it is during these moments of terror that California's rivers do the job of moving sediment and water.

Given the diverse landscape, geology, and climate of California, it should be no surprise that runoff characteristics vary greatly. Watersheds of comparable size in the same geographic area typically exhibit significant differences in response to storms. Some river basins shed their water quickly, leading to rapid and dramatic rises and falls within major rivers and streams. Other watersheds appear to be able to store water from storms, whether as snow, as groundwater, or in myriad topographic depressions, releasing it more gradually and producing less dramatic changes in river level. The nature and causes of these differences in runoff behavior are examined in this chapter, with an emphasis on the response of watersheds to storms.

MONITORING THE PULSE OF A RIVER: THE HYDROGRAPH

To state the obvious, when the rains come to California, the rivers rise. This is also a gross oversimplification of the process. Once precipitation falls, it must run a complex gauntlet on its way to becoming measurable discharge

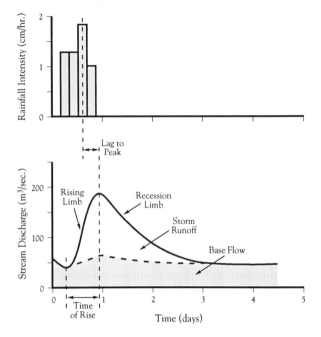

Fig. 5.1. Idealized hydrograph depicting changes in discharge
of a river in response to rainfall. (Modified from Dunne and
Leopold 1978.)

at the mouth of a watershed. The torturous pathways this rainfall takes
control the characteristics of runoff and the associated flooding. Hydrologists monitor the origin and intensity of discharge by studying a *hydrograph*
(fig. 5.1). A typical hydrograph is a plot of stream discharge (cfs or cms)
against time, expressed in hours or days. The hydrograph is usually compared to rainfall data in order to estimate the length of time between the
peak rainfall intensity and peak runoff. As outlined below, this *lag time* is a
vital element in floodplain management plans.

The shape of the hydrograph is a record of the response of watersheds
to rainfall events. The hydrograph is broken into two general segments: a
steep *rising limb* and a more gradual *falling limb* or *recession limb* (fig. 5.1).
The rising limb reflects the input of direct runoff from a storm. The more
or less synchronous arrival of peak storm runoff into the tributaries causes
the relatively rapid increase in discharge and the resulting steep rising
limb. The recessional phase of a flood event is more gradual, reflecting
the slow depletion of water that is temporarily stored in the basin on hillsides, in small tributaries, and in the shallow subsurface.

By careful analysis of rainfall data and flood hydrographs, hydrologists can glean a certain amount of information about the route that precipitation must travel before it becomes river discharge. In addition, hydrographs allow hydrologists to evaluate the response of different basins to similar storms. Rather than simply an exercise in understanding nature, the analysis of hydrographs is a vital first step in estimating the impact that changes in land use are likely to have on flooding within a basin. The following sections describe how runoff from storms is generated and how differences in physiography and climate within and between watersheds affect the timing and magnitude of discharge events.

PRECIPITATION

California's climate produces a mix of snow and rain that is irregularly distributed in both space and time (chap. 8). There are four aspects of the precipitation that falls on this state that control the timing and magnitude of runoff events: intensity, frequency, duration, and type.

There is a direct relationship between precipitation intensity (usually expressed as inches per hour) and the magnitude of runoff. As outlined below, watersheds are capable of absorbing low-intensity precipitation without producing abrupt changes in runoff. When precipitation intensity is high, the watershed's ability to absorb water is exceeded, leading to extensive amounts of runoff. For this reason alone, years with equal rainfall can produce substantially different total runoff amounts.

Rainfall duration, in concert with intensity, is also integral to the formation of runoff. The longer the rainfall event, the greater the total volume of water available to form runoff, especially if the longer duration is associated with high intensity. In the north coast basins of California, rain will occasionally fall almost continuously for a week or more, with average daily rainfall totals exceeding several inches or more (table 5.1). One week of rain in the north coast can often equal four years of the average annual rainfall for the south coast basins. However, it is rare that a single storm will be responsible for such lengthy periods of intense rainfall. The largest rainfall totals are all associated with the arrival of multiple storms over a very short period. As shown below, it is this unique condition of high precipitation intensities, duration, and frequencies that overwhelms the ability of watersheds to absorb rainfall, producing the state's largest runoff events.

Finally, the type of precipitation that occurs controls the nature of runoff events. In the high-altitude watersheds of the state, as much as half or more of the yearly precipitation falls as snow. This is especially true for cold, wet winters, when a large number of the storms that reach California originate in the Gulf of Alaska. The development of a snowpack acts to spread out or mute the effects of runoff associated with any given storm.

TABLE 5.1   California's Maximum Observed Rainfall Data

Duration	Depth (in.)	Location	Date
1 min.	0.65	Opids Camp	Apr. 5, 1926
2 min.	0.90	Opids Camp	Apr. 5, 1926
5 min.	2.10	Haines Canyon	Feb. 1, 1976
20 min.	3.35	Darwin	June 13, 1967
70 min.	7.10	Vallecito	July 18, 1955
80 min.	11.50	Campo	Aug. 12, 1891
2.5 hr.	8.00	Chatovich Flat	July 19, 1955
12 hr.	13.38	Opids Camp	Mar. 2, 1938
24 hr.	26.12	Hoegees	Jan. 22, 1943
2 days	36.10	Hoegees	Jan. 22, 1943
7 days	46.40	Honeydew	Dec. 1955
10 days	50.85	Mt. Baldy Notch	Jan. 1969
30 days	82.90	Honeydew	1955
60 days	107.90	Honeydew	1955
1 yr.	186.36	Ship Mountain	July 1977–June 1978

SOURCE: California Department of Water Resources Data.

On a seasonal basis, snowpacks tend to delay periods of maximum runoff well into the spring and early summer months (fig. 5.2). In contrast, when warm midlatitude storms strike California, snowfall is limited only to the highest elevations within watersheds, producing rapid runoff response.

BASE FLOW: WHY RIVERS RUN ALL YEAR

Even during the record droughts of 1976–1977 and 1987–1992, all of the major rivers in northern and central California flowed year-round. Dam releases augmented the rivers in many areas, but all of the major reservoirs recorded continuous inflow from their watersheds. This occurred despite a snowpack that was virtually nonexistent by mid-May during each of those years. Given that there is hardly any rain from May through October in California, this discharge cannot be ascribed to surface runoff. Rather, the water that flows through California's rivers and keeps many of them running in even the leanest of times is derived almost entirely from the subsurface.

Worldwide, groundwater makes up the largest source of unfrozen fresh water. In California, approximately half of the current water supply is derived directly from groundwater rather than rivers. The increasing pressure to develop groundwater resources has a number of long-term consequences, not the least of which will be a decline in flow within rivers.

Groundwater in California comes almost exclusively from precipitation. Water falling on the surface as rain or snow eventually percolates into the

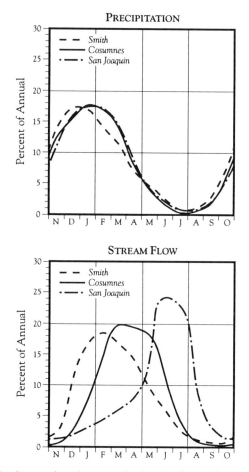

Fig. 5.2. Comparison between basins dominated by runoff derived from snowmelt (Cosumnes, San Joaquin) and runoff derived primarily from rainfall (Smith). Note substantial delay in peak runoff for basins whose precipitation primarily occurs as snowfall. (Modified from Cayan and Riddle 1992.)

ground and becomes part of the groundwater. The water that infiltrates into the subsurface and becomes groundwater is called *recharge*. When a well is drilled into the subsurface, water will eventually seep into it and fill it to some static level (fig. 5.3). The level that the water rises to denotes the top of the *groundwater table*. Below this level the pores or spaces in the rock or sediment will be filled entirely with water (*saturated zone*). Immediately above this level the capillary tension between rock and water wicks water upward out of the saturated zone and fills pore spaces. Termed the

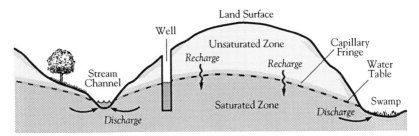

Fig. 5.3. Idealized distribution of groundwater table beneath land surface. Note that elevation of groundwater table mimics ground surface. (Modified from Dunne and Leopold 1978.)

capillary fringe, this zone can be several feet thick. The portion of the ground that lies above the capillary fringe, termed the *unsaturated soil-water zone,* or *vadose zone,* has only limited amounts of water in its pores.

If a body of sediment or rock provides a good supply of water, it is called an *aquifer.* Usually an aquifer is in the eye of the beholder. A single-family household may view the 3 gallons per minute that their well delivers as sufficient. Thus they are tapping into an aquifer. A farmer, whose needs are much greater, will not consider this yield sufficient and will not view this as an aquifer. In contrast to an aquifer is an *aquiclude,* or a unit or layer that inhibits the flow of groundwater. Mud and clay-rich sediments and rocks like shale and mudstone restrict the flow of water and commonly form aquicludes.

If you drill a number of wells in a region and map the level of the groundwater table, you will find that, in general, the surface of the water table matches the surface of the land (fig. 5.3). Like a river, differences in elevation of the water table produce differences in the amount of potential energy of the groundwater. The result is that groundwater, under the influence of gravity, flows downhill. Where river canyons dissect the landscape, they often intersect the water table, causing the groundwater to discharge into rivers through springs or direct seepage through the riverbed. This occurs commonly within the more humid regions of central and northern California where high recharge rates lead to development of elevated water tables. The portion of the total discharge within a river that is due to groundwater is termed *base flow.*

The amount of base flow discharge that a river receives is dependent on four factors: (1) the total amount of groundwater recharge in the region; (2) the *porosity* of the aquifer, or the total amount of water that the rock or sediment can hold; (3) the *hydraulic conductivity* of the aquifer, or the rate at which the water can move through the subsurface; and (4) the steepness or gradient of the water table. The difference in elevation between the highest point of the water table and the river canyons that drain

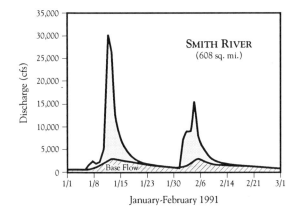

Fig. 5.4. Discharge for the Smith River during two storms in January and February 1991 and estimated base flow contribution. Note sharp rising limb and recession limb of hydrograph indicating rapid response of basin to storms. It should be noted that where runoff is captured by dams, it is more difficult to estimate base flow contributions because dam releases often mimic the pattern of base flow. (Graph based on U.S. Geological Survey Water Resources data.)

it becomes greatest during the winter and spring months, when recharge rates are exceptionally high. Thus the relative rate of groundwater discharge into streams is usually highest at those times, although snowmelt and direct runoff will typically have a larger effect. With the cessation of the rains and the complete melting of mountain snows, rivers begin draining the groundwater from their hillsides. As the gradient of the water table declines, the rate of discharge progressively slows. This removal of the groundwater from watersheds, which occurs much more slowly than the removal of surface runoff, is the source of flow during the summer and fall months for many rivers in California.

The groundwater table typically lies well below the rivers in the more arid regions of eastern and southern California and in the larger alluvial valleys of northern and central California. Seepage downward through the riverbed actually supplies water to the regional groundwater table rather than tapping it for base flow. This process is often reflected in the downstream decline in discharge of rivers in arid regions and is especially acute on arid alluvial fans or where intense groundwater pumping or other land practices have lowered the groundwater table adjacent to rivers.

The contribution of base flow to the discharge of streams can be estimated from hydrographs for relatively small streams that are not regulated by dams. Figure 5.4 shows a hydrograph for two storm events on the Smith River during the drought of 1991. The Smith River basin, which lies near the California-Oregon border, is a relatively small (608-sq.-mi.) watershed with only a minor snowpack and no significant dams. Most discharge on the Smith is associated with direct runoff immediately after storms; discharge that occurs between storms is dominated by base flow. During the drought of 1987–1992, groundwater tables dropped considerably within the basin, limiting the amount of base flow delivered to the river. Prior to the onset of rains in January 1991, the river reached a discharge low of less than 1,000 cfs, all of which was supplied by groundwater. The dramatic rise and fall of the Smith River during mid-January reflects the relatively quick hydrograph response of this basin.

OVERLAND FLOW

The magnitude and duration of runoff produced by any given storm varies greatly between and even within individual watersheds. Some of this variation can be ascribed to variations in the intensity of the rainfall that are produced by the watershed itself. Steep, high-elevation terrain will tend to wring more water out of Pacific storms than low-elevation terrain (chap. 8). But much of the difference in runoff characteristics is associated with the interaction between precipitation and the physiography, orientation, vegetation, soils, and geology of watersheds.

When the jet stream over the northern Pacific begins to shift to the south in November and early December, the winter rains and snows come to the parched landscapes of California. Without significant rainfall since May, six months of evapotranspiration have left the soils desiccated. These first rains fall on soils that act like a dried sponge, absorbing the moisture at a rate faster than it is supplied. Although the amount of precipitation that occurs in these early storms can be quite substantial, rapid infiltration rates allow it all to become part of the soil moisture or groundwater. As successive storms arrive, the pores of the unsaturated soil-water zone become increasingly full of water, reducing the rate at which they can absorb more. Eventually, the rate at which rain falls on the soil exceeds its ability to absorb it. It is at this critical juncture, when the *infiltration capacity* of a soil has been exceeded, that surface runoff begins to move across the landscape of California and into its rivers.

Infiltration Capacity

The shape of the hydrograph for any given river is dictated largely by the infiltration capacity of the watershed soils. Rather than reflecting a volume of water that can be incorporated into the soil, infiltration capacity refers to a rate (expressed in inches per hour) of absorption of water. The infiltration capacity of any soil changes with time. During winter storms,

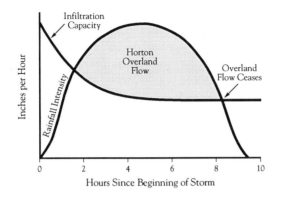

Fig. 5.5. Idealized relationship between rainfall intensity, infiltration capacity, and generation of runoff or overland flow.

soils with moderate moisture content will exhibit declining infiltration capacities. Depending on ambient conditions, approximately one-half hour to two hours after the beginning of the storm a soil will exhibit a steady but minimum infiltration capacity (fig. 5.5). Runoff occurs when rainfall intensity exceeds the infiltration capacity. Numerous factors control infiltration capacity, including the amount of moisture trapped in the soil prior to the onset of a rainstorm, the bedrock that the soil developed on, and the type of vegetation (or land use) that exists on the soil.

The greater the amount of moisture within a soil, the less its infiltration capacity. All of the large-scale flooding events in California's history have been associated either with large storms that followed close on the heels of other storms or with rain that has fallen on soils previously saturated by snowmelt (both conditions occurred in the floods of January 1995). Once soils within a watershed are saturated, it takes very little rain to exceed infiltration capacities. Without the damping effect of infiltration, which essentially acts to not only reduce the amount of surface runoff but spread it out over time, almost all of the rain goes directly and quickly into runoff. Thus for any given watershed the lag times of storm hydrographs will tend to be much less and the rising limb much steeper when soils are saturated. In addition, since a greater total volume of the precipitation makes it into runoff, the maximum or peak discharge from storms will also be much larger.

The response of soils to rainfall events is also dependent on their mineralogical composition and structure (chap. 6). In some north coast watersheds, the schists, metamorphosed volcanic and sedimentary rocks, and iron-rich igneous rocks decompose to form clay-rich soils. The low infiltration capacity of these soils leads to rapid saturation during storms and the development of voluminous runoff. The steep terrain of the north coast delivers this runoff quickly to local tributaries and streams, producing short hydrograph lag times and high peak runoff intensities. Most notorious of all of the rock types in California is the state rock, serpentinite. The soils that develop on serpentinite achieve saturation almost immediately during storms, producing dramatic surface runoff and erosion. In contrast to serpentinite soils, decomposition of Sierran granites produces sandy, well-drained soils with relatively high infiltration capacities. Hydrographs of low-relief watersheds developed in granitic terrains will typically have greater lag times, less intense peak discharges, and gentler rising and falling limbs.

In heavily vegetated watersheds that receive high yearly rainfall, the infiltration capacities can be quite high. The action of roots and the presence of abundant organic material within the soil keep the structure of the soil open and well drained. Because of this, many well-vegetated watersheds will produce relatively little direct runoff during moderate storms. In the less-vegetated, drier landscapes of southern California and the deserts, the infiltration capacity of the soils is typically low. Intense rainfall quickly saturates desert soils, producing rapid hydrograph responses, occasionally leading to flash flooding.

Overland Flow and Subsurface Storm Flow

Once rainfall intensity exceeds infiltration capacity, water begins to flow across the surface. Because the ground surface is uneven, water will initially collect in puddles and small swales. Water stored in this manner is termed *depression storage*. The amount of water that can accumulate in depression storage is highly variable, depending most on the nature of the land surface. Steep hillsides contain little depression storage, whereas low-lying areas can store as much as 2 inches of precipitation runoff. The magnitude of depression storage can influence the shape of a watershed's hydrograph. A large volume of available depression storage delays the arrival of runoff to the rivers, increasing lag times and decreasing the peak runoff intensity. In addition, water that accumulates in depression storage drains slowly following peak runoff. This tends to expand the hydrograph response to rainfall, lowering the slope and length of the rising and recession limbs.

Water will flow across the land surface of a watershed only when the infiltration capacity is exceeded and the depression storage is filled. Termed *Horton overland flow*, this is the principal source of high discharges in rivers and streams throughout much of California (fig. 5.6). Horton overland flow is shallow, sheetlike, and locally of very high velocity as it moves across the landscape. As discussed in the next chapter, this type of flow is also extremely effective at eroding loose soil and even bedrock. The intensity of

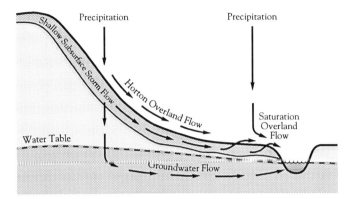

Fig. 5.6. Generalized depiction of the major sources of discharge in rivers. See text for discussion. (Modified from Dunne and Leopold 1978.)

Horton overland flow within any given watershed is highly variable. Steep areas with little vegetative cover to break up the sheetlike movement of runoff produce the highest rates of overland flow. Barren soils in construction sites or along compacted dirt roads are perhaps the best places to observe overland flow during intense storms.

The origin of the runoff that makes up the flood hydrograph can be complicated in watersheds that contain soils with high infiltration capacities. Since the groundwater table typically lies closest to the surface in areas immediately adjacent to streams and rivers (fig. 5.3), rainfall that infiltrates into floodplains and terraces close to stream courses will cause a local and rapid rise in the groundwater table. This rise produces a local increase in the gradient of the groundwater table, which, in turn, increases discharge into the adjacent river. Termed *subsurface storm flow,* this augmentation of base flow reaches channels more slowly and does not attain the peak discharges associated with Horton overland flow. As a result, hydrographs that are significantly affected by subsurface storm flow tend to be flatter, with gentler rising and recession limbs.

Where rainstorms are intense and groundwater tables are quite shallow, high infiltration rates can cause the groundwater table to rise until it reaches the ground surface. When this occurs, subsurface water is discharged directly onto the surface, forming the boglike conditions seen adjacent to many upland streams immediately after storms. Once this water begins flowing across the surface, any rain that falls on it contributes to the flow without infiltrating. This combined rainfall and groundwater discharge is called *saturation overland flow.* Since groundwater tables are usually shallowest adjacent to rivers and streams, saturation overland flow is capable of quickly and efficiently delivering water to river channels. Thus this flow tends to decrease the lag time of hydrographs and increase the peak intensities. However, because only a limited area of a watershed is likely to produce saturation overland flow, it still tends to contribute less to the hydrograph than Horton overland flow.

The hydrographs of most watersheds in California will reflect the aggregate results of all types of flow, with one type predominating over others. In general, for an "average" storm, in areas that have relatively sparse vegetative cover, whether due to more arid climate (such as in southern California) or land uses that have stripped vegetation (logging, mining, urbanization), runoff will be dominated by Horton overland flow due to generally low infiltration capacities. Subsurface storm flow and saturation overland flow are more important in more humid regions with higher infiltration capacities. Subsurface storm flow tends to predominate in upland rivers that have narrow alluvial valleys and steep hillsides with deep, highly permeable soils. In large alluvial valleys with shallow groundwater tables or relatively thin soils, extensive saturated areas produce abundant saturation overland flow.

SNOWMELT RUNOFF

In central and northern California watersheds that lie above 5,500 feet, much of the precipitation occurs as snow. The extensive snowpacks that develop in these watersheds are the most effective water storage systems in California. Indeed, without the snowpack we would be unable to use the state's water resources as effectively as we currently do. Yet, as has been shown by the drought of 1987–1992, the fortunes of agriculture, urban areas, and wildlife are tied directly to the nature of the state's snowpack.

Depending on the latitude and elevation of the watershed, snowmelt runoff can make up a substantial portion of the total runoff. In the Sierra Nevada and the Klamath and Trinity mountains, over 50 percent of the total runoff is derived from snow. From mid-November through early April, the cold temperatures at high altitudes coupled with the frequent (or infrequent) Pacific storms allow for the accumulation of a thick snowpack (figs. 5.7, 5.8). The growth of mountain snowpacks rarely occurs without disruptions. As discussed in chapter 8, warm, mid-Pacific storms often produce heavy rains at moderate elevations. When rainfall is intense enough, the mountains experience springlike conditions, including rapid melting of the snowpack. The combination of this snowmelt and intense, warm rains has produced some of the most damaging floods in the high-altitude watersheds of central and northern California.

Starting in early April, longer days and increased air temperatures con-

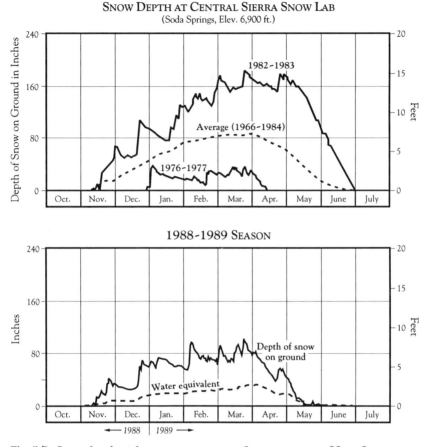

SNOW DEPTH AT CENTRAL SIERRA SNOW LAB
(Soda Springs, Elev. 6,900 ft.)

Fig. 5.7. Snow depth and snow water content for water year 1988–1989 as measured at the Central Sierra Snow Lab near Soda Springs, California, including highest, lowest, and average snow depths. Note that in an "average" year peak snow depth occurs at the beginning of April. (Based on California Department of Water Resources water supply summaries.)

spire to begin the melting of the snowpack. The melt-off of snow and its transmission to rivers takes place relatively quickly in most years. From an April 1 peak, the snowpack is greatly depleted by early June, and by early July it is virtually gone, with only a few remnants clinging to the highest altitudes. Because it takes several months to melt the snowpack in California, the snowmelt hydrographs are much different from those associated with rainfall events. Peak discharges tend to be considerably less, with shallow hydrograph limbs and a total hydrograph response involving months

Fig. 5.8. The thick blanket of snow that lies on the Sierra Nevada makes up the state's most valuable water reservoir. During the late spring and summer, the water stored in these high mountain snowfields is released to local creeks and rivers. By delaying the arrival of this runoff, snowpacks reduce the need for large reservoirs for water storage and flood control.

rather than days. With a few notable exceptions such as during the melting of the record snow accumulations of 1983, there is rarely any flooding associated solely with the spring snowmelt. This is one of the happier accidents of the unusual climate of California. Just about the time that increases in solar radiation become sufficient to initiate the melting of the snowpack, high pressure builds off the coast of California, deflecting major storms to the north and preventing catastrophic spring flooding that could be caused by the mixing of warm spring rains with melting snows.

Evolution of the Snowpack

The water watchers of California are perhaps the most intense snow observers in the world. The California Department of Water Resources (DWR) devotes a substantial portion of its meager yearly budget to measuring snow. It monitors the depth, density, temperature, and distribution of snow in California all winter and into the spring. The goal of all this snow watching is to estimate the amount of runoff that is going to be generated by these snows and when the runoff is going to arrive at the state's reservoirs.

As any skier knows, just as no two snowflakes are alike, no two snowfalls are alike either. The density of fresh snow is highly dependent on the air temperature during snowfall. The light powder cherished by skiers and snowboarders is produced when the air temperature is low. At 14°F, 1 cubic foot of freshly fallen fluffy powder will melt down to only 0.05 cubic foot of water. In contrast, at 32°F, 1 cubic foot of freshly fallen snow will melt to as much as 0.20 cubic foot of water. For this reason, measurements of snow depths that are typically reported in the local newspapers are unreliable indicators of the type of runoff year that can be expected.

Snow undergoes numerous physical changes shortly after it accumulates, all of which lead to increases in the overall snow density. Gravitational settling, wind packing, recrystallization, and melting are responsible for the metamorphosis of winter snowpacks, preparing them to release their water in the spring. During extended periods of cold in the middle of winter, the temperature of the entire snowpack falls below freezing. Periods of warming, such as during rainfall events, cause melting at the top of the snowpack. Meltwater that percolates into the snowpack refreezes when it comes in contact with ice that is below 32°F. The thicker and colder the snowpack, the better able it is to absorb and refreeze the melting that occurs.

Episodes of melting and refreezing have an impact on the overall condition of the snowpack. First, the refreezing causes ice crystals within the snowpack to enlarge (forming the dreaded "corn snow" typical of spring ski conditions). Second, the freezing process liberates latent heat, which acts to warm the overall snowpack. During the spring, a variety of heat sources contribute to this warming process. The most significant of these are absorbed solar radiation, which varies based on the season, latitude, forest canopy, and albedo (reflectivity) of the snow, and the sensible and latent heat exchanges that occur between the atmosphere and the snowpack. When heat sources are relatively high, the process of successive melting and refreezing rapidly changes the overall temperature of the snowpack. When the entire snowpack reaches 32°F, a portion of the percolating meltwater will not refreeze. Much of it will remain unfrozen in the pores of the snowpack, usually occupying between 2 and 8 percent of the total volume. At this point, when the entire snowpack is 32°F and contains abundant unfrozen water, the snowpack is said to be *ripe*. Any further addition of water, through rainfall or melting, causes runoff. When this coincides with the longer, warmer days of spring, the melt-off of the snowpack begins in earnest; as snow melts at the surface, the water that percolates does not refreeze but simply runs off (fig. 5.7).

Although snowpack ripening and melting is typically associated with spring conditions, some of the more significant floods in the history of California have been associated with warm rains falling on a ripe winter snowpack. The nearly catastrophic floods of 1986 that struck the Sacramento region involved unusually persistent subtropical rains that led to a rapid ripening and then sudden melt-off of a February snowpack. During January 1995, a series of subtropical storms similar to the February 1986 storms also led to flooding in central Sierran drainages, albeit with some important differences. Although the Sacramento region experienced localized flooding associated with small creeks and failure of urban runoff systems, there was minimal threat of flooding from the area's larger rivers. This was presumed by most to be due to the presence of large flood storage capacities in local reservoirs. However, substantial volumes of rainfall actually were stored in the snowpack. Near-record snowfalls and relatively cool temperatures during November 1994 left an unusually thick, relatively cold snowpack. During the early portions of the second week of January, when intense warm rains began to fall at elevations above 7,000 feet, most rain was captured and frozen into the snowpack. However, measurements at the Central Sierra Snowlab illustrate how close the residents of the region may have come to a repeat of 1986. By the end of the series of intense January storms, the snowpack at the 6,900-feet elevation was on the verge of melt-off. In one overnight period the researchers noted that of the 4 inches of rain that had fallen on the snowpack, almost 2.5 inches had simply run out from underneath it and into local drainages. This meant that the snowpack was still able to capture and hold some water, but it also indicated that the snowpack was fully ripe and ready for rapid melt-off. Fortunately for the American River drainage, as the snowpack approached melt-off, storm intensity and temperatures declined, preventing more extensive flooding.

Runoff of Snowmelt

Snowmelt reaches the streams and rivers of California through a variety of pathways. In most of the heavily vegetated watersheds, the high infiltration capacities of the soils preclude the formation of abundant surface runoff. Where this occurs, meltwater moves into streams primarily through subsurface flow. Where subsurface flow dominates, there will be a considerable lag time between periods of intense melting and associated peak discharges. If the groundwater table is shallow in a region undergoing rapid snowmelt, the infiltration of meltwater will cause the groundwater table to rise. Just as in intense rainfall runoff events, the intersection of the groundwater table with the surface produces saturation overland flow immediately beneath the snowpack. When this occurs, the overland flow will rapidly melt the overlying snowpack. In comparison with other basins, the lag times for this type of runoff are less while the peak discharges are greater than those associated primarily with subsurface flow. Where intense melting and percolation of water through the snowpack exceeds the infiltration capacity of soils, water is able to collect at the base of the snowpack, forming a saturated layer. Water within the saturated layer moves downhill rapidly as overland flow, discharging directly into streams and rivers. This type of runoff produces the shortest lag times and greatest peak intensities for meltwater runoff hydrographs and is typically associated with winter snowmelt flooding.

SUMMARY

While all discharge from California's rivers is derived from rain or snow, there are a variety of pathways that water can take on its way to becoming part of a river. Water that seeps into the ground and recharges aquifers can enter into rivers when the water table is intersected by a river channel or canyon. Termed base flow, the discharge of groundwater directly into rivers keeps them going during the long dry summer and fall in California. During storm events, rapid infiltration of water can cause groundwater tables to rise, leading to the discharge of subsurface storm flow into streams. During particularly intense storms, the groundwater table will intersect the surface, producing saturation overland flow. When rainfall exceeds the infiltration capacity of soils, water begins to flow across the surface, producing Horton overland flow. This type of flow is the source of most discharge during floods. In the mountainous regions of northern and central California, snowmelt runoff is an important contributor to the total amount of discharge within rivers. Runoff associated with melting snows does not occur until the snowpack is suitably ripe. Once melting begins, snowmelt water can flow along the base of the snowpack and directly into rivers or infiltrate to form subsurface flow.

When surface runoff is generated, it enters an elaborate plumbing system. The passage of this water through a watershed is measured on a hydrograph, which records the steep rise and gradual decline of discharge. The shape of the hydrograph that is generated by runoff events reflects the geomorphic, climatic, and geologic features of the watershed as well as the distribution of the various sources of runoff.

RELEVANT READINGS

Black, P. E. 1991. *Watershed Hydrology.* Englewood Cliffs, N.J.: Prentice-Hall.

Cayan, D., and C. Riddle. 1992. "Atmospheric Circulation and Precipitation in the Sierra Nevada." In *Managing Water Resources During Global Change,* ed. R. Herr,

711–720. AWRA 28th Annual Conference and Symposium: American Water Resources Association Technical Publication Series 92–4.

Dunne, T., and L. B. Leopold. 1978. *Water in Environmental Planning.* San Francisco: W. H. Freeman.

Freeze, R. A., and J. A. Cherry. 1979. *Groundwater.* Englewood Cliffs, N.J.: Prentice-Hall.

Kirkby, M. J., ed. 1978. *Hillslope Hydrology.* New York: John Wiley and Sons.

Manning, J. C. 1992. *Applied Principles of Hydrology.* 2d ed. New York: Macmillan.

Ward, R. C. 1990. *Principles of Hydrology.* 3d ed. New York: McGraw-Hill.

SIX

Sediment Supply

INTRODUCTION

As gravity drives runoff through and across a watershed, bed shear stress and the internal turbulence of moving water erode, transport, deposit, and eventually remove sediment. As noted previously, the work that a river does involves moving the sediment that is supplied to it. Changes in capacity and competence dictate where the erosion takes place and where the products of that erosion are likely to be deposited. Because of this, the shape and behavior of rivers is tied inextricably to the *sediment yield* of the watershed (usually expressed as tons of sediment per acre or square mile).

Almost all land uses in California have an impact on the amount of sediment that is supplied to rivers. Change in sediment yield of watersheds can come from seemingly disparate land use practices: agriculture, urbanization, flood control projects, logging. The effects of these changes, which can be far-reaching and occasionally problematic, are difficult to predict both spatially and temporally. However, the costs of ignoring the impacts of sediment can be substantial. Because of this, management of sediment production within watersheds has been a high priority of many of the land use planning agencies that operate in California. Yet the climate, unstable bedrock, and remarkable mountain-building rates within California's watersheds produce the highest yields in the country and some of the highest in the world. This makes the task of managing sediment production a particularly vital and onerous one.

The focus of this chapter is on how sediment is generated within a watershed, how it manages to find its way into rivers, and what the causes are for differences in sediment yield between different watersheds. Some of the land use changes that either increase or decrease the supply of sediment to rivers are covered in Part II.

WEATHERING: THE PRIMARY SOURCE OF SEDIMENT

In chapter 1, it was pointed out that there is a contest between the forces that build mountains and the forces that tear them down. Our oxygen- and water-rich atmosphere attacks the bedrock of California, altering and loosening the primary minerals, making them more vulnerable to erosion. Termed *weathering*, this process is the primary source of sediment delivered to the rivers of California.

Weathering is usually divided into two general domains: *chemical*, involving the decomposition of minerals through dissolution or alteration to another mineral, and *physical*, involving the actual disintegration of rocks and/or dislodgment of minerals. Although separate, the processes are often linked because they usually operate in concert to break down parent or bedrock material (fig. 6.1). Weathering within California is dominated by chemical processes. The generally wet climate and abundant vegetative cover accelerate the effects of chemical weathering. Physical weathering is limited in its overall impact but plays a major role in the production of sediment in the alpine and desert climates of the state.

The process of physical weathering involves the physical diminution of bedrock or parent material by breaking or fracturing it along zones of weakness. The breakdown of parent material by physical weathering takes place through a variety of processes. As rocks formed deep in the earth are eventually exposed at the surface through uplift and erosion, the decrease in pressure and stress causes rocks to fracture, often in layers parallel to the surface. Once fractured, water can seep into these rocks, hydrating clays or other minerals. This process can cause swelling of the minerals, disaggregating the rock. In semiarid and arid areas, salt crystallization can be an important physical weathering process. High evaporation rates of infiltrated water can lead to precipitation of a variety of salts. The force of crystallization of these minerals can be an effective physical weathering mechanism. Finally, in high-altitude areas, freezing of infiltrated water is a significant contributor to the weathering of rock.

Since the water vapor that forms rain spends a significant amount of time in contact with the atmosphere, it produces rainfall that is mildly acidic and highly oxygenated. When this rainfall lands on existing soils, it mixes with and augments water trapped within the unsaturated zone. The dead and decaying organic matter within soils and the plants and microbes that depend on it all exert a major influence on the chemistry of the rainwater, increasing its relative acidity and adding a number of complex organic acids.

As this chemically complex soil water percolates through the soil and underlying bedrock, it reacts with minerals. Depending on the composi-

PHYSICAL WEATHERING   CHEMICAL WEATHERING

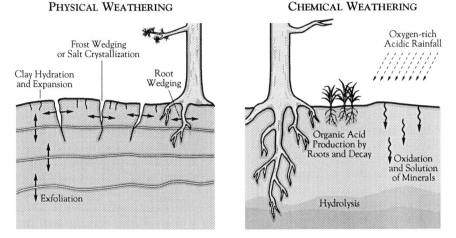

Fig. 6.1. Summary diagram depicting physical and chemical weathering processes that generate sediment for rivers. See text for discussion.

tion of the soil water and the mineralogy of the parent material, a variety of reactions can take place. The oxygen-rich nature of most soil water leads to "rusting," or oxidation of iron-bearing minerals, accelerating their breakdown. In addition, the dilute nature of most rainwater makes it ideal for dissolution of minerals that are typically soluble in soil conditions. Finally, the acidic nature of most rain and soil water makes it ideal for hydrolysis of minerals. During hydrolysis metallic cations (K, Ca, Mg, etc.) are displaced from mineral structures and replaced by hydrogen ions. This process initiates the conversion of the parent mineral to a clay and is an important process in the formation of soils.

The degree and rate of decomposition and disintegration of bedrock minerals to form soils depends on climate, vegetation, and rock type. The wetter the climate, the more dilute and oxygenated the solutions that move through the soils and the more rapid the breakdown due to oxidation and solution. Where dense stands of vegetation occur, the activity of microbes and plant roots within the soils increases the acidity of the solutions and provides numerous organic acids. This accelerates breakdown due to dissolution and hydrolysis. Finally, the rate of breakdown is dependent on the minerals that are attacked by the solutions percolating through the soils. Minerals that contain relatively few metallic cations (like quartz, SiO_2) tend to break down more slowly. In contrast, minerals like olivine and pyroxene, which contain abundant iron, magnesium, and other metallic cations, are highly susceptible to solution, oxidation, and hydrolysis. Rocks rich in these type of minerals break down rapidly due to weathering.

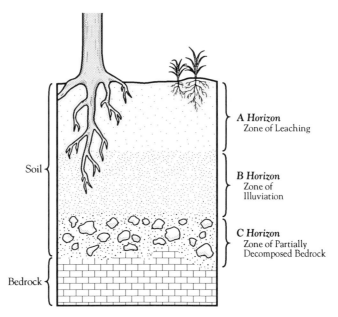

Fig. 6.2. Idealized soil profile illustrating the three principal
soil zones. (Modified from Griggs and Gilchrist 1977.)

SOILS: THE SOURCE OF MOST RIVER SEDIMENT

As the processes of hydrolysis, oxidation, and solution proceed over time,
they produce a mantle of unconsolidated mixtures of organic material,
clays, and remnant rock particles that differs considerably from the original rock mass. This material makes up the soil that covers most of the watersheds in California. As the process of converting bedrock to soil progresses, the soils develop a distinctive vertical arrangement of layers. This
arrangement, known as the *soil profile*, extends from the surface down to
the fresh, unaltered bedrock and is often best seen in road cuts and construction trenches.

In its most simplistic form, a soil profile can be subdivided into three
parts, usually designated as the *A, B,* and *C horizons* (fig. 6.2). The A horizon is the relatively thin, dark-colored layer at the surface that consists of a
mixture of humus, or organic material, and mineral matter, usually clays.
The A horizon is where most of the organic activity takes place within a
soil. Rainfall that falls on the ground passes through the A horizon first,
producing the most intense leaching and downward displacement of clays
and organic acids. For this reason the A horizon is often referred to as
the zone of *elluviation* or leaching. In contrast, the C horizon is typically

viewed as composed primarily of the parent material or bedrock. The C horizon, which is usually light colored due to the absence of abundant organic material, is where the initial breakdown of the bedrock is occurring. In between the A and C horizons is the B horizon. Material leached from the A horizon by percolating water accumulates in the B horizon, collecting as pockets of clay-rich material. Since the material leached from the elluviation zone accumulates in the B horizon, it is known as the *illuviation* zone.

In perhaps the ultimate exercise in button-sorting known to the physical sciences, the soil scientists (or pedologists) have sliced up the soil classification pie into myriad, infinitesimal divisions. It would be pointless to review the entire soil classification scheme here. Explanation of even the simplest classification groups, like *intrazonal hydromorphic planosols,* is beyond the goals of this text. The U.S. Soil Conservation Service has created a complex hierarchical classification scheme that recognizes ten orders, twenty-nine common suborders, and innumerable great groups and subgroups. The combinations are endless and, except for experienced pedologists, complicated to use. Suffice it to point out that these combinations reflect a variety of physical and chemical characteristics of soils as well as the climate zone in which they develop.

It should be no surprise that soils in California vary greatly in their thickness, structure, and composition. Climate, vegetation, topography, bedrock, and time all play a role in the development of soils. In general, older soils from shallow slopes in wetter climates tend to be thick, organic-rich, and better developed. Younger soils from more arid climates with steeper topography are thinner, with more poorly developed layering (fig. 6.3). Most important for the rivers of California is the resistance of soils to erosion. Thick, well-developed soils that have well-established vegetative covers tend to be more resistant to erosion. The binding action of roots and clays along with high infiltration capacities increase a soil's resistance to erosion and reduce its contribution of sediment into rivers. Poorly developed, relatively thin soils, whether due to climate, bedrock, or bad land use practices, tend to erode quickly, producing high sediment yields.

HOW EROSION WORKS

The transfer of the by-products of physical and chemical weathering into California's rivers takes place primarily by direct runoff of rainfall. In many steep watersheds with highly unstable soils and bedrock, mass wasting processes (discussed below) may contribute significant amounts of sediment during and after large rainfall events. Snowmelt, groundwater discharge, and subsurface flow contribute only minor amounts of sediment to rivers in California.

Fig. 6.3. Example of poorly developed soil profile from San Gabriel Mountains near Sylmar. Soils of this region are typically thin with poorly developed A and B horizons. These soils commonly have low infiltration capacities, producing prodigious amounts of runoff, and are usually prone to mass movements.

The erosional process can be divided into three general phases: (1) rainfall impact, where the kinetic energy of raindrops dislodges soil particles; (2) formation of Horton overland flow (chap. 5) and the transport of soil material as sheetwash; and (3) concentrated flow and scouring to form rills and gullies.

Rainsplash Erosion

To get a feeling for the significance of raindrops in erosion of soils, just try to look up the next time you are caught outside in a relatively intense rainstorm. Besides the torrents of water that miraculously find their way into your jacket, the pelting of your face by large drops quickly becomes quite painful. A big fat raindrop falling from the sky rapidly achieves terminal velocity. Because the drop has considerable mass and velocity, it will also possess significant kinetic energy. When this bullet from the sky strikes the ground, it transfers that kinetic energy to the soil particles, dislodging them. On relatively steep slopes, the splash that is formed by this collision reaches farther in the downhill direction than the uphill direction (fig. 6.4). In this way, rainsplash preferentially and systematically dislodges soil particles and transfers them downhill.

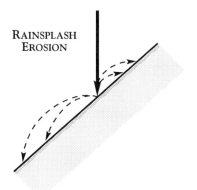

RAINSPLASH
EROSION

Fig. 6.4. Schematic diagram illustrating trajectories of soil particles dislodged by raindrop impact. Note that soil travels farther downslope than upslope, leading to a progressive downhill motion of soil particles.

The effectiveness of rainsplash erosion is dependent on the intensity of the rainfall, the steepness of the slope, the resistance of the soil to dislodgment, and, perhaps most important, the amount of vegetative cover. Trees, brush, and grass intercept rainfall, greatly reducing the kinetic energy and the ability of raindrops to dislodge and transport the soil. Agricultural operations, mining sites, some clear-cut logging, grazing, construction sites, and road cuts all leave bare ground with nothing to intercept the rainfall. Areas, especially grasslands and chaparral, that have been recently burned are also particularly susceptible to rainsplash erosion.

Erosion by Overland Flow

Although raindrop impact plays a major role in dislodging sediment, it is not particularly effective at transporting great volumes of material downslope. Rather, it is the action of water flowing across a slope that moves most sediment to rivers. As noted in the previous chapter, when the infiltration capacity of a soil is exceeded, water moves on the surface as Horton overland flow. Because the water forms a sheet across the slope, it is often referred to as *sheetwash*. As the water flows downhill, it steadily increases its depth and velocity until it reaches a point at which the shear stress of the water is sufficient to transport and, in many cases, erode sediment. The highest rates of hill slope erosion are accomplished by Horton overland flow.

Soil erosion by overland flow or sheetwash is accelerated where rainfall intensities are high and infiltration capacity is likely to be exceeded. The resistance of soil to erosion, the steepness, and the distance that flow travels across a slope each plays a role in determining the amount of erosion. However, the most important control on the amount of sediment transported by overland flow appears to be the amount and type of vegetative cover and any erosion control efforts that have been implemented. Any land use that reduces the amount and/or density of cover promotes the erosivity of overland flow. Vegetation on the slope effectively increases the roughness or frictional resistance to the flow. This acts to reduce the velocity of overland flow and break it up, decreasing its effectiveness.

Rill and Gully Erosion

Perhaps the most visually conspicuous type of erosion is that associated with the formation of rills and gullies. When water flows across a slope, minor irregularities in the surface can cause flows to coalesce. The localized concentration of flow increases the stream power and bed shear stress of the runoff, enhancing its ability to erode bedrock and soils. This leads to the formation of myriad tiny incisions or channels, called *rills*. If rills are not disrupted by the growth of vegetation, tillage, or vehicle traffic, they will continue to incise and coalesce with each significant overland flow event. This process leads to the development of progressively fewer and deeper channels cutting across the slope. Channels that are one or more feet deep are called *gullies*. Gullies can range in size from a few feet deep and tens of feet long to tens of feet deep and miles long (fig. 6.5).

Although rills and gullies form dramatic scars on the landscape, a number of geomorphologists have shown that their formation adds only a minor amount to the overall sediment budget of a watershed. However, the contribution of this process to local sediment budgets, especially in rivers adjacent to mining sites, construction sites, and road cuts, can be considerable and can represent a major hazard.

CALCULATING SEDIMENT YIELD

In making land use decisions for a watershed, planners need to be able to identify soils and geomorphic settings that are likely to produce considerable quantities of sediment. In addition, in order to assess cumulative impact, they must estimate how much sediment is likely to be supplied to local rivers when land use changes in a watershed. A variety of approaches have evolved to deal with these unknowns. A commonly used—and sometimes misused—approach involves the development of multivariate equations to estimate the total amount of erosion within a watershed. Based on studies at regional experimental stations, soil scientists will determine the amount of soil that is lost from a given field or hillside during a given storm for a given soil condition. The numerical relationship between these variables is then extrapolated to the range of landscape, rainfall, and soils

Fig. 6.5. Gully erosion forms intense scars of the landscape and locally supplies large amounts of sediment. Photograph illustrates initial formation of gullies across the landscape following a fire in southern California. These gullies will eventually coalesce to form fewer but increasingly larger gullies. Photograph courtesy of Robert Matthews.

that occur within a watershed. The "equation" that defines this relationship is called the *universal soil loss equation:*

$$A = RKLSCP, \tag{6.1}$$

where

- A = soil loss in tons per acre
- R = rainfall erosivity index, or a measure of the kinetic energy of rainfall
- K = soil erodibility index, or a measure of the ease with which soil is eroded
- L = hill slope length factor, or a consideration of the length over which the water has to flow
- S = hill slope gradient factor, or the steepness of the slope
- C = cropping management factor, or the impact of various crops or natural vegetation on the resistance of the soil to erosion
- P = erosion control practice factor, or a coefficient that corrects for the different types of erosion control practices employed.

The equation predicts only the amount of soil moved from its original site. It does not take into account the fact that once eroded, sediment is stored in a variety of localities within watersheds, including terraces, tributaries, bars, and channels. In addition, the equation does not identify the different mechanisms of soil erosion; it recognizes only the result, not the process.

Clearly, the universal soil loss equation has more fudge factors in it than the hydraulic engineering equations described in chapter 2. If the amount of soil loss measured does not match the calculated value, simply fiddle with any of six different variables until you get it right. In this regard, the general applicability of this equation is questionable, especially in such a diverse setting as California's watersheds. To get reasonable results, numerous experimental stations must be established to refine the equation's variables. Although fraught with difficulties and inaccuracies, the equation itself does offer a qualitative description of the factors that control the amount of erosion that occurs and which land use changes might have the greatest impact on it. In this manner, the equation offers a useful guide for land use planning decisions.

MASS WASTING

In response to the extraordinary erosion of agricultural soils during the Great Depression, government and university researchers began an intense program of study of the natural and land use factors that enhance surface erosion. The vast majority of this research was focused on the Midwest, where the damage was greatest. Because the slopes are low and the uplift rates are slight, few researchers paid attention to the role of mass wasting of slopes as a possible source of sediment. In the past few decades scientists from throughout the tectonically active areas of the Pacific Rim have been attempting to assess the role of landslides in watershed sediment yields. Predictably, the results are highly variable, depending on local climatic, topographic, and geologic factors. However, researchers have found that mass movement of sediment in very steep, heavily vegetated basins is one of the dominant sources of sediment supplied to rivers.

Mass movements fall into at least three general categories: *slides, flows,* and *heaves,* each with distinctive physical characteristics and mechanical properties. In slides, a relatively dry but cohesive mass of soil and/or bedrock moves rapidly downslope along a distinctive shear plane. In contrast, flows occur where the material is wetter but still relatively fast moving and involve internal mixing or shearing within the slide mass. In contrast to slides and flows, heaves occur where expansion and contraction of the soil leads to a very slow overall downhill motion. Although mass movements commonly fall into one category, many of the slides that occur in California's watersheds appear to be formed by a combination of processes (figs. 6.6, 6.7).

Causes of Mass Movement

Like water flowing downhill, gravity is the driving force behind the generation of mass movements. All day, every day, it is gravity that is attempting to pull down the steep mountain slopes of the state. Yet, with the exception of rare events, the hill slopes of California are not constantly falling down around our ears. Thus some balance must occur between the driving forces (referred to as the shear stress) and the internal forces of the hillside that act to resist mass movement (shear strength). As long as the shear strength of a slope exceeds or equals the shear stress, it will not succumb to gravity and fall down.

A variety of both natural and human-induced processes can lead to changes in the relationship between shear stress and shear strength of a hillside. Processes that act to increase the amount of shear stress on a hillside usually involve the addition of mass or an increase in the overall slope of the hillside, often through land use changes. This can include adding buildings to hillsides or increasing the amount of water stored in the hillside as groundwater or soil water either by decreased evapotranspiration due to vegetation removal or by increased channeling of surface runoff onto hillsides.

Decreases in shear strength of a slope are also caused by a variety of land use changes. Although land use changes that increase the water content of a slope lead to increases in shear stress, they are exacerbated by the tendency of the water to decrease shear strength within the slide and increase the buoyancy of the slide mass. In addition, shallow groundwater tables tend to decrease the frictional resistance along potential slide planes, acting much like a lubricant for the overall slide mass.

It is important to note that changes in land use do not *necessarily* cause landslides. Throughout the mountainous regions of California, the rapid rates of tectonic uplift and naturally unstable soils produce conditions that are prone to landsliding. Landslide mapping projects carried out by the U.S. Geological Survey, the California Division of Mines and Geology, and the U.S. Forest Service have shown that in some watersheds of the central and north coast a majority of the slopes consist of a mix of modern and ancient landslide material. Moreover, the natural evolution of most steep landscapes inevitably involves mass movements. As watersheds expand and deepen, the tendency of rivers to incise increases slope steepness and

SOME MASS MOVEMENTS COMMON TO
CALIFORNIA WATERSHEDS

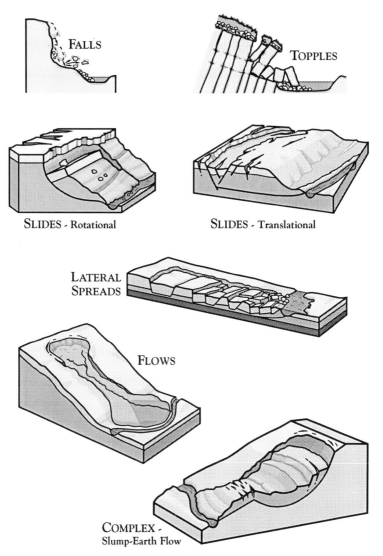

Fig. 6.6. Types of mass movements commonly noted in the watersheds of California. Falls, topples, rotational slides, and translational slides are typically relatively dry, while lateral spreads, flows, and slump-earth flows are relatively wet. All examples shown here move rapidly. All of these mass movements act to dam or alter the course of the state's rivers. In addition, in many watersheds mass movements are a major contributor to the overall sediment budget. (Modified from Varnes 1984.)

Fig. 6.7. Complex mass movement typically seen in unstable geologic units along the San Andreas Fault, central Coast Ranges. Note combination slump and earth flow features and multiple episodes of movement within slide mass. Photograph courtesy of Gerald Weber.

induces frequent landsliding. However, in many steep watersheds, there is a delicate balance between the shear stress that attempts to induce landsliding and the shear strength that resists it. This balance can be easily altered by land use practices such as urbanization, mining, farming, grazing, and logging, producing significant and widespread landsliding.

Impact of Mass Movements on Rivers

Mass movements have the potential to alter California's rivers substantially. Large slides in river canyons can form *landslide dams,* which change the gradient of a river and induce regional readjustments in grade, channel cross-section, and profile (fig. 6.8). The South Fork of the Smith River along the California-Oregon border and the California Salmon River of the western Trinity Alps have been dammed repeatedly by large slides, many of which are currently active and will dam the rivers again in the near future. The net effect of these dams has been similar to the creation of modern dams and reservoirs (chap. 16). Sediment is trapped upstream in the low-gradient stretch above the dam, while incision of the river takes

Fig. 6.8. Mass movements have the capacity to significantly affect rivers. The 1982 Love Creek Slide in the Santa Cruz Mountains (*top*), which killed 10 people, was a translational slide with associated debris flows. Photo courtesy of Gerald Weber. The slide and debris flow created a dam that temporarily blocked Love Creek (*bottom*) and flooded homes upstream. Constructed of a mixture of rock, soil, vegetation, and homes, this unstable mass was eventually breached. Catastrophic failure of landslide dams can lead to severe downstream flooding. Photograph from Griggs 1982.

place in the high-gradient stretch immediately at or below the dam. This erosion eventually removes the dam and the sediment trapped behind it, allowing the river to restore its original gradient. Occasionally, erosion will lead to collapse of these dams followed by catastrophic downstream flooding. The Noachian floods that follow modify the river canyons and floodplains in an instant. These rare events are greatly underappreciated in studies of California's more slide-prone watersheds.

Mass movements do not always dam rivers completely. More typically, the toe of a landslide or debris flow will impinge on the river, deflecting flow to one side and altering flow in the channel. By constricting the flow and increasing its velocity, the slides can induce bank erosion on both sides of the river. In most cases, the unconsolidated nature of landslide sediments makes them highly susceptible to erosion. Erosion of the toe by the river usually stimulates increased motion of the slide, adding even more sediment into the river. In this way, individual slides can serve as important point sources of sediment for extended periods of time until they are either completely eroded or stabilized.

Mass movements, both as sediment sources and as hazards, are a major headache for land use planners. It has been estimated that as much as 20 percent of the money spent on geologic hazards is spent on mass movements alone, exceeding the cost of flooding by one-half (California Department of Mines and Geology sources). During the last decade of this century, California alone will probably spend as much as $5 billion preparing for and cleaning up after landslides. There are sound engineering and geologic criteria for determining the types of locations where mass movements are likely to occur (regrettably, too seldom applied), but we are incapable of accurately predicting when and precisely where. Thus mass movement risk assessment is a game of chance. Compounding this is the fact that destructive mass movements often occur in bunches. Exceptionally large storms trigger numerous landslides and debris flows. Large earthquakes, if they occur during the wet season, may also trigger widespread mass movements. Numerous slides occurring at once would disrupt the equilibrium of any river system.

SEDIMENT SUPPLIED BY CHANNEL EROSION

As noted in chapter 4, river channels are hardly static. The tendency of rivers to store large amounts of sediment within point bars and longitudinal and transverse bars and on their floodplains makes the alluvial material of the river valley itself a potentially important source of sediment to a watershed. In high-gradient rivers that cut through narrow canyons, the amount of channel and floodplain sediment available to the river is not particularly large. Most of the sediment supplied by channel erosion is derived primarily from erosion of bedrock during incision of the channel.

However, where the river channel occupies a floodplain or incises through alluvial terraces, a substantial amount of the sediment budget for a basin may be provided by erosion of the banks of the river.

In a meandering river system, the lateral migration of a channel involves erosion on the steep, outside portion of the meander bend with matching deposition on the inside portion or point bar. This balance between erosion and deposition implies that there is no net change in sediment stored within a floodplain. Hence if sediment is being derived from erosion within the channel, then there must be a net depletion of stored sediment throughout the river system. A number of processes can cause a river to begin using its stored reserves of sediment. Increases in overall discharge and stream power or decreases in sediment supply (due to dams, usually) will induce channel changes that ultimately translate to increased erosion of alluvial deposits. However, the cannibalization of stored sediment in undammed California rivers usually occurs in response to large-scale events that have abruptly increased the amount of sediment temporarily stored within alluvial valleys. As is discussed below, the amount of sediment delivered by rare, catastrophic storms usually overwhelms the capacity and competence of rivers. This induces widespread channel aggradation and deposition on the floodplains. In the years following these rare events, the river attempts to restore grade or equilibrium by slowly eroding the stored material, thereby increasing the apparent long-term sediment yield.

OVERALL SEDIMENT BUDGET

The yearly amount of bedload and suspended load that reaches the mouth of any river represents a watershed's net sediment production. Although these data are useful when conducting regional-scale comparisons of erosion rates in watersheds, they fall far short of the information necessary for management of erosion within a watershed. As the above discussions illustrate, there is complexity in the way sediment is generated and routed through a watershed. For the purpose of assessing sediment sources within a watershed, it would be much more useful to evaluate sediment yield as the product of the following:

>   Sediment Yield by Overland Flow and Gullying
> + Sediment Yield by Landsliding
> + Sediment Yield by Bank Erosion in Channels
> − Sediments Added to Channels and Floodplains
> ───
> = Total Yearly Sediment Yield

Unfortunately, reasonably accurate estimates of the sediment contribution from these various sources are difficult to come by.

One of the most detailed and informative analyses of sediment sources and routing within a California basin was conducted by Harvey Kelsey on the Van Duzen River in northwestern California. The Van Duzen River occupies a moderate-sized (222-sq.-mi.), high-relief watershed with highly erosive bedrock. Rainfall values within the basin are high, commonly exceeding 100 inches on the ridgetops. Intense logging and grazing pressures within the watershed have exacerbated the naturally high erosion rates. The voluminous debris that moves through this basin has led to widespread destruction of anadromous fish habitat and poses a potential flooding risk.

Most of the sediment transport that occurs within the Van Duzen watershed takes place during the two to six most intense winter storms in any year, with 50 percent of the annual sediment transport occurring on average over only four days. Table 6.1 shows a simplified sediment budget and an analysis of sediment source areas for a 35-year period within the Van Duzen watershed. Some of the results are surprising. Apparently, almost half of the total sediment yield from the basin is derived from only 6 percent of the total land area within the basin. More than a quarter of the sediment is derived from sources that make up less than 1 percent of the total basin area. The major sources of sediment production appear to be (1) earthflow landslides (fast, wet) formed on grassy slopes; (2) debris slides and debris avalanches (fast, dry) on large, steep, forested slopes; (3) erosion of bedrock and alluvium along stream banks; and (4) gully formation and downcutting on rapidly eroding grasslands and grass-oak woodlands. The sediment budget developed by Kelsey did not treat erosion of stored sediment within channels as an important source because it was presumed that all of the sediment was derived from hill slopes during the 35-year period. However, a substantial portion of the current sediment yield from the Van Duzen River comes from reworking of this stored sediment.

A second aspect of the Kelsey study is the role that large storm events play in sediment production. As discussed above, large storm events, like those of December 1964, deposit large volumes of sediment in the main tributaries of rivers. This sediment is temporarily stored within the channel and then slowly removed by the less intense storms that follow. The sediment yields of many north coast basins showed a peak immediately following the 1964 floods, with a steady decline in subsequent years.

Although the relationship between sediment sources and sediment budget within the Van Duzen basin cannot be directly applied to watersheds outside of the area, the results of this study illustrate an important problem: a disproportionate amount of the sediment yield from a basin can be derived from relatively small but intensely eroding areas (i.e., 6% of the area produces 50% of the sediment; table 6.1). The erosion of the north

TABLE 6.1　Sediment Budget and Sediment Sources
for the Van Duzen River, 1941–1975

Sediment Budget	
Source	Amount (tons)
Sediment from Overland Flow and Gully Erosion	45,509,000
+	+
Sediment from Mass Movements	13,561,000
+	+
Sediment from Bank Erosion	3,045,000
–	–
Accumulation in Major River Channels	10,601,000
Net Sediment Yield	51,514,000

Sediment Sources in the Van Duzen Basin			
Sediment Sources	Sediment Yield (tons)	% Drainage Area	% Total Sediment Yield
Earth-flow Landslides	6,052,000	0.6	10
Debris Slides and Avalanches	10,630,000	0.4	17
Unstable Channel Banks	3,045,000	1.0	05
Gullied Terrain	11,418,000	4.1	18
Totals	31,145,000	6.1	50

SOURCE: From Kelsey 1980.

coast basins is not taking place as a slow, stately wearing away of the entire landscape. Sediment supply is dominated by point sources or unusually unstable areas characterized by mass movements and intense erosion. This means that uniform application of erosion control techniques for various land use practices is both unwarranted and unlikely to be successful in controlling sediment yield.

SUMMARY

The amount of sediment supplied to a river is a major control of the river's shape and behavior. The primary source of this sediment is the physical and chemical weathering of California's bedrock. Physical weathering involves the breakdown of parent material by fracturing and dislodging grains. Unloading during uplift, freezing and expansion of ice and salts, and hydration of expansive clay minerals all act to break and pry apart the rock. Chemical weathering of parent rock and the by-products of physical weathering produce the soils that mantle most of California's landscape. Oxidation, dissolution, and hydrolysis in conjunction with the organic acids produced by plant roots and the decay or organic material decompose parent material, converting it into the clays that make up soils. Well-developed, stable soils have three principal layers: (1) an A horizon, or zone of elluviation, characterized by abundant organic material and intense leaching; (2) a B horizon, or zone of illuviation, where material leached from the A horizon tends to accumulate; and (3) the C horizon, where bedrock is being actively altered and disaggregated.

Erosion of soils and bedrock and the routing of sediment into rivers take place through a variety of processes. The great kinetic energy of raindrops makes them effective at dislodging soil on bare slopes and transporting it downhill. Most transport of soil is accomplished by Horton overland flow when infiltration capacities are exceeded by rainfall intensities. Overland flow can coalesce to form rills and gullies, which also actively contribute to erosion. The widely used and misused universal soil loss equation illustrates the various geomorphic, climatic, and soil characteristics that promote erosion and high sediment yields.

Although not often considered, mass movements can be major contributors to the overall sediment budget of upland watersheds. Mass movements are categorized primarily by the amount of water they contain, the rate at which they move, and the amount of internal shearing that occurs. The stability of a slope is a function of the relationship between the shear stress that is being exerted and the shear strength of the potential slide mass. A variety of natural processes and land use practices can increase shear stress or decrease shear strength, promoting the formation of mass movements.

Erosion of the channel can also be a major source of sediment yield within a basin. Direct erosion of bedrock is a small but locally significant contributor to sediment budgets. Most of the sediment derived from channel erosion occurs when rivers tap into sediment stored within the channel and in terraces and floodplains. Catastrophic runoff events that overwhelm the competence and capacity of rivers may deposit large amounts of material within channels and on floodplains. During subsequent years the overall sediment yield of a basin may increase as these deposits are reworked by the river in its attempt to establish equilibrium or grade.

The net yearly sediment yield for a watershed is the sum of erosion by overland flow and gullying, erosion by mass movements, and erosion of channels minus the amount of sediment added to temporary or permanent storage within channels and floodplains. Detailed studies of north coast watersheds indicate that the bulk of the sediment yield is derived from relatively small, highly erosive areas.

RELEVANT READINGS

Brunsden, D., ed. 1971. *Slope Form and Process.* Institute of British Geographers Special Publication no. 3. Oxford: Oxford University Press.

Davies, T. R. H., and A. J. Pearce, eds. 1981. *Erosion and Sediment Transport in Pacific Rim Steeplands.* International Association of Hydrological Sciences Publication no. 132. Washington, D.C.

Griggs, G. B. 1982. "Flooding and Slope Failure During the January 1982 Storm, Santa Cruz County, California." *California Geology* 35: 158–163.

Griggs, G. B., and J. A. Gilchrist. 1977. *The Earth and Land Use Planning.* North Scituate, Mass.: Duxbury Press.

Hadley, R. F., and D. E. Walling. 1984. *Erosion and Sediment Yield: Some Methods of Measurement and Modelling.* Norwich, U.K.: Geo Books.

Kelsey, H. M. 1980. "A Sediment Budget and an Analysis of Geomorphic Process in the Van Duzen River Basin, North Coastal California, 1941–1975." *Geological Society of America Bulletin* 91: 190–195.

Laronne, J. B., and M. P. Mosley, eds. 1982. *Erosion and Sediment Yield.* Stroudsburg, Pa.: Hutchinson Ross.

Olshansky, R. B. 1990. *Landslide Hazard in the United States: Case Studies in Planning and Policy Development.* New York: Garland.

Selby, M. J. 1982. *Hillslope Materials and Processes.* Oxford: Oxford University Press.

Varnes, D. J. 1978. "Slope Movement Types and Processes." In *Landslides: Analysis and Control,* ed. R. L. Schuster and R. J. Krizek. Special Report no. 176. Washington, D.C.: National Academy of Sciences.

Varnes, D. J. 1984. *Landslide Hazard Zonation: A Review of Principles and Practice.* International Association of Engineering Geology, Commission on Landslides and Other Mass Movements on Slopes. Natural Hazards 3. Paris: UNESCO.

Wischmeier, W. H., and D. D. Smith. 1978. *Predicting Rainfall Erosion Losses: A Guide to Conservation Planning.* Agriculture Handbook no. 537. Washington, D.C.: U.S. Department of Agriculture.

Woldenberg, M. J., ed. 1985. *Models in Geomorphology.* Boston: G. Allen and Unwin.

SEVEN

River Network and Profile

INTRODUCTION

Imagine that you have been assigned the task of designing the optimum drainage network for a given California watershed. We know from the previous chapters that the plumbing system that you design must meet the following specifications: (1) runoff must obey the fundamental laws of physics; (2) the network must move all of the sediment and water out of the watershed in the most efficient manner while seeking to maintain a balance in energy expenditures; (3) the plumbing design must evolve with the watershed as it expands and matures; and (4) the plumbing system must also adjust to long- and short-term changes in climate. Supercomputers and legions of programmers are at your disposal for this seemingly simple job.

Where to start? Should you design a watershed that is drained by many small, straight channels of equal but relatively steep slope? This type of watershed should drain rapidly and efficiently but will have a great deal of trouble balancing energy expenditures. Conversely, it might be better to design a drainage network that looks like a tree: one large trunk river fed by a group of smaller rivers that are, each in turn, fed by an increasing number of even smaller tributaries. Although this would allow the river to distribute energy expenditures more uniformly, it also appears to be less efficient at rapidly transporting discharge and sediment out of the watershed. Presumably, the ideal river design would incorporate aspects of both end-member designs. What you are likely to discover from your efforts (as have numerous watershed "modelers") is that the potential variations are infinite.

It is logical to assume that nature has probably done a pretty good job of developing the optimum design for a watershed. Scrutiny of the topographic maps that cover California tell an intriguing story about this effort. Simply put, watersheds in California are like snowflakes and snowfalls: no two are exactly alike. The variation in the drainage networks and the slope of the rivers is extreme, seeming to run the gamut of possibilities. Thus it might be argued that the evolution of watershed drainage networks is a purely random process: nature has not engineered the perfect watershed and is simply creating rivers and channels in a haphazard (and presumably inefficient) manner, and any attempt to understand the design of a watershed or define laws that govern its development would therefore be futile.

An examination of California's watersheds indicates that there *is* some general order in this chaos. As a group, the low-gradient drainage networks along the western slope of the Sierras appear different from the high-gradient networks of the eastern Sierras; the wet north coast drainages contain drainage patterns that are not seen in watersheds of the desert regions of the south. Thus, although no two watersheds in California are alike, variation appears to take place within a limited range of possibilities for a given set of physical and climatic conditions. Given this knowledge, it may be possible to design a watershed; it is just that the solution is not unique. Any number of other designs that occur within a reasonable range are likely to be sufficient to do the job. Nature, in its development of watersheds, probably adheres to the same philosophy.

The origins of the differences and similarities of the network and profile of California's watersheds are examined in this chapter. The differences reflect variations in climate, geology, and tectonic setting; the similarities record the natural, deterministic process of water flowing across and eroding landscapes.

WATERSHEDS IN PLAN VIEW:
EVOLUTION OF DRAINAGE NETWORKS

In chapter 1 it was noted that the earth-atmosphere contest in California is currently being won by the earth forces: uplift rates and the processes that form mountains are outpacing the erosive capabilities of our atmosphere and climate. Because of this, watersheds in California have been developing on and in response to an ever-changing landscape. The driving forces for this evolution are mass movements and the water that flows across and within the landscape of California (chaps. 5, 6). Rainsplash, Horton overland flow, and saturation overland flow remove and transport sediment downslope. Without rivers or channels to carry this flow, it would move as sheets across the landscape, forming a relatively smooth topography lacking in steep canyons. But inhomogeneities in the topography cause flow to concentrate, first forming rills, which then coalesce to form gullies. Once gullies form, their ability to gather and concentrate surface runoff accelerates their incision and expansion. As rills become gullies, gullies coalesce to form the channels that eventually become rivers.

As channels grow, they intercept an increasingly larger amount of overland and subsurface flow, furthering their ability to erode and transport sediment. Because channels incise and expand laterally during their initial formation, they act to steepen the slopes of their watershed. This increases the volume and erosivity of overland flow and decreases the shear strength of landslide-prone hill slopes. In this way channels accelerate their own formation and drive the evolution of the landscape.

The initial formation of a drainage network within a watershed takes place at a surprisingly rapid pace. Studies in the midwestern and eastern United States have shown that drainage networks establish themselves within a few thousand years on highly erodible soils and bedrock. Despite their relatively fast appearance, there is not some preordained drainage pattern that develops on any given slope. Experimental and field studies have shown that during initial stages of formation, networks undergo nucleation and rapid expansion of the number and length of their channels (fig. 7.1 A, B). The skeletal drainage pattern that becomes established rapidly expands through upslope growth of the streams, followed by diversification and densification (fig. 7.1 B, C, D). Essentially, the growth of the network involves the subdivision of the entire watershed into increasingly smaller and more numerous subdrainages. Finally, at a relatively mature stage of development, the drainage network actually begins to consolidate (fig. 7.1 E, F). This takes place through *stream capture* or *stream piracy*, whereby upslope expansion of one tributary eventually leads to capture of runoff from another tributary. By reducing the slopes and stream gradients of the watershed and widening the main valleys, fewer large tributaries are needed to handle the runoff, maintaining a least-work design while continuing to balance energy expenditures.

Network expansion occurs by erosion at the *channel head*, or the upstream limit of well-defined channelized flow that is usually associated with incision into bedrock or soils. The mechanics of erosion at channel heads, called *headward erosion*, is highly variable in California's watersheds and involves both Horton overland flow and erosion due to rapid discharge of subsurface flow. The rate of headward erosion of channel heads is sensitive to changes in land use, climate, and tectonic uplift. For example, increases in the magnitude and intensity of runoff will accelerate the rate of growth of channel head cuts. Where changes increase the overall sediment load or decrease the amount of surface runoff, the rate of headward erosion

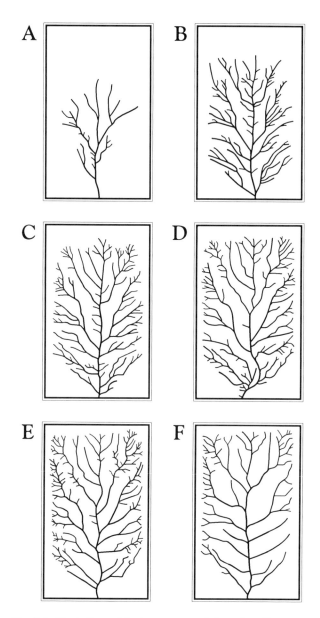

Fig. 7.1. Evolution of drainage network based on flume experiments. *A-B*, rapid expansion through headward erosion. *C-D*, network densification. *E-F*, consolidation through stream capture. (Modified from Schumm 1977.)

will decrease. In these cases excess sediment can cause channel heads to fill and eventually retreat downslope. The impacts of this on the overall watershed hydrology and sediment production are not well documented.

Lithologic and Structural Controls on Channel Network Development

There are a range of unequally distributed rock types within any large watershed in California. The location, composition, and history of formation of these rocks are all a function of the past and present tectonic activity of the region (chap. 9). The resistance of various rock types to erosion and mass movements has exerted considerable control over the evolution of California's drainage networks.

Within any given watershed, differential headward erosion rates concentrate network expansion in areas of least erosional resistance. Where contrasts in rock type occur, growth of the network can lead to sharp bends in the network channels. The numerous fault zones that cross California have perhaps the most striking impact on drainage patterns. Typically, faults will juxtapose rocks of significantly different erosional resistance. Headward growth of channels will often "work" along these differences for great distances, forming long, linear channel segments. In many areas, motion along the fault acts to weaken the erosional resistance of the geologic units that are sliding past each other. Headward growth along these zones of weakness will also produce distinctive straight channel segments.

The geologic influences on the patterns of channel networks are summarized in table 7.1 and illustrated in figure 7.2. The most common drainage network pattern in the smaller basins of California is known as *dendritic.* This treelike branching of channels occurs where the rock types are relatively homogeneous and do not differentially influence erosion rates (fig. 7.3A). Dendritic patterns most closely resemble the drainages that develop experimentally on uniform substrates (see fig. 7.1). In contrast, *trellis* and *rectangular* drainage patterns form where heterogeneous, well-stratified rock sequences or parallel fractures and faults dominate the evolution of the landscape. These patterns are common throughout the central and southern Coast Ranges of California as well as in portions of the Sierra Nevada. *Radial* and *annular* patterns are associated with the symmetrical erosion of edifices such as volcanoes or domes. These are common around Mount Lassen and Mount Shasta and reflect a relatively young, rapidly evolving landscape. In the Sacramento/San Joaquin Delta and on the lower portions of many alluvial fans, the division of the channel network into numerous individual channels produces a distinctive anastomosing channel network known as *distributary* (fig. 7.3B).

There is a tendency to draw conclusions about drainage network

TABLE 7.1   Typical Drainage Patterns Commonly Found in California

Type	Description	Controls	Regional Examples
Dendritic	Randomly oriented, treelike pattern	Homogeneous rocks Lack of major geologic structures	Common in upper elevations of Sierra Nevada, Klamath Mountains, and Peninsular Ranges
Radial	Streams flow away from center	Occurrence of isolated volcanic domes or cones	Mt. Lassen, Shasta, Diablo
Trellis	Primary drainages perpendicular to relatively straight main drainage Subsidiary drainages parallel to main drainage	Alternating parallel resistant and weak geologic units or parallel fault zones	Sierran foothills, northern and central Coast Ranges, Transverse Ranges
Distributary	Main stem divides into many channels	Rivers discharge onto low-gradient plain or permeable surface	Sacramento/San Joaquin Delta, numerous alluvial fans of arid southern California

patterns and the existing bedrock composition and geologic structure. However, it is important to remember that most rivers have had to carve through extensive thicknesses of geologic material to arrive at their present configuration. For example, 5 miles of rock have been stripped off the Sierra Nevada since the granites that make up its core were first formed. As the rivers have carved down through various geologic formations, each has left some imprint on the shape of the channel network. Where this imprint produces a lack of correspondence between drainage pattern and the geologic structure presently exposed at the surface, the river is presumed to be antecedent or superposed.

An *antecedent* river or drainage pattern is formed when a river is able to maintain its established course even though it is clearly being affected by tectonic uplift and changes in geology that could disrupt it. Antecedence tends to take place where broad, slow tectonic uplift allows gradual downcutting by the river. Antecedent rivers are those that appear to cross mountain ranges or hills without significant disruption in their pattern. Since most of California is undergoing fairly rapid rates of uplift, antecedent rivers and drainage patterns are rare. Where the course of a river or its channel network is clearly inherited from some previous structure and appears discordant with the existing rock type and structure of the watershed, the

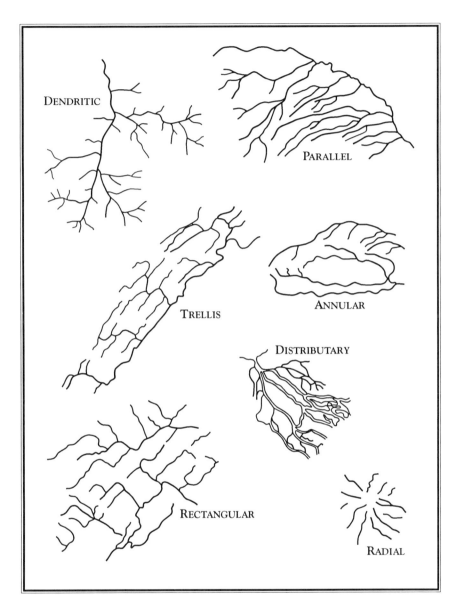

Fig. 7.2. General drainage patterns found in California. Parallel, annular, and rectangular patterns uncommon. (Modified from Morisawa 1985.)

Fig. 7.3A. Drainage patterns in California watersheds. *Above*: 1979 aerial photo-graph of upper Stony Creek, Mendocino County, illustrating dendritic drainage pattern typical of most upland watersheds in California.

river is said to be *superposed.* Since most of the bedrock rivers in California that are established in older rock units have sliced through different over-lying rocks during their development, many of the state's rivers show some effects of superposition.

DISCHARGE AND DRAINAGE NETWORK STRUCTURE

Once runoff is generated within a watershed, it feeds into the streams and rivers that route water and sediment downhill. The overall size, shape, and steepness of the basin influence how much water will run off and, in a gross sense, how fast it will run off. For each small drainage within a water-shed, there will be a flood hydrograph that reflects the local physical and climatic characters. As each of these drainages merges downstream, the flows that form these hydrographs are summed. Thus by the time all of this discharge passes through the mouth of the watershed, the measured flood hydrograph really records the aggregate sum of innumerable, much

Fig. 7.3B. *Above*: 1972 aerial photograph of Kings River in the southern San
Joaquin Valley illustrating distributary drainage pattern typical of large alluvial
fans. Single channel or braided rivers will commonly divide into multiple widespread channels as they spread out across low-gradient portions of alluvial fans.
Note the intensive development of the canal system that captures virtually all
of Kings River water and diverts it for agriculture. The Kings River used to feed
Tulare Lake, the largest body of freshwater in the western United States. Today,
the lakebeds have been converted to farms.

smaller flood hydrographs. Because the process of summing all of these
hydrographs takes place through an elaborate plumbing system, the structure and density of the network of streams and rivers that drain a watershed exert considerable influence on the nature of the flood hydrograph
and the ability of a watershed to move sediment.

   For much of this century geomorphologists have been engaged in an attempt to quantify the relationship between rivers and their watersheds. As noted in chapter 1, the analysis of basin morphometry involves measuring all that is measurable and then seeing what falls out, regardless of whether there is any logical reason to do this. This branch of science was brought to the forefront by Robert Horton, who devised *Horton's laws of drainage composition*. Numerous workers have modified Horton's original laws, thereby spawning myriad equations that quantify the physical characteristics of watersheds. Despite my disparaging comments, measuring morphometric relationships is valuable in that it allows objective, quantitative comparisons within and between watersheds. However, there is an inherent temptation to draw conclusions about process from these relationships that should be greeted with healthy skepticism.

It is beyond the scope of this book to cover all the mind-numbing measurements that can be made. Only a few of the most relevant and commonly used measurements are discussed here. Those wishing more are referred to the books and papers recommended at the end of this chapter.

Stream Order and Drainage Density

Within any watershed there is a seemingly chaotic distribution of drainages and tributaries of various sizes and shapes. The number of drainages, their relative size, and their spatial distribution presumably reflect an optimal design for removing runoff and sediment yield from a watershed. Horton demonstrated that the relationship between streams of different magnitude can be expressed in simple mathematical terms. Most important of these is the assignment of a *stream order* to stream segments within a basin that reflects their relative importance to the overall river system. The lowest-order streams are the creeks and ephemeral drainages; the highest-order segments are the trunk rivers or main river of a drainage. Since the initial efforts of Horton in the 1940s, a variety of approaches to "stream ordering" have evolved. Each of these techniques is fraught with some difficulties. The ordering system that is used most frequently in watershed studies is that first introduced by A. N. Strahler in 1952. The *Strahler ordering system*, illustrated here with an example from Santa Barbara's Mission Creek (fig. 7.4), is based on a division of a stream into segments. The stream segments that lack measurable tributaries (which often depends on the map scale being used) are designated first-order streams. Where two first-order streams join together, they form a second-order stream. Where a segment of a stream is joined by a lower-order segment (e.g., a third-order stream being joined by a second-order stream), the order does not increase. Only where two streams of equal order join together is the order number increased.

Although simple to use, the problem with this approach is that the

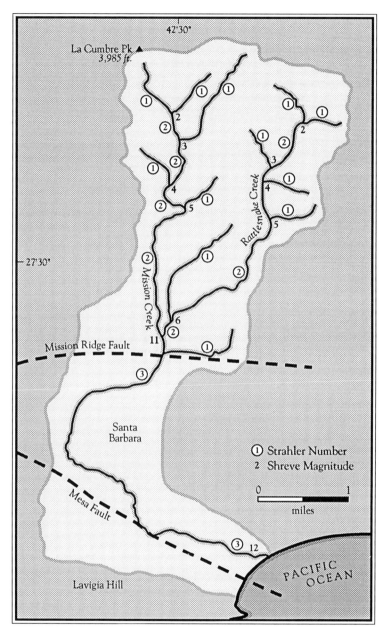

Fig. 7.4. Strahler order and Shreve magnitude for stream segments of Mission Creek, Santa Barbara, California. See text for discussion.

Strahler order does not account for all of the lower-order tributaries that have joined any segment. For example, one third-order tributary may have twenty first-order tributaries feeding into it while another third-order tributary may only have a few. Obviously, runoff is going to pass through these two systems differently. To deal with this inconsistency, in 1967, R. L. Shreve developed an ordering system (fig. 7.4) that recognizes the total number of tributaries that feed into any segment. In Shreve's system, streams consist of links, with the magnitude of any link being the sum of all the tributaries that feed into it. This means that at any point within a basin the Shreve magnitude is essentially equal to the sum of all the first-order streams upstream of that point.

Many of the linear features of river networks, such as the total number of streams in a basin and the average length of streams, are related to the Strahler order and Shreve magnitude of rivers. The most important relationship, however, is the relationship of stream ordering to sediment yields and the flood hydrograph. In general (read: with exceptions), low-order rivers tend to have rapid hydrograph responses to storms (fig. 7.5). Higher-order rivers, because of the numerous subbasins that feed into the main river and the tendency to store water on floodplains, will have flatter hydrographs. Because low-order rivers usually have numerous small tributaries, they also tend to produce higher overall sediment yields with low suspended load/bedload ratios.

One of the more significant influences on a river system is the network or drainage density. Drainage density is defined as the length of all channels within a basin divided by the total basin area. Of course, map scale tends to influence which features are chosen as channels and which are merely swales. However, the overall drainage density is quite variable among watersheds in California. It has been suggested that these differences reflect a minimizing of energy losses of flow over slopes and channels. For example, high drainage densities reduce energy loss due to overland flow or subsurface flow, whereas low drainage densities take advantage of the reduced frictional resistance associated with larger and deeper channels.

As noted above, rainfall and surface runoff are the principal controls on the generation of network density. High runoff rates coupled with highly erodible soils or bedrock produce extensive erosion and expansion of drainage networks. Where a high proportion of the rainfall that falls on a network runs off, high rates of erosion produce many channels. In some semiarid areas that have thin soils with low infiltration capacities, high runoff rates lead to the development of fine-textured, high-density networks (typically 40–400 measurable channels/sq. mi.). In contrast, in Sierran basins, the lower relative runoff rates produce channel densities that are usually much less (usually less than 15 channels/sq. mi.).

Because areas with high drainage densities tend to have short overland

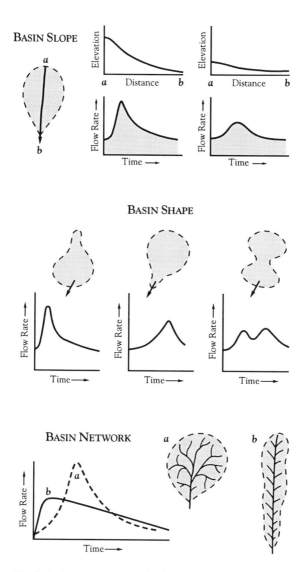

Fig. 7.5. Influences of basin slope, shape, and network on the shape and magnitude of flood hydrographs. (Adapted from figures in Saxton and Shiau 1990.)

flow transport distances, runoff makes it into the channel network quickly and efficiently. Since high drainage densities are usually coupled with thin soils that reach infiltration capacities quickly, flood hydrographs contain relatively short lag times, steep rising and falling limbs, and high peak discharges. In contrast, the long overland flow paths and high infiltration capacities of watersheds with low drainage densities produce more subdued flood peaks with greater lag times.

Basin Size and Shape

The size of a basin greatly influences the sediment yield and hydrograph response. It is perhaps a statement of the obvious that the larger the basin, the greater the amount of sediment and discharge that comes out of it. But this relationship is not arithmetic. As noted in chapter 6, relatively small areas tend to be major contributors of sediment to watersheds. As the size of the watershed increases, the influence of these point sources of sediment decreases. Because of this, the average sediment yield (tons/ acre) decreases with increasing size of the watershed (again, with notable exceptions like the Eel River). The same is true for discharge. Although the larger watersheds receive greater amounts of rainfall, the greater diversity of the landscape and increased sites for depression storage and infiltration usually lead to a decrease in the average runoff. In small watersheds, the hydrograph response to a storm depends primarily on the length of time it takes for water to run off slopes. In contrast, in large watersheds, the primary influence is the length of time it takes for water to feed through the channel network. Thus smaller catchments will usually have relatively short lag times with peaked hydrographs while large catchments are characterized by broad, flat hydrographs (see fig. 7.5).

The shape of a watershed also exerts considerable influence on the behavior of its river. Runoff flowing through elongate, narrow watersheds must travel through a much more extensive, higher-order channel network than a compact watershed of equal area. The longer travel paths tend to reduce the peak flow and increase the lag time of the hydrograph (see fig. 7.5).

WATERSHEDS IN PROFILE

The morphology and gradient of the channel within any stretch of river presumably reflect a balance of capacity and competence with overall sediment load, discharge, and the composition of bed and bank materials. Changes in discharge and size or quantity of sediment load will cause shifts within the channel to achieve maximum efficiency and balance. In all channel reaches, adjustments in capacity and competence are taking place through modification of the channel shape and gradient by deposition, channel incision, abandonment, or lateral migration. Each of these adjustments, in turn, influences or is influenced by adjustments in upstream and downstream reaches. In this way, rivers act like a single, mechanically linked system, constantly adjusting conditions throughout the length of the river in response to the discharge and sediment supplied by the watershed.

The *longitudinal profile* of a river is an integral part of this process of self-adjustment and balance. A typical profile is concave upward with a relatively short, steep-gradient channel near the head of the watershed, an intermediate length and slope reach in the middle, and a long, shallow-gradient channel in the lower reach (see fig. 7.5). The mouth of the river, where gradient equals zero, records the erosional *base level* for the watershed. Base level is essentially the lowest level to which a river can erode. For rivers that reach the ocean, present-day sea level is the same as base level (however, it is important to remember that sea level is in constant adjustment). The river cannot exist, much less erode, below sea level. For rivers that flow into lakes, the level of the lake surface is the effective base level.

Many authors have suggested that the concave profile of a river reflects the development of grade or equilibrium (chap. 1) within a watershed. The low discharge rivers of the upper parts of the watershed require steep gradients to maintain capacity and competence adequate for transporting sediment yields. But farther down the watershed, the addition of discharge from tributaries enables the sediment load to be transported by progressively lower slopes. In arid and semiarid areas of southern California and the Mojave Desert, seepage causes rivers to lose capacity and competence in the downstream direction. This may be responsible for the convex profiles typical of many of the rivers of this region.

The longitudinal profile of a river has proven too tempting to be left alone by those who wish to quantify the landscape. Many of the same geomorphologists who measured everything measurable found that a plot of river elevation against distance from the river mouth produced a scatter of points just crying to have a line fit to it. It has been proposed that a great deal of information can be gleaned from differences in the equations of lines that best fit these river profiles. Numerous mathematical functions have been reported which describe the longitudinal profiles of rivers. Some of these include exponential functions, power functions, log functions, and combinations of power functions (all of which can be fit to the profile shown in fig. 7.5). However, there is little consensus about what these different functions are really telling us.

Concavity, Base Level, and Knickpoints:
Adjustments in the Longitudinal Profile

In the medium and short term, the longitudinal profile of a *natural* (i.e., undisturbed) river is perhaps its stablest geomorphic feature. The concave shape reflects the adjustment of the river to (1) the climate of the watershed, which controls the amount of runoff (chap. 8); (2) the tectonic setting of the watershed, which controls its overall relief as well as changes in base level (chap. 9); and (3) the geology of the watershed, which controls sediment supply and the bedrock's resistance to erosion (chap. 9). Tectonic activity and climate in California are not static phenomena, and the bedrock of the state is as spatially variable as any in the world. In addition, it takes time for a river to complete the job of adjusting its profile to these independent variables (chap. 1). Because of this, the longitudinal profiles of California's rivers are in constant readjustment or dynamic equilibrium, never quite catching up to the changes that drive them.

As noted above, the adjustment of a profile involves incision and/or deposition within different river reaches and on different time scales. The "goal" of a river is to attempt to smooth the profile as much as possible and to establish the optimum concavity for the given sediment supply, discharge, and base level. Comparisons between different river profiles often illuminate differences in the physical conditions that drive the formation of profiles. The Tuolumne River (fig. 7.6) and Bishop Creek (fig. 7.7) both drain the upper elevations of the central Sierra Nevada. The channel heads that define these rivers both occur at approximately 12,000 feet in glaciated terrains that are cut into Mesozoic granitic rocks. Despite these similarities, the longitudinal profiles are strikingly different. The Tuolumne's profile is the broad, concave shape typical of most large Sierran and Klamath rivers, although there are numerous disruptions (discussed below). In contrast, the Bishop Creek profile approximates a straight line (also with disruptions). The underlying cause of the differences between these two profiles is tied to their tectonic setting and their overall stream order.

The Tuolumne River is developed on the broad, gentle western slope of the Sierra Nevada. It is a very high order river with numerous tributaries that increase its discharge in the middle and lower reaches. Thus progressively lower slopes are needed to handle the sediment load and discharge, producing the strongly concave profile. In contrast, Bishop Creek is a low-order river that receives the bulk of its discharge from snowmelt in the uppermost portions of the watershed; very few tributaries join the creek in its lower reaches. In addition, the watershed is developing along the very rugged, eastern escarpment of the Sierras where active range faults

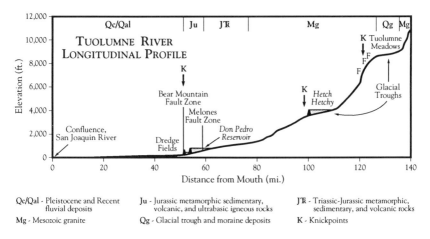

Fig. 7.6. Longitudinal profile of the Tuolumne River, west slope of the central Sierra Nevada. *F* designates significant waterfalls. (Based on U.S. Geological Survey topographic maps and California Division of Mines and Geology geologic maps.)

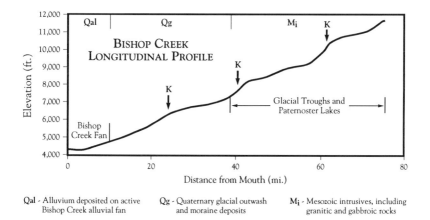

Fig. 7.7. Longitudinal profile of Bishop Creek, east slope, central Sierra Nevada. (Based on U.S. Geological Survey topographic maps and California Division of Mines and Geology geologic maps.)

Fig. 7.8A. *Knickpoints* are usually associated with changes in rock type or input of coarse debris from tributaries or mass movements. *Above*: Chamberlain Falls, North Fork of the American River, occurs at a sharp change in rock type. Immediately upstream of the falls there is deposition of gravels. At the falls and immediately downstream, the river is undergoing incision. Eventually, the break in gradient that forms the falls will migrate upriver, eliminating the knickpoint. Note the well-developed supercritical tongue of the rapid. The proposed multipurpose Auburn Dam would flood the North Fork of the American River to approximately this elevation. James McClain (UC Davis) guiding this Class IV drop during a class field trip. Photograph by author.

are producing exceptionally steep local slopes. The combination of steep slopes, small watershed area, and low-order river has led to the development of a very straight longitudinal profile.

The longitudinal profiles of the Tuolumne River and Bishop Creek also illustrate a key aspect of profile development. Rivers in California are constantly adjusting to local perturbations in their profile. These disruptions, known as *knickpoints*, usually consist of a long, low-gradient reach that abruptly gives way to a relatively short, steep-gradient reach (see figs. 7.6, 7.7), with the "knick" occurring at the change in gradient. For those of us adrenaline junkies who are wedded to scaring ourselves on California's whitewater rapids, a knickpoint is our best friend and most enjoyable nightmare. Virtually all of the best-known and most-loved/hated rapids in California occur at knickpoints (fig. 7.8A, B).

Fig. 7.8B. *Above*: Class VI Cassidy Falls, upper Kings River, occurs at a channel obstruction formed by accumulation of coarse debris above a sharp change in erosional resistance of the bedrock. John Lane (Outdoor Adventures, UC Davis) entering this Class VI rapid in the worst place possible. Amazingly enough, the boat did not flip, although it remained trapped in the supercritical-turbulent/ subcritical-turbulent transition for an extended period of time. Photograph courtesy of Alan Webster.

The asymmetric shape of most knickpoints (fig. 7.9) reflects a river's attempt to smooth its profile. The high-gradient portion immediately downstream of the knickpoint has a correspondingly high competence or stream power; thus the face of the knickpoint is likely to undergo head-ward erosion. In contrast, the low-gradient reach immediately upstream of the knickpoint has low competence, leading to sediment accumulation. In the ideal case, this ponding of sediment upstream and erosion of sedi-ment downstream leads to an upstream migration and eventual removal of the knickpoint. In reality, the processes or objects that formed the knick-point in the first place are likely to be more persistent, regularly renewing the knickpoint and preventing its upstream migration.

A variety of natural and human-induced processes produce knickpoints in river profiles. Where a river crosses a fault or sharp change in rock type, differences in erosional resistance will typically generate a knickpoint. The longitudinal profile of the Santa Ana River near San Bernardino (fig. 7.10)

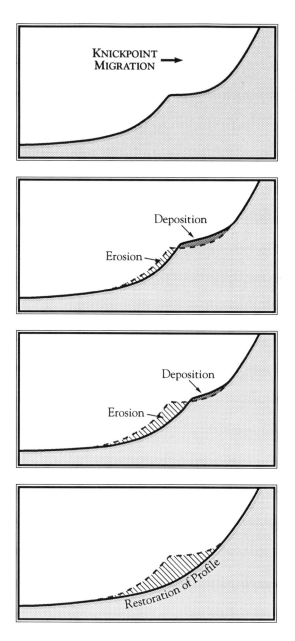

Fig. 7.9. Knickpoint removal by deposition upstream
of knickpoint and erosion downstream of knickpoint.
See text for discussion.

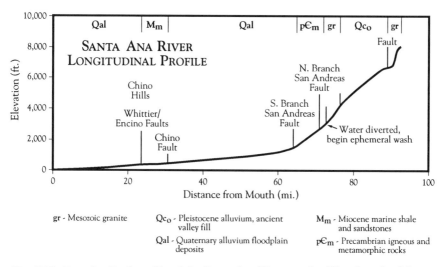

Fig. 7.10. Longitudinal profile of the Santa Ana River south of Los Angeles. Note subtle (but significant) breaks in slope associated with major fault zones. (Based on U.S. Geological Survey topographic maps and California Division of Mines and Geology geologic maps.)

shows the effects of the numerous active faults that cross southern California. The juxtaposition of rock types of different erosional resistance and rapid uplift adjacent to the fault zones clearly affect the shape of the profile. The Santa Ana River is actively attempting to adjust its grade by selectively eroding these knickpoints. However, this process is being continuously offset by movement along these faults (and several land use practices).

The Tuolumne River and Bishop Creek both record the effects of glaciations and volcanic eruptions within the Sierra Nevada. Within the upper reaches of both watersheds, extensive and recent glacial scouring and localized deposition of glacial tills have produced linear, low-gradient valleys. Known as glacial troughs, these valleys represent dramatic departures from the equilibrium profile. The downstream ends of these valleys form knickpoints that are actively being eroded by high-gradient, high-competence stretches of river that are commonly associated with the development of waterfalls. In the absence of future glaciations, these perturbations will eventually be removed and the profile will be smoothed.

In contrast to the localized adjustment of profiles associated with knickpoints, profiles will adjust simultaneously over extensive reaches of a river in response to long-term shifts in climate, tectonics, and base level. Sea level, which dictates the position of base level for many of California's rivers, is widely viewed as a static feature. After all, all of our geodetic surveys are tied to it as a reference datum; elevations are universally given as feet or meters above mean sea level. But sea level, like climate and tectonics, is not static. As geologists will readily point out, sea level is in a state of constant fluctuation. Changes in the volume of the ocean basins, changes in the volume of ice sheets, and the thermal expansion and contraction of the oceans cause sea level to rise and fall. Depending on the forces driving sea level change, it can be quite rapid (inches/hundred years) or quite slow (< 1 inch/thousand years). Regardless, the change in sea level dramatically affects rivers all over the globe by changing base level.

Most of the impact of base level changes occurs in the long, low-gradient stretch of a river (fig. 7.11). When sea level rises, it floods deltas and lowland areas, forming an estuary and causing the mouth of the river to retreat. This landward migration of a shoreline is called a *transgression*. If the supply of sediment is high enough, the response of a river will be to aggrade throughout its lower reaches, constructing a new profile tied to a higher base level. In contrast, if sea level falls, the shoreline may retreat seaward. Termed a *regression*, this lowering of base level will lead to an increase in the average gradient of the profile (fig. 7.11). The steeper gradient leads to increased stream power, which, in turn, causes the river to incise until it reestablishes its equilibrium profile.

Over the past few million years, sea level has been rising and falling at extraordinary rates. During the glacial maxima of the Pleistocene, sea level was so low that the mouths of California's rivers were located tens of miles farther west than at present. In the intervals between glacial maxima, the seas flooded interior valleys like the Great Valley and parts of the Los Angeles basin. Dramatic changes in climate accompanied each of these changes in sea level. The rivers of California have been constantly adjusting to these changes through incision and aggradation. Currently, most oceanographers and climatologists argue that sea level is rising, albeit slowly on a human time scale. Increases in global warming and associated melting of polar ice caps and thermal expansion of sea water would presumably increase this rate of rise. The nature of the response of California's rivers to this rise is debatable since almost all have extensive water (and sediment) diversions. Regardless, any rise in base level should lead to flooding in lowland areas and long-term changes in the equilibrium profiles of the state's rivers. The future of California's rivers is dealt with in detail in chapter 17.

SUMMARY

The drainage network and pattern, watershed size, and longitudinal profile all reflect the effort of a river to balance and minimize energy expenditures while transmitting discharge and sediment supply through and out

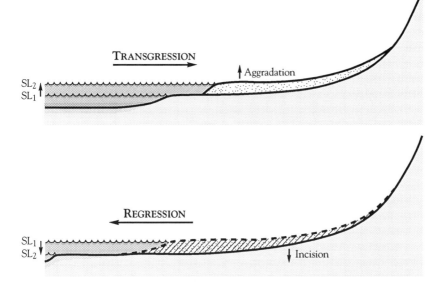

Fig. 7.11. Evolution of a longitudinal profile in response to changes in sea level. During rising sea level, elevated base level causes regional aggradation and landward transgression of the shoreline. During falling sea level, rivers undergo incision and shoreline regresses, moving seaward. SL_1 is initial sea level; SL_2 is ending sea level.

of a drainage basin. The development of a drainage network takes place through erosion at the channel head. The resistance of the bedrock to erosion and the distribution or structure of the bedrock greatly influence the development of drainage patterns. The complex plumbing system that eventually forms through the expansion of drainage networks dictates the shape and magnitude of the flood hydrograph.

Streams can be classified based on their Strahler order and Shreve magnitude. The Strahler order, which is the most widely used, defines a hierarchy of stream segments within a watershed, with low-order streams having few branching tributaries and high-order streams containing numerous, multibranched tributaries. High-order streams have flatter hydrographs with longer lag times. Low-order streams tend to produce higher and coarser sediment yields and steep hydrographs. The shape and the size of a watershed also greatly influence runoff processes. As watershed size increases, the runoff and sediment yield per acre declines. Long, narrow watersheds appear to have more subdued hydrograph responses to storms than more equant watersheds. Drainage density of a watershed also appears to greatly influence hydrograph response. Higher drainage densities produce higher peak flows and shorter lag times than low drainage density watersheds.

The longitudinal profile of a river is in slow, constant adjustment to watershed conditions. Profiles are typically convex upward in shape with a steep gradient at the head and a low gradient at the mouth. Variations in the shape of profiles reflect the response of the river to the overall tectonic, climatic, geologic, and base level conditions. Changes in these conditions can produce regional shifts in profiles involving widespread river aggradation or incision to reestablish the ideal concavity. Local disruptions in profile associated with faulting, changes in lithology, or glacial processes are termed knickpoints. Rivers attempt to remove knickpoints and smooth the local longitudinal profile by erosion on the steep, downstream side of the knickpoint and deposition in the low-gradient upstream area.

RELEVANT READINGS

Abrahams, A. D., ed. 1986. *Hillslope Processes.* London: G. Allen and Unwin.

Beven, K., and M. J. Kirkby, eds. 1993. *Channel Network Hydrology.* New York: John Wiley and Sons.

Horton, R. E. 1945. "Erosional Development of Streams and Their Drainage Basins: Hydrophysical Approach to Quantitative Morphology." *Geological Society of America Bulletin* 56: 275–370.

Kirchner, J. W. 1993. "Statistical Inevitability of Horton's Laws and the Apparent Randomness of Stream Channel Networks." *Geology* 21: 591–594.

Leopold, L. B. 1993. *Base Level Rise: Gradient of Deposition.* Berkeley: Laser Pages Publishing.

Morisawa, M. 1985. *Rivers.* New York: Longman.

Rhodes, D. D., and G. P. Williams, eds. 1979. *Adjustments of the Fluvial System.* Dubuque: Kendall/Hunt.

Saxton, K. E., and S. Y. Shiau. 1990. "Surface Waters of North America: Influence of Land and Vegetation on Streamflow." In *Surface Water Hydrology,* ed. M. G. Wolman and H. C. Riggs, 55–80. Vol. O-1 of *The Geology of North America.* Boulder: Geological Society of America.

Schumm, S. A., ed. 1977. *Drainage Basin Morphology.* Stroudsburg, Pa.: Dowden, Hutchinson & Ross.

Shreve, R. L. 1967. "Infinite Topologically Random Channel Networks." *Journal of Geology* 75: 178–186.

———. 1974. "Variation in Mainstream Length with Basin Area in River Networks." *Water Resources Research* 10: 1167–1177.

Strahler, A. N. 1957. "Quantitative Analysis of Watershed Geomorphology." *American Geophysical Union Transactions* 38: 913–920.

EIGHT

Climate and the Rivers of California

INTRODUCTION

The preceding chapters of this book have emphasized the process-response nature of rivers and their landscapes. All aspects of the day-to-day operation of a river and its efforts to achieve balance and efficiency are tied into a complex negative feedback system wherein change in one parameter is compensated for by change in another, which, through a series of incremental adjustments, may ultimately restore the system to its original state. Within any natural, negative feedback system there are processes that are fully independent; they influence the system and are not influenced by it. For the rivers of California, these independent variables are the state's climate, geology, and tectonics. While generally unaffected by river processes, these three independent variables are not fully independent of each other. The present tectonic setting and the history of tectonic activity have dictated the nature and distribution of the state's geology (*geology* as used here refers to the distribution, structure, and type of rocks and sediments that make up the state). These same tectonic processes influence the climate of the state by controlling where mountain ranges occur and at which latitude California resides. Ultimately, by controlling the configuration of the Pacific Ocean, tectonics has controlled the pattern of atmospheric circulation that delivers precipitation to California.

My ambition in this chapter is to synthesize the role that climate plays in shaping rivers and their watersheds. The impact of climate on the design and function of rivers cannot be overstated since it is precipitation patterns that control the amount of energy supplied to any river system. However, this discussion is, by necessity, a generalized summary that regrettably leaves out a number of the more crucial and interesting details.

The suggested readings listed at the back of this chapter provide a general background and some of those key details.

CLIMATE IN THE LAND OF EXTREMES

During the period between November and May, I and many of my colleagues and friends are avid California weather watchers. Dutifully, every night, as if our intense interest might somehow affect the outcome, we stare at the satellite images and fancy 3D graphics that tell us our weather future over the next three to five days. With glassy-eyed devotion, we listen to the weather forecaster describe the movement of "troughs" and "ridges," "upper level lows," and "fronts" with admirable ease. Our interest is understandable. The wet weather in California is confined to a remarkably limited number of storms over a short period of time. It is a do-or-die, all-or-nothing climate. Either you get the rain in the winter or you have a drought. There is no making up for it during the rest of the year.

California's Mediterranean climate (a misnomer, really, because it rains in the summer in the Mediterranean region) produces exceptional spatial and temporal variations in rainfall (fig. 8.1). From the average of 100+ inches of rain per year on the mountains near the Smith River to the average of 2 inches of rain per year near the New River and the Whitewater River, the longitudinal rainfall gradients are immense. In addition, even along lines of equal latitude there are tenfold variations in precipitation. The 50+ inches of yearly precipitation that falls above Huntington Lake in the southern Sierra Nevada tapers off to 5 inches at Bishop in Owens Valley less than 40 miles away. This seemingly erratic distribution of rainfall is magnified by the feast or famine tendencies of our climate. It is bemusing to listen to the weather forecasters talk about cumulative seasonal rainfall as some percentage of "normal," placing great import on whether we are currently above or below "normal." This is a gross abuse of the language. "Normal" for the land of extremes is just that, extreme: extremely wet or extremely dry. What the weather forecaster really means is percent of seasonal *average* or the *mean.* The average, for that matter, is also meaningless because it is the average of extremes and thus has a large standard deviation. Rarely does yearly rainfall come even close to these seasonal averages. To illustrate, the estimated annual discharge based on tree ring data over the last 400+ years is shown in figure 8.2. What is significant about discharge and related rainfall for any given year is not whether something is above or below average but the magnitude of the departure away from that average. Maybe we should discuss rainfall totals as a percentage of *abnormal* instead. The point of this is to emphasize the seemingly arbitrary distribution of precipitation in California. This deluge versus drought climate runs the rivers and shapes the landscape in its own unique way.

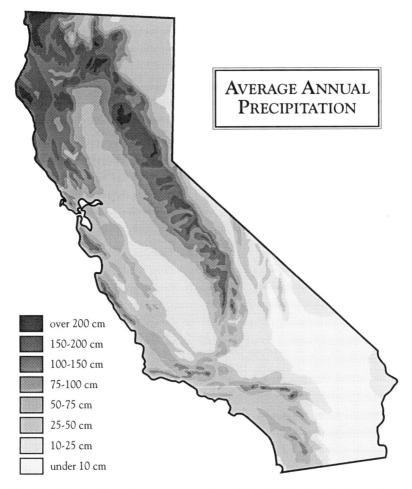

AVERAGE ANNUAL
PRECIPITATION

over 200 cm
150-200 cm
100-150 cm
75-100 cm
50-75 cm
25-50 cm
10-25 cm
under 10 cm

Fig. 8.1. Distribution of average annual rainfall in California. (Redrawn from California Department of Water Resources maps.)

Atmospheric Circulation and the California Climate:
A Global Perspective

Heat from the sun supplies the energy that runs the hydrologic cycle. Surface net radiation varies from day to night, winter to summer, pole to equator. The result is an earth unequally warmed, with most of the heat concentrated near the equator and little left over for the poles. The circulation of the atmosphere acts to try to balance this heat inequity by transferring warm air from the equator to the poles and returning cold air

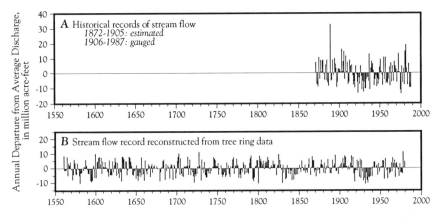

Fig. 8.2. Annual departure from average stream discharge of the Sacramento River Basin Index. *A,* Historical records of stream flow (estimated 1872–1905; gauged 1906–1987). *B,* Stream flow record reconstructed from tree ring data, 1560–1980. (Modified from Hunrichs 1991.)

from the poles to the equator. This transfer process, while driven by differential heating, is greatly influenced by the spin of the earth, the distribution of the continents, and, to a lesser extent, tidal forces.

The general circulation patterns of the atmosphere are illustrated in figure 8.3. Elliptical circulation cells transfer air toward and away from the poles. These cells, known as the Hadley, the midlatitude Ferrel, and the Polar, vary in intensity and geometry with the seasons. The position of high and low pressure centers is controlled by interactions at the margins of these cells. Where surface convergence leads to rising air, such as at the boundary between the Ferrel and Polar cells, low pressure conditions dominate (fig. 8.3). Where upper-level convergence causes air to fall, such as at the join between the Hadley and Ferrel cells, high pressure develops. Superimposed on these cells are winds that flow subparallel to lines of latitude. These include the west-flowing tropical trade winds, the midlatitude westerlies, and the polar easterlies. This overall circulation structure, which broadly determines global climate, is disrupted by smaller-scale perturbations. Cyclonic (low pressure) and anticyclonic (high pressure) circulation is responsible for the change in atmospheric circulation patterns that ultimately produce day-to-day changes in weather.

When the temperature difference between the poles and the equator is small, such as in the summer, atmospheric circulation is somewhat sluggish, with fewer perturbations in pattern. This type of circulation, known as *zonal,* leads to mostly west-east airflow in the midlatitudes. In contrast, when the differences are high, such as in the winter, circulation becomes

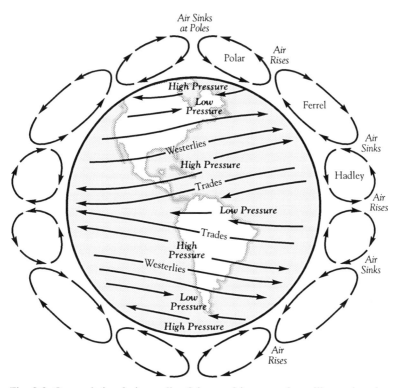

Fig. 8.3. General circulation cells of the earth's atmosphere illustrating the mechanism of heat transfer between the poles and the equator. (Modified from Washington and Parkinson 1986.)

more vigorous, generating more intense disruptions in airflow. Known as *meridional* flow, this condition produces extensive north-south oriented flow. During meridional flow, these disruptions sweep like high amplitude waves across the midlatitudes. The high pressure areas, which form the crests of these waves, are called *ridges*. These are responsible for moving warm air northward to the colder latitudes. The troughs of these waves are appropriately referred to as low pressure *troughs*. Because troughs move cold air southward to warmer latitudes, they are generally associated with stormy conditions. (See fig. 8.4.)

Extratropical cyclones (meaning storms born outside of the tropics) provide the bulk of the rain that falls on California. Most of these are derived from a region stretching from the Gulf of Alaska south to the latitude of the Hawaiian Islands in the western Pacific. Occasionally, moisture associated with tropical storms will feed into California from the south, creating locally intense rainfall and associated flooding events in southern

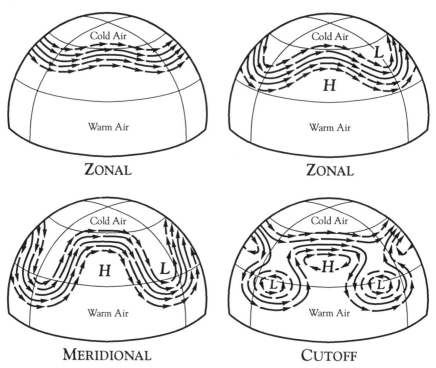

Fig. 8.4. Generation of troughs and ridges during zonal and meridional flow.
(Modified from Lins, Hare, and Singh 1990.)

California deserts. These storms do not have a major impact on the larger
rivers of California.

The birth of extratropical cyclones is complex. In essence, they are
formed as the atmosphere attempts to reduce large temperature gradients. When air resides over large uniform areas like the Gulf of Alaska or
the Hawaiian Islands, the "air mass" that forms takes on the character of
the area in which it originated. The air masses can be tropical (warm) or
polar (cool) in character and maritime (moist) or continental (dry). Temperature gradients tend to be greatest along frontal zones or the narrow
boundaries that separate air masses. There is a nearly continuous frontal
zone that separates tropical air from polar air. During January, this zone
stretches from about the latitude of the Philippines in the western Pacific
northwestward to British Columbia. Most extratropical cyclones form along
the sharp temperature gradient along this frontal zone. Once spawned,
these cyclones move westward as a wave under the general influence of the
jet stream winds of the midtroposphere. On the west side of this cyclone,

cold polar air moves equatorward; on the east side, warm tropical air moves poleward. This is why California winter storms are typically wet and warm in the beginning and cold and dry at the end.

Most of the winter storms that affect the west coast of North America are spawned along the polar front in two general regions: the Gulf of Alaska and the mid-Pacific north and west of the Hawaiian Islands. Some of the most frequent storms are from the Gulf of Alaska where a cold, maritime air mass develops during the winter months. Because these storms are generally cold (dominated by the transfer of cold air from the pole to the equator), they hold less total moisture. As these storms move southward, the temperature gradients that spawned them in the first place are slowly reduced. Thus the intensity of these storms usually decreases as they move southward, leaving proportionately less rainfall in the southern portions of the state.

Storms that are spawned in warmer, mid-Pacific regions usually follow along the polar front until they reach the west coast of North America. Shifts in the location of the polar front and in the configuration of low and high pressure cells in the Pacific (discussed below) dictate where these warmer, moisture-laden storms make landfall. When the jet stream-controlled storm track shifts southward, storms enter California with greater frequency. Two general types of midlatitude storms strike California. The first are the storms with long but relatively narrow frontal areas. During these storms regions of intense atmospheric circulation less than 100 miles wide but thousands of miles long may stretch from California to the Hawaiian Islands, rapidly transferring heat and moisture from the low to the midlatitudes. The rapid transfer of warm, subtropical moisture along narrow frontal bands produces highly localized and relatively short-lived but extremely intense rainfall and localized flooding. The great storms of 1986 in the Sierra Nevada region east of Sacramento and the storms of 1982 in the San Francisco Bay/Santa Cruz region were of this type. In contrast, there are the more regional storms that produce widespread high rainfall amounts and flooding. This is usually accomplished by numerous back-to-back storms. Groups of cyclones, known as a family, will be spawned at the same time along the mid-Pacific polar front. These cyclone families will strike the west coast with a frequency of about one every 36 hours or less. Because of storm frequency, infiltration capacities do not recover between storms but lead to exceptional amounts of runoff. The great floods of 1955–1956 and 1961–1962 in northern California and in 1995 in all of California are examples of these storms. Both the regional and the localized mid-Pacific storms are probably the most significant in the shaping of the rivers in California.

During a "typical" year, the mid-Pacific cyclones that water central and northern California will occasionally intrude in southern California. In "atypical" years, the position of blocking "highs," or ridges, along the west coast and the upper-level flow that moves cyclones across the Pacific increase the frequency of storms in southern California, producing numerous flooding events. The wet years in southern California are usually associated with a southward shift in the jet stream. The troughs associated with the formation of fronts will dig farther to the south as they move into California, tapping into warmer, more moist air. The high yearly rainfall totals reflect both the increased frequency of storms and their greater moisture content. During many drought winters, a strong, relatively stationary ridge will develop over British Columbia and the Gulf of Alaska. In "average" years, cyclones generated in the mid-Pacific will move over the top of these ridges, passing well to the north of California. Occasionally, storms will pass underneath this ridge and enter directly into southern California, producing relatively little precipitation in northern and central California and voluminous rains in the south. Where these storms occur in clusters, or as families, the most intense rainfall events are likely to occur, such as in the winters of 1968–1969, 1977–1978, and 1979–1980.

EL NIÑO EVENTS, DROUGHTS, AND FLOODS

The factors that determine whether California has a wet or a dry winter are a subject of continuing debate and numerous vigorous research programs. Most workers agree that the temperature in the uppermost 1,000 feet of the ocean (usually referred to as sea surface temperatures, or SSTs) acts as a fundamental control on the climate of California. A number of recent studies have documented how changes in SSTs have controlled the position and intensity of major atmospheric circulation cells. Areas characterized by high SSTs tend to develop stationary low pressure cells (rising, moist air), while low SSTs lead to the formation of high pressure cells. These cells, in turn, control the frequency of extratropical cyclone genesis and, more important, their pathways as they move eastward across the Pacific.

Extreme periods of drought and wet in California can be tied to SST-driven shifts in the location and intensity of major pressure cells (fig. 8.5). During the winter of most years, a large atmospheric low pressure system develops in the central northern Pacific in the region surrounding the Aleutian Islands. During average or above average years, this low pressure center weakens and shifts southward. The southern position of this pressure center shifts the storm track to the south, increasing the frequency of mid-Pacific and Alaskan storms that reach California.

During dry years, the central northern Pacific low pressure cell intensifies and shifts northward toward the Bering Sea (see fig. 8.5). This, coupled with the establishment of a weak high pressure cell offshore of

Fig. 8.5. Location of major low pressure center near the Aleutian Islands during above average and below average precipitation years in California. (Modified from Peterson, Cayan, Dileo-Stevens, and Ross 1987.)

California, acts to direct storms into northernmost Canada and Alaska, creating widespread drought in central and northern California. As noted above, during drought conditions in central and northern California, storms will often move south or underneath the weak high pressure system that resides offshore of California, leading to above average precipitation in southern California. In rare cases, such as the record drought of 1976–1977, the intensity of the offshore high pressure cell acts to deflect almost all storms, leading to statewide drought conditions.

Although it is easy to point to changing SSTs and the position of the central northern Pacific low pressure system as the major cause of fluctuations in California's climate, these changes are really only one small part or symptom of large-scale circulations that affect the entire northern Pacific. These *teleconnections* between changing ocean temperatures, currents, and the atmosphere over the Pacific are the source of our long-term trends in precipitation. For the past 10 years considerable attention has been focused on events in the far western Pacific that may greatly influence global climate patterns, including California's climate. For many years oceanographers and atmospheric scientists have recognized that major changes in SSTs in the central Pacific and even the Indian Ocean are tied to dramatic local and regional climatic events. During "normal" years, the continuous east-to-west trade winds tend to blow warm surface waters across the Pacific, accumulating them in a pool of exceptionally warm water (> 84°F) in a band stretching from north of Australia across the Indian Ocean to southeastern Africa. For reasons that are not abundantly clear, in some years the trade winds that restrict this pool of water to the western Pacific and Indian Ocean appear to slacken. As the trades weaken, short-lived westerlies begin to blow back across this pool. The effect of this surface wind change is to propel the warm water pool eastward, spreading warm surface waters over a much larger area of the Pacific. (See fig. 8.6.)

The back-and-forth motion of this warm water pool is known as the Southern Oscillation. One consequence of the Southern Oscillation is the well-known but poorly understood El Niño. El Niño represents a period when warm water moves east across the Pacific. A number of strange atmospheric and oceanic processes appear to be associated with this movement of warm water. The Peruvians noted that these strange events usually appeared around Christmastime and gave the process the name El Niño (meaning Christ child). Intervening non–El Niño periods (referred to as "La Niña" by those unaware of the origin of the term) occur when the warm water pool is collected in the west. Besides substantially controlling the SSTs of much of the central and northern Pacific, the El Niño/ Southern Oscillation (ENSO) transfers a great deal of heat and moisture to the atmosphere. This is accomplished by advective heat transfer and convection associated with the convergence of the trade winds and monsoonal winds. The outflow from this convection process occurs well up in the atmosphere, where it is transferred north and south through the Hadley cells (see fig. 8.3). As it moves away from the equator, this hot and wet air feeds into and ultimately affects the tropospheric jet stream.

During El Niño events, the vigorous exchange of heat between the Southern Oscillation and upper atmosphere moves eastward out into the central portions of the Pacific. The net effect of this is to greatly alter the jet stream patterns, which, in turn, controls weather patterns all over the globe. The direct effect of El Niño on northern Pacific SSTs and

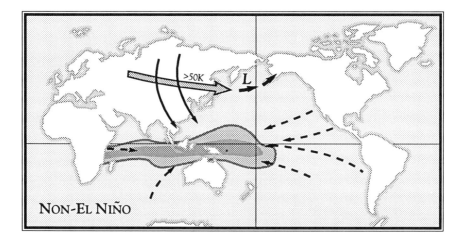

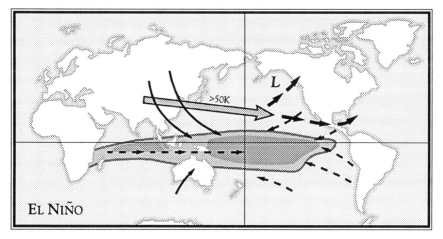

Fig. 8.6. Distribution of the warm water pool associated with the Southern Oscillation and changes in global jet stream patterns. Moist Pacific surface trade winds and Australasian monsoons (thin arrows) converge here, causing convection that feeds warm, wet air into the northern Pacific. Midatmosphere westerly jet stream winds (thick arrows) are affected by this introduction of air from the Southern Oscillation. The eastward displacement of the warm water pool marks El Niño events and is associated with stronger monsoons and weaker trade winds. Change in position of convection greatly affects jet stream paths and rainfall patterns in California. (Modified from Philander 1992.)

weather is complex. Much more moist, warm air is moved into the northern Pacific by the expanded pool of warm, equatorial water. The impact on the rivers of California simply depends on where that moist air and the associated storms are likely to make landfall as they move eastward across the Pacific. The answer to this question has remained elusive.

There have been numerous El Niño events recorded this century. The mother of all El Niño events occurred during the winter of 1982–1983. Precipitation in central and southern California that year was exceptional, with a record-breaking snowpack in the central and northern Sierra Nevada and some locally spectacular winter and spring flooding. The total volume of runoff from California also set a record that year. Fortunately for Californians, much of the moisture had accumulated as snowpack, allowing runoff to occur over many months rather than all at once. During the winter of 1994–1995, El Niño appears to have reestablished itself, feeding warm, moist air from the central Pacific into the jet stream that sweeps storms to California. Several climatologists have pointed to El Niño as the cause of the severe flooding seen statewide in January 1995. Based on the unusual weather of 1982–1983 and 1994–1995, it is logical to assume that El Niño events produce lots of precipitation and even some disastrous flooding. Given that we need only monitor barometric pressures and sea temperatures to know when an El Niño is forming (accomplished with satellites now), it should be simple to predict when the "good" years are likely to occur. Unfortunately, atmospheric science is not there yet. The midlatitude effects of El Niño events appear to be terribly complicated. For example, a moderate El Niño event occurred in 1976–1977. This coincided with a record *low* rainfall year in California. Four other "unusual" precipitation years occurred during the period 1975–1982. None coincided with El Niño conditions. The whopping big floods of 1955 and 1964 that produced some of the largest flood damage in California's history clearly occurred between El Niño periods, not during.

In 1992, an El Niño began to develop in the Pacific. Several scientists predicted that this would break the drought that had gripped California since 1987. Of course, 1992 came and went, leaving California in a sixth year of drought and in a political crisis. As that year passed without major rainfall, at least one climatologist remarked to the news media that maybe rainfall in California was simply random. Some years we got lucky, some years we didn't, and there was no telling which year was going to be the best despite all our efforts. Of course, this is scientific heresy, but at present it is the utilitarian view of long-range weather prediction. Right now, the most reliable criteria for medium-range predictions appear to be SSTs immediately offshore of California and Alaska, but even this approach is highly inaccurate. Extensive research projects are currently under way to numerically model the interaction between El Niño and the atmosphere. Eventually we will tease some reliable predictions out of this and understand how El Niño events control midlatitude weather, but at present our reach exceeds our grasp, and, for that matter, when it comes to El Niño events, we may be grasping at straws. The consensus view is that El Niño events are probably responsible for much of the weird weather in California, but at present it is not possible to accurately reconstruct the teleconnections between the Southern Oscillation, the SSTs in the central north Pacific, and the frequency and intensity of storms that arrive in California.

OROGRAPHIC EFFECTS

Although the frequency and intensity of the storms that reach California exert ultimate control over regional variations of precipitation, the irregular landscape of California plays a major role in extracting moisture from storms as they come in off the Pacific. The changes in precipitation patterns caused by the landscape are known as *orographic effects.*

As moist lower atmosphere air enters California, it is forced up and over the mountains. As air rises to higher altitudes and is subjected to lower atmospheric pressures and temperatures, it loses its ability to hold water as vapor. The excess vapor that can no longer be held condenses and precipitates as either rain or snow (fig. 8.7). In this way, the mountains of California are capable of wringing vast amounts of water out of otherwise ordinary storms.

Most southern Californians know that as air sinks the increase in pressure causes it to heat and dry out. The hot, bone-dry Santa Ana winds that parch southern and central California are a product of this *adiabatic heating.* The same warming and drying process takes place as air clears the crest of a mountain range (fig. 8.7). The cool, damp air that spills across mountain crests sinks rapidly due to its relatively high density. As it sinks along the lee face of the mountain it heats adiabatically, allowing the air to hold more water vapor. This increased ability to hold vapor leads to rapid decrease in the amount of precipitation wherever air is sinking.

The tendency for rain or snow to occur when air is rising and to cease when air is sinking produces the strong latitudinal gradients in precipitation seen throughout California. This *rainshadow* effect can be seen in the valleys of California that are flanked on the west by moderate to large mountain ranges. For example, yearly rainfall averages around 60 inches on the summit of the Santa Cruz mountains. Less than 10 miles away, near San Jose, this figure drops off to less than 15 inches. The entire southern end of the San Joaquin Valley is a virtual desert (< 6 inches average precipitation/year). Although not particularly high, the Transverse Ranges and

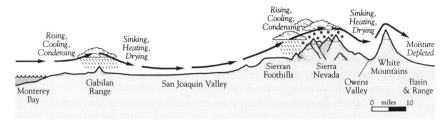

Fig. 8.7. When warm, moist air from the Pacific comes ashore and rises over the Coast Ranges, it loses moisture. As it descends into the Central Valley, it heats and dries out. Eventually, it rises again over the Sierras where it cools and condenses, forming rain and snow. By the time this air reaches the Owens Valley and the Great Basin, it has been thoroughly dried out.

the central Coast Ranges that lie to the west do an effective job of keeping this region dry even though it lies close to the Pacific.

California's mountainous landscape not only extracts moisture from storms but also exerts considerable influence on the regions to the east. By the time Pacific air has risen over the crest of the Coast Ranges and then either the Klamath, Sierra Nevada, San Gabriel, or San Bernardino Mountains, a great deal of its moisture has been depleted. Even though some of the mountain ranges of easternmost California and the Great Basin are almost as tall as the Sierras (e.g., the White-Inyo Range), air that rises over them has been rendered dry and capable of producing only a fraction of the precipitation totals seen on comparable Sierran peaks. This large-scale rainshadow effect is the principal reason for the relative dearth of large rivers in eastern California and most of Nevada.

Besides enhancing precipitation totals, the orographic effects of California's mountain ranges control the type of precipitation. The rapid cooling of air masses as they rise over the larger mountain ranges leads to precipitation of snow, rather than rain. The type of precipitation that occurs strongly influences the timing and magnitude of runoff (chap. 5). The extensive snowpack that accumulates during the winter months acts like a very large reservoir, storing potential runoff long after the storm event. In this way, the mountains of California not only extract large amounts of water from storms but also store the water, releasing it slowly over the spring and early summer. If California was as topographically featureless as portions of the Midwest, its overall water picture would be completely different. Without the orographic influence of mountain ranges, it would receive but a fraction of the total precipitation that it presently does, and, more important, almost all of the state's runoff would be confined to the few winter months when it receives most of its precipitation. California would be a very different and altogether less interesting place.

SUMMARY

The energy flow for the rivers of California is provided by the state's diverse and changeable climate. The storms that supply precipitation to California are generated by the attempts of the atmosphere to balance differential heating of the earth. Circulation cells transfer heat from the equator to the poles and cold from the poles to the equator. Interactions at the margins of these cells spawn low pressure (cyclonic) and high pressure (anticyclonic) centers that are driven west-to-east across the Pacific by the jet stream. The birthplace of extratropical cyclones dictates the amount and type of precipitation that reaches California. Storms spawned in the central and western Pacific are warm and moist, supplying abundant rain. Storms spawned in the Gulf of Alaska are typically colder and drier, with a greater amount of snow.

The factors that determine which type of storms reach California and with what frequency are complex. The position and intensity of low and high pressure cells appear to be tied to sea surface temperatures immediately offshore California and in the Gulf of Alaska. These SSTs, in turn, are probably influenced by atmospheric circulation patterns controlled principally by SSTs in the equatorial Pacific and Indian oceans. Changes in SSTs in the Pacific and Indian oceans, termed El Niño/Southern Oscillation events, appear to control the amount of moisture and heat transferred from the equatorial regions to the northern Pacific. The teleconnections between California's erratic weather and these ENSO events is still poorly understood, however.

The impact of storms on the rivers of California is a function of latitude and relief. On average, storms strike the northern portion of the state more often than the southern, with higher precipitation totals in the north. When storms sweep across the state, the location of mountain ranges influences strongly both the amount of precipitation and the type. By causing cyclonic air masses to rise, cool, and condense, the western slopes of mountains receive high amounts of rain and snow, leading to large, perennial rivers. In contrast, air masses tend to warm and dry as they descend the eastern slopes of mountains, reducing the amount of precipitation and producing smaller, more ephemeral rivers.

RELEVANT READINGS

Ahrens, C. D. 1993. *Meteorology Today: An Introduction to Weather, Climate, and the Environment.* 4th ed. St. Paul: West.

Diaz, H. F., and V. Markgraf, eds. 1992. *El Niño: Historical and Paleoclimatic Aspects of the Southern Oscillation.* Cambridge: Cambridge University Press.

Hunrichs, R. A. 1991. "California: Floods and Droughts." *U.S. Geological Survey Water Supply Paper W2375*: 197–206.

Lins, H. F., F. K. Hare, and K. P. Singh. 1990. "Influence of the Atmosphere." In *Surface Water Hydrology*, ed. M. G. Wolman and H. C. Riggs. Vol. O-1 of *The Geology of North America*. Boulder: Geological Society of America.

Peterson, D. H., D. R. Cayan, J. Dileo-Stevens, and T. G. Ross. 1987. "Some Effects of Climate Variability on Hydrology in Western North America." In *The Influence of Climate Change and Climate Variability on Hydrologic Regime and Water Resources*, ed. S. I. Solomon, M. Beran, and W. Hogg, 45–62. International Association of Hydrological Sciences Publication 168, Vancouver, B.C., Canada.

Philander, S. G. 1992. "El Niño." *Oceanus* 35: 56–65.

Trewartha, G. T., and L. H. Horn. 1980. *An Introduction to Climate*. 5th ed. New York: McGraw-Hill.

Washington, W. M., and C. L. Parkinson. 1986. *An Introduction to Three-dimensional Climate Modeling*. Mill Valley, Calif.: University Science Books.

NINE

Tectonics and Geology
of California's Rivers

INTRODUCTION

As discussed in the previous chapter, the state's climate, geology, and tectonic setting are the fully independent forces that drive the rivers of California. All adjustments in a natural river system, including its morphology and behavior, can be traced to these forces. Ultimately, it is the tectonic history and setting of a watershed that is so very important. The history of tectonic activity dictates the nature and distribution of geologic units that make up a watershed. Modern tectonic processes are superposed on this geologic assemblage, lifting it up and forming the mountain ranges or "templates" that rivers carve into.

This chapter reviews the concept of plate tectonics. A more complete description of this remarkable theory is contained in most introductory geology texts. The emphasis here is on the nature of tectonic interactions at plate boundaries and how this might control the evolution of watersheds. The latter part of the chapter examines the rivers of California and the major hydrologic regions in light of their general tectonic, geologic, and climatic context.

PLATE TECTONICS:
THE UNIFYING THEORY OF THE GEOLOGIC SCIENCES

During my career in academia, I have had the good fortune to watch the geosciences undergo their most dramatic revolution since the early observations of James Hutton, Sir Charles Lyell, and Charles Darwin. This revolution stemmed from empirical analysis of the obvious. If you hold a globe in your hands, you cannot help but notice that the continents that surround the Atlantic Ocean all fit together nicely, like pieces of a jig-saw puzzle laid next to each other on a table. It takes no stretch of the imagination to fit these continental masses back together again by simply shrinking the Atlantic Ocean. The stretch is imagining how this might be accomplished.

Early in this century Alfred Wegener, a German meteorologist, was the first to cogently assemble the evidence for the separation of Africa from South America. In addition to the interlocking shape of the two conti-nents, he documented their shared flora and fauna and strikingly similar geologic history, making a well-argued case for the opening of the Atlantic Ocean in the Mesozoic. Termed *continental drift* at the time, Wegener's hy-pothesis was ridiculed by many of the premier intellectuals of the age and he was largely ignored as something of a crank. During the middle part of this century, however, improvements in geophysical techniques turned this crank into a visionary.

By the mid-1960s, it was well established that the floor of the Atlantic Ocean was expanding in an east-west direction, with Europe and Africa pulling away from North and South America. This expansion was shown to be accomplished through *seafloor spreading*, or the formation of new crust at the irregular submarine mountain range that runs down the cen-ter of the Atlantic. The recognition of this process and the confirmation of Wegener's seemingly outrageous hypothesis solved innumerable geo-logic puzzles and ushered in what has to be considered the most prolific era in the geologic sciences. New discoveries and creative new hypotheses began emerging daily, and whole new approaches to solving geologic problems were developed.

Today, the hypothesis of continental drift has evolved into the theory of *plate tectonics*. Geologists and geophysicists have discovered that the outer portion of the earth is made up of a series of mostly rigid plates, 50 to 70 miles thick, that are in constant motion relative to each other and to any fixed point on the earth. The movement, or "tectonics," of these plates ex-plains the creation of most physiographic features that we see on the earth today and the distribution and character of the earth's many rocks and, to a degree, its fossils.

The portion of the earth that makes up these mobile plates is called the *lithosphere*. Beneath the lithosphere is a relatively soft zone, known as the *asthenosphere*, that deforms easily if stress is applied to it (fig. 9.1). The con-trast in strength or rigidity between the lithosphere and the asthenosphere allows the outer portions of the earth to glide around independent of its interior. In addition to the physical contrast between the lithosphere and the asthenosphere, the outer portions of the earth can also be subdivided on the basis of overall composition. The stony, outermost skin of the earth is appropriately called the *crust*. The composition of the crust is highly

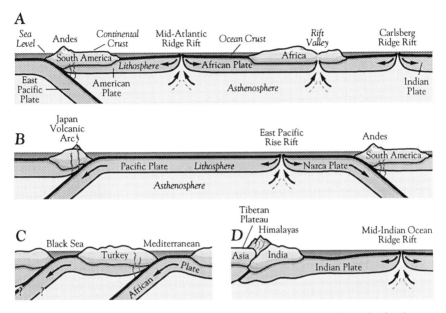

Fig. 9.1. Generalized diagram depicting the major types of lithospheric plate boundaries seen on the earth today and the relationship between crust and mantle. (Modified from Press and Siever 1986.)

variable. The *continental crust* is made up of a mixture of metamorphic, sedimentary, and igneous rocks that tend to be rich in silica and alumina-bearing minerals like quartz and feldspar. Overall, the chemical composition of the continental crust is similar to granite. In contrast, the *oceanic crust*, which occurs beneath the world's major oceans, is more like basalt, containing abundant amounts of iron- and magnesium-bearing minerals.

At the base of the crust there appears to be a significant change in composition, with an overall increase in the type and number of iron- and magnesium-bearing minerals. Stretching from the base of the crust to a depth of more than 1,900 miles, this region is referred to as the *mantle*. The lithosphere encompasses all of the crust and part of the upper mantle, while the asthenosphere is confined to a layer in the upper mantle (fig. 9.1).

At least nine major lithospheric plates, in addition to innumerable smaller plates, can be recognized on the earth. Some of these plates carry the continental crust; others carry only the oceanic crust; and many contain both. The type of crust that resides on a plate controls the surface expression of the crust and its interactions with other plates at its edges. The crust beneath the continents is much thicker (about 25 miles) than the crust beneath the oceans (less than 5 miles). In addition, the granitic material that makes up the continental crust is, in contrast to the oceanic crust, less dense. The relatively rigid crust and uppermost mantle that make up the lithosphere rest on the soft, deformable material of the asthenosphere. Under the pull of gravity, each type of crust sinks to a certain depth in the same manner that a boat does when placed in water. Like a barge filled with coal, the thin, relatively dense crust of the oceanic lithosphere creates a low profile with only minimal draft. In contrast, the thick but buoyant crust that lies atop the continental lithosphere acts like a tall tugboat with a deep draft but high freeboard. This floating balance between lithospheric plates of different composition is called *isostacy* (which means "equal standing") and explains why the continental crust stands in great relief compared to the oceanic crust.

PLATE BOUNDARIES

For the rivers of California, the key aspect of plate tectonics is the nature of interactions at the boundaries of plates containing different types of crust. The types of rocks that make up our state either have been created at plate boundaries or have been greatly modified by their proximity to a boundary. More important, California's modern landscape directly reflects the melting, folding, faulting, and uplift of these rocks in response to processes that operate at the edges of plates.

Most mountain ranges, volcanoes, and earthquakes are associated with interactions along plate boundaries. For this reason, attention has been focused on identifying and classifying plate boundaries as a way of making order out of the apparent chaos of tectonic activity. Figure 9.1 illustrates the principal types of plate boundaries that occur in the world today and have operated throughout the past. In general, these can be classified based on the character of the plate interaction and the composition of the crust that makes up part of the lithosphere.

Plate interactions fall into three overall categories: *divergent,* in which plates move away from each other; *convergent,* in which plates collide with each other; and *transform,* in which they slide past each other.

Divergent Boundaries

Divergent plate boundaries are zones of tension where *rifting* of the crust takes place. Rifting occurs where the crust faults and is pulled apart, often forming deep valleys surrounded by mountains. The tension in the crust often allows *magma* (molten rock) to rise close to the surface, heating the crust and causing it to expand, creating mountains. In addition, the faulting also allows magma to erupt on the surface, forming volcanoes. The East African Rift, the cradle of human evolution, is one of the most frequently cited examples of this type of boundary. When rifting proceeds far enough and two separate plates start to form and pull away from each other, new material is added to the edge of each of the plates as magma wells up from deep in the mantle. The new, dense, and thin lithosphere formed by this process is oceanic in composition and will typically form ocean basins, like the present Atlantic. (See fig. 9.1.)

Convergent Boundaries

There are thousands of miles of rifts on the earth's surface that are generating new oceanic lithosphere. Since the earth is not expanding, the production of new lithosphere at rifts must be compensated by consumption of old lithosphere elsewhere. This occurs at the convergent plate boundaries. When two plates that are floating on top of a plastic asthenosphere collide, something has to give. Where the relatively dense lithosphere of oceanic plates collides with the buoyant lithosphere of continental plates, the oceanic plate will be forced downward. The same is true for collisions between two oceanic plates when one is typically more dense and less buoyant than the other (fig. 9.1). As this lithosphere is forced down into the asthenosphere, the increasing temperature causes melting and eventual assimilation of the lithosphere into the mantle. In this way, lithosphere that is generated by upwelling mantle at ridges is eventually recycled.

The area where one slab of lithosphere slithers underneath another is known as a *subduction zone.* Some of the world's largest earthquakes and most dynamic geomorphic and bathymetric features occur near subduction zones. The deepest depths of the world's oceans occur at *trenches* where subduction takes place. One of the best-known examples, the Marianas Trench, is associated with subduction of an oceanic plate beneath another oceanic plate.

As a slab of oceanic lithosphere is subducted, sediment and volcanic rocks that reside on top of the crust are scraped off onto the adjoining plate. The remaining material is carried deep into the earth where it is assimilated through melting. Most important, there is usually some water trapped inside this subducted material. If water is added to rocks, the temperature at which they melt is lowered. Therefore, the transfer of water deep into the earth at subduction zones usually creates regions of concentrated melting and the formation of magma. Because molten rock is less dense than solid rock, the magma will often rise toward the surface. If the magma cools slowly within the earth, it forms a *batholith,* or large body of crystalline igneous rock like granite and gabbro. Where rising magma reaches the surface, it will erupt, forming a linear volcanic mountain range such as those that rim subduction zones.

The characteristics and composition of the volcanic mountain ranges that form at subduction zones reflect the types of plates that are colliding. Where oceanic lithosphere subducts beneath oceanic lithosphere, the upwelling magma forms *island arcs,* or arcuate chains of islands similar to Japan (fig. 9.1). Since the crust and mantle that are melting to form these islands are rich in iron- and magnesium-bearing minerals, the resulting batholiths and volcanic rocks are composed predominantly of gabbro and basalt. Where oceanic lithosphere subducts beneath continental lithosphere, the eruptions form *continental arcs,* similar to those of the Andes of South America (fig. 9.1). The silica- and aluminum-rich continental crust that is melted at the subduction zone produces granitic batholiths and andesitic volcanic rocks.

The real attention-grabbing interactions occur when objects or plates collide but refuse to subduct. For example, the Galápagos Islands, which are volcanic islands developed above a region of upwelling mantle beneath the Nazca Plate (known as a *hotspot*), and the South American continent are moving toward each other. Like a package on a conveyor belt, this island chain will eventually be carried to a collision with South America at the subduction zone off Peru and Chile that is currently creating the Andes. When islands or island arcs run into the edge of a continent, the collisions can produce considerable upheaval along the continental margin, causing rocks to bend and break thousands of miles inland. However, the sine qua non of all collisions are the ones that occur between continents. Today, India is plowing northward into the gut of Asia. Since the Asian and Indian plates are composed of buoyant continental lithosphere, they are each resisting subduction beneath the other. The result of this unwillingness to yield is the world's highest terrestrial mountain range, the Himalayas, where mountain-building rates are some of the highest recorded and the bending and breaking of the rocks is extreme.

Transform Boundaries

Along many plate boundaries, lithosphere is being neither created nor consumed. Instead, there is conservation of material where plates simply slide past each other along vertically oriented faults. These types of plate boundaries are known as transform margins (fig. 9.2). The very high rates of plate motion along many of these boundaries (> 2–3 in./yr.) produce regionally extensive faults and more frequent but often less damaging earthquakes than those associated with subduction zones.

In an ideal, homogeneous world (the Valhalla of most engineers), the conservation of motion along transform faults would release all of the stress that builds up along the plate boundary by movement on a single fault strand, leaving the adjacent landscape unaffected. However, the relative direction of motion of plates is rarely parallel to their transform boundaries. This, plus differences in the structure and composition of the rocks

Fig. 9.2. Streams offset by strike-slip motion along the San Andreas Transform. Here crustal blocks are sliding horizontally past each other. Photograph by Sandra Schultz Burford, U.S. Geological Survey, from Wallace 1990.

that occur along transform boundaries, causes them to be quite complex. Most large transforms consist of multiple shorter fault strands that split and join with other fault strands. The concentrated occurrence of these subsidiary faults adjacent to the main transform defines a *fault zone* in which the buildup of stress along the plate margin is accommodated through numerous faults over a fairly large area.

Fault zones become particularly wide where transform boundaries kink or bend. Depending on the relationship between the motion of the plates and the orientation of these bends (fig. 9.3), deformation and associated faulting adjacent to the transform can lead to the formation of mountain ranges (compressional settings) and deep basins (extensional settings).

Triple Junctions

Throughout the above discussion the emphasis has been on the single surface that separates two plates. If you divide up the surface of a sphere into a series of plates, it is a geometric certainty that three different plates are likely to intersect at some point. The point at which three plate boundaries connect is known as a *triple junction* (fig. 9.4). Since there are three types of boundaries, there are a total of ten possible combinations that can

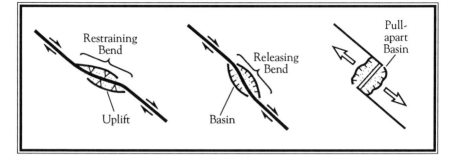

Fig. 9.3. Motion along irregular transform margins can lead to the development of mountain ranges and basins adjacent to the main transform. Where relative plate motions lead to development of combined transform and divergent margins, isolated spreading centers separated by transform fault segments can occur. (Modified from Crowell 1974.)

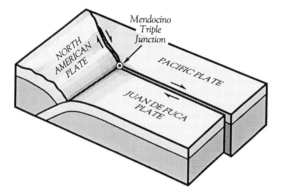

Fig. 9.4. The Mendocino Triple Junction of northern California: a transform-transform-subduction zone triple junction located at the intersection of the North American Plate, the Pacific Plate, and the Juan de Fuca Plate. This is a mobile triple junction that is currently moving northward, turning off subduction of the Juan de Fuca Plate as it goes.

make up a triple junction (e.g., divergent-convergent-transform, divergent-divergent-divergent, divergent-transform-transform, etc.). Some of the triple junction combinations are very stable and will not change their configuration unless there is a change in the direction of motion of their plates. However, if one or more of the triple junction boundaries is a subduction zone, then the triple junction itself will move and its geometry will change. Because of this, the margin of a plate may "experience" a triple junction of varying form that migrates through time. As this triple junction moves along the edge of the plate, the adjacent area may be subjected to widely varying conditions, creating a complex geologic history.

PLATE BOUNDARIES AND THE GEOLOGY OF CALIFORNIA'S WATERSHEDS

The rocks that make up California control many aspects of the sediment yield, discharge, and gradient of the state's rivers. The geologic jigsaw puzzle that we see today (fig. 9.5) is the cumulative product of more than one billion years of activity along what is now the western edge of the North American Plate (the current edge has not *always* been oriented north-south). Constructing and fitting together the jigsaw pieces we see today involved numerous collisions and subductions, several separations, and frequent transform motions along the boundary. With each type of plate boundary interaction, a unique suite of rocks was formed. Thus the tectonic history of California's margin is read through the rocks exposed at the surface today. It is not practical (or relevant) to review the entire plate tectonic history of California in this book. The large-scale changes in activity at the plate margin are summarized below to provide a general framework for the geology of the state and its watersheds. A generalized time scale is provided in figure 9.6.

Divergent Boundary Rocks

During the late Precambrian and early Paleozoic, before the plants invaded the land surface and changed the way rivers work (fig. 9.6), western North America was dominated by a divergent boundary. The net result of hundreds of millions of years of passive activity at the edge of the continent led to the formation of a setting broadly similar to that seen along the east coast of the United States today. California occupied a broad, low-gradient continental edge in which vast quantities of sediment, supplied by low-gradient rivers, accumulated in alluvial valleys, coastal plains, and marine environments along the subsiding continental margin. During much of this time, North America lay within the tropics, leading to the deposition of limestones and other types of chemical sediment typical of warm, low-latitude settings. The long history of burial, heating, bending, and uplift of these sediments has hardened them into tough, erosionally resistant metamorphic rocks. The remnants of these deposits can be found today throughout the eastern half of California. They are particularly prominent in parts of the eastern Sierra Nevada, the San Bernardino Mountains, the Great Basin, and the Mojave Desert. Because few significant rivers flow across these geologic units they do not exert a great deal of influence.

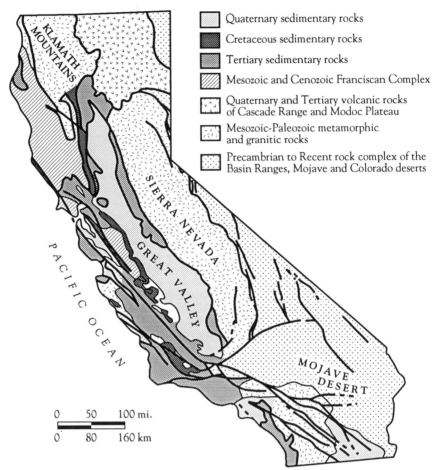

Quaternary sedimentary rocks

Cretaceous sedimentary rocks

Tertiary sedimentary rocks

Mesozoic and Cenozoic Franciscan Complex

Quaternary and Tertiary volcanic rocks
of Cascade Range and Modoc Plateau

Mesozoic-Paleozoic metamorphic
and granitic rocks

Precambrian to Recent rock complex of the
Basin Ranges, Mojave and Colorado deserts

Fig. 9.5. Generalized geologic map of the state of California showing regional associations of geologic units. A more detailed (and useful) geologic map is available from the California Division of Mines and Geology. (Modified from California
Division of Mines and Geology sources.)

Convergent Boundary Rocks

During the middle of the Paleozoic (fig. 9.6), the divergent margin that
had dominated the tectonics of western North America became a convergent margin. Off and on for approximately 300 million years the formation of new rocks and the alteration of old rocks along the western edge
of the continent were controlled by subduction-related tectonics. Two
general suites of rocks formed during this time: those associated with the

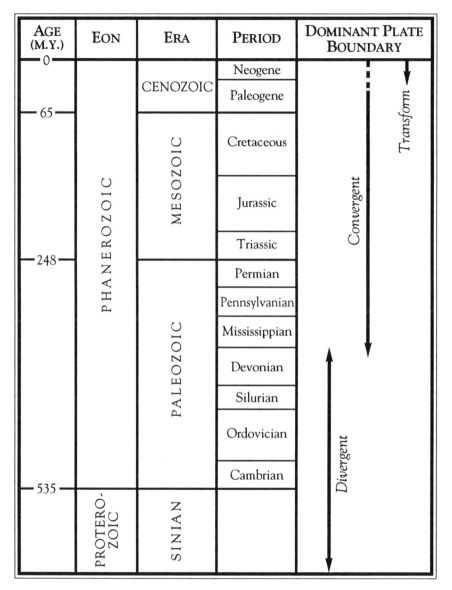

AGE (M.Y.)	EON	ERA	PERIOD	DOMINANT PLATE BOUNDARY
0	PHANEROZOIC	CENOZOIC	Neogene	Transform
			Paleogene	
65		MESOZOIC	Cretaceous	Convergent
			Jurassic	
			Triassic	
248		PALEOZOIC	Permian	
			Pennsylvanian	
			Mississippian	
			Devonian	Divergent
			Silurian	
			Ordovician	
			Cambrian	
535	PROTERO- ZOIC	SINIAN		

Fig. 9.6. Timing of divergent, convergent, and transform margin tectonics that dominated California for more than 600 million years.

subduction of oceanic lithosphere beneath the continental lithosphere of North America and those emplaced by or otherwise associated with collisions at the continental edge.

For much of the late Paleozoic and Mesozoic and all of the early Cenozoic, the western margin of North America plowed into and over the oceanic lithosphere of the ancestral Pacific Ocean. The subduction of oceanic lithosphere beneath North America led to the formation of distinctive assemblages of sedimentary, metamorphic, and igneous rocks. In a manner analogous to the development of the modern Andes and Cascades (fig. 9.1), large continental arcs formed above the subduction zones. The melting associated with subduction led to the formation of large granitic batholiths capped by volcanic edifices. Rocks into which these batholiths intruded were heated and transformed into metamorphic rocks. In the region immediately adjacent to the subduction zone trench, sediments that had been deposited on the ocean floor were routinely scraped off and piled against the continent, forming large accumulations of intensely deformed sedimentary and volcanic strata with stray bits of ocean crust converted to serpentine. Eroded material of the continental arc and the material that had been added to the continent by subduction routinely collected in basins that lay adjacent to the arc, forming thick accumulations of sandstones and shales.

Today, the rocks left behind by the subduction of oceanic lithosphere dominate the geology of California and its watersheds. The large Mesozoic granitic batholiths and andesitic volcanic rocks of the Klamath Mountains, Sierra Nevada, San Gabriel and San Bernardino mountains, and the Peninsular Ranges of southernmost California are all associated with melting of lithosphere in a subduction zone. The deformed Mesozoic and Cenozoic shales, cherts, volcanic rocks, and serpentinite of the northern and central Coast Ranges and portions of the central and northern Sierra Nevada were all formed as material was scraped off the subducting lithospheric slab. Finally, large deposits of Mesozoic sandstone and shale underlie the Central Valley and crop out along the eastern edge of the central and northern Coast Ranges and portions of the Transverse Ranges near Santa Barbara. These voluminous deposits accumulated in deep ocean basins that separated the subduction zone on the west from the continental arcs to the east.

During the period when convergent margin activity dominated western North America, numerous geologic "objects" managed to collide with the edge of the continent. The "objects" are all features typically associated with oceanic lithosphere, including island arcs, seamounts, and even large slabs of ocean crust. As they collided with the continent, their size and/or buoyancy prevented them from being carried beneath the continent at the subduction zone. In this way, geologic features, or *terranes,* that may have formed great distances from California were periodically added to the North American continental margin.

The emplacement of island arcs, seamounts, and other geologic features had large-scale repercussions for western North America. Many of these collisions produced widespread deformation and heating of the rocks, often resulting in episodes of extensive mountain building, or *orogenesis*. Each orogeny, or single mountain-building event, shuffled the existing rocks through regional faulting and created new rocks either through erosion and deposition, metamorphism, or even igneous activity.

The rocks associated with multiple collisions between North America and various geologic features from the ancestral Pacific form prominent features in a number of the state's major mountain ranges. Much of the late Paleozoic and Mesozoic age metamorphic and volcanic rocks of the central and northern Sierra Nevada were formed by collisional events. Extensive portions of the central and western Klamath Mountains and portions of the northern Coast Ranges are also a product of these collisions.

Transform Boundary Rocks

The same subduction processes that dominated California for so many years also brought a fundamental reorganization of the plate boundary during the middle Cenozoic. Between 20 and 30 million years ago, North America began to override the spreading ridge that separated the Pacific Plate from the Farallon Plate (fig. 9.7). This collision, which initiated at about the present latitude of Los Angeles, divided the Farallon Plate into the Juan de Fuca Plate and the Cocos Plate as the Pacific Plate continued to converge on North America. The relative sense of motion between the Pacific Plate and the North American Plate caused the new plate boundary to change from a subduction zone to a transform margin. This confusing relationship is explained in more detail in the relevant readings listed at the end of this chapter. Two mobile, unstable triple junctions developed as the Pacific Plate/North American Plate margin expanded. The northern juncture between the Juan de Fuca/Pacific/North American Plate is known as the Mendocino Triple Junction because of its present location near the town of Mendocino (fig. 9.7). The expansion of the transform fault separating the North American and Pacific plates caused the two triple junctions to migrate away from each other, with one headed south toward Mexico and the other headed north toward Oregon.

Throughout the mid- and late Cenozoic, the conversion of California's convergent margin to a transform margin produced widespread changes in the type of rocks formed within the state. The end of subduction meant an end to the development of large granitic batholiths and the cessation of the type of volcanism commonly associated with arcs. As subduction was

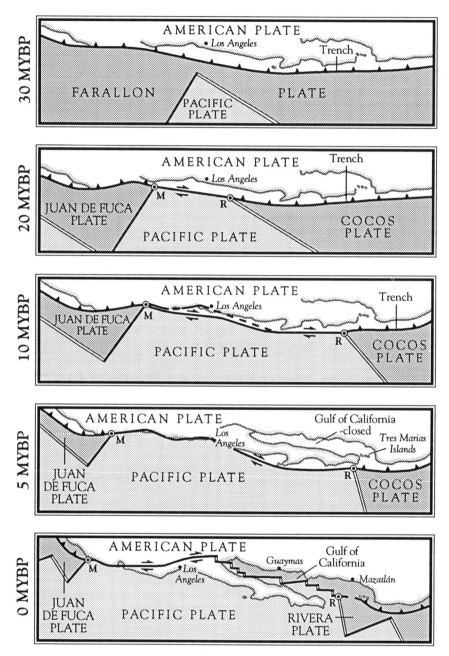

Fig. 9.7. Cenozoic evolution of the western margin of North America. Conversion of the subduction margin to a transform margin took place and is taking place as the Pacific Plate intersects the North American Plate. (Modified from W. Dickinson, in Ernst 1981.)

shut off by the migrating triple junctions (fig. 9.7), kinks and bends in the expanding transform produced numerous, smaller mountain ranges and deep basins. Many of these basins accumulated great thicknesses of oil-rich marine sediment, while others were filled with coarse alluvial material.

Most mid- and late Cenozoic rocks that occur abundantly throughout the Coast Ranges of central California and the Transverse and Peninsular ranges of southern California were formed in short-lived basins created by motion along the developing transform margin. Many of these rocks are sedimentary in origin, reflecting the erosion of nearby mountain ranges. Others are volcanic, indicating that tension in the crust associated with the irregular motion along the transform allowed magma to erupt at the surface.

Plate Boundaries of Today

With the possible exception of a continent-continent collision (and this is debatable), California has experienced all types of plate interactions. Today, the oblique convergence between the Pacific Plate and the North American Plate has led to the development of three general types of plate boundaries within or close to the borders of California (fig. 9.8). Each of these boundaries is presently controlling the development of the region's landscape.

Although the southward migration of a triple junction ended subduction in southern California, the present plate boundary has not been entirely converted to a transform boundary. Instead, in the southernmost portion of the state, the plate boundary has elements of both a transform and a divergent boundary. Along the center of the Gulf of California and northward into the Salton Sea, the boundary consists of segments of spreading, offset by long segments of transform motion. The result is that Baja California is being pulled away from mainland Mexico and areas like the Salton Sea are being actively rifted. This same combination of transform and divergent motion appears to extend into the Mojave Desert and the Colorado Desert regions as well.

Northwest of the Salton Sea, the divergent boundary that dominates the Gulf of California and southeastern California gives way to the state's most prominent plate boundary, the San Andreas transform fault zone. Motion along this world-famous fault occurs in a wide zone, affecting faults that lie well offshore and well inland of the actual transform boundary. Bends and kinks in this fault and the related dispersal of stress have produced the numerous small mountain ranges and steep-sided valleys that dominate the south and central coasts of California. It has even been shown that aspects of the uplift of the Sierra Nevada and formation of the Basin and Range are probably related to the stress fields that have developed along the San Andreas transform.

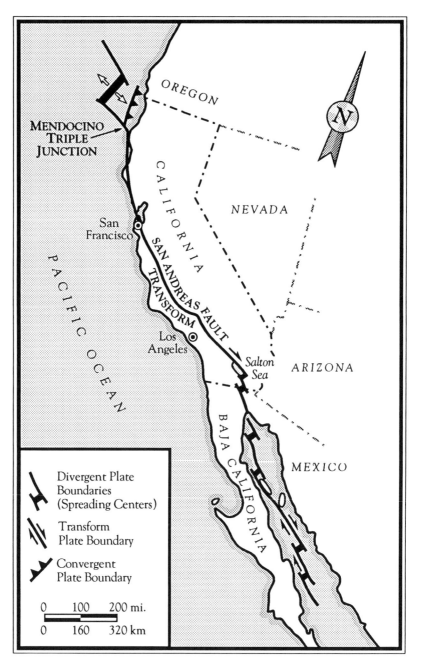

Fig. 9.8. Plate boundaries affecting California's landscape today. Note three principal types: convergent of northern California, transform of central and southern California, and divergent-transform of southeastern California and the Gulf of California. (Modified from Norris and Webb 1990.)

In the northwestern corner of California, the San Andreas transform takes a sharp bend as it meets the Mendocino Triple Junction. North of the triple junction, the Juan de Fuca Plate is currently sliding eastward beneath the North American Plate. The subduction tectonics of northernmost California controls much of the character of the region. The high rates of uplift in the northern Coast Ranges record the faulting and bending associated with subduction. More significantly, active volcanoes such as Mount Shasta and Mount Lassen and the basalts of the Modoc Plateau all owe their existence to melting of the subducted slab of lithosphere that lies deep beneath them.

CALIFORNIA'S RIVERS IN CONTEXT

Each watershed is unique. The mosaic of geologic units, recent and past tectonic activity, and frequency, intensity, and type of storms that strike any watershed dictate its primary characteristics and the evolution of its rivers. With almost a dozen major climate zones and more than a billion years of activity along a plate boundary, it should be no surprise that California contains the most diverse assemblage of watersheds of any state in the United States. From the dry washes of the Mojave Desert to the temperate rain forests of the north coast, no two California watersheds are alike. This variability is both a blessing and a curse for those who must manage California's land and water resources. The blessing stems from the physical and biological diversity of the state's watersheds and rivers and the ability of these watersheds to produce voluminous amounts of surface runoff and groundwater. The curse stems from the difficulty involved in managing this diversity and exploiting the resources. Since each watershed is unique, blanket planning and engineering solutions are likely to meet with highly variable success (see pt. II).

In this section the nature of California's diverse watersheds and rivers is reviewed in light of the tectonic, geologic, and climatic context outlined above. It would take most of the rest of this book and perhaps another of equal size to cover all the pertinent details of each watershed. There are over sixty major drainages in California and more than one thousand smaller but equally important ones. Instead of laboriously discussing each watershed, I have grouped them based on their occurrence within the major hydrologic regions as defined by the California Department of Water Resources (fig. 9.9). These regions define geographic areas where watershed conditions are broadly similar and runoff has a like destination.

The climate, tectonic setting, geology, sediment yields, and runoff characteristics of California's nine hydrologic regions are summarized in tables 9.1 through 9.6. This summary of the context of California's rivers cannot possibly do justice to their diversity and grandeur. Limited space (and

Fig. 9.9. Hydrologic regions of California based on divisions established by the California Department of Water Resources. Each region exhibits similar precipitation, runoff, geologic, and tectonic conditions. (Based on Department of Water Resources maps.)

patience) precludes a complete treatment. For a more detailed look at the state's individual watersheds, refer to the Relevant Readings listed at the end of this chapter. A particularly useful reference is the recent publication by the California State Lands Commission entitled *California's Rivers: A Public Trust Report* (1993). A copy of this report can be purchased directly from the State Lands Commission for $15.

TABLE 9.1   North Coast Hydrologic Region

Climate	Highest yearly rainfall totals in California, with areas near the Oregon border receiving nearly 200 inches. High-intensity, long-duration rainfall events common. Precipitation dominated by rainfall with heavy snowfall limited to Klamath Mountains and Trinity Alps. Intense orographic effects in mountain ranges near coast.
Tectonic Setting	Area located north of Mendocino Triple Junction dominated by subduction zone tectonics with high rates of uplift in Coast Ranges close to subduction zone and active volcanoes in nearby Cascade Range. Area south of Mendocino Triple Junction dominated by mountain building along compressional sections of San Andreas Transform.
Geology	Geologic units record past and present subduction zone tectonic activity. Near-modern and ancient subduction zone rocks dominated by mixtures of volcanic and sedimentary units with isolated serpentinite units. In area to east, older rocks composed of granitic and metamorphic rocks with younger rocks dominated by volcanics. Subduction zone rocks highly unstable and prone to landslides and erosion.
Sediment Supply	State's highest total sediment yields. Caused by combination of unstable rock types/soils, high rates of uplift, high total rainfall, and land use practices that promote erosion, such as logging and grazing.
Runoff Characteristics	Rivers have highest peak discharges recorded in state. Smaller, coastal watersheds like Navarro, Mad, Smith, and Eel exhibit rapid hydrograph response with limited base flow and snowmelt. Eastern, larger rivers like Klamath and Trinity have more subdued hydrograph response and high overall base flow and snowmelt runoff.

Major Rivers

River	Length (mi.)	Watershed Area (sq. mi.)	Peak Discharge (cfs)	Date
Eel	200	3,120	752,000	Dec. 23, 1964
Gualala	35	290	55,000	Dec. 22, 1955
Klamath	210	12,100	557,000	Dec. 23, 1964
Mad	90	490	81,000	Dec. 22, 1964
Mattole	56	340	90,400	Dec. 22, 1955
Navarro	19	300	64,500	Dec. 22, 1955
Noyo	35	130	26,600	Mar. 29, 1974
Russian	105	1,480	102,000	Feb. 18, 1986
Salmon	46	750	100,000	Dec. 23, 1964
Scott	68	650	54,600	Dec. 22, 1964
Shasta	52	790	21,500	Dec. 22, 1964
Smith	50	630	228,000	Dec. 22, 1964
Trinity	170	2,860	231,000	Dec. 22, 1964
Van Duzen	63	275	48,700	Dec. 22, 1964

SOURCES: U.S. Geological Survey Water Data Reports and California State Lands Commission.

TABLE 9.2 Sacramento, San Joaquin, and Tulare Lake Hydrologic Regions

Climate	Region dominated by strong orographic influence of Sierra Nevada and southern Cascade Mountains. High yearly precipitation totals, with approximately 50% occurring as snow. Highest precipitation occurs in Mount Shasta and northern Sierra Nevada. Rare, mild mid-Pacific storms produce intense winter snowmelt and runoff.
Tectonic Setting	Watersheds of northern portion dominated by subduction-related Cascade volcanism. Sierra Nevada undergoing rapid uplift associated with range-front faults along eastern escarpment. All runoff flows to regional tectonic depression of Central Valley bounded on east by Sierra Nevada and west by active uplift of Coast Ranges. Rapid uplift of both Sierra Nevada and Coast Ranges probably associated with development of San Andreas Transform.
Geology	Geologic units record past and present subduction zone tectonic activity. Cascade volcanoes forming above subducting Juan de Fuca Plate. Granitic rocks and most metamorphic rocks of Sierra Nevada formed during subduction prior to development of transform. Rapid Pleistocene uplift and global cooling led to development of glaciers throughout Sierra, altering longitudinal profiles of most river systems and depositing tills.
Sediment Supply	Overall sediment yield of watersheds low. Widespread vegetative cover (fir/pine forest in upper elevations, foothill scrub and oak savanna in lower elevations) and relatively stable rock type/soils reduce total sediment budget. Local intense sediment yields associated with various land uses including logging, grazing, hydraulic mining, urbanization.
Runoff Characteristics	Rivers of Sierra Nevada have largest lag times and most subdued peak runoffs due to accumulation of snowpack. All major rivers characterized by extensive spring runoff due to snowmelt and year-round elevated base flow.

Major Rivers

River	Length (mi.)	Watershed Area (sq. mi.)	Peak Discharge (cfs)	Date
American	265	2,000	180,000	Nov. 21, 1950
Bear	77	295	48,000	Feb. 17, 1986
Clavey	35	170	19,400	Jan. 13, 1980
Cosumnes	80	725	45,100	Feb. 17, 1986
Feather	175	4,580	150,000	Feb. 19, 1986
Kern	164	2,400	40,000	Nov. 19, 1950
Kings	133	1,745	85,200	Dec. 23, 1955
Merced	135	1,275	13,600	Dec. 5, 1950
Mokelumne	160	660	27,000	Nov. 22, 1950
Pitt	200	5,000	30,000	Feb. 20, 1986
Sacramento	327	24,000	620,000	Feb. 19, 1986
San Joaquin	330	13,540	79,000	Dec. 9, 1950
Stanislaus	161	1,100	62,500	Dec. 24, 1955
Yuba	96	1,350	180,000	Dec. 22, 1964

SOURCES: U.S. Geological Survey Water Data Reports and California State Lands Commission.

TABLE 9.3   San Francisco Bay and Central Coast
Hydrologic Regions

Climate	Strong latitudinal and orographic rainfall effects. Northern portion of region has high rainfall totals over mountain ranges (> 50 in.). Interior valleys exhibit rainshadow effects. Region prone to very intense rainfall from mid-Pacific storms. Snowfall insignificant. Southern portion of region receives half precipitation of north. Rare, intense storms associated with subtropical moisture produce significant runoff events in south.
Tectonic Setting	Area dominated by compressional and extensional tectonics associated with San Andreas Transform. Coast Ranges undergoing rapid uplift in compressional regions. Transverse Ranges of southern portion undergoing counterclockwise rotation and uplift associated with San Andreas Transform. Orientation of faults controls location and orientation of major river valleys.
Geology	Northern area composed of geologic units formed during ancient subduction zone tectonics and during formation of extensional basins along San Andreas Transform. Southern area composed primarily of rocks associated with evolution of San Andreas Transform. Subduction-related units dominated by sedimentary and volcanic rocks with abundant serpentinite. Transform-related units dominated by poorly consolidated sedimentary rocks and less abundant volcanic rocks.
Sediment Supply	High total sediment yields from many watersheds. Caused by combination of unstable rock types/soils, high rates of uplift, and occurrence of high-intensity rainfall events. Southern area rivers commonly carry debris flows during high runoff.
Runoff Characteristics	Small, steep watersheds have very short lag times and high peak runoffs. Limited seasonal base flow and no significant snowmelt runoff. All rivers of region prone to intense flooding during winter storms.

Major Rivers

River	Length (mi.)	Watershed Area (sq. mi.)	Peak Discharge (cfs)	Date
Arroyo Seco	40	385	28,300	Apr. 3, 1958
Carmel	35	250	9,950	Feb. 28, 1983
Cuyama	91	1,130	17,800	Feb. 25, 1969
Estrella	55	800	32,500	Feb. 24, 1969
Nacimiento	65	325	7,340	Feb. 25, 1969
Pajaro	40	1,190	24,000	Dec. 24, 1955
Salinas	180	4,160	83,100	Feb. 26, 1969
San Lorenzo	25	137	30,400	Dec. 23, 1955
Santa Ynez	70	845	80,000	Jan. 25, 1969
Sisquoc	45	445	23,200	Dec. 6, 1966

SOURCES: U.S. Geological Survey Water Data Reports and California State Lands Commission.

TABLE 9.4   North and South Lahontan Hydrologic Regions

Climate	Moderate to low total precipitation with semiarid conditions dominating southern region. Intense rainshadow effects from Sierra Nevada. Most runoff in region derived from snowmelt and base flow associated with high altitude watersheds of eastern Sierra Nevada. Rare, intense summer storms provide bulk of runoff in ephemeral desert drainages.
Tectonic Setting	Northern region dominated by east-west crustal extension and regional uplift of Basin and Range coupled with high rates of uplift of Sierra Nevada along eastern escarpment. Produces extensive internally drained valleys. Mojave Desert and associated areas of southern region undergoing both east-west extension associated with Basin and Range and northwest-southeast shear associated with San Andreas Transform. Extension in both regions leading to development of numerous recent volcanic centers.
Geology	Geologic units of region highly variable, reflecting long history. Precambrian and early Paleozoic igneous, metamorphic, and sedimentary rocks record development of divergent margin. Extensive Mesozoic granitic rocks and associated metamorphic rocks formed by convergent margin processes. Cenozoic sedimentary and volcanic rocks formed in isolated basins associated with Basin and Range extension and San Andreas Transform development. Overall, most rock types relatively stable.
Sediment Supply	Due to low overall precipitation totals and influence of snowmelt runoff sediment yields relatively low. In Sierran drainages where abundant glacial tills being reworked get locally high yields. Ephemeral semiarid drainages get coarse debris flows.
Runoff Characteristics	With exception of Owens River all watersheds relatively small, steep. Snowmelt-dominated drainages of eastern Sierra characterized by prolonged spring runoff and high base flow. Ephemeral drainages have rare flood flows with rapid hydrograph response and exceptionally coarse load. Base flow nonexistent in some drainages.

Major Rivers

River	Length (mi.)	Watershed Area (sq. mi.)	Peak Discharge (cfs)	Date
Carson	46	280	15,100	Jan. 31, 1963
Mojave	100	2,120	18,000	Jan. 26, 1969
Owens	120	1,965	na	na
Susan	59	185	5,850	Jan. 24, 1970
Truckee	60	930	17,500	Nov. 21, 1950
Walker	47	360	6,500*	Dec. 11, 1937

SOURCES: U.S. Geological Survey Water Data Reports and California State Lands Commission.

*Based on West Walker River Flows

TABLE 9.5 South Coast Hydrologic Region

Climate	Climate dominated by Mediterranean influences—frequent dry years interspersed with rare high precipitation years. Bulk of runoff associated with rainfall from intense, subtropical storms. State's highest 24-hour rainfall totals come from San Gabriel and San Bernardino mountains, which exert major orographic influence. Limited snowpack accumulations.
Tectonic Setting	Watersheds of region dominated by past and present activity along San Andreas Transform. High rates of uplift in Transverse Ranges and San Gabriel and San Bernardino mountains adjacent to or associated with San Andreas system. Location and motion of major faults controls geometry and orientation of larger watersheds. Numerous fault strands disrupt longitudinal profiles of major rivers.
Geology	Diverse assemblage of geologic units. Granitic and related metamorphic rocks of Peninsular Ranges and Transverse Ranges formed by subduction processes similar to those that formed Sierra Nevada, although south coast rocks emplaced by movement on San Andreas system. Abundant Mesozoic and Cenozoic sedimentary rocks formed in dismembered marine and nonmarine basins along San Andreas. Sedimentary rock units prone to landsliding and locally high erosion rates.
Sediment Supply	Intense urbanization and flood control projects in many south coast watersheds have reduced potential sediment yields. Combination high relief, unstable soils, limited vegetative cover, abundant wildfires leads to locally high sediment yields. Debris flows and mudflows common in smaller drainages.
Runoff Characteristics	Most rivers of region are ephemeral with limited base flow and snowmelt contribution. All rivers dominated by highly erratic flow conditions and frequent flooding. Urbanization and watershed conditions lead to short lag times and intense peak discharges.

Major Rivers

River	Length (mi.)	Watershed Area (sq. mi.)	Peak Discharge (cfs)	Date
Los Angeles	97	830	129,000	Feb. 16, 1980
Rio Hondo	20	125	38,800	Jan. 25, 1969
San Diego	45	439	75,000	Jan. 27, 1916
San Gabriel	59	350	46,600	Jan. 25, 1969
San Jacinto	38	725	16,000	Feb. 17, 1927
San Luis Rey	51	575	95,600	Jan. 27, 1916
Santa Ana	93	1,700	46,300	Mar. 3, 1938
Santa Clara	75	1,616	68,800	Jan. 25, 1969
Ventura	33	190	63,600	Feb. 10, 1968

SOURCES: U.S. Geological Survey Water Data Reports and California State Lands Commission.

TABLE 9.6 Colorado Desert Hydrologic Region

Climate	Region receives state's lowest yearly precipitation totals (< 2 in./yr. in some regions). Strong rainshadow effect of Peninsular Ranges coupled with southernmost location limit rainfall to a few storms per year. Most runoff occurs during intense summer tropical storms or during periods when subtropical jet stream shifts northward.
Tectonic Setting	Northern half of region lies within Mojave Desert (see table 9.5) where east-west extension and northwest-southeast shear is producing numerous isolated fault blocks and mountains. In southern half, San Andreas Transform is broken up into spreading segments associated with northward extension of East Pacific Rise and opening of Gulf of California. Incipient spreading centers forming large depressions like Salton Trough and Imperial Valley that capture most runoff.
Geology	Diverse geology throughout region. Similar in composition to much of the Mojave Desert area (table 9.4). Present divergence producing voluminous volcanic rocks and limited Cenozoic granitic rocks. Abundant Mesozoic granitic and metamorphic rocks reflect subduction zone processes active before San Andreas Transform. Widespread accumulation of alluvium in large, fault-bounded basins.
Sediment Supply	Overall low sediment yields due to arid climate. Ephemeral drainages prone to flooding and debris flows during intense precipitation events.
Runoff Characteristics	Most rivers of region are ephemeral with little to no base flow except in areas adjacent to high mountains of South Coast Hydrologic Region. Colorado River, which marks eastern edge of hydrologic region, is "technically" largest river in California, although little of its watershed resides within California.*

Major Rivers

River	Length (mi.)	Watershed Area (sq. mi.)	Peak Discharge (cfs)	Date
Alamo	52	695	4,500	Aug. 17, 1977
New	60	1,000	3,000	Aug. 17, 1977
Whitewater	25	1,500	2,500	Jan. 25, 1969

SOURCES: U.S. Geological Survey Water Data Reports and California State Lands Commission.

*By this point in the book the reader will have noticed that I have judiciously ignored the granddaddy of the rivers of the Southwest, the Colorado. The reasons for this neglect are severalfold. Unlike all other rivers in California (with the exception of the upper Klamath), the Colorado watershed basically exists outside the boundaries of the state. By the time the Colorado River makes it to the southeasternmost border of California, its formative processes have pretty much done their job. Rainfall, snowfall, runoff, water diversions, tectonics, etc.: this story takes place in Colorado, Utah, Arizona, and New Mexico.

SUMMARY

The rocks of California's watersheds and the location and size of mountain ranges are tied to the state's past and present tectonic setting. Since California lies at the western edge of the North American Plate, interactions along the plate boundary have dictated much of the geologic history of the region. Three general types of plate boundaries have been and are currently active within California: convergent boundaries, where oceanic lithosphere is subducted beneath the continental lithosphere of North America; divergent boundaries, where tension within the lithosphere causes plates to pull away, forming new lithosphere; and transform boundaries, where plates slide past each other along vertically oriented transform faults.

The complex geologic jigsaw puzzle that makes up modern California today records at least three different episodes of interactions at the plate boundary. During the late Precambrian and early Paleozoic, the western edge of North America was a divergent boundary with a well-developed continental shelf. Starting in the mid-Paleozoic, the margin converted to a convergent boundary characterized by subduction and episodic collisions and mountain-building events. In the mid-Cenozoic, the collision between the Pacific Plate and the North American Plate began the conversion to a transform margin. Expansion of the transform through migrating triple junctions created much of the landscape that we see in central and southern California today. In far northern California, subduction zone processes still dominate the development of the landscape of the region.

The rivers of California can be grouped based on like characters within the hydrologic regions designated by the California Department of Water Resources. Each region consists of a unique combination of precipitation patterns, geologic structure, and active tectonics that has shaped their watersheds and rivers.

RELEVANT READINGS

Burchfiel, B. C., P. W. Lipman, M. L. Zoback, and W. G. Ernst, eds. 1992. *The Cordilleran Orogen: Coterminous U.S.* Vol. G-3 of *The Geology of North America.* Boulder: Geological Society of America.

Crowell, J. C. 1974. "Origin of Late Cenozoic Basins in Southern California." In *Tectonics and Sedimentation,* ed. W. R. Dickinson. Society of Economic Paleontologists and Mineralogists Special Publication 22. Tulsa: SEPM.

Ernst, W. G., ed. 1981. *The Geotectonic Development of California.* Englewood Cliffs, N.J.: Prentice-Hall.

Gerrard, A. J. 1988. *Rocks and Landforms.* London: Unwin Hyman.

Harbaugh, J. W. 1975. *Northern California: Field Guide.* K/H Geology Field Guide Series. Dubuque: Kendall/Hunt.

Howard, A. D. 1979. *Geologic History of Middle California.* Berkeley, Los Angeles, and London: University of California Press.

Ingersoll, R. V., and W. G. Ernst, eds. 1987. *Cenozoic Basin Development of Coastal California.* Englewood Cliffs, N.J.: Prentice-Hall.

Norris, R. M., and R. Webb. 1990. *Geology of California.* 2d ed. New York: John Wiley and Sons.

Press, F., and R. Siever. 1986. *Earth.* 4th ed. New York: W. H. Freeman.

Sharp, R. P. 1976. *Southern California: Field Guide.* K/H Geology Field Guide Series. Dubuque: Kendall/Hunt.

———. 1978. *Coastal Southern California: Field Guide.* K/H Geology Field Guide Series. Dubuque: Kendall/Hunt.

Sharp, R. P., and A. F. Glazner. 1993. *Geology Underfoot in Southern California.* Missoula, Mont.: Mountain Press.

Wallace, R. E. 1990. *The San Andreas Fault System, California: An Overview of the History, Geology, Geomorphology, Geophysics, and Seismology of the Most Well Known Plate-Tectonic Boundary in the World.* U.S. Geological Survey Professional Paper no. 1515.

And the books by John McPhee

1981. *Basin and Range.* New York: Farrar, Straus, Giroux.

1983. *In Suspect Terrain.* New York: Farrar, Straus, Giroux.

1993. *Assembling California.* New York: Farrar, Straus, Giroux.

PART II

Learning the Lessons
Land Use and the Rivers of California

TEN

Rivers of California

The Last 200 Years

INTRODUCTION

The characteristics of each watershed in California are the result of a billion years of landscape evolution driven by changes in climate and the interactions of tectonic plates along the western margin of North America. As noted in chapter 1, with the arrival of the Europeans and the discovery of gold the rules that govern the development of rivers were altered. Part II of this book examines some (but not all) of the important land uses that have changed or are presently changing the watersheds and rivers of California. This chapter presents a brief summary of the major political, economic, and demographic shifts of the last 200 years that have modified the state's landscape.

The emphasis of Part II is on how and why land use practices change the natural variables that control the behavior and character of the state's rivers. One variable that was not discussed in detail in Part I is water quality. This is primarily because water "quality" is in the eye of the beholder. Ideal water quality for human consumption may be vastly different from ideal water quality for the delta smelt, desert pupfish, or striped bass. Moreover, with the exception of its influence on riparian vegetation, water quality has little input into geomorphic systems. Yet the issue of declining water quality is currently driving many decisions about the future of California's rivers, especially in the Sacramento/San Joaquin Delta. Brief discussions of water quality are therefore included in the following discussions of land use impacts.

1800–1900: ARRIVAL OF THE EUROPEANS AND THE DISCOVERY OF GOLD

The first Europeans to come to the region that is now California encountered a diverse landscape little changed by the Native Americans that had occupied it for more than 10,000 years. Like the Native Americans whom they eventually displaced, the first Europeans also did little to alter the face of California. The Franciscan missions located throughout the state produced crops through irrigation diversions and Native American slave labor. However, the sparse population and the relatively primitive water resource development techniques of the Spanish produced limited change in the rivers. As population centers like San Francisco and Monterey began to grow in the late 1700s and early 1800s, there were increases in logging, farming, and grazing in the state, but for the most part, these operations were small and had little overall impact.

Without question, it was the discovery of gold in 1848 that forever (at least in human terms) altered the landscape of California. The explosive growth in California's population that followed the discovery of gold and the methods used to extract the resource changed the natural processes that governed the state's rivers. No longer would the rivers operate in blithe disregard for the organisms dependent on them. In a geologic blink of an eye, a billion years of California river processes were transformed.

The events of the last half of the nineteenth century set the stage for many of the river-related problems that confront us today (fig. 10.1). The gold rush brought thousands of miners to the Sierra Nevada to muck through streambeds and river terraces. In the first few years large amounts of gold were extracted from the state's rivers. Because the techniques used to extract the gold were relatively simple and small in scale, the cumulative damage to the rivers was limited. Within a few years of the first discovery of gold, the in-stream and near-stream placer deposits played out. As the miners began to abandon the Sierra Nevada goldfields, many chose to stay and pursue hard rock gold or other minerals. Still others moved to new California gold mining operations in the north coast region or simply left the golden state to pursue the silver rush in Nevada. However, most simply walked away from mining. In a trend that would persist until the 1990s, these visitors who had come to get rich quick abandoned thoughts of returning home and chose to settle in California. Many discovered opportunity in the rich farmlands, many sought jobs in the cities, and some found work in the timber industry. In all, the rapid assimilation of the forty-niners into the economy of California gave all of its industries a boost toward the twentieth century.

As is discussed in the following chapter, in 1853 miners discovered that ancient Eocene-aged placer deposits in the central Sierra Nevada contained small amounts of gold. Widespread hydraulic mining of these deposits transferred mountains of debris into the rivers of California. As this wave of sediment moved through the tributaries and eventually into the main stems of the Sacramento and San Joaquin rivers, it plugged the chan-

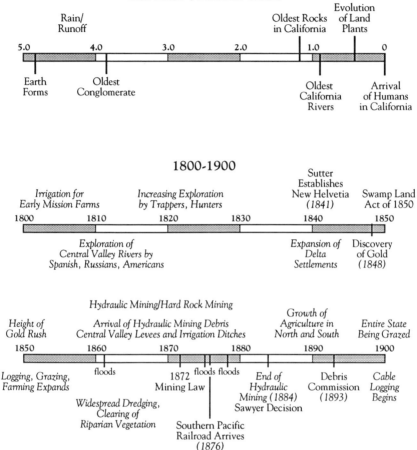

Fig. 10.1. Generalized time line depicting major "events" up until 1900 that have affected or are currently affecting the rivers of California.

nels and poured onto the farms that had colonized the fertile floodplains. Although legal action eventually halted hydraulic mining, the rivers that drain the Sierra Nevada (arguably the most important in all of California) were significantly changed.

As the placer mining era gave way to the hydraulic mining era, demand for timber increased dramatically. Large-scale timber operations in the Sierra Nevada and the north coast supplied lumber to the miners and the growing cities of California. At the same time, grazing operations, which had started with the large ranchos of the Spanish, began expanding throughout California from the high mountain meadows of the Sierras to the dry deserts of the Mojave. The timber operations and grazing operations changed the type and density of vegetation that covered the California landscape, eliminating a number of species and altering whole ecosystems. These changes, and their attendant runoff and erosion problems, began the decline in wildlife habitat that bedevils these industries today.

The debris produced by hydraulic mining led to flooding in the Central Valley during the 1860s and 1870s with catastrophic consequences. In his diary of the Whitney Party, William Brewer reported that the Central Valley had become an inland sea 20 miles wide and 250 miles long during the floods of 1865. Farms and cities were completely inundated, with significant losses in property and life. These flooding events, which were repeated many times toward the end of the nineteenth century and the beginning of the twentieth century, inspired private and government initiatives to reduce the impacts of flooding and mining debris. The approach inevitably involved the realignment of the rivers, most often in direct conflict with the natural processes that shape them. These blunt instrument approaches included channeling and the construction of ever-greater levees. Later, the ultimate blunt instrument, dams, would be pressed into service to contain the mining debris and to hold back floodwaters.

The channelization and leveeing of California's rivers, along with the arrival of the railroads, encouraged the development of vast tracts of land for agriculture. By the turn of the century, increasingly larger landholdings in the Central Valley and the valleys of southern California were producing highly profitable, diverse crops. The dry-land wheat farms that were so successful in the middle part of the century gave way to fruit orchards, vineyards, and row crops, all with growing national markets. The diversification and growth in the size of these farms coupled with several severe droughts increased pressures for the development of irrigation systems. Reclamation became a booming business, and irrigation colonies appeared all over southern California and later in the Central Valley. Diversion dams and increasingly elaborate irrigation canals were constructed. The government stayed out of the water development business during this time, except to settle the innumerable legal disputes that cropped up over water rights.

Expansion of the urban centers of California began to outpace the growth in farms during the latter part of the nineteenth century. By 1900, approximately half of the total population of California had left the rural areas and moved to the cities, with more than 60 percent of these urbanites living in the south coast region. In defiance of logic, growth was taking place as far removed from water sources as possible. This growth and the inevitable need for water set the stage for some of the major political battles of the twentieth century and served as the impetus for large-scale goverment-managed water projects.

1900–1950: "RECLAMATION" AND FLOOD CONTROL

The period from 1900 to 1950 brought the most far-reaching changes to the state's rivers (fig. 10.2). During these 50 years, the state of California survived two world wars, a depression, one of two "droughts of the century," and a continuing population boom. The increasing demand for water and power to feed the state's growth cemented local, state, and federal governments in the development of one of the most ambitious water engineering schemes in the world.

Changes in the ideology of the state and federal government along with climatic and economic events coincided to spur the "reorganization" of California's rivers. Since the arrival of the hydraulic mining debris, flooding in the Central Valley had long been a way of life. Crop damage during flood events was simply the "collateral" damage associated with occupying the floodplains. However, as more and more farms were developed on the Central Valley floodplains and corporate agriculture began to grow, an increasingly noisy populace was becoming intolerant of flooding. Beginning in 1902 and again in 1904, 1906, 1907, and 1909, the Sacramento Valley farmers were hit by a series of devastating floods. The Army Corps of Engineers, through the California Debris Commission, asked Congress and the state of California for funds to support an aggressive effort to reduce flooding and restore navigation to the sediment-choked Sacramento River. Called the Sacramento Flood Control Project, this was the most comprehensive and, in many ways, far-sighted approach to flood control ever undertaken. Congress and the state agreed, and the "reclamation" (as if they were somehow being restored to their former use!) of the fertile floodplains of the Sacramento Valley and a complete reconfiguration of the river's channel system were begun.

While the Army Corps was grappling with plans to reclaim the Central Valley, the electrification of California was in full swing. Pacific Gas and Electric, along with other investor-owned power agencies, scrambled to meet the power needs of the growing urban centers of California. At the beginning of the twentieth century, hydroelectric dams became the preferred method of power generation. Hundreds of these dams appeared throughout California during these times, especially in the watersheds of the Sierra Nevada where year-round water supplies were most dependable. Although most of these dams were small, the cumulative impact on the sediment supply and discharge of the state's watersheds was profound.

Prior to 1900, both Los Angeles and San Francisco had depended on private water companies to supply their needs. Increasingly complex (and

1900 - Present

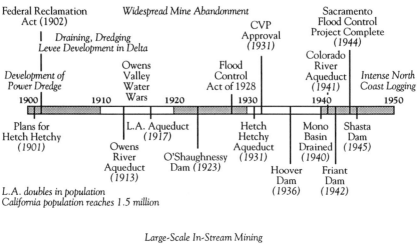

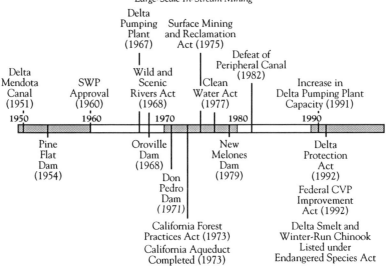

Fig. 10.2. Generalized time line depicting important historical events of the twentieth century that have affected or are affecting California's rivers.

bizarre) water rights laws, a lack of private capital, and growing demands for irrigation made it harder and harder for private companies and water colonies to expand. It was becoming evident in the early 1900s that government at all levels was going to have to step in to solve the problem. Two unrelated water initiatives, one in San Francisco and one in Los Angeles, were begun which would greatly affect urban water politics in California.

In the early 1900s, the city engineer of San Francisco, Marsden Mansen, proposed that the city develop a reservoir and water delivery system that would meet its long-term needs. In a self-destructive fit of administrative pique, he rejected fourteen possible high-quality and economically feasible sites and chose to construct a reservoir in the Grand Canyon of the Tuolumne River. Hetch Hetchy Reservoir was to be located within the boundaries of the newly designated Yosemite National Park, a location as seemingly far removed from San Francisco as possible and requiring an extensive and costly water delivery system. This choice set off more than a decade of political fireworks. In addition to intense political wrangling over costs, it spawned the modern environmental movement in California and the West. With the help of John Muir, Hetch Hetchy became the symbol of resistance of environmental groups to water development projects. Eventually and against considerable odds, Hetch Hetchy was approved by the voters in San Francisco. After years of cost overruns and numerous bond issues to support them, water finally flowed to the Bay Area in 1934.

While San Francisco struggled in its attempts to develop its own water system, Los Angeles quietly and efficiently went to the Owens Valley, captured and transferred almost all of the runoff of the eastern Sierra Nevada, and created the foundations for the stratospheric growth of the Los Angeles basin. As most California historians acknowledge, William Mulholland delivered water to Los Angeles. As the head of the city's municipalized water system, Mulholland convinced the voters of Los Angeles to provide all of the money for the Owens Valley Project up front, placing the city perilously close to receivership. Despite the risk-taking, under Mulholland's direction, the project was completed rapidly and within its budget—making a number of prominent Californians fabulously rich in the process. When it opened in 1913, the amount of water delivered by the Owens Valley aqueduct was four times what Los Angeles needed. This excess water was then spread around into the orchards of the San Fernando Valley. The growth generated by this water quickly used up any excess. As Los Angeles began to expand its landholdings in Owens Valley in anticipation of shipping more water to the Southland, it became embroiled in violent water wars with local landowners. Eventually, and despite considerable resistance, Los Angeles purchased most of the land and water rights in Owens Valley, exporting most of the runoff from the watershed as well as the groundwater.

At the same time that Los Angeles was fighting its water wars in the Owens Valley, acute water shortages associated with the drought of the 1920s and rapid population growth made it imperative that additional sources be developed. In 1924, Los Angeles established a consortium of water districts, known as the Metropolitan Water District, to tap into the Colorado River. Approved in 1928, the Colorado River Project in conjunction with the expansion of the Owens Valley Project brought vast quantities of water to the Southland, fueling the growth of one of the world's largest and most prosperous urban areas.

Although the efforts of San Francisco and Los Angeles to develop water projects in California had an impact on several of California's prominent rivers, it was the election of President Teddy Roosevelt and passage of the Reclamation Act of 1902 that dramatically changed them. Roosevelt, who had an engineer's view of "wasted" water in the West, actively promoted the federal government's role in the development of large water projects and prompted government agencies to begin thinking about long-range possibilities. The symbol of Roosevelt's view and the tool by which he promoted it is embodied in the Reclamation Act of 1902. This act, which created the often-maligned Bureau of Reclamation, was designed explicitly to provide subsidized irrigation water to farmers and to stimulate economic development and population growth wherever the federal government chose to build their dams. In the early part of the century, the Reclamation Act got off to a slow start, with relatively few large-scale federal water and flood control projects. The depression and the eventual election of President Franklin D. Roosevelt changed all this. The economic demand for New Deal construction projects became the catalyst for the chaotic, *disorderly* development of the West's major rivers.

The Reclamation Act and the large-scale public works projects it promoted also got a great boost from floods that occurred on the Mississippi River during the 1920s. At this time, the Army Corps saw the opportunity to include flood control in the mission of the agency. The Flood Control Act of 1936 gave the corps the green light to spend vast sums to protect all those who chose to reside on the floodplains. Of course, these sums had to be justified on a cost/benefit basis, but that rarely proved an obstacle to the creative economists and engineers of the corps.

While the Reclamation Act was being promoted throughout the West and new and ever-larger water projects were being considered, farming in the San Joaquin Valley and southern California was undergoing rapid expansion. To meet the demand, newer and larger irrigation districts were being developed. The arrival of electricity and gasoline-powered engines allowed many farmers to pump groundwater as well as withdraw water from local rivers and streams: a trend that developed toward an innate dependency on increasing amounts of irrigation water. When the depression and drought years of 1928 to 1935 finally struck this region, there was tremendous overdrafting of groundwater and a complete exhaustion of surface supplies, creating more demand for government-run water development.

During the 1920s, powerful agricultural interests began campaigning for construction of a very large irrigation project for the Central Valley.

Despite their efforts, numerous legal, financial, and political obstacles kept their ambitions fettered for more than a decade. When the depression finally came to California, the political landscape changed and the state legislature approved the construction of the Central Valley Project, ostensibly to stimulate the economy. Because of the weak economy, however, California could not pay for the CVP. With the New Deal in full swing, the stage was set for the Bureau of Reclamation to step in and take over the project. The construction took much longer than anyone had predicted, but by 1951 a large segment of the CVP, including Shasta Dam, Friant Dam, and the Delta-Mendota and Friant-Kern canals, was completed. The amount of water diverted by the CVP had changed the nature of runoff from more than 40 percent of the surface area of California. In turn, it began delivering subsidized, low-cost water to large portions of the Central Valley.

The tumultuous years between 1900 and 1950 witnessed an explosive growth in California's population and an increasing appetite for power and water for growing urban centers and agriculture. At the same time, increasing urbanization of California along with agricultural expansion onto floodplains created a rising demand for flood control structures. The federal, state, and local governments responded by channelizing, dredging, and leveeing the state's rivers and developing the foundations for the world's most complex, expensive water transfer system. The rivers of the state were blocked, harnessed, and reconfigured with dramatic and long-term consequences.

1950–1970: BOOM TIME

The aggressive development of California's rivers that had taken place in the first half of the twentieth century did not abate in the 1950s (see fig. 10.2). The growth in urbanization following World War II spilled onto floodplains throughout the state. When widespread flooding occurred in northern California in 1955, the damage was almost as large as the political response. New calls for flood control dams were answered by numerous small projects and one very large one, the Feather River Project, which would eventually lead to the construction of Oroville Dam. But the Feather River Project turned out to be just the beginning of the grandest effort to rearrange California's water, the State Water Project. A nightmare of water rights and political infighting, the SWP was probably the institutionalized birth of the division between the water-rich, population-poor northern half of the state and the water-poor, population-rich southern half of the state. Under the stewardship of Gov. Edmund G. Brown, Sr., Californians approved the SWP by the slimmest of margins, with widespread support in southern California carrying the day.

At the same time that the state was aggressively developing its own water resources, the federal government was accelerating its plans. In 1949, the Bureau of Reclamation published a study of Central Valley "needs" (both real and imagined) and recommended development of no less than thirty-eight individual dam sites. In the two decades following the release of this report, most of these projects were completed, including the large San Luis Reservoir, Folsom Dam, and the Trinity River Diversion. A great deal of concrete was poured into California's rivers between 1950 and 1970.

Increases in water development projects were not the only factors changing California's rivers during the 1950s and 1960s. The growth in population following World War II spurred considerable demand for building materials. Logging operations grew rapidly in the north coast and the Sierra Nevada, topping out near 6 billion board feet annually during the 1950s. The period between 1950 and 1970 also saw the rapid removal of most of the old-growth forests in California and widespread damage to streams and riparian corridors. Almost all of this logging was clear-cut, tractor yarding, which is the most damaging kind (chap. 12). Since most of this logging took place on private lands and few people visited the remote forests of California, little attention was paid to the downstream consequences. However, by the 1970s, the damage from a century of intense logging and poor land use management practices was becoming increasingly apparent. By the end of the 1960s, a growing population increasingly interested in visiting and preserving the wildlands of California coupled with declining salmon fisheries and wildlife brought new scrutiny of the state's logging industry.

The increases in demand for lumber in the 1950s and 1960s were matched by burgeoning demand for sand and gravel. To supply the explosion in dam, canal, and road building, as well as the growth in urban centers, the channels, floodplains, and terraces of the state were mined, removing a key ingredient in the equilibrium that rivers maintain. Since dams were already trapping sediment normally supplied to rivers by their watersheds, the removal of "stored" sediment created numerous local and regional impacts (chap. 11). While sand and gravel was becoming the state's top mineral resource, operators and owners of gold, mercury, and copper hard rock mines were either walking away from their properties or selling them to whoever showed up to take over their responsibility and, most important, their liability. As groundwater filled these mines and rainfall percolated through their tailings piles, they began to discharge a highly toxic brew into the state's rivers, destroying wildlife habitat and directly affecting the drinking water supplies of millions of people.

The statewide boom in mining, logging, farming, urbanization, and dam building of the 1950s and 1960s set the stage for the clash of interests that has dominated river politics over the past 25 years.

1970–PRESENT: THE WAR OF THE SPECIAL INTERESTS

The period between the beginning of the New Deal and the depression and the authorization of the last major SWP dam (the New Melones on the Stanislaus River) must be viewed as the "golden years" by western water developers and engineers. With a state and federal government that simply could not say no and fragmented political forces incapable of effectively opposing water developments, there was an orgy of planning, designing, and constructing. Although unforeseen at the time, these glory days of unrestrained growth eventually had to come to an end. Several things conspired to arrest the momentum of water development. First, the rest of the country slowly began to catch on to the fact that most of the benefit derived from these huge projects was being accrued by large irrigation districts who received subsidized water to grow low-value crops on, in many cases, substandard land. Second, it was clear by the 1970s that water projects were no longer needed to prop up California's economy. The state was booming, becoming one of the largest economies of the world. Recognizing this, presidents after Dwight D. Eisenhower began to reduce and eventually eliminate authorization of new dams in the Bureau of Reclamation's budgets. Third, even if desired or needed, new water projects were becoming prohibitively expensive. All of the best dam-building sites already had dams on them. New sites required more engineering and higher costs for construction. The cost/benefit ratios that were fudged in the past to make projects "feasible" simply could not be fudged enough to make up for the increased costs. Finally, the nail in the coffin of large-scale water projects may have been the rise in the environmental movement. Numerous organizations began highly successful political and legal efforts to end large water projects in California. In conjunction, these four factors—subsidized water, lack of need for economic development, increasing financial costs of development, and the rise of the environmental movement—sounded the death knell for large-scale water projects in the state.

Since 1970 it has become increasingly apparent that the reconfiguration of California's surface water and the land use changes that have occurred in the state's watersheds have produced a complex, often intractable environmental and water quality problem. Despite the prognostications of the water developers, increases in water quantity did not translate to increases in quality for all. Today, the Sacramento/San Joaquin Delta, the epicenter of California water politics, is in a state of decline. This decline is measured not solely by the listing of a few species of fish under the Federal Endangered Species Act but by an overall decline in the quality of the water that is pumped out of it—water that supplies the needs of two-thirds of California's population (chap. 16). In a state of political paralysis and obsessed with self-preservation, the governing bodies of

California have been unable to effectively deal with this decline. The federal government has attempted to step in to resolve the water quality issues by threatening to force the state to clean up its own mess. As this book was being written, the federal government and the state of California had called a truce in their war of regulations in the delta (actually, the federal government gave in). This truce, however, represents a political, rather than scientific, solution to the delta problems. Because of this, new battles will undoubtedly surface in the near future.

In the 1970s, the logging industry, which labored away in relative anonymity for most of a century, began to compete with a number of special interests for use of the state's wildlands. The intense regional loss of salmon spawning habitat in the north coast, the sedimentation in logged watersheds that threatened old-growth stands and small urban areas, the clear-cuts throughout the forested regions of California—all drew unwanted attention to an industry that was overharvesting the state's declining forests and, in most cases, severely damaging the local rivers. Emergence from the protective mantle of obscurity also befell the mining and sand and gravel industries. As the rate of sand and gravel mined from the state's rivers began to exceed the ability of watersheds to replenish the losses, significant changes began to be recorded. Increased channel incision and bank erosion, local flooding, bridge failures, falling local groundwater tables, and losses in critical wildlife habitat were all tied to excessive aggregate extraction. At the same time, declining water quality in rivers all over the state were linked to the more than three thousand abandoned mines. Cleanup of these mines, an almost impossibly expensive and time-consuming task, became a new priority and yet another drain on government resources.

Perhaps no industry in California has enjoyed the new spotlight less than agriculture. Grazing impacts were recorded throughout the state, with damage to the riparian corridor cited as a major cause of the decline of native trout species. The profligate overuse of pesticides and fertilizers on farmlands created serious local and regional water quality problems, especially in the state's water wells. The selenium pollution at Kesterson Reserve, caused by a system that encouraged pouring cheap irrigation water on marginal soils, was a public relations nightmare for the agricultural industry as well as the government that supplied it with water. But nothing focused the spotlight as much as the drought years of 1987–1992. It was during these years that urbanized California woke up to the haves versus the have-nots in the state's water picture. Decreased runoff, increasing demand for water to support declining wildlife and fisheries, and increases in urban demand have produced a fundamental challenge to agriculture's previously sacred stranglehold on more than 80 percent of the developed surface water in the state.

The convergence of political, environmental, and economic circumstances of the last 25 years has brought California's rivers to a confluence. The following chapters describe how and why land uses at issue today have an impact on rivers.

RELEVANT READINGS

California State Lands Commission. 1993. *California's Rivers: A Public Trust Report.* Sacramento: California State Lands Commission.

Davis, M. L. 1993. *Rivers in the Desert: William Mulholland and the Inventing of Los Angeles.* New York: HarperCollins.

Hagwood, J. J. 1981. *The California Debris Commission: A History of the Hydraulic Mining Industry in the Western Sierra Nevada of California, and of the Governmental Agency Charged with Its Regulation.* Sacramento: U.S. Army, Corps of Engineers.

Palmer, T. 1982. *Stanislaus, The Struggle for a River.* Berkeley, Los Angeles, and London: University of California Press.

————, ed. 1993. *California's Threatened Environment: Restoring the Dream.* Washington, D.C.: Island Press/Planning and Conservation League Foundation.

————. 1986. *Endangered Rivers and the Conservation Movement.* Berkeley, Los Angeles, and London: University of California Press.

Reisner, M. 1986. *Cadillac Desert: The American West and Its Disappearing Water.* New York: Viking.

Reisner, M., and S. Bates, 1990. *Overtapped Oasis: Reform or Revolution for Western Water.* Washington, D.C.: Island Press.

Worster, D. 1985. *Rivers of Empire: Water, Aridity, and the Growth of the American West.* New York: Pantheon Books.

ELEVEN

Mining and the Rivers of California

INTRODUCTION

The birth of the golden state is inextricably linked to its mining industry. The discovery of placer gold in Sierran streambeds spurred the most significant immigration event in the history of California. By land and by sea, people from all over the world flocked to California, creating the first of many waves of newcomers and establishing the roots of our diverse culture. The exaggerated reports of vast wealth and the hectic pace of immigration played a major, if not decisive, role in the unusually rapid approval of California's statehood.

Since the initial discovery of gold, California's mining industry has grown and diversified. Today, gold makes up only about 17 percent of the value of nonfuel minerals produced within the state. Unlike the wild and glamorous 1800s, today's mining industry is dominated by the production of more mundane mineral resources. The state's insatiable need for building materials has fueled a boom in mining operations that produce decidedly *un*glamorous commodities such as cement, sand and gravel, and crushed stone. These products make up about half of the value of all nonfuel mineral (used loosely here) production in the state, totaling approximately $1.3 billion annually.

Throughout its history in California, the mining industry has maintained a complex and often dysfunctional relationship with the state's rivers. Water is involved in almost all types of mining, whether as a necessary ingredient for production or as a waste product. Because of this, mining has had and still has a universally negative impact on the state's rivers. Of the many mining techniques that have been used or are currently being used in California, three stand out as perhaps the most detrimental for the state's rivers. The first, hydraulic mining, was active during the latter part of the nineteenth century. By washing mountains of sediment into the central Sierran rivers, this technique led to a complete reconfiguration of the Sacramento River and the Sacramento/San Joaquin Delta. Although enjoined more than a century ago, the impacts of hydraulic mining are still apparent today. The second major impact stems from the innumerable abandoned mines that are currently discharging some of the state's most seriously polluted fluids directly into the rivers. Many of these mines have no owners and have been dumped on the government, producing a costly bureaucratic and economic headache that is far from being cured. The last of the major impacts associated with mining stems from the state's largest mining industry, sand and gravel. Today, hundreds of operators are extracting aggregate from the floodplains and channels of the state's rivers. These seemingly innocuous, low-tech operations have produced dramatic changes in river behavior and have pitted mine operators against farming, urban, and environmental interests.

HYDRAULIC MINING: 1853–1884

The impact of gold mining on the rivers of California is unprecedented. As most California schoolchildren know, James Marshall discovered gold at Sutter's sawmill on the South Fork of the American River in January 1848. Within a year, a gold rush that transfixed the world was in full swing. For the first few years miners found abundant quantities of gold in the riverbeds of the central Sierra Nevada. All of this placer gold had been concentrated in these deposits by hydraulic segregation. The exceptionally high density of the gold particles raised their critical shear velocity over material of comparable size (chap. 3), causing it to accumulate in sand-filled scour pools at meander bends or adjacent to bars. The gold's high density also tended to keep it in the traction carpet during high discharge events of coarse bedload streams. This allowed the gold to infiltrate between the stationary, coarse material of the streambed, effectively trapping it in the pore spaces between large clasts. The early placer gold miners quickly recognized the reasons for the irregular distribution of placer gold within river sediments, becoming some of the first practicing hydrologists and sedimentologists of the state.

Within the first year of the gold rush, the easily accessible gold was mined out of the Sierran streams. As the search for in-stream placer gold intensified and more and more miners arrived in the Sierras, groups began to organize their efforts on a larger and larger scale. They often built dikes or small check dams to divert the river during the summer and fall, leaving the gravels bare and easy to process. Although these small-scale diversion dams had immediate, short-term impacts on the Sierran rivers, the overall effects were usually erased by erosive high winter flows.

As the easily accessible placer gold began to play out, miners logically began to search for other sources of gold. By accident, they stumbled upon ancient river channels that contained gold trapped in the same kind of sediments that they were currently mining in the Sierran rivers. These channels, which are more than 40 million years old, were formed by rivers that flowed out of the Idaho/Nevada/Utah region and across a relatively subdued ancestral Sierra Nevada range. Known as the Eocene *auriferous gravels*, these deposits are widespread in the Yuba, Bear, and American River drainages of the central Sierra Nevada.

At first, the proven methods of shovel, pick, and wheelbarrow were used to mine the auriferous gravels. Intense weathering had made these ancient deposits soft and easy to work. However, the relatively small amount of gold within the gravels made them unprofitable to mine using traditional methods. Soon, however, the miners devised increasingly ingenious methods, usually involving water, to extract the gold. Ultimately, the invention of the canvas hose and later the sheet metal pipe allowed miners to impound water upstream of their diggings and transfer it under great hydraulic head until it was sprayed forcefully against the canyon walls with huge nozzles called monitors.

During the 1860s and on into the 1870s, the monitors washed away entire hillsides in the Sierra Nevada (fig. 11.1). The runoff from these operations was processed through large sluices, which allowed the segregation of the gold from the gravels. The sediment-laden discharge from these operations was fed directly into the rivers of the Sierra. Few worried about the response of the rivers to this dramatic increase in sediment supply. This may have been in part because the outwash from the early hydraulic mining operations was fed into small creeks and tributaries. In average runoff years this excess load overwhelmed the competence and capacity of these drainages, leading to dramatic local aggradation or ponding of the sediment. By trapping sediment in the tributaries, the impacts on the larger trunk river systems went unnoticed.

The first portent of changes to come arrived in January 1862 when locally heavy rainfall in the Sierra Nevada moved mining sediment out of the tributaries into the main trunk rivers and eventually out into the Central Valley. Even without the addition of mining sediment, these floods would have been devastating. In the Central Valley, the growing farming communities discovered that they had built on an active floodplain. All of the Central Valley rivers overtopped their natural levees, and most manmade levee systems also failed. The torrents of water that came rushing out of the Sierras also carried a significant fraction of the hydraulic mining debris with it. Along with the floodwaters, mixtures of mud, sand, and cobbles poured onto the floodplains of the Central Valley. Upstream almost all of the diversion dams and canals that were set up to supply water

Fig. 11.1. Hydraulic mining activity during the 1800s added 1.5 billion cubic feet of sediment to the rivers of the central Sierra Nevada. *Top*: This was accomplished by directing high-pressure streams of water against gold-bearing ancient gravel deposits. Photograph from Gilbert 1917. *Bottom*: The sediment-laden runoff was collected in sluices, processed for gold, and discharged into large tailings piles or directly into local creeks, rivers, and drainages. Photograph from Ferrer 1990; originally supplied by the Siskiyou County Historical Society.

to the hydraulic mining operations were destroyed and washed into the Central Valley. It was a deluge of Noachian proportions.

The coarse mixtures of debris that made it onto the floodplains of the Central Valley were an initial clue that something was amiss in the Sierran watersheds. Usually, the water that flows onto the floodplain is dominated by fine-grained suspended load. Coarse-grained material is typically confined to the highly competent, deeper portions of the channel (chaps. 3, 4). The excessive amount of sediment supplied to Central Valley rivers overwhelmed their capacity. This led to deposition of material within the active channels, eventually reducing their ability to contain coarse sediment. The bedload-rich flows that spread across the floodplains simply could not be contained by the aggraded river channels. The source of this excess sediment was, for the most part, the outwash from hydraulic mining.

Although a number of farmers raised concerns about the debris coming out of the Sierras in 1862, their complaints were largely ignored, perhaps because the worst drought of the nineteenth century set in immediately after the flood. From late 1862 through 1865, the Sierras received well below average precipitation. Although there was usually enough water to run the hydraulic mining operations, the rivers lacked the competence and capacity necessary to transport outwash sediment to the Central Valley. Without direct, measurable evidence, it was hard to prove that hydraulic mining was responsible for the flooding of 1862. In addition, much of the growth in the farming communities was due, in part, to the gold rush itself. Thousands of miners consuming farm goods made some farmers reluctant to bite the hand that they fed.

Hydraulic mining in the Sierras boomed during the late 1860s and on throughout the 1870s. Each year, increasing amounts of debris would inundate farms during local flooding events. Soon the entire Central Valley was engaged in a giant private levee-building operation to keep floodwaters out of farms and cities. In the long run, the haphazard development of levees actually exacerbated flooding problems. By reducing the ability of floodplains to absorb excess discharge, levees increased peak flood flows, creating greater flooding damage in reaches with small or natural levees (chap. 15). Then, in the winter of 1875, the impacts of hydraulic mining came to a deadly climax. The towns of Yuba City and Marysville had suffered severe damage from the floods of 1862 and 1865. In response, each town created levees along the Yuba River to protect itself. In the years between 1865 and 1875, the Yuba River had aggraded rapidly to a point where the riverbed itself lay above the town. On January 19, 1875, a moderate flow within the sediment-choked Yuba River channel breached these levees, sending a torrent of coarse debris through the town and practically destroying it. When the waters receded, it was clear to all that the debris was derived from the mining operations. The next winter was nearly a carbon copy. Although Marysville and Yuba City had built even higher levees to protect themselves, the farms and towns that lay downstream, including Sacramento, were hard hit by flooding associated with channel aggradation.

The impacts of hydraulic mining sediment were not simply concentrated in the towns and farms that lay along the base of the Sierras. Prior to 1865, river traffic from San Francisco had been able to travel up into the Feather River drainage as far as the town of Oroville. This rapidly became impossible. Even travel to Sacramento was becoming increasingly difficult, especially within the delta region where channel aggradation had been widespread and flooding had become a regular occurrence. The coarse sediment load of the Feather River was so great that it actually dammed the Sacramento/Feather River confluence. This sediment dam created widespread flooding of farms that were far removed from any direct contact with the hydraulic mining sediment.

As the flooding and levee building continued in the Central Valley, there was increasing political and, eventually, legal pressure to end hydraulic mining. The verbal battles of the late 1800s between farmers and miners bear a striking resemblance in tone and language to those between loggers and environmentalists today. Eventually, a series of lawsuits (the first environmental lawsuits in California history) were filed by the farming interests against the mining operations. In the fall of 1882, Edward Woodruff filed suit against the North Bloomfield Mine of the Yuba River seeking an end to hydraulic mining. Judge Lorenzo Sawyer presided (agonized?) over this case for eighteen months. In 1884, he issued a permanent injunction against hydraulic mining on the Yuba, bringing a virtual end to one of the most destructive resource extraction techniques ever practiced in California.

Long-Term Impacts

In 1892, Congress created the California Debris Commission. The commission, composed largely of U.S. Army Corps of Engineers officers, was charged with the task of clearing California's rivers of hydraulic mining debris, restoring navigation to the Sacramento River, and designing catchment systems that would allow hydraulic mining to resume. The latter task proved impossible on a large scale and was eventually abandoned. Following severe floods in 1902, 1904, 1906, and 1907, the Debris Commission began a valleywide dredging operation to enhance flood control and to increase the ability of the rivers to scour the mining debris.

Although dredging and levee construction were devastating to aquatic and riparian communities (see chap. 15), in many respects the Debris Commission's efforts worked fairly well. Dredging in the Sacramento River

channel coupled with the effects of channel scouring through leveed portions of the river appeared to have restored the elevation of the riverbed
near Sacramento to its original level by as early as 1927. G. K. Gilbert, a
patriarch of North American geology and geomorphology, studied the mining debris problem in the Yuba and Sacramento River drainages. His results, published in 1917, represent one of the first and most-cited studies
of river responses to changes in sediment load. Gilbert postulated that the
mining debris would pass through the Sacramento River and Delta system
much in the same way a flood wave would. He wrote,

> the flood of mining debris is analogous to a flood of water in its mode of
> progression through a river channel. It travels in a wave, and the wave grows
> longer and flatter as it goes. Where the channel is too small to contain it, the
> water wave spreads out over adjacent lands, and the volume thus escaping
> from the channel is temporarily stored, so as to regulate the flow at points
> below. The debris wave differs from the water wave in the fact that its over-
> flow volume is permanently lodged outside the river channel, and in the ad-
> ditional fact that the material of the wave is not homogeneous. From the
> start there is a sorting of the debris, and the finer parts ravel faster than the
> coarser. (Gilbert 1917:31)

Based on this model and measurements of a time series of low-flow elevations of the riverbed, Gilbert predicted that the rivers would return to
their previous elevations by 1967.

Several recent studies have tested Gilbert's hypothesis. The low-flow elevations of the Sacramento and Yuba rivers show a "recovery" of the Yuba
by around 1950 and the Sacramento by 1930. The conclusions of these
studies were that Gilbert was generally correct in his predictions and that
sediment loads of these rivers had presumably returned to normal. However, a more detailed analysis of this question by L. Alan James of the University of South Carolina has produced some surprising and contradictory
results.

Careful surveys of mountain streams and rivers that were affected by hydraulic mining debris indicate that a substantial volume of this material is
stored in terraces and floodplains. Aggradation of the rivers in the late
1800s was so dramatic that a range of potential new sediment storage sites
were created and filled. Following the cessation of hydraulic mining, incision left much of this material behind, perched above the rivers in various sediment reservoirs. Today, this material is being slowly reworked and
added to the sediment load of these mountain rivers (fig. 11.2A, B).

In addition, the restoration of the elevation of river channels in the Central Valley is an artifact. First, the higher sediment loads of the tributaries
feeding into the Sacramento are muted by the elaborate network of reservoirs that intercept this sediment. Measurements indicate that many of
these dams are trapping large amounts of mining debris. The accumula-

Fig. 11.2A. Impacts of hydraulic mining on California rivers. *Above*: Widespread aggradation associated with the passage of the hydraulic mining sediment wave on the Yuba River led to repeated flooding during the late 1800s and early 1900s. Photograph from Gilbert 1917.

tion of this material is reducing the life expectancy of these dams (chap. 16). Second, the response of the residents of the Central Valley to the deposition of mining debris on the floodplains was to build levees. When those levees failed, the residents simply built higher ones. As discussed in chapter 15, the construction of levees increases stream power and competency, leading to scouring of the channels. Thus the river system has not naturally "healed" itself as some predicted it would. Instead, a large portion of the mining debris that was delivered to the Central Valley has, in reality, yet to be moved through since it is currently stored beneath the levees and on the floodplains.

Hydraulic mining led to a complete reorganization of the rivers that flow out of the central Sierras and a reconfiguration of the Central Valley, forever (in human terms) altering the landscape of California. In all, more than 1.5 *billion* cubic feet of mining debris were washed into the Central Valley from just five rivers, with more than 40 percent coming from the Yuba River alone. Perhaps the most ironic aspect of this episode in California history is that despite extraordinary investments in large engineering operations to capture gold, very little was actually recovered. Estimates vary, but the total value (in today's dollars) of the gold produced by hydraulic mining between 1860 and its ignominious end in 1884 is less than

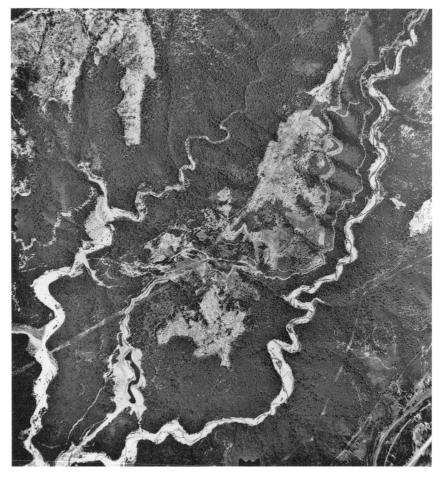

Fig. 11.2B. *Above*: 1972 aerial photograph of Bear River and Greenhorn Creek, Tahoe National Forest. Note hydraulic mining scars in the center of photo. The light-colored channel fills consist of quartz-rich hydraulic mining sediment, indicating that the river has yet to recover and that a large volume of sediment remains trapped in the Bear River drainage. USDA aerial photograph.

$5 billion, a fraction of the value of just one year's oil production in California. No single industry in the history of California has generated more long-term environmental damage for such a meager economic return.

ABANDONED AND INACTIVE MINES

Following the initial discovery of placer gold in the streams of California, prospectors began combing the hills for a greater variety of minerals. Unlike placer gold, most of the mineral riches were buried underground, requiring the excavation of large pits or the construction of elaborate underground mines. Many of these mines exploited gold-rich quartz veins within the Mother Lode Belt of the Sierran foothills. Others focused on the extraction of silver, copper, zinc, lead, tungsten, and more. In part, growth of hard rock mining in California was tied directly to placer gold mining. Mercury, or quicksilver, was used to separate gold during the milling process. By a providential twist, while the Sierras turned out to be rich in gold, the Coast Ranges were rich in the mercury needed to process it, spawning a coeval mercury rush in the late 1800s.

Of all the resource industries in California, hard rock mining has traditionally shown itself to be perhaps the most myopic. Spurred on by the giveaway of public lands promoted by Congress in the 1872 Mining Law, this capital-intensive, high-risk industry has been governed by an overriding need for immediate return on investments. Because all ore bodies are limited in scope, every mining operation is destined for extinction. Only the very largest mining companies can afford long-range planning; but the need to extract as much profit as quickly as possible governs most operations.

According to R. Humphries of the State Water Resources Control Board, there are more than 15,000 abandoned hard rock mines within the state's borders. The companies that developed these mines got in, got their resources, and got out as quickly as possible. In an attempt to minimize the expense of their operations, they either walked away without conducting any cleanup and reclamation (effectively transferring it back to the government) or, commonly, sold the property to a buyer who usually lacked the resources to clean it up. Today, around 2,500 of these mines have the potential to create significant environmental problems. Of these, approximately 150 are actively discharging some of California's most polluted fluids directly into its rivers and streams.

Most of the abandoned problem mines are associated with copper and mercury mining, although some zinc, silver, and gold mines are important contributors. The copper mines that have proven the most troublesome are located in the Lake Shasta area and the foothills of the Sierra Nevada; the most significant mercury mines are in the Clear Lake area of the Coast Ranges. One of the state's most notorious polluters is Iron Mountain Mine near Lake Shasta. Despite Herculean efforts to clean up this mine (including its listing as one of the state's top EPA Superfund sites), the Regional Water Quality Control Board estimates that the mine and its tailings supply 1,200 pounds of copper and 800 pounds of zinc to Keswick Reservoir *every day*. Besides their mineral content, the common link in problem mines is their location in generally high rainfall areas and steep terrain. When oxygenated groundwater and rainfall seeps into abandoned mines or passes through tailings piles, a number of chemical reactions take place (fig. 11.3A, B). Where the mines or their dumps contain considerable amounts of iron sulfides (like pyrite, FeS_2), the water oxidizes the minerals, converting them to sulfates and iron oxides. This process releases many of the toxic metals that were previously bound up in the sulfide minerals. In addition, the water/rock reactions acidify the water and intensify the leaching of metals. Because the problem mines are located in areas that receive significant rainfall, the reaction products are regularly discharged into local streams.

The cocktail that is produced by these reactions, known generally as *acid mine drainage,* can be lethal to local aquatic communities. The impact is highly variable, because natural environmental factors like total discharge, dissolved oxygen concentration, temperature, and hardness and alkalinity of the water all influence the toxicity of the drainage when it mixes with surface waters. In general, base metals like copper, zinc, and lead become much more toxic to fish and other aquatic life in water that has higher temperature, contains reduced dissolved oxygen, and is acidic. Since most mine drainage is already extremely acidic (often with a pH of less than 2–3; as low as 0.5 at Iron Mountain Mine), it lowers the pH of the receiving waters, increasing the overall toxicity of the discharge.

The impact of mine drainage also varies greatly during the year. It is logical to assume that during low-flow periods, such as summer and fall, the ability of base flow to dilute the effects of acid drainage would be reduced and the impacts would be greatest. However, most studies have found that the most significant pollution takes place during high rainfall events in the winter and spring. Apparently, the slow movement of fluids through mine tailings and the ore-bearing rocks that surround the mine allows a great deal of contact between groundwater and reactive minerals. When high rainfall comes, the infiltration of rainwater displaces the groundwater that has been in contact with the sulfides. This acidic, older groundwater is then discharged into local streams and rivers through a variety of pathways (fig. 11.4). In this way, plumes of acidic, metal-laden water pass through river systems immediately following storms and overwhelm the effects of dilution.

The response of aquatic communities to acid mine drainage is not universally the same. Many species bioaccumulate metals (i.e., store them in their tissues) until they reach a threshold of toxicity. For example, trout and salmon are much more susceptible to the buildup of toxic metals than many of the "less desirable" fish species, like bluegills. Similarly, there are significant differences within and between benthic invertebrates, algae, and bacteria. Despite these differences, the overall diversity of aquatic communities can be used as a general indicator of the biological health of a river system. Statewide monitoring programs generally show that the greater the amount of acid mine drainage, the lower the diversity of the aquatic

Fig. 11.3A. Iron Mountain Mine, Shasta County, one of the state's top EPA Super-fund sites. *Above*: Mine site illustrating runoff of material from mining area. Hold-ing ponds are incapable of preventing direct runoff into Keswick Reservoir.

Fig. 11.3B. *Above*: Tailings from older mine workings. Leachate from tailings is discharging into local streams and eventually into Keswick Reservoir, a major source of drinking and irrigation water in California. Photographs courtesy of Robert Matthews.

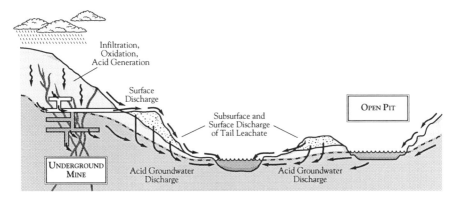

Fig. 11.4. Origin of acid mine drainage from underground and open pit mines in California.

fauna. In extreme cases, this leads to near-complete sterilization.

The impacts of mine drainage are not restricted to riverine biological communities. The top problem mines, like Iron Mountain, Mammoth, Balakala, Keystone, and Penn, discharge directly into the Sacramento and San Joaquin rivers. Besides poisoning an ever-dwindling salmon population, these mines supply toxic metals to the river system that provides water to two-thirds of the state's population. Unfortunately, although the wildlife impacts of acid mine drainage are well documented, it is presently unclear how much of an effect these mines have on the quality of the state's drinking water. State agencies have documented high levels of copper in the Sacramento/San Joaquin Delta. It has long been assumed that this excess copper is coming from the numerous abandoned copper mines in the Central Valley watershed. However, to date there have been no definitive studies that have been able to trace the copper back to these mines. In addition, it has been pointed out that farmers throughout the Central Valley apply tons of copper sulfate to their orchards every year. Runoff from farms has undoubtedly increased the overall copper content, but it is unclear how much. It is this kind of scientific uncertainty that clouds the acid mine drainage issue and keeps legions of lawyers employed.

The enactment of the California Surface and Mining Reclamation Act in 1975 coupled with increased enforcement of federal and state water quality standards should lessen long-term impacts of new hard rock mines. However, these new acts do not undo the damage of the past one hundred fifty years. The logical solution to acid mine drainage and the fouling of California's rivers is to clean up the abandoned mine sites and prevent further runoff. Like all environmental remediation efforts, it is far easier to set this as a goal than it is to carry it out. Cleanup of even a few dozen of the worst mines runs into the tens of millions of dollars, far outstripping government budgets. As noted above, it is difficult, if not impossible, for the various government agencies to place blame accurately for these mines. In many cases the mines have changed hands often, and, most commonly, the present owners lack the financial resources to effect any significant change. There is rarely a deep pocket to fund the cleanup operation. Rather, it appears that despite intense study and legal wrangling over the past 20 years, we are likely to see little significant reduction in the impact of mined land drainage.

IN-STREAM SAND AND GRAVEL MINING

According to California Division of Mines and Geology reports, there are over nine hundred companies in California that are involved in the extraction and processing of aggregate. The "ore" for the vast majority of these companies is the deposits of sand and gravel that occur within channels and on the floodplains and terraces of the state's rivers. Over the past 10 years more than a billion short tons of material have been removed. According to G. Mathias Kondolf of UC Berkeley, this may represent as much as ten times the amount of bedload supplied to rivers by the state's watersheds. The problems that arise from aggregate mining stem from the concentrated removal of material from stream channels and from pits located close to them.

Limited research has been conducted over the past few decades on the effects of in-stream mining both within and outside California. A number of rivers in California are changing in response to aggregate mining operations and are the focus of controversy. In northern California, the Russian River, Cache Creek (fig. 11.5A), Redwood Creek, Stony Creek, and a host of others are being actively mined with a range of adverse impacts. In southern California, the Santa Clara River, the Tujunga River (fig. 11.5B), and many of the rivers that drain the San Gabriel and San Bernardino mountains are also being mined. Some of the impacts from these operations have involved considerable damage to local bridges and other structures.

As I have stated throughout this book, the work that a river does includes eroding, transporting, and depositing sediment. The river's behavior and its form reflect a dynamic adjustment to sediment yields and discharge conditions. Not surprisingly, the extraction of sand and gravel from a riverbed disrupts this work. The complex feedback system that governs a river's response to these disruptions often ensures that the local removal of aggregate produces changes in river morphology and behavior over a significantly greater area than the extraction site itself.

The consequences of in-stream aggregate mining on rivers are reviewed

Fig. 11.5A. Aggregate mining operations. *Above*: Cache Creek, Yolo County. Widespread dry-pit active channel mining and bar-skimming operations have significantly altered the overall sediment budget of Cache Creek, threatening adjoining farm areas, groundwater, and local infrastructure (see text for discussion).

briefly here. More extensive treatments of this issue are contained in the articles and books listed in the Relevant Readings section at the end of this chapter. The impacts of aggregate mining on river systems are rooted in the tendency of miners to remove material at a rate that exceeds replenishment from upstream sources. The readjustment of a river to new local sediment budgets can lead to a number of changes in conditions within the channel and along the floodplain. These changes often prove to be detrimental to land uses that are completely unrelated to and, in many cases, quite distant from aggregate mining operations.

On-site Impacts

There are three general types of in-stream aggregate mining operations in California that have a significant impact on rivers. These are (1) *dry pit, active channel mining,* in which bulldozers, scrapers, and loaders excavate pits on ephemeral streambeds; (2) *wet pit, active channel mining,* in which draglines or hydraulic excavators remove material from below the water

Fig. 11.5B. *Above*: Terrace pit mining, shown here, attempts to avoid the active channel. However, during high flows braided rivers will usually break through berms that separate these pits from the active channel. As shown in the Tujunga Wash area of southern California, this can cause extensive downstream and up-stream damage. Photographs courtesy of Rand Schaal, pilot.

table or directly from a perennial stream channel; and (3) *bar skimming,* in which the tops of gravel bars are removed without excavating below the summer water table level. The usual approach to in-stream mining involves the development of one or more extraction pits within the river channel during the dry season (see fig. 11.5). Water that continues to move through the river is usually diverted around the pits by temporary berms. Aggregate material is often processed adjacent to or within the channel of the river. Aggregate mines are also commonly established outside the active stream channel on the floodplain or on adjacent river terraces. Depending on the depth of the pit and the elevation of the water table, these operations can be wet or dry.

The argument that many aggregate extraction companies make in defense of their industry is that they are exploiting a renewable resource. Ideally, as winter flows enter the pits, the sharp increase in channel size will cause a rapid decline in competence, leading to rapid deposition of sediment within the pit. Eventually, during the course of a winter, localized deposition should fill the pit and restore the original bed profile of the river without any long-term impacts.

In rivers where the total sediment budget is very large and aggregate extraction rates are low, the ideal notion of aggregate as a yearly renewable resource may be valid. However, in practice, this is rarely the case. Studies of a number of northern California rivers where estimates of bedload transport rates and sediment budgets can be accurately measured indicate that sand and gravel in most of the heavily mined rivers is being depleted at a rate far greater than it is being replenished. Although California's watersheds are notorious for their high sediment yields, the state's innumerable dams and the urbanization of the watersheds have decreased the amount of coarse sediment available to most rivers. On many of the larger rivers, such as the Sacramento and the San Joaquin, the ability of dams to trap sand-sized and coarser material means that the most desired material has been virtually eliminated from the rivers (see chap. 16). This plus the tendency of operators to extract as much material as the market will bear—without regard to replenishment—has led to environmental and structural damage throughout the lower reaches of rivers in California.

During winter flows, the temporary berms that aggregate operators construct to channel low water flows are inevitably eroded, allowing the thalweg of the river to reestablish itself through the extraction pit. Where the pit is separated from the main river channel by a temporary dike, high flows will occasionally break through and pass through the mined area. As noted above, once a river colonizes a pit, the channel geometry is greatly altered (fig. 11.6). During intermediate flows, the upstream end of the pit will behave in a manner similar to a knickpoint. The steeper gradient generates an increase in stream power and competence, leading to headward

Water enters pit during rising stage

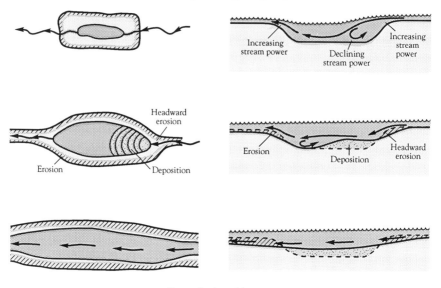

Smoothed profile

Fig. 11.6. Evolution of in-stream aggregate mining pits as winter flows enter pit. Note headward erosion of the pit and downstream erosion as the river attempts to reestablish original profile.

erosion as the river attempts to smooth its overall longitudinal profile. Immediately downstream of this knickpoint, the sharp decrease in slope and the increase in channel cross-sectional area of the pit reduce stream power, leading to rapid deposition of bedload (the filling of the pit envisioned by gravel operators). Downstream of the extraction pit, the flow has excessive stream power, leading to scouring of the channel downstream. Thus through headward erosion and downstream scour the river attempts to smooth the disruption that a pit forms in its profile.

Scouring and filling of aggregate pits is not limited to the thalweg or axis of any channel. The excess competence at the upstream and downstream ends of the pit causes the channels at both ends of the pit to scour laterally as well as vertically. Where bank materials lack cohesion or stabilizing riparian vegetation (the usual case adjacent to mining operations), intense bank erosion and eventual bank collapse can occur.

The on-site or near-site consequences of the development of aggregate pits are well documented in California's rivers. Perhaps the most spectacular example comes from Tujunga Wash where it empties into the San Fernando Valley near the Verdugo Hills. In this region, Tujunga Creek spreads out into a braided ephemeral river at the head of an alluvial fan. Extensive aggregate mining operations at the head of this fan produced large pits more than 50 to 75 feet deeper than the thalweg of the creek. Historically, low flows occupied a single channel on the fan. Unreinforced berms diverted these flows away from the pits. During the winter of 1969, the entire southern California region was inundated by a series of intense, closely spaced storms. Since braided rivers balance their energy expenditures by occupying multiple channels, it should have been no surprise to local mine operators when the creek broke through the berms and flowed into the aggregate extraction pits. Intense headward erosion took place where flows entered the pits, lowering the channel by more than 14 feet for more than one-half mile upstream. This erosion caused the failure of three major bridges by undercutting their abutments and led to the complete destruction of six homes. Since the pits acted as a trap for sediment, intense scouring also occurred downstream, eventually cutting into and destroying a very long section of four-lane highway.

The events seen in 1969 at Tujunga Wash have been repeated throughout California on numerous occasions. The usual casualties of a river's attempt to reestablish its gradient appear to be bridges, roads, and water supply lines, which are destroyed by scouring. CalTrans has been actively studying methods to limit the effects of in-stream mining on bridges in a number of California rivers. At the time of this writing, CalTrans was concerned about possible mining-induced failure of one hundred fifty bridges on twenty-five streams in California (reported in the *Sacramento Bee,* March 14, 1994). Costly remedial measures are almost always required, including, in some cases, the relocation of roadways and construction of new bridges. Ironically, like hydraulic mining and abandoned mines, the cost of these remedial measures is often far greater than the value of the resource extracted.

In addition to potentially devastating impacts on local structures, there are immediate on-site impacts to riparian and aquatic communities. Most aggregate mining operations process material adjacent to their extraction pits. The screening and crushing of the material can be done using both wet methods, in which water is mixed with the aggregate as it is sieved, and dry methods, in which the aggregate is simply passed through dry. Both processes can increase turbidity in the mined river, reducing water quality. This, in addition to the direct removal of gravel from the riverbed, destroys local spawning habitats as well. Finally, few mining operations stick solely to the active channel. Many colonize terraces or floodplains adjacent to the channel. These operations inevitably involve removal of riparian growth. The loss of a riparian canopy increases water temperature and reduces habitat diversity, while increasing the susceptibility of the banks to erosion.

Off-site Impacts

Although aggregate extraction operations create considerable local impacts, the regional or cumulative effects of these operations have produced the most political and economic fallout. The cause of the problem is straightforward: widespread removal of sand and gravel coupled with sediment-trapping dams have reduced supply to the point that rivers that have highly competent flows during the winter are cannibalizing their own sediment previously stored in floodplains and terraces (chaps. 3, 6).

Rivers move a great deal of coarse bedload each year during high-flow stages. As the sediment moves downstream it pauses in point bars, longitudinal and transverse bars, and channel beds. As sediment is removed from these bars, it is replaced by sediment from upstream. This transport process can involve centuries of alternating deposition and transport before a particle either makes it to the ocean or is lost to the system by disaggregation or deposition on a floodplain. However, when sediment supply is cut off, the various temporary storage sites lose their yearly replenishment, becoming progressively depleted until they eventually disappear.

The inability of a river to replenish the bars and channels with coarse sediment initiates regional channel degradation. On the lower Russian River, where aggregate extraction has produced numerous local impacts, the cumulative effects are extreme. Some channel reaches that once contained large, actively migrating gravel bars are currently devoid of any significant bedforms and the river is flowing directly over bedrock. Because winter flows within the river have excess stream power and competence, bank erosion has become a serious problem in many portions of the Russian River drainage, threatening the destruction of several major bridges and claiming an ever-increasing share of the farmland. Channel lowering, which has exceeded 20 feet in some areas, has exacerbated this problem (fig. 11.7).

Along Cache Creek in Yolo County west of Sacramento, 50 years of aggregate mining can be directly correlated to channel incision of more than 12 feet (fig. 11.8). There is a positive side to this bed lowering: the flood capacity of the channel has been expanded, lessening the need for more flood control structures. However, this bed lowering has been the center of considerable regional squabbling. Along with the widespread exposure of bridge abutments and the erosion of fertile farmland, there has been a significant impact on the groundwater of the region. As noted in chapter 5, in alluvial valleys the surface of the groundwater table is tied closely to the elevation of adjoining rivers. As channels incise to greater depths, the groundwater surface lowers along with it. In this way, a significant volume of potential groundwater storage is lost. At the same time, the gradient of the groundwater table becomes steeper, leading to a more rapid draining of the local aquifer.

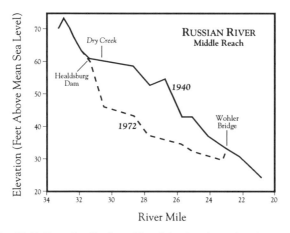

Fig. 11.7. Longitudinal profile of the Russian River below Healdsburg Dam depicting channel incision associated with heavy in-stream gravel mining between 1940 and 1972. (Modified from Collins and Dunne 1990.)

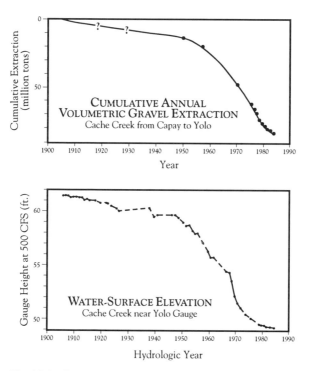

Fig. 11.8. Comparison of gravel extraction rates and bed surface lowering along Cache Creek in Yolo County. (Modified from Collins and Dunne 1990.)

Groundwater degradation associated with channel incision appears to have affected the Cache Creek drainage. Prior to streambed lowering, a well-developed riparian corridor and a number of nut and fruit orchards lined the creek. All of these depended on a relatively shallow groundwater table. By lowering the groundwater table more than 12 feet, portions of the riparian vegetation and some orchards were lost. This increased bank instability accelerated the processes of lateral erosion in some areas.

Disruption of groundwater supplies in some mined areas is not associated solely with channel incision. In many drier areas, a substantial portion of the local recharge of aquifers comes directly from the river itself (chap. 5). The dredging of material from a riverbed along with on-site processing of sediment can produce extensive turbidity within streams and rivers. During low summer and fall flows, deposition of the clay and silt on and within existing gravel beds can reduce their permeability and, ultimately, their ability to recharge aquifers.

SUMMARY

Throughout the history of California, its mining industry and its rivers have been in conflict. Hydraulic mining of the last century poured so much debris into the rivers of the Sierra Nevada that it permanently altered (in human terms) the state's largest watershed. More than a century of get-in-and-get-out hard rock mining has dotted California with abandoned mines that discharge some of the state's most toxic waters directly into the rivers. Today, in-stream aggregate mining is carting away the sediment that makes up the beds and banks of rivers throughout California, destroying bridges and ruining aquifers, wildlife habitat, and spawning grounds. By all standards, mining in California has not been river-friendly.

The impacts of hydraulic mining and in-stream aggregate mining are rooted in their effect on the sediment budgets of rivers. Hydraulic mining, which had its heyday between 1853 and 1884, dramatically increased the sediment budgets of central Sierran streams and rivers. The addition of abundant coarse material overwhelmed the capacity of the rivers, causing them to temporarily store sediment by deposition within channels and floodplains. The loss of channel capacity and aggradation of river courses led to widespread flooding of Central Valley towns and farms. In the more than 100 years since the end of hydraulic mining, most rivers have reestablished their original gradients. This has occurred because dams have trapped mining sediment and levees have promoted channel scouring. Much of the original sediment that was hydraulically mined remains trapped behind dams, within terraces, and on the leveed floodplains of the Central Valley watershed.

The impacts of in-stream aggregate mining are associated with the tendency of operators to mine sediment at a faster rate than it is replenished. Urbanization and the widespread damming of California's watersheds have reduced overall sediment budgets. Excessive aggregate mining leads to sediment-starved rivers. Excess stream power causes a number of on-site and off-site impacts. When rivers occupy aggregate pits during winter flows, they attempt to smooth their profiles by headward erosion at the upstream end of the pit, deposition of sediment within the pit, and scour of the downstream end of the pit. This smoothing of the profile leads to bridge and road failures upstream and downstream of the mining site. On a regional scale, the decline of sediment yields leads to widespread incision, bank erosion, and loss of gravel bars. The incision lowers local groundwater tables, and bank erosion reduces riparian cover.

The impact of hard rock mining on the rivers of California is associated primarily with the failure of mining companies to control the discharge of acid mine drainage into rivers. Oxidation of ores by percolating rainwater releases toxic metals and acidifies groundwater or tailings leachate. Subsurface flow and surface discharge directly from mines and tailing piles can reduce or eliminate aquatic diversity in nearby streams and rivers. The intensity of this sterilization depends on background environmental conditions as well as the amount and type of acid mine drainage.

RELEVANT READINGS

Bull, W. B., and K. M. Scott. 1974. "Impact of Mining Gravel from Urban Streambeds in the Southwestern United States." *Geology* 2: 171–174.

Collins, B., and T. Dunne. 1990. *Fluvial Geomorphology and River-Gravel Mining: A Guide for Planners, Case Studies Included.* California Division of Mines and Geology Special Publication no. 98.

Evoy, B. L., and M. Holland. 1989. *Surface and Groundwater Management in Surface Mined-Land Reclamation.* California Division of Mines and Geology Special Report no. 163.

Ferrer, T. 1990. "The Liberty Gold District." *California Geology* 43: 123–133.

Gilbert, G. K. 1917. *Hydraulic-Mining Debris in the Sierra Nevada.* U.S. Geological Survey Professional Paper no. 105.

Hagwood, J. J. 1981. *The California Debris Commission: A History of the Hydraulic Mining Industry in the Western Sierra Nevada of California, and of the Governmental Agency Charged with Its Regulation.* Sacramento: U.S. Army, Corps of Engineers.

James, L. A. 1989. "Sustained Storage and Transport of Hydraulic Gold Mining Sediment in the Bear River, California." *Annals of the Association of American Geographers* 79: 570–592.

———. 1991. "Incision and Morphologic Evolution of an Alluvial Channel Recovering from Hydraulic Mining Sediment." *Geological Society of America Bulletin* 103: 723–736.

Kondolf, G. M. 1993. "The Reclamation Concept in Regulation of Gravel Mining in California." *Journal of Environmental Planning and Management* 36: 395–406.

Kondolf, G. M., and W. V. G. Matthews. 1993. *Management of Coarse Sediment on Regulated Rivers*. California Water Resources Center Report no. 80.

Kessler, S. E. 1994. *Mineral Resources, Economics and the Environment*. New York: Macmillan.

Sandecki, M. 1989. "Aggregate Mining in River Systems." *California Geology* 42: 88–94.

Scott, K. M. 1973. *Scour and Fill in Tujunga Wash: A Fanhead Valley in Urban Southern California, 1969*. U.S. Geological Survey Professional Paper no. 732-B.

Sengupta, M. 1993. *Environmental Impacts of Mining: Monitoring, Restoration, and Control*. Boca Raton: Lewis.

TWELVE

Logging California's Watersheds

INTRODUCTION

When John August Sutter arrived in California in 1839, he recognized great economic opportunity in the vast natural resources of the region. With a large land grant in hand, he established a fort and thriving farming community near the confluence of the Sacramento and American rivers. In order to supply lumber to his community and to expanding markets in the San Francisco region, Sutter established a sawmill near the small town of Coloma along the South Fork of the American River. When Sutter's foreman, James Marshall, discovered gold in the mill's tailrace, this seemingly insignificant enterprise generated a chain reaction that dramatically altered the economic, cultural, and natural landscape of California (see chaps. 10, 11). It is fitting that this sawmill that so significantly changed California would also prove to be the birthplace of the modern, large-scale logging industry. The gold rush in the Sierra Nevada and the Klamath Mountains, followed later by a silver rush in Nevada, created an insatiable demand for timber. According to the California Department of Forestry and Fire Protection, at the time that Sutter built his mill, California produced approximately 20 million board feet of lumber per year. Less than 30 years later, California was producing nearly 700 million board feet annually, with most going to the mining operations. Today, California produces about 5 billion board feet of timber—about half of the state's total demand.

The first gold miners to reach the Sierra Nevada were opportunistic loggers with no regard for such issues as sustained yields, habitat degradation, and cumulative impacts. Wherever gold was mined, the riparian corridors were simply stripped of trees to build sluice boxes, shelters, wagon roads, and towns. Although this produced considerable local impacts, the limited extent of in-stream placer gold kept these impacts from affecting a wider region. When the hydraulic mining industry began to expand in the late 1850s, the impacts of logging became more widespread. Hydraulic mining of the Sierran watersheds required extensive water diversions. According to county records cited in the *California Water Atlas*, by 1867 more than 4,000 miles of ditches and canals had been constructed to feed the mining industry, with Nevada County alone containing more than 1,000. Wherever these ditches went aboveground, they were constructed of wood. In addition, the processing facilities of the hydraulic mining operations were all constructed of lumber. At the same time that the hydraulic mining operations were creating a large demand for lumber, other forms of mining were starting to expand. Hard rock mines, particularly the gold mines of the Mother Lode and the silver mines of Nevada, needed large timbers to shore up shafts and adits. In particular, large, old-growth stands of trees were needed for the heavy beams of these mines. The volume of timber needed for both hydraulic and hard rock mining was far greater than local forests and local operators could supply. To meet this need and the expanding needs of growing urban areas, sawmills and large timber operations cropped up throughout the forests of California. Today, visitors to Lake Tahoe can still see the effects of the mining-induced expansion in the logging industry. Prior to the silver rush in Nevada, the forests surrounding Lake Tahoe were dominated by pines. During the late 1800s the entire basin was logged to support the silver mines of Virginia City. Mark Twain describes the beauty and extent of these pine forests (to which he accidentally set fire) in his book *Roughing It*. The successional forests that grew back following the removal of the pines now consist of a mix of fir and pine, with the firs dominating the wetter regions. Poorly adapted to the local climate, firs are dying in great numbers throughout the Tahoe basin as a result of the drought of 1987–1992.

Although hydraulic mining is the source of the catastrophic changes that took place in Central Valley and Sierran rivers during the late 1800s, there is little doubt that the widespread logging and grazing of this period exacerbated these changes. Most often, the impact of logging and grazing was felt on a local scale. High erosion rates, declining water quality, and loss of resources spurred the legislature to develop some of the first environmental laws to protect watersheds from "reckless and wasteful cutting" and "the ravages of goats and sheep."

Today, grazing (discussed in chap. 13) and timber harvesting are regulated by a welter of local, state, and federal laws and agencies. Despite this regulation, these industries are still dogged by controversy over their land use management practices. For the rivers of California, the removal of vegetation from steep, upland watersheds inevitably alters the supply of run-off and sediment. The cumulative effects of these alterations can be either subtle or dramatic, but they always produce changes in the morphology and behavior of rivers as they adjust to their new conditions. These changes and their attendant impacts on fisheries, wildlife, water supply, flood control, and infrastructure cause much of the concern about logging.

The influence of logging practices on the rivers of California has been the subject of research over the past two decades. Most of the attention has been focused on the highly erosive watersheds of the North Coast Hydrologic Region, which supply two-thirds of the state's total timber production, although logging impacts in the Sierra Nevada have been receiving an increasing share of the spotlight. The role of the timber industry in changing the rivers of California can be broken up into two general classes: *on-site impacts* and *cumulative impacts.* On-site impacts are associated directly with the types of logging techniques used, the physiographic, geologic, and climatic setting of the logging operations, the amount of vegetation removed, and, perhaps most important, the construction of roads. Cumulative, or off-site, impacts reflect the aggregate effects of many past and present timber operations within any given watershed.

TIMBER HARVEST TECHNIQUES

According to the California Department of Forestry and Fire Protection (CDFFP), approximately 250,000 to 300,000 acres of timber will be logged annually during the 1990s. Although the amount of potentially productive forests is split roughly evenly between private landowners and the national forests, timber harvesting is most intense on private land. Because logging on private lands generally exceeds the rate of new growth, the contribution of timber from private land will decline over the next few decades as the mature and old-growth stands are progressively removed. This will shift the future emphasis to national forest lands.

The amount of timber removed during logging operations is highly variable. According to R. Johnson of the CDFFP, contrary to popular belief, less than 5 percent of the logging in California involves complete removal of all trees, or true clear-cutting. The selective cutting of trees of a certain age or size dominates most logging operations. Although not strictly clear-cut, almost all trees are removed in most tracts. A small number of seed or shelter trees are usually left for a period of time after initial logging to promote growth of new trees. These trees are removed when new stands become established. This is, in effect, a form of clear-cutting, only spread out over a period of 10 to 15 years.

The drought of 1987–1992 and the associated fires killed vast numbers of trees in California, primarily within the Sierran forests. In the Lake

Fig. 12.1. Tractor yarding, the most damaging harvest method, involves dragging felled trees downhill to a yarding area. Compaction of large, downhill-converging road and skid trail network produces high sediment yields and runoff. Photograph by author.

Tahoe basin, more than half of the standing timber has died or is unlikely to survive due to drought-induced insect infestation. This has brought an increased emphasis on salvage logging, which involves selective removal of dead or dying trees.

The techniques used for extracting trees vary throughout California. The most common and least expensive approach is *tractor yarding* (fig. 12.1). Here, a network of skid trails are cut through a forest to allow tractors to drag felled trees downhill to a central yarding area where the logs can be transferred to logging trucks. This skid trail network is usually quite extensive and involves clearing vegetation from significant amounts of land. In steep areas that are difficult for tractors to negotiate or in regions that are considered environmentally sensitive, *cable yarding* is often used. There are two general variations on the cable yarding technique (figs. 12.2, 12.3). The first, called *highlead cable yarding,* involves attaching cables to felled trees and dragging them uphill to a central yarding area or landing. The second, called *skyline cable yarding,* involves suspending the felled trees above the ground as they are hauled uphill to the yarding area. Both highlead and skyline cable yarding are more expensive and of-

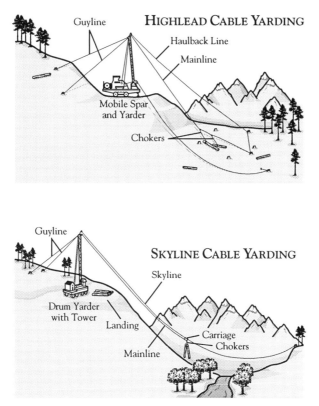

Fig. 12.2. Examples of cable yarding techniques used in environmentally sensitive areas. Highlead cable yarding (top) drags logs uphill to a yarding area, while skyline cable yarding (bottom) suspends logs aboveground, causing less soil compaction and vegetation disruption. (After Huffman 1977.)

ten unfeasible in selective cut or salvage operations. Although not used extensively in California, cable yarding is one of the most popular techniques in the Pacific Northwest. Within the last decade, a few companies in California have started to use helicopters for transporting logs to yarding areas. This method is by far the most expensive but is growing in popularity in extremely rugged or environmentally sensitive regions.

ON-SITE IMPACTS

The on-site impact of most logging operations on rivers stems from two separate but related activities: vegetation removal and road building. This impact is summarized in figures 12.4 and 12.5. Although the scorched

Fig. 12.3. Example of logging techniques in the Redwood Creek drainage near Redwood National Park. Areas where highlead cable method (*C*) was used are located below main haul road (*A*). Tractor yarding method (*T*) was used in area at the top of photo. Note downhill convergence of tractor yarding skid trails on yarder sites. Photograph by David Van de Mark, from Huffman 1977.

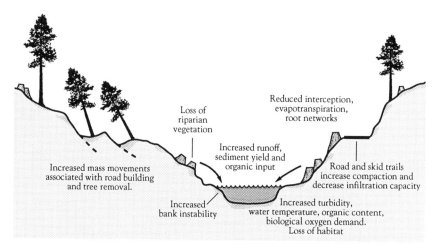

Loss of riparian vegetation

Reduced interception, evapotranspiration, root networks

Increased runoff, sediment yield and organic input

Increased mass movements associated with road building and tree removal.

Road and skid trails increase compaction and decrease infiltration capacity

Increased bank instability

Increased turbidity, water temperature, organic content, biological oxygen demand. Loss of habitat

Fig. 12.4. Generalized depiction of impacts associated with logging in environmentally sensitive areas.

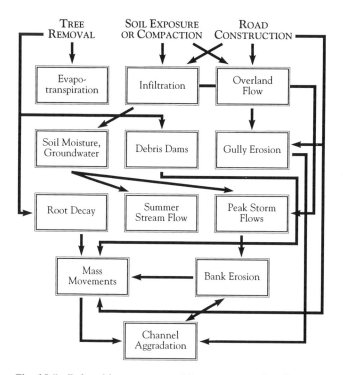

Fig. 12.5. Related impacts caused by tree removal, soil exposure and compaction, and road construction within logged areas. Note complex negative feedback within system.

earth look of most recently logged areas would logically point to vegetation removal as the cause of the most significant impact, it is the road building that ends up doing most of the damage to river systems.

Logging Roads and Skid Trails

Virtually all logging areas have some kind of road network. The density of this road network, the steepness of the terrain, the stability of the slopes, and the erodibility of the soil all combine to make roads major sediment and runoff contributors.

The construction of logging roads and skid trails exposes bare soil to raindrop impact. As noted in chapter 6, the kinetic energy of raindrops is exceptionally high and capable of dislodging soil particles. When this occurs on steep slopes, raindrop impact alone can rapidly dislodge and transport soils that lack cohesion. Although raindrop impact is capable of dislodging abundant soil material on these roads, overland flow creates most of the erosion. The repeated passage of tractors and logging trucks over skid trails and roads compacts the soil. Studies have shown a wide variation in the amount of compaction, depending on the texture and composition of the soils as well as the overall soil moisture content. In general, clay-rich, wet soils compact most intensely (up to 40% or more) and dry sandy soils the least. Compaction usually takes place through the crushing or filling of pores within the soil. As porosity decreases, the permeability and, ultimately, the infiltration capacity are reduced. Thus when rain falls on these roads their infiltration capacity is quickly exceeded, producing voluminous Horton overland flow.

Because most logging takes place in relatively steep, rugged terrain, roads and skid trails must, by necessity, also be steep. Overland flow moving across these steep roads leads to rapid erosion, eventually forming rills and gullies. The impact of this overland flow in most logging sites is reduced by decreasing the slope of the roads and placing water bars to deflect flow off the road. Where proper road construction techniques have been ignored, these roads will actually become small streams during runoff events, discharging sediment-laden waters directly into creeks and drainages located on the site.

In addition to increasing erosion, logging roads and skid trails promote the formation of mass movements (fig. 12.6). The cutting of logging roads on steep hillsides often leads to an overall increase in the slope, which, in turn, increases the shear stress (chap. 6). If additional logging roads discharge onto slopes above these roads, they can contribute to this problem by increasing the weight of the slope (increased shear stress) and decreasing its internal shear resistance. This is one reason that landslides increase in frequency following logging in steep, inherently unstable sites.

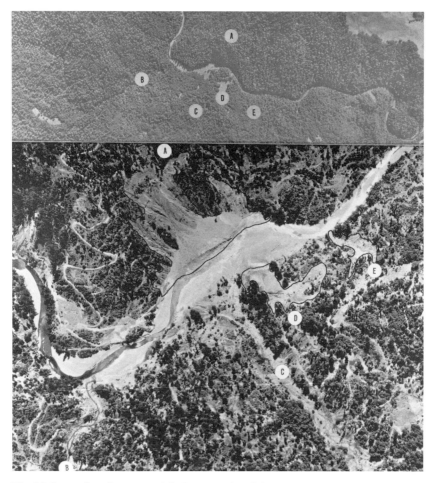

Fig. 12.6. 1948 and 1972 aerial photographs of the Mattole River approximately 5 miles upstream of Honeydew, Humboldt County. Mass movement *A* was not visible in 1948 but became a significant producer of sediment by 1972. Note aggradation and loss of riparian vegetation in streams *B, C.* Sediment may be stored in these tributaries until large runoff events. Slides *D* and *E* are new. Photograph from California Department of Water Resources 1974.

Sediment and runoff from logging roads, along with increased production of sediment from landslides, feed into local drainages and creeks. The magnitude of the impact on these drainages depends on the natural instability of the logging site and, perhaps more important, the logging technique used. Tractor yarding creates the most damage within watersheds. Because tractors drag felled trees over the landscape, there is widespread

soil compaction associated with road networks. In addition, tractor yarding inevitably involves road networks that converge downhill toward a
yarding area. Overland flow across these converging skid trails act much
like a drainage network. As skid trails merge, overland flows are summed,
greatly increasing the stream power of the flow and its ability to erode material. Although highlead cable yarding also involves extensive skid trails
that converge on a yarding area, its impact is less for three reasons: (1)
road and skid trail networks are usually smaller; (2) dragging logs across
the soil by cable rather than tractor compacts the soil less; and (3) the
skid trails converge uphill toward the yarding area, rather than downhill
(figs. 12.1, 12.2, 12.3). The latter causes overland flow on the skid trails to
be dispersed across the hill, rather than concentrated. Because few, if any,
skid trails are involved in skyline cable yarding and helicopter yarding,
these techniques tend to produce the least on-site impacts.

Vegetation Removal

The on-site impacts of the removal of vegetation vary in intensity, depending primarily on their proximity to river and stream courses and the
steepness of the terrain. When logging takes place within the riparian corridor, there is intense disruption of streams and rivers (fig. 12.4). Many
studies have shown that the removal of the forest canopy in riparian areas
leads directly to increases in water temperature, organic content, biological and chemical oxygen demand, and local sediment yields. In addition,
the removal of this vegetation reduces habitat diversity along the stream
banks and promotes bank instability and erosion.

In some logging operations, slash and large logs are either deposited
directly in creeks and rivers (currently prohibited) or washed in during
high runoff events. Although the presence of this material increases the
diversity of the riverine habitat, excessive amounts create local debris jams
(fig. 12.7). These jams, which can be found virtually anywhere logging has
occurred, act as small dams that inhibit fish migration and degrade spawning habitat. Because the debris jams typically trap sediment, they form a
localized knickpoint in the longitudinal profile of the river (chap. 7). By
trapping sediment, the jams promote erosion and channel scouring immediately downstream and deposition and channel widening upstream,
often leading to bank erosion and further disruption of the riparian corridor. The failure of these debris jams during high-flow events can create
substantial flooding downstream as well as damage to structures that are
struck by the larger debris.

When logging takes place away from the riparian corridor, the removal
of large trees can significantly alter the runoff and groundwater characteristics of the site's slopes. Some studies have shown total soil moisture is ac-

Fig. 12.7. Debris jams, typical of logged regions, prevent upstream migration of fish, alter sediment supply, and form local flooding hazards during high runoff events. This particular debris jam occurred at a bridge crossing of Soquel Creek in the town of Aptos in the winter of 1982. It caused widespread flooding upstream and downstream of the bridge. Failure of these kinds of debris jams can be catastrophic. Photograph courtesy of Gerald Weber.

tually increased by the removal of trees because evapotranspiration is decreased. This, in turn, decreases the infiltration capacity and promotes the generation of excessive runoff. The removal of trees and vegetation also decreases the amount of direct interception as well as potential sites for surface retention and ponding, further enhancing the runoff from the site.

The deep root structures of large trees play a vital role in maintaining slope stability in very steep watersheds. It takes years for roots to decay following logging, but a number of studies have shown that mass movements increase once root decay progresses to a certain level. In conjunction with the road and skid trail network, this can lead to significant long-term increases in the formation of mass movements on some sites. Where these mass movements enter directly into tributaries and stream courses, severe local impacts can occur.

Although it seems logical to expect that the removal of vegetation would greatly increase the erosion rates of soils, it turns out to have a relatively minor overall affect. The piles of slash that are commonly distributed throughout the logged sites and the rapid regeneration of shrubs and grasses act to intercept overland flow and raindrops on logged sites, reducing the amount of erosion that takes place.

CUMULATIVE IMPACTS OF LOGGING ON RIVERS

For much of this century and the last, the default view of logging operations was that because each operation represented such a small portion of the overall watershed, the net impact of any one harvest was really quite small and unworthy of much concern. However, over the past three decades, foresters, loggers, and environmentalists have become increasingly aware of the importance of assessing off-site and downstream impacts of logging operations. Known generally as cumulative impacts, these are the long-term effects that accumulate over many years within a watershed. Because they represent the sum of numerous past and present logging operations, the nature of these impacts may be substantially different from on-site impacts.

Through lengthy legal wrangling, it has been determined that the California Environmental Quality Act (CEQA) in conjunction with the Forest Practices Act (FPA) dictates that Timber Harvest Plans must assess the overall impacts of their project in light of past, present, and future projects. Nearly 20 years after CEQA was enacted, most individuals connected with the logging industry would agree that determining the contribution of an individual operation to cumulative impacts has proven an elusive and politically contentious goal. Although often difficult to quantify, the cumulative impact of logging in California's watersheds can be tied directly to changes in the parameters that fundamentally control river behavior: runoff and sediment yield.

Changes in Runoff Characteristics

Intuitively, it would seem that the removal of vegetation and the construction of logging roads should substantially alter the overall runoff characteristics of a watershed. After all, the compaction of soils and the reduction in evapotranspiration and interception should increase the volume of runoff that occurs as overland flow and as subsurface flow. The rapid delivery of this runoff to drainages and streams throughout a logged watershed should logically increase peak flows and decrease the lag time of storm hydrographs. Ideally, the magnitude of these changes should be a function of the size of the watershed and the amount of the area that is cut over.

This subject has been studied in watersheds and forest experiment stations across the country, producing a bewildering array of seemingly contradictory results. Researchers have documented both increases and decreases in lag times and peak flows following logging. Most studies, however, have demonstrated that there is a general decrease in the lag time of peak flows following storm events, confirming the preconceived notions. Most studies have also shown that peak discharges and total flow volume tend to increase for high-frequency events (recurrence intervals of less than 20 years). The surprising result of studies conducted in the Pacific Northwest and northern California is that logging operations do not appear to substantially increase the peak discharge or total volume of the very large storm events (those with recurrence intervals greater than 20 years). The reason behind this counterintuitive result may lie in the differences in the way watersheds produce runoff from storms of varying intensity. During low-intensity storm events, runoff appears to be strongly influenced by the relatively small proportion of the watershed that contains soils likely to produce abundant overland flow. Thus in watersheds that are logged, the amount of disturbed area producing high runoff is likely to have a great influence on the characteristics of the watershed's hydrograph. In contrast, during very large storm events, all of the watershed is involved in producing runoff, not just the select areas containing disturbed or impermeable soils. Widespread production of Horton overland flow, saturation overland flow, and subsurface flow essentially masks the local contributions from roads and skid trails.

An additional complication in predicting cumulative effects arises where snowmelt makes up a significant portion of the total runoff. As discussed in chapter 8, most storms in California produce rainfall to high altitudes at the beginning, followed by a lowering of the snow level as cold air fills in behind the front. Where a substantial, ripe snowpack exists, warm rains can produce very large amounts of runoff. Where rain falls directly on a snowpack, such as in clear-cut areas, melting and runoff can take place rapidly. In contrast, a dense forest canopy intercepts rainfall, delaying storm flow peaks associated with snowmelt. The reverse effect controls runoff during the spring. As any skier knows, areas lacking forest cover will accumulate the most snow and retain it longer into the spring. The high albedo, or reflectivity, of open areas limits the amount of absorbed solar radiation, reducing the rate of snow ripening. In this way, clear-cut logging can act to reduce and delay peak discharges associated with spring snowmelt runoff.

The long-term cumulative impact of changes in discharge characteristics is difficult to predict. Presumably, the magnitude and frequency of large flows will be generally unchanged by logging. Since these catastrophic runoff events play a vital role in shaping the landscape in forested watersheds, it can be argued that there is likely to be little net long-term effect from logging. However, if equilibrium channel patterns and cross sections are primarily formed during bankfull stage conditions (chap. 4), then increases in the peak discharge and decreases in lag times of these more frequent flows should cause channels to adjust. These adjustments may involve channel scouring and widening to accommodate the larger flows. It is impossible, however, to resolve these changes without considering the second major variable, sediment supply. As is shown below, logging produces increases in the sediment yield of a watershed. Geomorphic changes that occur in response to logging are driven by the combined effects of changes in runoff characteristics and increases in sediment supply.

Changes in Sediment Supply

Most forest research literature that attempts to evaluate cumulative impacts of logging focuses on the effects of excess sediment production. Direct measurements of runoff from logging sites have shown staggering increases in sediment yield, commonly ten times more than in unlogged areas. Most of the increase in sediment supply comes from a dramatic increase in the total suspended load, although severalfold increases in bedload are also not uncommon. The overall amount of increase in sediment yield depends on the amount of area that is cut over, the inherent erosivity of that area, and the type of harvest techniques used, with tractor yarding generating the highest sediment yields.

High rates of uplift, high rainfall, and unstable rock types in the North Coast Hydrologic Region produce exceptionally high natural sediment yields. Logging and grazing within these watersheds have exacerbated the existing conditions, producing some of the highest sediment yields measured in the United States. As noted in chapter 6, erosion and sediment transport is variable in space and time. Although the intermediate discharge events shape the equilibrium condition of a river, the rare events have produced dramatic alterations in the channel and floodplains of most of these watersheds. The length of time it takes for a river system to recover or return to equilibrium conditions depends on the size and frequency of the flows that follow these rare events and the length of time until the next rare event.

As with the generation of runoff, most sediment in undisturbed watersheds is derived from a relatively small but highly unstable proportion of the total watershed area. Logging within a watershed increases the number of sites that produce high sediment loads and the amount of sediment supplied from preexisting unstable sites. However, like the natural systems, logged areas vary greatly in the amount of sediment they supply. A relatively small percentage of the logged areas tend to supply a disproportionate amount of the total sediment associated with logging. The impacts of these unstable areas need to be identified and carefully monitored to assess cumulative impacts.

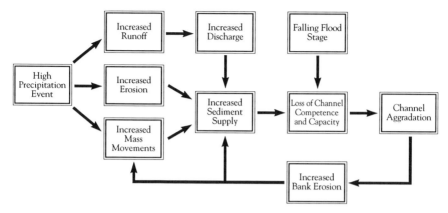

Fig. 12.8. Feedback in response to exceptionally large rainfall events. (Based on research conducted in north coast watersheds.)

Regardless of its source, once sediment enters a watershed's drainage network, its transport is driven largely by the rare runoff event. Work on watersheds of the north coast (chap. 7) indicate that the sediment derived from unstable or logged sites tends to overwhelm the capacity of adjacent creeks and drainages. In this way, during "normal" years material is effectively trapped and stored within the low-order tributaries of a watershed in much the same way hydraulic mining gravels were stored in Sierran tributaries during drought. The local effects of this storage can produce considerable water quality and wildlife habitat impacts.

When the unusual runoff event does arrive, a chain reaction of events occurs which can significantly alter the watershed (fig. 12.8). First, intense rainfall not only produces high runoff rates but also increases the amount of erosion and the contribution of sediment from mass movements (fig. 12.6). Second, the highly competent, sediment-charged flows are capable of entraining material stored in the low-order tributaries and transporting it to the main trunk river. Failures of debris jams are common during these events and can augment the total sediment load significantly. Third, the simultaneous arrival of this exceptionally large wave of sediment in the main trunk river produces an effect similar to that recorded during the period when hydraulic mining debris was being discharged from the Sierra Nevada. As the stage of the trunk river begins to fall, competence and capacity are rapidly exceeded, leading to widespread deposition of material and reduction in channel capacity through rapid channel aggradation. Fourth, the loss in channel flow capacity causes the river to expand laterally by eroding its banks. In steep, unstable drainages like those of the north coast, this bank erosion will commonly trigger widespread mass movements, further increasing the sediment load of the river and promoting widespread channel aggradation and more landsliding.

Given the nature of the chain reactions that take place during very rare flooding events, it is difficult to accurately assess the cumulative impacts of logging within a watershed. Because sediment tends to pond in low-order drainages, monitoring programs may only detect local impacts that have little effect on the overall watershed. Since the probability is low that extreme events are going to occur during any monitoring period (see chap. 14), a true measure of the impacts is unlikely to be made. Rather, most monitoring programs require extrapolation of effects from low-flow to high-flow conditions. However, since the scouring of material ponded in tributaries only occurs when runoff of suitable intensity is reached, the relationship between more frequent, less intense storms and less frequent, more intense storms is not likely to be linear. For these reasons it seems prudent to overestimate the effects of increased sediment supply when assessing cumulative impacts.

Changes in Water Quality and Wildlife Habitat: Salmon versus Lumber

The cumulative downstream effects of logging on wildlife habitat have been generating controversy in California for the past thirty years. The precipitous decline in salmon and other fish stocks has been the centerpiece of debate during this time, although other threatened or endangered species such as the spotted owl have played important roles. The loss of salmon represents a major problem for one of the state's important fisheries industries. In addition, the salmon is an important "indicator" species, reflecting the overall health and biological diversity of the state's rivers. The collapse of salmon populations in California is associated most directly with dams and other water diversion projects that have either degraded habitat or acted as barriers to migration (chap. 16). However, dams play much less of a role in the loss of salmon in the Klamath River and other north coast drainages. In this region, where much of the fall-run Chinook salmon spawns, it appears that the cumulative effects of a century of logging and, to a lesser extent, grazing and mining, have been the principal cause of population decline.

The high sediment yield and high runoff associated with logged areas conflicts with the very specific spawning needs of salmon (see fig. 12.4). Adult female salmon deposit their eggs in redds, or nests, within the coarse gravels of riffles and bars. Over a period of twenty to forty days the eggs mature within riffles and bars, becoming alevins or sack-fry. These sites are ideal for maturation of the salmon eggs for two principal reasons: (1) the relatively swift currents that move across riffles and bars maintain the low temperatures and high dissolved oxygen levels necessary for salmon egg development; and (2) their coarse, porous nature allows the eggs to reside within the interstices in the gravel, protecting them from entrainment by the rapid currents while maintaining water circulation. Once mature, the salmon emerge from the redds (at this point they are known as fry or juveniles) and feed on insects and plankton until they are large enough to make the trip to the Pacific Ocean and begin the long cycle of growth before returning to spawn in their natal stream.

Only a minor portion of the sediment that is supplied to rivers by erosion in logged regions is coarser than sand. Typically, two-thirds or more of the sediment is dominated by fine-grained silt and clay, or the material that is moved as suspended load. As the capacity and competence of river flows are exceeded by input of sediment from logged sites, fines are deposited on or infiltrate into the gravel-covered riffles and bars of the river, reducing water circulation within the coarse sediment. Where widespread aggradation takes place following major runoff events, the sites of accumulation of gravel are often completely buried by fine sand and silt, completely eliminating salmon spawning grounds.

The on-site impact of removal of riparian vegetation has a cumulative effect as well. Salmon eggs and fry require stable, cool water temperatures and high levels of dissolved oxygen. The removal of the forest canopy within riparian corridors can lead to increases in overall water temperature of the river. In addition, where logging practices allow large amounts of debris to collect within the river channel, the organic decay and excess nutrient load leads to excess biological and chemical oxygen demands, often to the detriment of salmon eggs and fry.

SUMMARY

For much of this century the primary goal of most federal and state agencies that have managed the forests of California has been to maximize the extraction of resources. The result has been widespread overharvesting of the state's forests and the predictable alterations in the character of the state's rivers and the degradation of wildlife habitat, species diversity, and water quality. The impacts of logging on the state's rivers can be divided into two general groups: on-site impacts directly associated with timber harvesting techniques and the watershedwide cumulative impacts of logging practices in the past, present, and future.

The magnitude of on-site impacts from logging is associated with the environmental factors of the site, including climate, geology, physiography, and soils, as well as the type of harvesting techniques used. Tractor yarding, with its widespread skid trails that converge downslope, creates the most impact. Highlead and skyline cable yarding produce less significant impacts, and helicopter yarding causes the least disturbance. Road building and the development of skid trails increase the amount of runoff and sediment yield from the site. Road building and tree removal appear to increase the development of mass movements as well. Logging within or adjacent to the riparian corridor is most detrimental to fisheries and wildlife habitat due to increases in water temperature, turbidity, and biological and chemical oxygen demand.

Off-site, or cumulative, impacts within logged watersheds are difficult to measure and predict. Most studies have documented decreases in lag times associated with the amount of logged area. For small and intermediate runoff events, logging appears to increase the total volume of runoff as well. However, logging appears to have no significant impact on the total volume of runoff arising from very large storm events. The largest cumulative impact from logging comes from sharp increases in sediment yield. During high runoff events, higher sediment yields can lead to widespread channel aggradation, which, in turn, can lead to lateral migration of channels and increased rates of landsliding.

Declining salmon stocks in the north coast region are tied, in part, to the local and cumulative impacts of logging. High sediment yields have led to accumulation of fines within spawning gravels. In addition, increases in water temperature and declining oxygen levels associated with logging have contributed to the degradation of spawning habitats.

RELEVANT READINGS

California Department of Forestry and Fire Protection. 1988. *California's Forests and Rangelands: Growing Conflict over Changing Uses.* Sacramento: California Department of Forestry and Fire Protection.

California Department of Water Resources. 1974. *Management for Fishery Enhancement on North Coastal Streams.* Sacramento: California Department of Water Resources.

Hewlett, J. D. 1982. *Principles of Forest Hydrology.* Athens: University of Georgia Press.

Huffman, M. E. 1977. "Geology for Timber Harvest Planning, North Coastal California." *California Geology* 30: 195–201.

Lisle, T. E. 1989. "Sediment Transport and Resulting Deposition in Spawning Gravels, North Coastal California." *Water Resources Research* 25: 1303–1319.

Meehan, W. R., ed. 1991. *Influences of Forest and Rangeland Management on Salmonid Fishes and Their Habitats.* American Fisheries Society Special Publication no. 19, Bethesda, Md.

Newcombe, C. P., and D. D. MacDonald. 1991. "Effects of Suspended Sediments on Aquatic Systems." *North American Journal of Fisheries Management* 11: 72–82.

Reid, L. M., and T. Dunne. 1984. "Sediment Production from Forest Road Surfaces." *Water Resources Research* 20: 1753–1761.

Salo, E. O., and T. W. Cundy, eds. 1987. *Streamside Management: Forestry and Fishery Interactions.* Institute of Forest Resources Contribution no. 57, University of Washington, Seattle.

Swanston, D. N., and F. J. Swanson. 1976. "Timber Harvesting, Mass Erosion, and Steepland Forest Geomorphology in the Pacific Northwest." In *Geomorphology and Engineering*, ed. D. R. Coats, 199–221. New York: Dowden, Hutchison and Ross.

Walling, D. E., T. R. Davies, and B. Hasholt, eds. 1992. *Erosion, Debris Flows and Environment in Mountain Regions.* IAHS-AISH Publication, vol. 209.

Wright, K. A., K. H. Sendek, R. M. Rice, and R. B. Thomas. 1992. "Logging Effects on Streamflow-Storm Runoff at Caspar Creek in Northwestern California." *Water Resources Research* 26: 1657–1667.

THIRTEEN

Food Production and the Rivers of California

INTRODUCTION

Like the timber industry, the birth of large-scale agriculture in California can be tied to the gold rush. Thousands of hungry miners with money to spend spawned a dramatic, overnight expansion in farming and grazing operations. As the gold played out and the miners began to leave the Sierras, many recognized the potentials of the fertile, largely unoccupied floodplains of the Central Valley and chose to explore new careers in agriculture.

By the turn of the century, California was well on its way to becoming one of the world's most productive agricultural regions. Despite numerous setbacks from floods and droughts, large-scale, highly successful farming operations were established throughout the Sacramento/San Joaquin, Salinas, San Gabriel, and San Fernando valleys. At the same time, cattle and sheep grazing had spread to all corners of California, including the deserts of the Mojave and the lush bottomlands of the north coast. The economy of California, which had been accelerated by the discovery of gold, was now dependent primarily on its agricultural industry. The urbanization of California and the associated rise in manufacturing and tourist jobs during the middle and latter parts of this century have diminished the relative economic importance of grazing and agriculture. Today, only a small percentage of the state's population is directly involved in agriculture. In addition, the $20 billion in basic agricultural goods produced yearly in California represents less than 3 percent of the state's total economy. Of course, many of these goods are remanufactured and transported, adding to the overall value. Yet as any elected official in California will note, despite its diminished economic importance, the agricultural industry retains considerable political clout.

The transformation from the small farms and ranchos of the early 1800s to the large-scale agriculture of today has altered the rivers of California more than any other industry. Nearly one-third of the land area of California is devoted to agriculture. Almost one-third of that area is covered by crops that require irrigation. The demand for irrigation consumes 80 percent of the state's developed surface water and an unknown but probably greater percentage of the state's groundwater. The innumerable dams and canals that feed this demand have led to a wholesale reorganization of the state's rivers, altering their hydrology, biology, and water quality.

Although the largest impact of the agriculture industry on the state's rivers has been indirect, involving changes in hydrologic conditions some distance from where the extracted water is eventually used, there are a number of impacts that are more directly attributable to the nature and extent of agricultural practices. Grazing and tilling lead to excessive rates of erosion and runoff, and alterations of the riparian corridor cause changes in bank stability and wildlife habitat. The widespread use of pesticides and fertilizers degrades water quality throughout the state, as do salt and toxic metal-bearing return flows from agricultural drains. The problem of nonpoint source pollution from farms cannot be overstated. The Environmental Protection Agency (EPA) has estimated that agriculture is the single largest contributor of nonpoint source pollutants nationwide, with nutrients and sediment having the greatest impact on the nation's rivers and water supply. This legacy is no better in California: the State Water Resources Control Board estimates that agriculture generates more than half the water pollution in the state today.

It is unreasonable to suggest that the damming of California's rivers and all large-scale transfers of water are an impact driven solely by agricultural demands for irrigation water. Urban water needs and flood control interests play an important role. Because of this shared responsibility, the impacts of dams and diversions are reviewed in a later chapter (chap. 16). Here, I examine the more direct impacts of the agricultural industry on the rivers of California, including the effects of overgrazing and farm runoff.

THE GRAZING OF CALIFORNIA'S WATERSHEDS

California's cattle and sheep industry has grazed the state's wildlands for more than two centuries. According to the California Department of Forestry and Fire Protection, approximately half of the 85 million acres of today's wildlands are being actively grazed by sheep and cattle operations. The impacts of grazing on the wildlands and rivers of the West and in California in particular are currently the focus of acrimonious debate. In virtually every area where grazing is occurring or has occurred in the

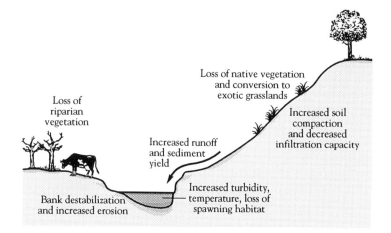

Fig. 13.1. Generalized depiction of impacts of grazing on rivers.

recent past, there are tangible, easily recognizable impacts. In general, the nature of these impacts can be divided into two groups (summarized in fig. 13.1): (1) erosion and increased runoff associated with removal of cover and the compaction of soils, and (2) deterioration of the riparian corridor and aquatic habitats where grazing activities are closely adjacent to stream courses.

Grazing-induced Increases in Erosion and Runoff

Throughout the western United States, livestock grazing has been recognized as a significant contributor to increased sediment yields and runoff from watersheds. In almost all cases, the root cause of these increases is overgrazing and the conversion of native vegetation to grassland vegetation. Although both sheep and cattle graze on California's wildlands, there has been a long-term decline in sheep production. Today, grazing operations in California are dominated by two types: cow-calf operations, in which a brood cow herd is maintained year-round, and stocker operations, in which weaned calves from cow-calf operations are purchased for grazing on range and pasture and then sold to feedlots.

The cause-and-effect relationship between overgrazing and increases in sediment loads and discharge in rivers is remarkably similar to the effects of logging in watersheds. As in logging operations, the excessive removal of vegetation by grazing reduces interception and evapotranspiration, leading to an increase in runoff from all sources. In a process that is analogous to the effects of tractor yarding, grazing leads to compaction of soils and declines in infiltration capacity. A full-grown beef cow ready for market typically weighs more than 1,000 pounds. Depending on the texture and wetness of the soil, these future Big Macs can produce compaction comparable to that measured on logging roads and skid trails. Wet, boggy areas are particularly susceptible to damage. Once compacted, the combination of limited vegetative cover and low infiltration capacity produces high rates of erosion associated with overland flow and raindrop impact (chaps. 5, 6). Perhaps the most notable impact is the tendency of overgrazed areas to develop extensive gully networks. The initiation of gullying is typically associated with compaction and vegetation removal that occurs along animal trails. Like the skid trails formed by tractor yarding, these pathways often converge downslope, usually toward watering areas such as streams, wells, or springs. Their convergence increases the impact of overland flow, enhancing the formation of rills and gullies. Once established on grazed slopes, gullies can take decades to recover, even if grazing is stopped completely.

Although overgrazing by itself can produce significant increases in sediment supply and runoff, a variety of natural and human-made factors make the watersheds of California uniquely prone to grazing impacts. In the more rugged watersheds of central and northern California, grasslands are typically located on highly unstable soils and rock types. For example, in the Eel River drainage, which is known for its extensive stands of redwoods, there are large grassland areas that are currently being grazed. The lack of trees in these areas is associated with the occurrence of extremely expansive, serpentine-rich soils that are prone to erosion and, more important, mass movements. Grazing on these unstable lands only exacerbates their natural instability and has led to sharp increases in local sediment supply.

Two centuries of grazing and the introduction of a variety of exotic grasses have eliminated almost all of the native grasslands in California. The exotic grasses that cover the foothill and valley areas used for grazing are all annuals that dry up in the late spring and early summer as soil moisture declines. Unlike stocker operations, cow-calf operations need to hold a brood stock over from year to year. Thus during the late summer and early fall when little forage grows within the grasslands of central and southern California, grazing pressures can become severe. To compensate, some operators move their herds to the higher elevations, typically in the Sierra Nevada, where shrubs and perennial grasses within wet meadow areas provide adequate forage. Yet these wet meadows have been shown to be the most sensitive to disruption from grazing animals.

One of the most significant effects of grazing has come from the conversion of chaparral, hardwood, and sagebrush lands into grasslands. As any plant ecologist will point out, the native grasses, shrubs, and trees of

California are the best adapted for the state's unique climatic and soil conditions. These native species do the best job of intercepting runoff and stabilizing soils. Unfortunately, most grazing operators and the agencies that regulate them view native trees and brush as a nuisance that inhibits the production of exotic annual grasses. The conversion of the watersheds of California to grasslands began during the gold rush as Sierran herds were expanded to meet increasing demands for meat and hides (in reality, Native Americans routinely burned areas of California to enhance or maintain grasslands, although not on the scale of that seen in the nineteenth and twentieth centuries). During the 1940s, a concerted effort was launched by state and local governments to significantly "improve" California's rangelands by eliminating vast tracts of native vegetation. Between 1945 and 1973, landowners were paid by the government to clear nearly one million acres of hardwood woodland (primarily oak) for range improvement. Herbicides were applied throughout the state to improve "degraded" (i.e., natural) sagebrush lands and other brush-covered lands so that exotic annual grasses could become established. Today, a moratorium on some herbicide use has increased the emphasis on controlled or prescribed burning to improve degraded lands, although air quality restrictions often limit these as well.

The naturally unstable soils, the limited ability of the landscape to support livestock during the summer months, and the widespread conversion of California's wildlands to rangelands dominated by exotic annual grasses have made the state's watersheds highly susceptible to alteration from overgrazing. Regrettably, there are insufficient data to determine the extent of the problem on federal lands here in California. However, the U.S. Soil Conservation Service estimates that more than 40 percent of California's private grazing land is undergoing accelerated erosion due to overgrazing and poor management. Because of the lack of basic data, it is difficult to gauge the overall impact of the increases in runoff and sediment load on the rivers of California.

Grazing in the Riparian Corridor

The most contentious issue facing the livestock industry is associated with grazing in the riparian corridor. More than any other activity, this pits the grazers against a number of competing interests, including water supply, fisheries, and wildlife habitat management.

During the summer months, as annual grasses dry out or are removed by grazing, livestock will increase grazing pressures within riparian corridors, where green forage and a reliable supply of water are located. Grazing in and adjacent to stream courses can affect all components of a river system through reduction or even complete removal of riparian vegetation. Livestock commonly feed on the seedlings of trees and brush within the riparian corridor, severely inhibiting regeneration. Perhaps more important are the effects of trampling. The large, sharp hooves of cows break down the banks of streams, expose the roots of trees and shrubs, and crush seedlings.

The consequences of the destruction of the riparian corridor can be far-reaching for both wildlife habitat and related land uses. As in logged areas, the riparian corridor forms an important buffer between a creek and the surrounding slopes of the watershed. Sediment-laden overland flow may be intercepted by the dense vegetation that is located along stream courses, muting its effects on the river systems. By removing riparian vegetation, the impacts of runoff and sediment yields from surrounding grazed lands are enhanced, producing significantly higher total sediment yields, increased peak flows, and decreased lag times.

The destabilization of banks is of more direct importance. As noted in chapter 4, the development and maintenance of river meanders depends partially on the erosional resistance of the bank material. Riparian vegetation plays an integral part in this stabilization. Loss of vegetation and trampling reduces the cohesiveness of the bank materials and its resistance to scour. This can (and often does) lead to accelerated erosion of riverbanks, local increases in sediment input, meander abandonment, and, ultimately, the complete transformation of a meandering system into a braided system. When these local effects are combined with the higher sediment yields and runoff from adjacent grazed lands, the overall hydraulic and sediment transport character of the river can be severely changed, producing a prolonged and possibly catastrophic period of readjustment.

In addition to causing changes in the behavior of a river, grazing within the riparian corridor appears to have a major effect on wildlife and fisheries habitat. A 1991 position paper of the American Fisheries Society has suggested that concentration of livestock along riverbanks is the number one cause of habitat degradation for trout in the western United States and the primary cause of the decline in native trout species. The reasons for the decline in fish populations are similar to those noted in chapter 12 for logging. Removal of riparian vegetation leads to increases in water temperature, reduction of input of large organic material, and decreases in habitat variability. All of these are vital to maintaining high primary productivity and a food chain suitable for sustaining fish. In addition, the increased erosion associated with bank destabilization and increased sediment yield from surrounding areas increases turbidity, which reduces photosynthesis and smothers spawning habitats with fine sediment.

Throughout California there have been several small-scale efforts to begin restoring the riparian corridors of streams damaged by grazing. Most of these efforts have focused on either preventing access to riparian and wetland areas through fencing or limiting riparian access to periods when the corridor is less likely to be adversely affected. In most cases, if left alone, riparian corridors will usually reestablish themselves, although not always with the original plant and animal species. Unfortunately, this recovery period can be very long and the extent of the damage can be quite widespread. To illustrate, U.S. National Forest Service inventories of riparian and wetland areas in the Inyo National Forest indicate that 90 percent are damaged in some form by grazing. Of the fish-bearing streams surveyed, two-thirds were rated poor to medium in habitat quality; of the more than three hundred reaches of streams surveyed in the Golden Trout Wilderness Area, 90 percent were considered fair to poor. The unsettling aspect of these surveys is that most of the damage was caused by grazing more than 50 years ago and there are no immediate prospects for recovery. No matter how careful present and future management techniques are, the adjustment of California's rivers to the impacts of grazing is likely to take a very long time.

AGRICULTURAL RUNOFF

As pointed out in the introduction to this chapter, the greatest impact on the state's rivers comes from the innumerable dams, canals, and levees that support the agricultural industry and, to a lesser extent, the urbanization of California (chaps. 15, 16). A secondary but important impact is associated with the conversion of California's floodplains and hillsides into farms. Almost 11 million acres of California's watersheds have been stripped of their native vegetation and put to the plow. The local and regional impact of this large-scale reconfiguration of the landscape is highly variable, depending on the types of agricultural practices, the farmer's efforts to control erosion and runoff, and the climate, topography, and soils of the region. In general, the local impacts of farms on the state's rivers can be divided into two classes (summarized in fig. 13.2): (1) river alterations associated with drainage reconfigurations and increases in runoff and sediment yields, and (2) water quality impacts associated with pesticide applications and irrigation practices. An additional impact, associated with the widespread removal of riparian vegetation, river channelization, and the construction of levees, is covered in chapter 15.

Runoff and Sediment Yields

Much of the impact of agriculture on California's rivers is governed by the seasonal nature of rainfall. It is an arguably cruel twist of fate that the optimal growing season for crops is not the rainy season. Because of this, more than 80 percent of the farming acreage in California is irrigated.

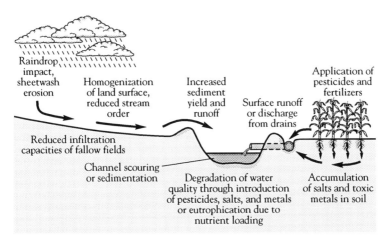

Fig. 13.2. Generalized depiction of river impacts associated with agricultural practices used in California.

During the fall, at the end of the growing season, most fields are allowed to lie fallow. Even in those fields where perennial crops are grown, such as orchards and vineyards, intensive weed management programs remove most vegetation. Thus millions of acres of land are bare at the arrival of rain in late fall (fig. 13.3A).

Depending on soil conditions and slope, bare ground produces runoff rates second only to impermeable surfaces such as asphalt and concrete. The lack of vegetation removes the runoff damping effects of interception and evapotranspiration. In addition, the lack of humus and roots within the soil coupled with the compacting effects of heavy farm machinery lead to greatly reduced infiltration capacities. Within hours of the beginning of a rainstorm, Horton overland flow can occur on the bare soil of fallow fields and orchards.

The increases in runoff intensity associated with bare soil are exacerbated by a number of other farming practices. The conversion of wildland to farms or irrigated pastureland typically involves a complete reconfiguration of the drainage network. The seemingly random distribution of creeks and drainages that occurs in most prime agricultural areas is anathema to the orderly squares and rectangles needed for most farm operations (fig. 13.3B). Following removal of native vegetation, farm operators will usually fill or realign most of the small, ephemeral drainages that cross their land. The net effect of this process is to homogenize the landscape by reducing the number of first- and second-order drainages (chap. 7). Because of this, overland flow takes a more direct and unencumbered path to larger

Fig. 13.3A. Farms make up a major portion of the watersheds of California's rivers. The majority of the floodplains of the state's larger perennial rivers are dominated by farms. *Above*: Fallow fields of Salinas Valley in late fall at the beginning of the rainy season. Exposed fields yield high runoff rates and sediment yields. Photograph by author.

creeks and rivers. In addition, the homogenization of the landscape reduces the amount of depression storage (chap. 5). Both of these changes, in conjunction with decreases in infiltration capacity, can lead to dramatic increases in peak discharge and decreases in lag times of the flood hydrographs of local creeks and rivers, with the net result of more frequent and more intense downstream flooding and channel scouring.

Although farmers and land use planners are concerned about changes in the timing and intensity of runoff from farms, the issue of greatest concern is soil erosion. George Washington, Thomas Jefferson, and a host of other pioneering agriculturists recognized erosion as a fundamental cause of declining farm productivity and advocated measures to control it. Following the dust bowl of the Great Depression, numerous government agencies have been assisting farmers in the control of soil erosion. Of course, this has not been out of any sense of obligation toward rivers per se but primarily as a way to maintain soil fertility and higher crop yields. An important erosion management tool has been the application of the fudge factor–filled universal soil loss equation (described in chap. 6). This notoriously inaccurate regression equation, with its innumerable assumptions,

Fig. 13.3B. *Above*: The drainage networks of most tributaries are "homogenized" in most intensively farmed regions, Sacramento Valley. Photograph courtesy of Rand Schaal, pilot.

has been widely used to estimate the best management practices for reducing erosion.

It is no startling revelation that the farms of California are introducing prodigious amounts of sediment into the state's rivers. The U.S. Soil Conservation Service has been encouraging farmers to use better soil management practices for over 50 years with mixed results. By far the worst sediment producers are the agricultural row crops that are augmented by irrigation during summer months. During winter months, when fields are bare, raindrop impact, coupled with overland flow, leads to exceptionally high rates of erosion. Because of the homogeneous landscape, sheetwash erosion and rilling are primarily responsible for the entrainment and transport of sediment. Unlike other land uses that increase sediment yields, erosion associated with agricultural practices is not restricted to the winter months. Throughout California the inefficient use of irrigation water produces large amounts of summertime runoff. In the San Joaquin Valley, the Soil Conservation Service has documented sediment yields from irrigation in excess of 14 tons per acre. This figure is comparable to the Eel River basin, which produces one of the highest sediment yields in North America.

Almost all of the sediment that is discharged from farms is silt to clay in size. As discussed above, the introduction of abundant fine-grained suspended load into rivers degrades aquatic habitats through increases in turbidity and smothering of potential spawning areas. During the summer and fall months when competence and capacity levels of most creeks and rivers are at their lowest, sediment-rich irrigation runoff will not only severely degrade habitats but will also produce significant channel aggradation.

Water Quality Impacts

The waters that drain from farms into the rivers of California not only carry large volumes of sediment, they also contain a witch's brew of organic and inorganic compounds that, while not directly changing the hydraulic behavior of a river, can adversely affect water quality and wildlife habitat (fig. 13.4). There are three general groups of pollutants that run off of the state's farmlands: pesticides, nutrients, and toxic metals. Each type has its own unique transport history through aquatic and riparian communities. The review presented here is, at best, cursory. For further information, refer to the Relevant Readings section at the end of this chapter.

Pesticides and Herbicides. According to the State Water Resources Control Board, more than 160 million pounds of pesticides and herbicides are

Fig. 13.4. Agricultural drains from farms, such as these in the Sacramento/San Joaquin Delta, collect agricultural runoff and discharge it directly into the state's rivers. Pesticides, nutrients, and toxic salts and metals degrade downstream water quality, adversely affecting wildlife habitat and drinking water supplies. Photograph courtesy of Rand Schaal, pilot.

used annually by California's farmers, representing a third of the total used in the United States. In addition, the variety of pesticides is vast: there are more than ten thousand different brands approved for use in California by the Department of Pesticide Regulation. Once applied, these pesticides are transported to rivers through multiple pathways, including the atmosphere, surface runoff, and subsurface flow. Most pesticides reach rivers as soluble phases that are either dissolved in the water or, more commonly, adsorbed onto the surface of fine-grained soil particles. In this way, the high sediment yields typical of runoff from most farmed areas facilitate the transport of pesticides into rivers.

The chemical behavior of pesticides in natural systems, their impacts on aquatic and riparian systems, and the extent of their occurrence in the rivers of California are surprisingly poorly known. It is prohibitively expensive to screen the state's waters for all the different types of pesticides that occur, and the evaluation of their environmental impact takes a great deal of time and manpower. Thus most monitoring programs focus only on chemicals that are either known to be a problem or judged most likely to be a problem. Today, the Toxic Substances Monitoring Program of the State Water Resources Control Board surveys only forty-five organic chemicals, such as pesticides and PCBs, at ninety-one stations throughout the state. Although it is one of the more comprehensive programs in the country, it is hardly sufficient for a state as large and complex as California.

The class of pesticides that has proven to be the most troublesome are the *organochlorine pesticides*. In California and much of the rest of the world, the environmental levels of organochlorine pesticides tend to be much higher than those of other pesticides because of their widespread use and their complex chemical and metabolic pathways. Most organochlorine compounds are insoluble in water but turn out to be highly soluble in fats and hydrocarbons. Because of this, they accumulate in biological tissues, reaching much higher levels than those of the surrounding water and sediments. To complicate this, these pesticides tend to stick or adsorb onto soil particles and organic material, which allows them to be transported in rivers and later stored in sediment. The best-known organochlorine pesticide, DDT, was banned in the 1970s. However, concentrations of its metabolic by-products, DDD and DDE, are still high in many environments, especially in arid areas. Indeed, in statewide sampling of freshwater fishes conducted by the State Water Resources Control Board in 1990, the DDT group of organochlorine pesticides exceeded National Academy of Science recommended levels in twelve of the state's river monitoring stations.

The impact of most pesticides and herbicides on aquatic organisms is usually noted first at or near the top of the food chain. The tendency of larger predators, like fish, to bioaccumulate these substances can produce die-offs that seem to affect only one species. For example, herbicides used on rice fields in northern California have produced spectacular die-offs in carp and striped bass populations on the Sacramento River without appearing to significantly affect other organisms.

The good news for the rivers of California is that most of the newer pesticides and herbicides that are reaching the market are highly unstable and break down quickly in natural environments. Research in California has shown that controlling surface discharge following the application of these substances allows sufficient time for the compounds to break down. The bad news is that the biological and water quality effects of the breakdown products themselves are poorly understood.

Nutrients.   Despite the seeming fertility of California's farmlands, farmers apply more than 1.2 *trillion* pounds of fertilizer annually to the watersheds of the state (based on statistics of State Water Resources Control Board). That is about 35 pounds of fertilizer for every man, woman, and child in this state. In most rural and many suburban areas in California, a significant amount of the degradation in surface water and, more commonly, groundwater quality can be traced directly to this profligate overuse of fertilizers. The problems generated by this runoff are exacerbated by runoff from the large feedlots in the Central and Imperial valleys. Accurate statistics on the amount of runoff that is generated by these operations are not available. However, to put this into perspective, it has been estimated that the potential pollution load from a typical, moderate-size feedlot exceeds that of a small city. Yet, unlike cities, the "sewage" produced by feedlots is commonly allowed to run off directly into rivers without any treatment.

The nutrients in runoff from farms and feedlots that are most frequently cited as the cause of the degradation of waterways are nitrogen and phosphorus. Unlike pesticides, nitrogen and phosphorus occur naturally in small amounts in all riverine settings and are an essential ingredient in most living organisms.

There are elevated levels of nitrogen (usually as nitrates) and phosphorus (usually as dissolved orthophosphates and polyphosphates) wherever farm and feedlot runoff is discharged into river courses. Nitrates and phosphates not only increase the productivity of crops; they also stimulate the growth of algae and other photosynthetic plants in rivers. In many aquatic plant communities, phosphorus and nitrogen are the limiting nutrients for primary productivity. For example, water hyacinths, spurred by the high nitrate and phosphate contents of the Sacramento and San Joaquin rivers, have become a hazard to navigation and water flow within parts of the delta. More significantly, excess nitrate and phosphate levels cause the *eutrophication* of rivers. Algal "blooms" associated with the introduction of nutrients from agricultural runoff can lead to very high biological oxygen demands and a reduction in total dissolved oxygen. In areas where current velocities are low and turbulent mixing and oxygenation of the water is nonexistent, this reduction in oxygen levels can produce anaerobic conditions, particularly near the channel bottom where decaying material collects. While not directly toxic to wildlife, the changes in water quality that are caused by the introduction of nitrates and phosphates severely alter or eliminate habitat. In extreme cases, intense eutrophication during warm weather periods can lead to large-scale fish kills.

An important side effect of excess nutrient levels in California's rivers is the production of trihalomethanes (THMs), a suspected cancer-causing agent that appears in drinking water in many portions of the state. Apparently, chlorine, the most widely used disinfectant for domestic drinking water supplies in California, combines with natural organic matter to form THMs. The high organic content of river water in agricultural areas is due, in part, to agricultural runoff and may pose a long-term problem. This problem is likely to become particularly prominent in the Sacramento/San Joaquin Delta, where two-thirds of the state's drinking water is mixed with voluminous agricultural runoff.

Salts and Toxic Metals. California agriculture's dependence on irrigation has created a large-scale experiment in aqueous geochemistry. In semiarid regions, such as the Imperial Valley and the southern San Joaquin Valley, the ready availability of both surface water and groundwater has promoted cultivation of crops on soils that can only be regarded as marginal. Rather than simply growing crops elsewhere, the usual solution is dilution. By pouring vast quantities of subsidized, inexpensive irrigation water on these soils, farmers have been able to minimize their negative aspects and generate a crop. The direct consequence of this approach for the rivers of California comes when this salt- and metal-rich irrigation water is returned to the rivers.

The best and perhaps most heralded example of the consequences of farming and irrigation in marginal areas comes from the southern San Joaquin Valley (fig. 13.5). As discussed in chapters 8 and 9, this region lies in one of the more intense rainshadows in the state. The central Coast Ranges and Transverse Ranges intercept most of the moisture that approaches the area from the Pacific, producing rainfall totals in the valley that average less than 6 inches per year. The dramatic uplift of the Coast Ranges in this region has produced a steep front along the western side of the San Joaquin Valley with large alluvial fans that are fed by ephemeral streams that originate near the crests of the mountains.

During most years, there is little surface runoff on these alluvial fans. Runoff that does occur is usually limited to the coarse alluvial streams

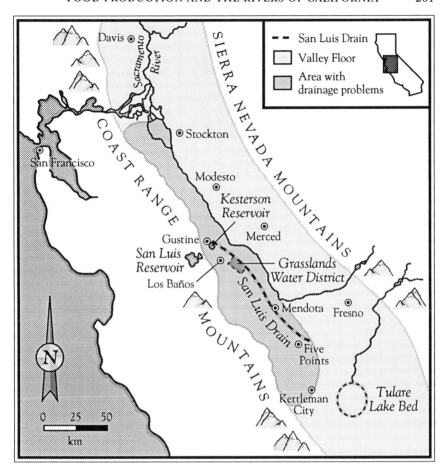

Fig. 13.5. Map of the San Joaquin Valley depicting areas with poorly drained, saline soils. (Modified from Tanji, Lauchli, and Meyer 1986.)

near the upper reaches of the fans. The distal portions of the fans, located near the center of the valley, are dominated by very fine grained soils that receive little surface runoff or precipitation. The mineralogic composition of these soils, in conjunction with the low annual rainfall, makes them highly saline.

Under "natural" conditions, the groundwater that underlies these alluvial fans is derived primarily from infiltration in the upper parts of the fan, near the mountains (fig. 13.5). Prior to widespread farming of this area, recharge water flowed from west to east, following the general topography (see chap. 5), toward the base of the fans, discharging locally at the surface through artesian wells and contributing vital base flow to the San Joaquin River.

This great experiment in geochemistry began as early as the late 1800s when farmers began pumping groundwater and using it for irrigating crops grown on the marginal, saline soils of the region. To make these soils arable, disproportionately large amounts of groundwater had to be applied in order to leach salts from the root zone. Intense groundwater pumping reached a maximum in the 1950s, causing water tables beneath the alluvial fans to drop dramatically. The decline in water tables led to a reorganization of the recharge and groundwater flow of the region. During periods of intense pumping and irrigation, horizontal recharge in the lower portions of the alluvial fans was replaced by downward flow of irrigation water. This fundamental change in the source of recharge dramatically altered water quality. As each acre-foot of irrigation water percolated through the soil, it reacted with organic and inorganic constituents, taking many of them into solution. Surface evaporation and transpiration concentrated these soil waters, further degrading their quality. As these saline waters percolated through the unsaturated zone, they often precipitated salts, but they did so below the root zone of the crops. Where salt-laden groundwater made it to the lowered groundwater table, it was often recycled back to the surface by groundwater pumping and irrigation. The result of this recycling is the buildup of salts and other chemicals in the unsaturated zone and in the groundwater of the region.

In the late 1950s and 1960s, surface water was brought into the southern San Joaquin Valley to replace declining groundwater. Farmers of the region must have felt that their problems were solved with the arrival of this clean, salt-free surface water derived principally from the Sierra Nevada. Unfortunately for them and the rivers of the state, the application of surface water created a whole new set of problems. This inexpensive water was applied liberally to the salty soils of the region. Meanwhile, the groundwater wells, which had apparently created so much of the problem, were turned off. The consequence of this reduced groundwater pumping and widespread application of surface water was a dramatic and rapid rise in the regional groundwater table. In many areas, the water table that rose close to the surface brought with it the salts and chemicals that had been leached from the soils by the previous irrigation practices. More important, the presence of a shallow, saline groundwater table increased the formation of salts in soils by increasing the amount of water available for evaporation. Instead of the previous problem with groundwater tables that had dropped too low, the San Joaquin farmers were now faced with groundwater tables that had risen too high.

The usual way to deal with shallow, saline groundwater tables is to install drains or perforated pipes that capture water as it percolates through the soil. Getting rid of this captured water usually involves discharging it into local rivers and streams. These agricultural drains, which are essential for many lowland farms, are a fixture in large valleys throughout California. The water that they discharge, however, is notoriously high in salts as well as organics and nutrients from agricultural fertilizers. Where abundant, these drains degrade local water quality so much that surface water supplies cannot be used for drinking *or* irrigation (this has been especially true in the lower reaches of the Colorado River). The well-organized farmers of the southern San Joaquin Valley lobbied the federal government for help with this problem. The proposed solution was to collect the discharge from the drains and export it directly to San Francisco Bay, thereby reducing the degradation of San Joaquin River water quality. The San Luis Drain (fig. 13.5) was designed to remove the offending discharge. Despite years of construction, the project ran out of funds and was never completed. This is where the real difficulty began.

Uplift of the Coast Ranges west of the San Joaquin Valley has exposed Miocene- and Pliocene-aged marine mudstones to erosion and weathering. The clays and silts that originally made up these shales now make up the fine-grained lower portion of the alluvial fans that formed along the eastern flank of the Coast Ranges. All the salts and metals that typically occur in marine shales were carried with these muds and silts. One metal in particular, selenium, has proven to be a big problem.

Selenium is a ubiquitous trace metal in sedimentary rocks and soils. Normally, it is relatively insoluble, especially in acidic soils, and it typically will not bioaccumulate. But the irrigation practices of farmers in the southern San Joaquin Valley produced (unwittingly) the ideal conditions for mobilizing selenium and producing one of the more intractable pollution problems facing wildlife and water quality agencies in California today.

The high evaporation rates of the southern San Joaquin Valley and the generally saline soils react to produce high pH (basic) soil water conditions. Selenium, which is insoluble at moderate to low pH, becomes soluble at high pH. Studies of shallow groundwater along the western edge of the San Joaquin Valley show a direct correlation between high pH, saline groundwaters, and selenium concentrations. The irrigation and drainage practices applied to these marginal soils led to increases in pH and associated increases in selenium in the agricultural drains (fig. 13.6). Had these drains discharged directly into the San Joaquin River or had they made it directly to San Francisco Bay as originally planned, the selenium problem might not have appeared until much later. Instead, the incomplete San Luis Drain stopped at the southern end of the Kesterson National Wildlife Refuge, effectively turning the refuge into an extensive agricultural disposal facility.

None of the water that was discharged directly into the Kesterson refuge was inherently toxic to wildlife. Typical San Luis Drain water contained less than 300 parts per billion selenium—levels not normally known to

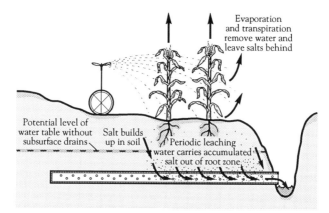

Fig. 13.6. Processes responsible for buildup of salts and
toxic metals within poorly drained soils. (Modified from U.S.
Department of Interior, Bureau of Reclamation, 1984.)

cause problems. However, high evaporation rates and lack of an outlet led
to the concentration of selenium, usually in surficial organic detritus and
the upper few inches of soil. Normally, the selenium would have remained
immobile and would not have affected wildlife. However, as a number of
researchers found, high pH and the presence of abundant organic and inorganic sulfides mobilize selenium, making it available for transmission
through the food chain and allowing it to be bioaccumulated by birds and
other wildlife within the refuge. The consequences of this bioaccumulation are particularly well known—illnesses and reproductive deformities
among the waterfowl of the refuge.

The selenium problem experienced at the Kesterson refuge is not
unique. A number of studies, including one initiated by the *Sacramento
Bee*, have shown that the conditions that produced the high selenium concentrations are occurring or are expected to occur in semiarid, marginal
farming areas throughout the western United States. It is unlikely that the
Kesterson disaster will be the last one to be associated with agricultural
drainage.

SUMMARY

California is a national and international giant in agricultural production.
Born out of the gold rush, this industry has fueled the economy of California for most of the last century. The value of the basic goods produced
by this industry today represents less than 3 percent of the total economy.
Yet this industry uses approximately 80 percent of the state's surface water

and an unknown but probably equivalent amount of groundwater and is responsible for more than half of the state's water pollution. For these reasons, the industry recently has been receiving unfavorable scrutiny.

Grazing currently occurs on over half the state's wildlands. The impacts of grazing are associated with erosion and increased runoff caused by removal of vegetation and compaction of soils. Increases in sediment yield, development of gullies, loss of native vegetation, increases in peak discharge, and decreases in lag times are common in watersheds that are heavily grazed. The most notable impacts are found in the riparian corridor. Trampling and grazing of vegetation adjacent to rivers degrades water quality and decreases bank stability, causing significant adjustments in channel morphology and dynamics.

Although the largest impact from farming can be traced to the dams and water diversions that supply irrigation water (chap. 16), agricultural runoff has important local and regional impacts on rivers. Irrigated fields and the tendency to allow fields to be fallow during the rainy season produce increases in sediment supply to local streams and rivers. More important, there are a number of water quality impacts associated with runoff from farms. The 160 million pounds of pesticides applied annually to California's farms can affect water quality significantly. Bioaccumulation of these compounds has affected a number of species. The 1.2 trillion pounds of fertilizer applied to California's farms have increased the nutrient loading of the state's rivers. High nitrogen and phosphorus levels lead to eutrophication of rivers, especially during warm months. The tendency to apply cheap irrigation water to marginal farmlands has produced extensive runoff of salts and toxic metals in the semiarid farming regions of the state. Agricultural drains, which remove these salts and metals after leaching of soils, usually discharge into rivers, thereby degrading water quality. Where drains discharge into holding ponds or lakes, accumulation of selenium and other metals can lead to high levels of toxicity.

RELEVANT READINGS

Armour, C. L., D. A. Duff, and W. Elmore. 1991. "The Effects of Livestock Grazing on Riparian and Stream Ecosystems." *Fisheries* 16: 7–11.

Bren, L. J. 1993. "Riparian Zone, Stream, and Floodplain Issues: A Review." *Journal of Hydrology* 150: 277–299.

Chaney, E. D., W. Elmore, and W. S. Platts. 1990. *Livestock Grazing on Western Riparian Areas*. Washington, D.C.: U.S. Environmental Protection Agency.

Charbonneau, R., and G. M. Kondolf. 1993. "Land Use Change in California, USA—Nonpoint Source Water Quality Impacts." *Environmental Management* 17: 453–460.

Conway, G. R., and J. N. Pretty. 1991. *Unwelcome Harvest: Agriculture and Pollution.* London: Earthscan.

Deverel, S. J., and S. K. Gallanthine. 1989. "Relation of Salinity and Selenium in Shallow Groundwater to Hydrologic and Geochemical Processes, Western San Joaquin Valley, California." *Journal of Hydrology* 109: 125–149.

Engberg, R. A., and M. A. Sylvester. 1993. "Concentrations, Distribution, and Sources of Selenium from Irrigated Lands in Western United States." *Journal of Irrigation and Drainage Engineering* 119: 522–536.

Gilliom, R. J., and D. G. Clifton. 1990. "Organochlorine Pesticide Residues in Bed Sediments of the San Joaquin River, California." *Water Resources Bulletin* 26: 11–24.

Naiman, R. J., H. Decamps, and M. Pollock. 1993. "The Role of Riparian Corridors in Maintaining Regional Biodiversity." *Ecological Applications* 3: 209–212.

Paveglio, F. L., C. M. Bunck, and G. H. Heinz. 1992. "Selenium and Boron in Aquatic Birds from Central California." *Journal of Wildlife Management* 56: 31–42.

Saiki, M. K., M. R. Jennings, and R. H. Wiedmeyer. 1992. "Toxicity of Agricultural Subsurface Drainwater from the San Joaquin Valley, California, to Juvenile Chinook Salmon and Striped Bass." *Transactions of the American Fisheries Society* 121: 78–93.

Sedgwick, J. A., and F. L. Knopf. 1991. "Prescribed Grazing as a Secondary Impact in a Western Riparian Floodplain." *Journal of Range Management* 44: 369–374.

Tanji, K., A. Lauchli, and J. Meyer. 1986. "Selenium in the San Joaquin Valley." *Environment* 28: 6–11.

U.S. Department of Interior, Bureau of Reclamation. 1984. *Drainage and Salt Disposal.* Information Bulletin 1, San Luis Unit, Central Valley Project Sacramento. Sacramento: U.S. Department of Interior.

Weres, O., A. R. Jaouni, and L. Tsao. 1989. "The Distribution, Speciation and Geochemical Cycling of Selenium in a Sedimentary Environment, Kesterson Reservoir, California, U.S.A." *Applied Geochemistry* 4: 543–563.

FOURTEEN

A Primer on Flood Frequency

How Much and How Often?

INTRODUCTION

Land use planners and civil engineers are faced with an untenable problem. We, the general public, have charged them with the task of planning for floods that are going to occur who-knows-when and are going to be who-knows-how-big. Since planners and engineers lack a reliable crystal ball, or the requisite software for accurate disaster predictions, they are forced to make lots of estimates, which are really nothing more than best guesses based on an analysis of historical data. This natural disaster guessing game is founded in large measure on probability statistics. The *fundamental* question that is asked by those who help us prepare for the inevitable is, What are the odds that a flood of a given magnitude will occur in any given year or over the lifetime of any given project? Based on the calculation of those odds (discussed below), a cascade of interrelated land use planning and engineering decisions are made. All of these decisions are an attempt to balance risk of disaster against the cost of planning for or preventing it.

Although hard to imagine, the seemingly innocuous pursuit of probability statistics has controlled many aspects of the modification of California's rivers. The greatest impact stems from the efforts to designate the 100-year floodplain and to develop justifications for flood control projects. Small changes in probability can affect local and regional economies and the way in which projects are packaged and sold to the taxpayers. For the rivers of California, these statistics are fundamental because they control, at least in part, the size and location of dam, bypass, and levee projects intended for flood control and the portions of the state's floodplains deemed "suitable" for urbanization. Given the importance of these probability statistics to a broad range of river impacts and the floods of 1995, I devote an entire chapter to them.

FEMA, THE U.S. ARMY CORPS OF ENGINEERS, AND THE 100-YEAR FLOODPLAIN

Over the years that it has been in existence, the Federal Emergency Management Agency (FEMA) has been in the business of bailing people out after natural disasters. The past 10 years have been banner years for FEMA. There have been several large earthquakes, a number of extraordinary hurricanes and remarkable wildfires, and a series of spectacular floods, culminating with the 1993 floods on the Mississippi and the 1995 floods in California. FEMA has rescued thousands of unlucky individuals by doling out billions of dollars in aid. However, the events of the past 10 years have prompted some serious questioning of our approach to natural disasters. All of FEMA's good works aside, why should people who live in areas that are prone to natural disasters be subsidized by the more prudent people who live out of harm's way? The default answer is usually that (1) natural disasters are simply too unpredictable to allow complete risk-free planning; (2) people should not be penalized for being unfortunate enough to be in the wrong place at the wrong time; and (3) it is more cost-effective from a revenue perspective to revive local economies and tax bases as quickly as possible.

The massive and rapid urban sprawl of this century has led to the occupation of flood-prone lands throughout California, placing millions in harm's way (fig. 14.1A, B). After all, floodplains are naturally flat, making them ideal building sites, and their proximity to water and the industry that develops around it makes them particularly magnetic. But floodplains, by definition, are also regularly occupied by floods. It was noted in chapter 5 that the configuration of a river channel is tied most closely to the discharge that produces bankfull stage, Q_b. In undammed, natural rivers, this discharge level occurs an average of every 1.5 to 2 years; any discharge that is greater than Q_b will breach the natural levees and inundate the floodplain. This means that peak flows that occur an average of every 2 years or more will cause flooding in natural river systems. Clearly, building right on the floodplain next to a river channel does not represent the pinnacle of foresight and planning. But, of course, this has not stopped vast numbers of otherwise intelligent people (the unfortunate residents of Guerneville come to mind).

Recognizing that people occasionally choose to court disaster, FEMA instituted the National Flood Insurance Program in the 1960s. This program requires that local planning agencies develop land use planning in the floodplain. Specifically, FEMA forces local communities to adopt mea-

Fig. 14.1A. Examples of flood damage in Santa Cruz County during the January floods of 1982. *Above*: Collapse of the foundation of a house due to bank undercutting along Soquel Creek during the flood. Houses in this stretch of river had been inundated and undercut in earlier floods. However, housing sites were rebuilt on imported fill. The recurrence interval for this flood was calculated to be 14 years. Urban encroachment onto the floodplain, coupled with debris jams that formed at several bridges (see fig. 12.7) of this creek, caused most damage. Photograph courtesy of Gerald Weber.

sures to prohibit new development within the 100-year floodplain and to require that any preexisting developments purchase federally subsidized flood insurance. Like any bureaucratic mandate, there are loopholes. Development can occur within the "flood fringe," or margins, of the floodplain as long as it is elevated above the level of the 100-year flood and does not, by decreasing the cross-sectional area of the channel, increase the flood height significantly. In concept, this is a sound and economic approach to land use planning. It is cheaper in the long run to simply avoid disasters rather than to repeatedly clean them up. In this way, market incentives are strong for developers to avoid building on floodplains and to reduce the government's long-term costs.

With the help of the U.S. Army Corps of Engineers and engineering firms across the country, FEMA has been developing floodplain hazard maps throughout the United States that designate the 100-year floodplain. This "line in the sand" influences billions of dollars in development and

Fig. 14.1B. *Above*: Collapsed bridge over the San Lorenzo River, downtown Santa Cruz. Scouring around old bridge pilings during high discharge led to subsidence and collapse. Arrow denotes highwater line during flood. (From Griggs 1982.)

infrastructure costs. But why the *100*-year floodplain, and how valid is its designation? The choice of 100 years rather than 200 or 400 is, to put it quite simply, arbitrary. It is not as if people living 10 feet outside of the dreaded 100-year floodplain are safe and those living 10 feet within it are threatened. Flood magnitudes form a continuum with no natural break at the 100-year mark. In addition, next door neighbors can pay vastly different insurance rates based on the remarkably *precise* location of the line delineating the 100-year floodplain. As will be shown below, the precision of the 100-year floodplain maps is not matched by their accuracy. These maps are based on statistical best guesses, and the errors are often quite large. To compound the problem, the margins of the 100-year floodplain are in a constant state of flux as new data are added to the analysis every year and watershed conditions change. This is especially true when large flooding events occur which exert a great deal of influence over the flooding data set. Despite these problems, FEMA has blithely gone forward designating poorly constrained and highly inaccurate 100-year floodplains throughout the country and indirectly dictating the fate of many of the nation's rivers.

Once a 100-year floodplain has been designated or a significant flood occurs which causes severe property damage, there is usually an intense lobbying effort to build flood control structures. At this point, the Army Corps of Engineers will usually step in to determine the optimal size and design of the flood control project. The approach that the corps uses is what they call *expected value analysis*. This technique calculates an estimated annual damage for floods that occur either with a particular flood control project or without. The average annual amount of damage prevented (figured over a very long period of time) less the annualized cost of the project itself represents the project's net benefit (or loss). For example, the larger the flood event, the greater the potential annualized damage. Thus it would seem prudent to build as large a flood control structure as physically possible to contain these very large flows. However, at some point, the costs of building that larger structure are going to begin to outweigh the value of damage prevented. Expected value analysis attempts to determine the size of a flood control project that creates the maximum benefit with the least cost.

In principle, this approach makes sense. Yet, like the designation of the 100-year floodplain, the hard and fast calculations necessary for expected value analysis stem from the inescapably inaccurate but terribly precise estimates of flood frequency. However, according to the corps and other agencies, the actual goal of the expected value analysis approach is to accurately estimate (and therefore reduce) damages over the country as a whole, rather than at any particular site. By applying the technique to many projects, it is assumed that the consequences of error in flood frequency estimation are reduced and that the aggregate estimated expected damages are correct. Of course, this artful dodge is of small comfort on the local scale, where errors in flood frequency estimation can have substantial economic and social impacts.

FLOOD FREQUENCY: MYTHS AND MISCONCEPTIONS

Since the floods of 1986 in Sacramento (discussed below), a very large segment of California's population has been directly affected by the methods used to estimate flood frequency. Daily lives and the potential, expenditure of billions of dollars for flood control have depended on these estimates. Yet only a vanishingly small percentage of the population understands the concepts that govern flood frequency calculations. The majority either choose to "leave it to the experts" or, worse yet, are singularly misinformed.

There are a number of myths and misconceptions (and a lot of fancy terminology) that limit the general public's access to understanding flood frequency. These are grouped here into four general flood frequency concepts. The first two concepts are statements of the obvious; the last two are more subtle and require lengthy explanation. Each, however, reflects the nature of probability statistics and the pitfalls of relatively small data sets.

Flood Frequency Concept 1: *The probability that a 100-year flood will strike a river in California is the same every year, regardless of how long it has been since the last 100-year flood.*

The vast majority of the general public has little appreciation of what the term *100-year* (or for that matter, 200-year, 400-year, etc.) floodplain actually means. On undammed rivers, the level of inundation of a floodplain is primarily associated with the magnitude of the peak discharge for a given flood. The 100-year floodplain on these rivers is therefore a function of the discharge level that is likely to be equaled or exceeded an average of once every 100 years. This relationship is not so simple for dammed rivers. Since runoff is stored behind flood control dams, the duration of high discharge is ultimately more important than peak discharges. High-intensity but short-lived peak discharges can usually be absorbed by flood control reservoirs and released slowly later. However, when high discharge occurs over several days, the storage capacity of reservoirs is lost, leading to high and occasionally destructive downstream releases. Thus the estimated 100-year flood downstream of a dam is likely to be associated with long-term high runoff, rather than one single large storm.

Regardless of the upstream conditions, the 100-year, 200-year, and 400-year floodplains are defined by a statistical estimation of the likelihood, or probability, that a certain discharge will be equaled or exceeded in any given year, whether as a peak flow or as volume of flow over several days. This is usually expressed as the *exceedance probability,* or *P.* The inverse of exceedance probability, *1/P,* is known as the *recurrence interval,* or *T.* For example, the calculated probability that a peak discharge of 130,000 cfs will occur on the lower American River near Sacramento is .014. This means that in this or any other year there is a slim, 1.4 percent chance that the flows that visited the area in 1986 will be equaled or exceeded. The inverse of this probability, 1/.014 = 70, is the recurrence interval of that flow. A 70-year recurrence interval means that when studied over a hypothetically very long period (say, thousands of years), the 130,000 cfs flow will occur an *average* of every 70 years.

A recurrence interval of 70 years does *not* mean that the flow will be exceeded every 70 years, like clockwork. There is still an alarmingly large segment of the population that naively believes that just because Sacramentans had a 70-year flood in 1986, they are going to be spared a similar flood until the year 2056. They are just as likely to be hit by a 130,000-cfs flow this year as they were in 1986. A simplistic but rational way to view this is to consider how many 130,000+ cfs flows are likely to occur over a 7,000-year period. If they have a 70-year recurrence interval, then 100 of these flows will occur. Whether the 100 flows are spread roughly evenly throughout the 7,000 years or whether they all occur within the first 100 years is immaterial; their exceedance probability and recurrence interval remain the same. It must be remembered that the recurrence interval is really not a predictor of the interval between flows but is only a way to express the likelihood or probability that a flow will occur. During the floods of January 1995, the nightly news held a constant reminder of how misconstrued the notion of the 100-year floodplain is. In the Laguna Creek area of Sacramento, one woman was filmed railing against a local developer, claiming that she had been told that they "weren't supposed to be flooded for 100 years." On the same evening, a man in Guerneville, on the Russian River, was filmed complaining that he had been told that they had a 100-year event just nine years ago in 1986 and that the flooding should not have been back so soon. To both these people and, I suspect, thousands of Californians like them, concept 1 directly applies: the probability that a 100-year flood will strike a river in California is the same every year, regardless of how long it has been since the last 100-year flood.

Flood Frequency Concept 2: *It is not a certainty that the 100-year event will occur sometime in the next 100 years (although it is pretty likely).*

When you discover that your house is located on the 100-year floodplain, you are usually told that in any given year there is a 1/100 or .01 probability that the floodplain will be inundated. In my numerous conversations with people about this, they always seem to feel that these are pretty small odds and that they are in good shape. Despite this apparent good fortune, it is reasonable to ask what the probability is that at least once in your lifetime you will be inundated. What is the probability that you will be flooded sometime during the life of your mortgage? Because this represents accumulation of probability over a number of years, the statistics are a bit different. There is a simple equation that calculates the probability, P, that a given-size flood with a recurrence interval of T years will occur or be exceeded within the next n years:

$$P = 1 - [1 - 1/T]^n. \tag{14.1}$$

For example, suppose that you have the great fortune of living your entire life (say, 70 years) on the American River floodplain in Sacramento. What are the odds that during your lifetime you will see a 70-year flood or greater? During any single year of your life, the odds were 1/70 or a .014 probability, which seems like comfortably slim odds to most. However, according to equation 14.1, over your entire lifetime the probability is .63, almost a two-in-three chance, that you'll be flooded. The same relationship applies for any recurrence interval; there is a two-in-three chance that the 100-year flood will occur over the next 100 years, a two-in-three chance that the 200-year flood will occur over the next 200 years, and so on. Moreover, during the 30-year life of your mortgage, there is a .35 probability, or more than a one-in-three chance, that you will be flooded by the American River. Millions flock to gambling halls and bingo parlors to risk money on odds worse than these, yet many developers and home owners will steadfastly maintain that the year-to-year odds are really in their favor and that they should not be prohibited from living in the floodplain. In reality, the odds are pretty good that they *are* going to be flooded in the long term; it is just unlikely in any single year.

Flood Frequency Concept 3: *In California, where historic data sets are small, the 100-year floodplain is likely to grow following a major flooding event.*

To fully understand this concept, it is essential that the techniques used for estimating recurrence intervals be reviewed. Naturally, a subject as important as flood frequency is examined by innumerable statisticians who continuously refine the techniques, quibble over the details, and use a language about as intelligible as Sanskrit to most lay people. Moreover, as I discovered when writing this chapter, these same statisticians become quite bent out of shape when someone attempts to simplify their somewhat opaque science. Their concern has merit, however, since in statistics the Devil resides happily in the details. Yet, to make this discussion palatable, I have chosen to ignore some of the details. For more enlightenment and a lot of turgid prose, see the Relevant Readings listed at the end of this chapter.

The fundamental assumption inherent in calculating exceedance probabilities is that runoff is randomly distributed in time and that the data set used represents a sample of these random or independent events. Although it often appears that years of high rainfall and drought cluster, there is no evidence (yet) that there is a predictable pattern. If there were, we could not state that in any given year the probability of a 100-year event is always the same. Climate changes and trends in climate will alter the reliability of calculations, but we have yet to document their occurrence sufficiently to gauge their impact over the design life of any given project (see chap. 17).

Usually, random data form a "normal" distribution (the typical bell-shaped curve) wherein most of the data fall near some mean value, with fewer and fewer data points occurring farther and farther away from the mean. Peak discharge or annual flood data are not normally distributed; small flows occur proportionally more often than large flows. Thus flows of different magnitude are not likely to be normally or equally distributed around the mean since there are going to be lots of small flows and few very large flows. To properly analyze the statistics of these data, it must be log-transformed into a bell-shaped distribution. If the data are a true representation of the range and distribution of discharges, they will all fall on a straight line on graph paper that plots the log of discharge against the exceedance probability for that discharge.

To illustrate this process, stream flows for the California Salmon River were taken from the U.S. Geological Survey Water Resources Data volumes. These volumes, which are available in most university and government libraries and on compact discs, list daily average discharges for the hundreds of stream gauges that are monitored throughout California. On larger rivers (and for the purposes of this illustration), these averages can be considered as peak daily discharges. The Salmon River of the Klamath River watershed was chosen as an example because it has an extensive flow record (about twice that of the typical California river) and contains no significant dams and human alterations of its flow (it is also prone to seasonably high flows and terrific Class V spring whitewater rafting).

To evaluate trends in the relationship between exceedance probability and peak discharge, the data from the Salmon River were plotted on log-probability graph paper (fig. 14.2). Before plotting the data, the peak annual discharge for each year of record is ranked, with the highest being ranked first and the lowest being ranked last. Each ranked discharge is then plotted against its calculated exceedance probability using the *Weibull plotting position formula*:

$$P = m/(n+1), \tag{14.2}$$

where P is exceedance probability, m is its rank, and n is the number of years of record. This can either include or exclude any intervening years when flow measurements were not made. Of course, the inverse of P is T, the calculated recurrence interval, so

$$T = (n+1)/m. \tag{14.3}$$

For example, the Christmas floods of 1964 produced 100,000 cfs discharge on the Salmon River. Since this discharge is first-ranked in a data set consisting of 64 years, its exceedance probability is 1/(64+1), or 0.15. The inverse of .015 is the recurrence interval, 65 years. The smallest peak flow occurred during the drought of 1977, reaching only 1,280 cfs. The exceedance probability for this flow is 64/(64+1), or .98; its recurrence interval would therefore be 1.02 years.

In an ideal and perfect world, where our data set is normally distributed and accurately reflects the distribution of discharge values, the data points from the Salmon River would all line up along a straight line. This line, known as the *frequency curve*, could then be used to estimate the peak discharge of the 100-year event (exceedance probability of .01) by reading

SALMON RIVER

Basin Area = *751 sq. mi.*

Water Years in Record: *1912-1915, 1928-1957, 1959-1988*

Exceedance Probability

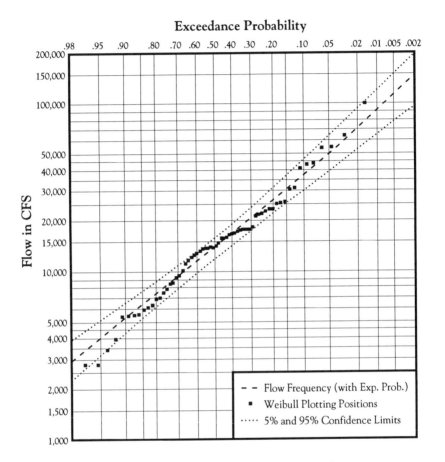

Flow in CFS

- - Flow Frequency (with Exp. Prob.)
- ■ Weibull Plotting Positions
- ..... 5% and 95% Confidence Limits

64 Events Between 1912 and 1988

Expected Probability Flow (cfs)	Exceedance Probability	Recurrence Interval	Confidence Limits Flow (cfs)	
			.05	.95
146,000	.002	500	199,000	95,000
111,000	.005	200	150,000	76,400
89,200	.01	100	119,000	63,800
70,600	.02	50	92,300	52,500
50,100	.05	20	63,700	39,200
37,300	.10	10	46,200	30,300

it directly from the graph. Of course, it is not a perfect world and there is always some scatter to the data, requiring us to fit a line that best approximates its distribution.

The fitting of a frequency curve to discharge and exceedance probability data is the most precarious step in determining flood frequency and designation of the 100-year floodplain. The data are plotted on a log-probability scale. This means that subtle changes in the slope of the curve can produce major differences in estimated flow magnitudes for the larger events. In general, a "best fit" line is calculated which essentially averages the scatter of the data points. Figure 14.2 shows the calculated best fit line for the 64 discharge values from the Salmon River. Based on the position of this line, the estimated flow for the 100-year event is 89,200 cfs, smaller than the record flow of 100,000 cfs but greater than all other recorded flows on the Salmon River.

Flood frequency concept 3 states that the 100-year floodplain that we are adapting ourselves to this year is likely to grow following a major flooding event. The fluid nature of the line in the sand that defines the edge of this floodplain is a natural outgrowth of the statistical approach used to define the 100-year floodplain. For example, every year that passes adds a new data point to the graph. Rather than simply being plotted on the graph independent of the other data points, this point causes all others to shift, inevitably changing the slope of the frequency curve. However, the impact of new data depends on the size of the original data set and the magnitude of new discharge values.

By increasing the value of $n + 1$ (eg. 14.2) the addition of any new data will affect the Weibull plotting position of all data points in the data set. For moderate-sized data sets like the Salmon River, the effect of increasing $n + 1$ by 1 is relatively minor. However, the magnitude of the impact of new data is also dependent on the ranking of the discharge. When a new discharge value is added to a data set, it lowers the ranking, or increases the value of m (eq. 14.2), of all smaller peak discharges. For example, if a peak flow of 10,000 cfs were to occur on the Salmon River next year and be added to the data set, it would rank 46th out of 65 data points. This means that the value of m for all data points previously ranked 46th or above will be increased by 1.

Increasing the value of m for the smaller peak discharges is unlikely to have a significant impact on the slope of the frequency curve since there

◀ Fig. 14.2. Flow frequency curve for the Salmon River based on data for 64 years. Based on the flow frequency curve, the estimated discharge for the 100-year event on the Salmon River is 89,200 cfs. (Redrawn from plots generated courtesy of U.S. Army Corps of Engineers Hydrologic Engineering Center, Davis, California; raw data for plots supplied by author.)

are numerous peak discharge values that are comparable in size, muting the overall effect of the shift. However, when exceptionally large discharge values occur, the impacts on the slope of the frequency curve can be substantial because (1) high-ranking flows shift the values of m for a large portion of the data set, and (2) their plotting position, well removed from the mean of the data set, exerts a disproportionate influence on the slope of the curve.

To illustrate, suppose that a discharge equivalent to the calculated 100-year event were to arrive next winter on the Salmon River (fig. 14.3). After all, it is just as likely to occur next winter as it is fifty winters from now. When this flow does arrive, it would be ranked second in a data set of 65 and plotted with a calculated exceedance probability of $P = 2/(65+1) = .03$, roughly equal to a 33-year recurrence interval, not a 100-year interval. Although the addition of this large discharge event would have minimal impact on the plotting position of the highest-ranked flow, it will significantly change the plotting position of other large flows. For example, the previously second-ranked flow in 64 becomes the third-ranked flow in 65, increasing its plotted exceedance probability from .03 to .05. The previously third-ranked flow becomes the fourth-ranked, increasing its plotted exceedance probability from .05 to .06, and so on. The net effect of the addition of a high-ranking discharge event is to shift all of the data points on figure 14.3 to the left, with substantial shifts occurring in the plotting position of the rare, large events.

The tendency of rare events to produce significant shifts in the plotting position of high discharge values ensures that when unusually large flooding events occur in a river system, the recalculated frequency curve is going to be markedly different. In California, where discharge data sets are small (usually less than 100 years), these rare events will inevitably lead to an increase in the slope of the frequency curve. This means that based solely on the local frequency curve, the estimated discharge for the 100-year event will increase following a large flooding event, leading to an *expansion* of the designated 100-year floodplain. This is the reason that 100-year floodplains mysteriously seem to expand following large floods.

Of course, the statisticians of the Army Corps of Engineers and other agencies that deal with flood frequency recognize the pitfalls of small data sets, such as those that are used here in California, and the tendency of large flooding events to disproportionately influence the frequency curves. A variety of statistical methods are used to reduce built-in errors (this subject is beyond the scope of this chapter; see Relevant Readings). To offset the impact of small data sets, the local data are compared to, and adjusted to reflect, regional data. This has the net effect of increasing the amount of data used to constrain the frequency curve and reducing the impact of rare events. Unfortunately, given the relatively recent colonization of Cali-

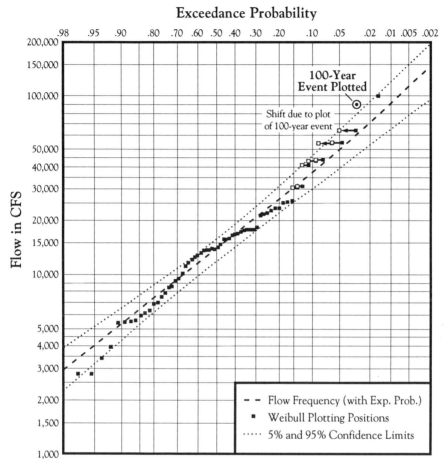

Fig. 14.3. Potential impact of unusually high discharge event on the flood frequency curve for the Salmon River. If a flow equivalent to the calculated 100-year event identified in fig. 14.2 were to occur, it would cause a shift in all of the data points. Arrows indicate the magnitude of the shift for the top-ranked flows. Shifts for lower-ranked flows would be minimal. A refitted frequency curve would have a steeper slope and thus a significantly greater discharge for the 100-year event. In this way, unusually large flow events lead to increases in the size of the 100-year floodplain. (Modified from fig. 14.2.)

fornia, data sets are limited, muting the effectiveness of this technique. Additionally, regional historic data are analyzed to better constrain the recurrence intervals of the unusually large events. Based on newspaper accounts, highwater marks, and personal accounts of flooding, statisticians can estimate the magnitude of peak discharges in the past. These data, which are highly subjective and potentially inaccurate, can also be used to help constrain the recurrence intervals of large flows. Finally, in rare cases, paleoflood studies and tree ring analyses can be used to develop a long-term record of large floods.

Regardless of these adjustments, in California, where the data sets are small, addition of new data is inevitably going to lead to adjustments in the frequency curve. Exceptionally large flooding events are likely (meaning, with exceptions) to end up increasing the slope of the calculated frequency curve, leading to increases in the size of the estimated 100-year floodplain.

Flood Frequency Concept 4: *It is a virtual certainty that the defined 100-year floodplain is not the actual 100-year floodplain.*

The scatter in the data shown in figure 14.2 reflects the potential for error in estimates based on the calculated frequency curve. After all, it is unlikely that the period of time that we have sampled represents precisely the distribution of yearly peak discharges that might occur over very long periods. This is like using the people in one subway car to give you an estimate of the size distribution of all the citizens in New York City who ride the subway. You would get a distribution, but it would be especially inaccurate for the extremes in size, whether very large or very small. To deal with this problem, statisticians usually designate *confidence limits* for the line that best fits their distribution. Confidence limits, shown in figure 14.2, define an envelope that is parallel to the calculated frequency curve and that contains almost all of the scatter in the data. The lower line that defines the envelope is the 5 percent confidence limit; in the view of a statistician, all but 5 percent of the data will likely fall above this line. The upper line is the 95 percent confidence limit; all but 5 percent of the data will likely fall below it.

The size of the confidence limits tells us something about the alleged accuracy of the frequency curve itself. For the Salmon River data set, the 100-year event is calculated to be 89,200 cfs. However, there is a 95 percent probability that the 100-year event will be less than 119,000 cfs and a 95 percent probability that the 100-year event will be greater than 63,800 cfs (this translates to a 90% probability that the 100-year event lies between these two figures). All these probabilities get confusing, but what is important to note is that in reality, the 100-year event probably lies somewhere between 63,800 and 119,000 cfs—a full 55,200 cfs potential variation!

The "uncertainty" of frequency analysis as expressed by the size of confidence limits is only part of the story. The boom period of dam planning and construction in California took place during the first half of this century. For many of the state's rivers, there was only a limited data set available for estimating flood recurrence intervals. The small size of the data sets presumably produced large potential error, which would have been reflected in the confidence limits. In an ideal world, these large confidence limits would have been taken into account in the design of dams.

But what if the limited period that has been sampled is so small that it is not representative of the range and distribution of expected flood values? The Salmon River discharge data have been split into two subsets to illustrate this (fig. 14.4): discharge data that predate 1950 and discharge data that postdate 1950. Although there was a prolonged drought during the depression, the climate of the first half of this century was kinder and gentler than the latter half, with a maximum peak discharge of only 26,000 cfs as compared to the 100,000 cfs of 1964. Figure 14.4 illustrates the problems that occur when only limited data sets are available. For the first half of the century, the estimated 100-year flood would have been 45,000 cfs. For the second half of the century, the 100-year flood would be 112,000 cfs: two and one-half times greater. Worse yet, the two frequency curves lie completely outside of each other's so-called 95 percent confidence limits. Even the envelopes defined by the confidence limits do not overlap for the high discharge events. Even if modified with data from regional and historical analyses (outlined above), there are still likely to be substantial differences in the estimated frequency curves of the two subsets.

Confidence limits and the accuracy of frequency curves for any given river depend in part on the extent of the available data. Even large data sets (by California standards) are likely to have large confidence limits. In addition, long-term random shifts in rainfall and discharge patterns are likely to be an inescapable artifact embedded in the record. Depending on the period of the record analyzed and the chance occurrence of the rare, very large event, the flood frequency curves can be vastly different. For these reasons, it is a virtual certainty that the defined 100-year floodplain—the planning tool of the twentieth century—is not the actual 100-year floodplain at any given point in time.

FLOOD RECURRENCE AND THE AMERICAN RIVER: A CASE EXAMPLE

For many northern Californians, 1986 was figuratively and literally a watershed year. The intense, mid-Pacific storm that parked in the area of the American River canyon in February of that year produced this century's greatest single storm runoff event in the central Sierras (although the floods of 1865 may have been greater). A combination of factors, including intense runoff in the American River drainage, very high discharges on the Sacramento River, and failure by the Bureau of Reclamation to

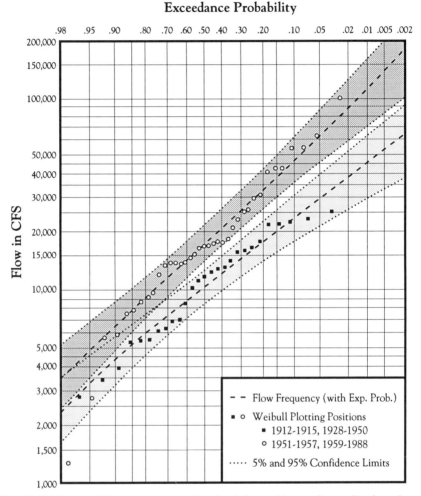

Fig. 14.4. Two flood frequency curves for the Salmon River at Somes Bar based on flow records before 1950 (light shading, squares) and after 1950 (dark shading, circles). Note substantially different estimated discharges for 100-year flood events. (Redrawn from plots generated courtesy of U.S. Army Corps of Engineers Hydrologic Engineering Center, Davis, California.)

properly operate Folsom Dam as a flood control structure, created a major flooding threat for the Sacramento area.

The February 1986 storm created hardship for many parts of northern California. However, its greatest economic impact was not associated with flooding. Instead, a far greater cost has been through the impact that these floods had on the statistics used to develop flood hazard maps within the

Sacramento region and the resultant fractious political fallout over both construction of the Auburn Dam and the continued development of the American River floodplain.

When Folsom Dam was completed in 1957 and the system of levees and canals was completed along the Sacramento and American rivers, the state capital and the floodplains surrounding it had protection against runoff from a very large storm. Based on deterministic models of runoff in the American River basin, the Army Corps of Engineers estimated that Folsom Dam could control the runoff of storms that would occur an average of only once every 250 years. Floods that occurred in 1955, 1963, and 1965 indicated that the corps' deterministic models were wrong and that the dam could really only provide 120-year flood protection. However, outside of the corps, few were concerned about the Sacramento area floodplains. After all, the mythical 100-year floodplain still lay just inside the tops of the levee system that borders these rivers, meaning that the FEMA National Flood Insurance Program did not apply and therefore would not hinder growth.

By all published measures at the time, the statistically defined 100-year event, indeed the 120-year event, arrived in February 1986. It was a close call, but it was assumed that the flood control systems operated within the original design criteria (with a few glaring glitches) and the residents were spared a calamity. As part of a reevaluation of the flood protection provided by Folsom Dam (begun before the floods of 1986), the Army Corps of Engineers took a second look at the flood frequency statistics. After all, the dam had been designed in 1949 and the flood frequency curves had been calculated from data gathered from 1905 through 1948 (fig. 14.5). With the inadvertent stroke of a statistician's hand, the estimated discharge associated with the 100+-year flood of 1986 became the 70-year flood. When the results were released, the levees no longer contained the 100-year floodplain and nearly 300,000 people and numerous large developers found themselves within the glare of FEMA and the National Flood Insurance Program.

The Sacramento area represents a case study of the four essential flood frequency concepts outlined above. The floods of 1986 shook the region loose from its false sense of security of 100-year flood protection. The flood whose odds were so slim that it seemed hardly worth worrying about predictably appeared at a moment that could not be predicted (concepts 1 and 2). Miraculously, the region was spared considerable damage. Prior to and after the floods of 1986, analysis of flood frequency was begun by the corps. Because of their size, the floods of 1986 exerted a great deal of influence on the frequency curve. The 1986 peak discharge was immediately downgraded from the 120-year flood to the 70-year flood (concept 3). In addition to the floods of 1986, the new data set included

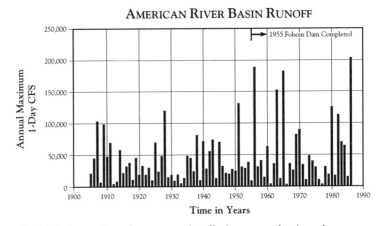

Fig. 14.5. Annual maximum one-day discharge on the American
River 1905–1986. Postdam flows reflect inflow into Folsom Reservoir.
Note significant differences in distribution of peak flows prior to and
after completion of Folsom Dam. (Courtesy of U.S. Army Corps of
Engineers.)

several large flows that occurred after the construction of Folsom Dam
(fig. 14.5). The new data set, which added these large flows to the relatively low flows that dominated the first half of this century, produced a
higher calculated slope of the frequency curve (concepts 3 and 4). A steep-
ened frequency curve means an increase in the estimated discharge for
the 100-year event. New FEMA flood hazard maps show a tremendous expansion of the 100-year floodplain, which created political chaos in the
floodplain regions of Sacramento.

Since the development of the new flood hazard maps for Sacramento,
there has been a great deal of political squabbling about how best to cope
with the pressure to develop the floodplain. A variety of measures have
been proposed to provide regions like the Natomas area with 100-year
flood protection, including raising and strengthening levees, making more
room in Folsom Reservoir for runoff, and building the Auburn Dam. Few
of these proposals directly confront the issue of the accuracy, or better yet,
the usefulness, of the 100-, 200-, or 400-year floodplain designation. The
potential errors in the calculations are extreme and no line in the sand is
located correctly, nor will that line remain static in the future (concepts 3
and 4).

Once floodplain maps are drawn up, they rapidly become embedded in
local law and land use planning. This is not the fault of the agencies that
draw up the maps; they usually give the proper disclaimers for their calculations (i.e., don't shoot the messenger). Indeed, at the time of this writ-

ing, the Army Corps of Engineers and the Water Resources Council had recently dropped the term "100-year flood" from their lexicon, recognizing the inherent pitfalls and misunderstanding associated with it. Rather, it is the engineers' and planners' craving for hard numbers and the development interests who want to colonize floodplains that drive the conversion of honest estimates of chance into precise but highly inaccurate predictors of the future. What is most disturbing is that many communities actually promote colonization of the edge of the 100-year floodplain, permitting concentrated development right up to the line in the sand as if this line will somehow protect the inhabitants. This approach to planning is a tragedy in the making.

The concept of the 100-year floodplain is deeply ingrained in law and planning strategies throughout the United States. Invented as a guideline about thirty years ago, use of this planning tool has run its course and probably run aground. It is time to devise more realistic approaches to floodplain management that acknowledge the pitfalls of calculating exceedance probability and show a healthy respect for built-in errors. To a lesser extent, the same can be said for the corps' expected value analysis. The precise calculations that are made for estimated flood damage with and without flood control structures are based in large measure on flood flow frequency calculations with extremely large errors. At present, there is no better technique for making these estimates. In light of that, it seems prudent to focus on the range of expected values for each project rather than designing them for a single, specific event.

SUMMARY

Government agencies such as FEMA, the Army Corps of Engineers, and others that attempt to reduce risk from flooding are dependent on estimates of the probability that large floods will be equaled or exceeded in any given year. Flood frequency analysis assumes that the recorded annual peak discharge values for any river represent a random sample. Using the Weibull plotting position formula, the exceedance probability for a given peak flow is plotted against its discharge. Supplemented by historical and regional analyses, the line that best fits the plot of all annual peak discharges is designated a flood frequency curve and is used to estimate the size of discharges associated with floods of a given recurrence interval.

Four important generalizations can be made about flood frequency analysis. First, the possibility that a 100-year flood will strike a river in California is the same every year, regardless of how long it has been since the last 100-year flood. Second, it is not a certainty that the 100-year event will occur sometime in the next 100 years, although it is likely. Third, in California, where historical data sets are small, the 100-year floodplain will usually expand following a major flooding event. Finally, it is a virtual certainty that the defined 100-year floodplain is not the actual 100-year floodplain.

RELEVANT READINGS

Baker, V. R., R. C. Kochel, and P. C. Patton, eds. 1988. *Flood Geomorphology.* New York: John Wiley and Sons.

Black, P. E. 1991. *Watershed Hydrology.* Englewood Cliffs, N.J.: Prentice-Hall.

Cruff, R. W., and S. E. Rantz. 1965. *A Comparison of Methods Used in Flood-Frequency Studies for Coastal Basins in California.* U.S. Geological Survey Water Supply Paper no. 1580-E.

Dunne, T., and L. B. Leopold. 1978. *Water in Environmental Planning.* San Francisco: W. H. Freeman.

Feldman, A. D. 1979. *Flood Hydrograph and Peak Flow Frequency Analysis.* U.S. Army Corps of Engineers, Hydrologic Engineering Center Technical Paper no. 62.

Griggs, G. B. 1982. "Flooding and Slope Failure during the January 1982 Storm, Santa Cruz County, California." *California Geology* 35: 158–163.

Linsley, R. K., and J. B. Franzini. 1979. *Water Resources Engineering.* New York: McGraw-Hill.

Manning, J. C. 1992. *Applied Principles of Hydrology.* 2d ed. New York: Macmillan.

Rahn, P. H. 1994. "Floodplains." *Bulletin of the Association of Engineering Geologists* 31: 171–182.

U.S. Water Resources Council. 1981. *Guidelines for Determining Flood Flow Frequency.* U.S. Water Resources Council Bulletin no. 17B.

Ward, R. C. 1990. *Principles of Hydrology.* 3d ed. New York: McGraw-Hill.

FIFTEEN

The Urbanization of California's Rivers

INTRODUCTION

California's population has expanded from approximately 1.5 million at the turn of the century to more than 34 million today. Like most modern cultures, the people who have been crowding into California have not chosen to spread out; less than 6 percent of the population live in rural regions, while the rest of us inhabit the extensive metropolitan areas of the state.

Despite our tendency to crowd into cities, the urbanization of California has taken place horizontally, not vertically. Daily, inexorably, the farmlands and wildlands of the state are converted into parking lots, strip malls, and u-store-it facilities. As a result, we have paved or reshaped the many surfaces that supply water to our rivers, and, more important, we have built our homes and mini-marts on the floodplains that surround them.

This process of urbanization has had profound, long-term impacts on the rivers of California. By creating innumerable impermeable surfaces, we have altered the sediment load and discharge regime of our rivers. Channel changes and alterations in flood hydrographs have been the natural response as the rivers have adjusted to their new conditions. These adjustments inevitably run afoul of the desires and well-being of those who live on the floodplains. The usual response is to build complex, large, and expensive engineering structures that control a river's behavior. Each of these structures, in turn, exacerbates the imbalances associated with urbanization of the watershed, often leading to a call for more engineering solutions.

This chapter reviews the impacts of urbanization on the behavior and water quality of rivers and the types of engineering solutions that are usually proposed. Dams, the most often proposed and most expensive flood control solution, are covered in detail in the next chapter.

URBAN STORMWATER RUNOFF

Urbanization involves the widespread application of impermeable materials to the surface of a watershed. Roofs, sidewalks, streets, and parking lots have negligible infiltration capacities. Rain that falls on urbanized areas is rapidly converted to overland flow, which discharges into local rivers and streams through complex surface runoff subsystems.

The conversion of farms and wildlands to urban uses involves wholesale clearing of native vegetation or crops. Most developments take years to complete, during which time the soil is laid bare or, at best, becomes covered by weeds and grasses. As shown in chapter 6, rainfall impact coupled with overland flow produces high rates of erosion on bare soils. Watersheds that are undergoing conversion to urban uses will typically have sediment yields that are one hundred times higher than rates for natural areas. This influx of sediment from urban areas overwhelms the competence of local tributaries, leading to local aggradation. Once urbanization is complete, erosion rates fall back to near-normal or even less than normal because of the stabilization of the land surface and the sewering of runoff. Some communities in California have set up guidelines or construction codes for reducing erosion and sediment runoff during construction. Most of these communities are located in steep, upland watersheds. However, outside of the Lake Tahoe region and a few select communities where erosion hazards are a serious concern, these codes are often ignored.

A second direct impact of urban runoff comes from the fact that the innumerable impervious surfaces of an urban area collect dust, dirt, and, most important, abundant urban pollutants. The range and type of these pollutants is broadly similar and, in some cases, greater than wastewater discharged from municipal sewage plants. Technically, any water that is discharged from a municipal area must meet federal and state water quality standards. The California State Water Resources Control Board had issued a directive that would require regional water quality boards to establish standards for urban stormwater. In addition, municipalities would be required to monitor their runoff and propose mitigation measures. At the time of this writing, this directive had been rescinded by the courts because economic impacts had not been fully explored.

Pollutants from stormwater runoff come from three general sources: (1) catch basins where runoff is temporarily stored during storms; (2) sewers in systems that combine treated or untreated effluent with stormwater runoff; and (3) the land surface of the watershed.

Catch basins within urban areas collect and redirect runoff from gutter systems. Between storms a certain amount of water remains in these basins either as a residual from storm runoff or as water collected during dry-weather runoff (e.g., that water you *meant* to get on your lawn but sprayed onto the street instead). The water that collects in these basins during dry-weather runoff is heavily polluted and rapidly becomes septic and anaerobic because of its disproportionately high organic nitrogen and phosphorus content. As soon as runoff enters the catch basin, this liquid is displaced and discharged into local tributaries. This produces highly localized shock pollution at the beginning of runoff from a storm. In large rivers like the American and the Sacramento, the effects of this shock pollution are minimized by dilution. However, the aquatic systems of small urban tributaries are highly susceptible to this form of shock pollution, especially in the fall when base flow levels are low and most habitats are stressed.

The most important contributor of pollutants to urban runoff is the surface of the urbanized area itself, primarily the streets, gutters, roofs, and parking lots that feed directly into storm sewers. A variety of pollutants accumulate on these surfaces. Vehicle exhaust from urban traffic produces lead, chlorides, and nitrates as well as increased chemical oxygen demand (COD) of the surface runoff. Street litter, animal feces, fertilizers, and debris washed into streets from yards add greatly to the total organic content, fecal coliform levels, suspended solids, and biological oxygen demand (BOD) of the runoff. In addition, tire wear produces extensive petroleum-based residues. The impact of this material on the quality of surface runoff depends largely on the amount of buildup that has occurred between rainstorms. Surprisingly, the rate of buildup tends to be highest in the first few days after a rainstorm, tapering off steadily after 10 days.

THE URBAN HYDROGRAPH

Most urban planners and engineers view rainfall and surface runoff as an annoyance that threatens homes and infrastructure and generally inconveniences urban life. The goal of local development designs is to shed runoff as quickly and efficiently as possible. The hydraulic efficiency of the region's natural drainage network is usually "improved" to get water off the streets and parking lots rapidly. This involves reducing the length of overland flow by capturing runoff in gutters and virtually eliminating depression storage by passing runoff rapidly through a system of culverts and channels.

The voluminous earthmoving and the systematic decapitation of hills and burial of valleys that seem to accompany most developments eliminate many of the natural channels and tributaries that cross a landscape. In this way, urbanization *technically* acts to reduce the overall drainage density, Strahler order, and Shreve magnitude of the natural channel system (chap. 7). In reality, however, each of the myriad gutters and storm sewers acts as a new low-order tributary, offsetting the effects of channel filling.

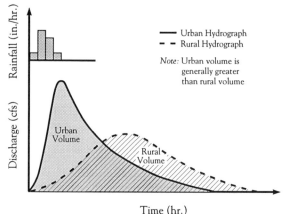

Fig. 15.1. Changes in shape and magnitude of hydrograph associated with urbanization of a watershed.

This increases the overall drainage density and magnitude and enhances the ability of the urban landscape to shed water.

The combination of increased hydraulic efficiency, lower infiltration capacities, higher total runoff, and increased drainage density and magnitude in urbanized areas can have a significant effect on local drainages and a potentially large cumulative impact on a watershed. Innumerable studies have shown that urbanization produces an immediate effect on flood hydrographs (fig. 15.1): lag times decrease, the magnitude of flood peaks increases, and total runoff volume increases. The impact on the hydrograph translates to significant alteration of flood frequency. Peak discharge values for floods of a given recurrence interval tend to increase in direct relation to the amount of the watershed that is covered by impervious surfaces and the amount of the area that is served by storm runoff sewers (fig. 15.2). This appears to be especially true for floods of higher frequency.

The relationship between urbanization and flood peaks is illustrated well in the Los Angeles basin. The Los Angeles River, which carries runoff from the Los Angeles basin, is essentially a concrete-lined ditch (fig. 15.3). During most of the year the "river" is occupied by runoff from the over-watered lawns of the area. During the winter, urban runoff from the San Fernando Valley and portions of the city of Los Angeles is funneled through several large catchment basins that ultimately feed into the Los Angeles River. Over the last 40 years, the agricultural lands of the San Fernando Valley have been steadily paved over and sewered, increasing the amount of runoff and the magnitude of the flood peaks. This kind of increase influences the calculated flood frequency curves for this region (see fig.

LOS ANGELES RIVER

Exceedance Probability

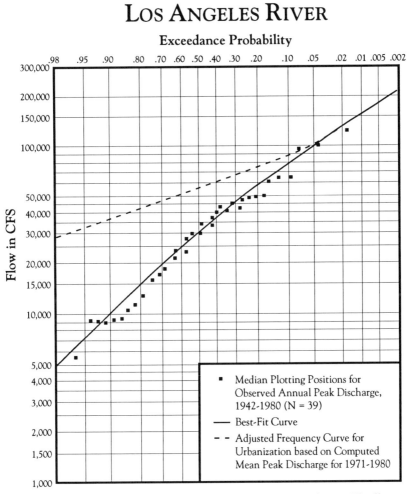

Fig. 15.2. Discharge frequency curve for the Los Angeles River at Wardlow Road. (Modified from Evelyn 1982.)

15.2). Since data from the preurbanized watershed are analyzed along with data from the urbanized watershed, the flood frequency curve is unlikely to reflect current conditions.

Today, elaborate computer-based mathematical models are available to calculate and plan for storm runoff in large urban areas. The goal of these programs is to manage runoff (and, less frequently, sediment and pollutants) on a basinwide scale and analyze the effectiveness of existing systems. Unlike models of rivers, urban runoff models can be relatively accurate because the variables are well known. This has allowed planners to gauge the effects of new development and to design mitigation measures. The goal of most measures is to increase the lag time and dampen the peak discharge of runoff events by mimicking the natural process of depression and floodplain storage of runoff. Retention ponds and lakes, temporary on-site storage of runoff, settling basins, and debris basins all serve to undo what the myriad impervious surfaces of urbanized areas create. Unfortunately, even the best drainage plans cannot offset the combination of exceptional rainfall intensities and widespread urbanization. During most of the flooding in January 1995, attention was focused on flooding adjacent to urban creeks and rivers. However, a significant fraction of the flood damage that occurred was associated with failure of urban drainage systems, not high river discharges. In addition, many urban drainage systems depend on being able to discharge into local creeks. Since many creeks and rivers were at or above flood stage during the high rainfall events, the storm sewers were unable to discharge any water, leading to intense localized street flooding.

FLOOD CONTROL THROUGH CHANNELIZATION
OF RIVERS

As noted in chapter 14, throughout California there is a centuries-old contest between those who want to live near rivers and the natural processes that form floodplains. When floods inundate the floodplains of California, the response has been to pour vast sums of money into channeling the flow of rivers or building flood control dams and bypasses so that urbanization of the floodplain can continue unencumbered—at least until the next big flood.

In the urban environment, channelization is the most common approach to ill-behaved rivers and creeks. This can involve dredging or lining of existing drainage channels, wholesale removal of riparian vegetation or snags, straightening and changing the gradient of channels, and adding embankments and levees along the margins of the channel or floodplain (fig. 15.4). The logic of all of these approaches is simple and based on the continuity of flow equation ($Q = vA$) and the Manning equation ($v = [1.49R^{2/3}s^{1/2}]/n$) (discussed in chap. 2). You can increase the amount of discharge that a channel can handle by enlarging its cross-sectional area or by making the water run through it faster or, more typically, both. This is almost always accomplished through major surgery on the fluvial system.

Channel Modifications

From the point of view of this geologist, it appears that the nation's civil engineers are incapable of accepting the natural design of rivers as an

Fig. 15.3. The Los Angeles River, a typical urban river in southern California. Extensive use of concrete lining to maintain
channel stability, increase channel capacity, and lower roughness. Photograph from Kahrl 1979.

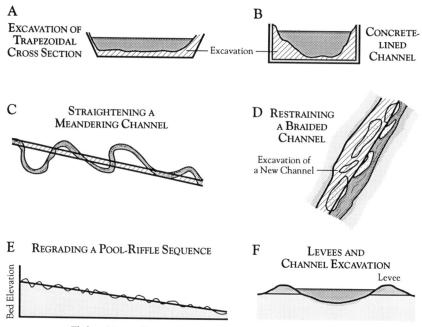

Fig. 15.4. Types of channelization techniques typically used in urban areas. (Modified from Brookes 1988.)

adequate engineering solution (fig. 15.5A). In the engineering literature the modification of rivers is routinely referred to as "river improvement," as if nature just didn't quite get it right the first time. In California's urban areas the traditional approach to river improvement is to dredge, straighten, and line a river channel.

Dredging is usually the first approach. By increasing the cross-sectional area of the channel, more discharge can be accommodated by the channel before bankfull stage is reached. There are a number of engineering hurdles associated with dredging channels, not the least of which is maintenance of bank stability. Scouring along the base and margins of channels can cause slumping of channel walls. In addition, the removal of riparian vegetation reduces bank cohesion, increasing the susceptibility of the channel margins to erosion and failure. Given the unstable nature of most dredged channels, a river can quickly undo the effects of channel dredging.

To prevent channel erosion or failures, channel cross sections are often sculpted to form a trapezoid. This cross-section geometry reduces scouring by limiting flow separation along the channel margins. In addition,

Fig. 15.5A. A classic example of "river improvement" in an urban area: Walnut Creek in the town of Walnut Creek. *Above*: Natural (or nearly so) riparian vegetation and channel geometry of Walnut Creek.

Fig. 15.5B. *Above:* Army Corps of Engineers "improvements" involving channel straightening, dredging, and lining to increase flow capacity. In many cases, these concrete-lined channels do not perform to specification. Introduction of coarse sediment loads will lead to increased bed roughness, decreasing flow velocities, and increasing flow depths. Photographs courtesy of Robert Matthews.

the trapezoidal shape decreases the slope of the channel margin, reducing the likelihood of its failure. To further inhibit channel margin scouring, engineers will often line channels with cobble- to boulder-sized material, called *riprap* or *rock revetment*. In highly urbanized areas, where channel stability is essential, the channel is lined with concrete or sprayed with grout (fig. 15.5B).

In addition to increasing the stability of urban channels, linings are often applied to reduce bed roughness and increase flow velocities. In some small urban channels, engineers have attempted to create channels that produce supercritical flow during high discharge (chap. 2). However, the introduction of sediment into these channels and the formation of a mobile bed will usually increase bed roughness, reduce flow velocities, and restrict the flows to subcritical conditions. For this reason, many of the initial estimates of the flow capacities of these channels have turned out to be greatly in error.

Along with dredging and lining river channels, one of the most often applied "improvements" involves channel straightening, including the wholesale removal of meander bends. The goal of channel straightening is virtually always based on the same general principle as channel dredging and lining: to move more water through a channel faster and more efficiently. When a meandering channel is straightened, the length of the channel axis is reduced. This has the net effect of increasing the slope of the channel, which, according to the Manning equation, should increase the flow velocity and reduce the cross-sectional area occupied by the flow. The added "bonus" often associated with channel straightening is the decrease in the total area of the floodplain that is occupied by the channel, which increases the area available for development along the floodplain.

Channel Diversions

Where channel capacities simply cannot be increased, the usual approach is to develop channel diversions. This can involve construction of "new" river channels that divert water from a main channel course, route it through or around urban areas, and either return it to the river downstream or discharge it directly into the ocean, a lake, or a settling basin. The second approach is to develop large-scale flood bypass areas. In California, the largest bypass system is along the Sacramento River. Designed in 1911 in response to flooding caused by hydraulic mining debris (chap. 11), the Sacramento Flood Control System utilizes a combination of large dams and extensive tracts of floodplain to reduce peak discharges during floods. When discharge within the Sacramento River near Sacramento exceeds approximately 100,000 cfs, weirs divert water into the Yolo and Colusa Bypass areas (fig. 15.6). These floodplain areas, which are open only to farming, are capable of absorbing as much as 400,000 cfs or more from the Sacramento River (fig. 15.7). Water not lost by infiltration and evaporation in these bypasses is either returned slowly to the river through the weir system or transferred southward in large bypass channels. In conjunction with large dams (discussed in the next chapter), the goal of these bypasses is to mimic the natural process of a floodplain within a river system. As discussed previously, the storage of water on the floodplain mutes the peak discharge and increases the lag time of the flood hydrograph, reducing the impact on flood control structures.

Levees

Whenever channel dredging or straightening occurs, it is usually accompanied by construction of levees (fig. 15.8). The goal of levee development is straightforward: by increasing the elevation of the margins of the channel, the flow capacity is increased to a point that high-volume flows do not inundate the urbanized floodplain. Modern levee systems and associated dikes and floodwalls are designed to increase channel capacity to handle a flood of a given recurrence frequency (chap. 14), usually called

Fig. 15.6. Sacramento Flood Control System in the Sacramento metropolitan area in 1975. River on right is the lower American River below Folsom Reservoir. Dark color is due to lack of suspended sediment (trapped by dam; see chap. 16). Light-colored river is the Sacramento. Large, light-colored area on the left is the Yolo Bypass, which diverts the bulk of the flow of the Sacramento River during flood stage. Photograph from Kahrl 1979.

the *design flood.* For flood control projects constructed by the U.S. Army Corps of Engineers, the size of the levee is dictated by a balance between the cost of construction and the amount of damage that is prevented by that construction. Levees built by local communities are often designed with just enough freeboard to meet National Flood Insurance Program limitations for development on the 100-year floodplain. As pointed out in chapter 14, this is a recipe for disaster.

There are two general approaches to levee systems (fig. 15.9). The first involves construction of levees as part of the channelization and straightening of a river. Here, the levees form an extension of the banks of the

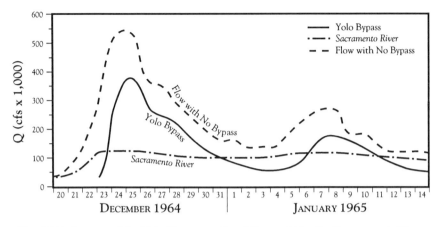

Fig. 15.7. Impact of the Yolo Bypass on flood flows within the Sacramento River during the floods of December 1964 and January 1965. (Modified from Kahrl 1979.)

Fig. 15.8. Levees along the Sacramento River north of Sacramento. The goal of most levees is to increase channel capacities, increase flow velocities, inhibit lateral migration of the river, and, in this case, aid diversion of water for irrigation. Photograph courtesy of Rand Schaal, pilot.

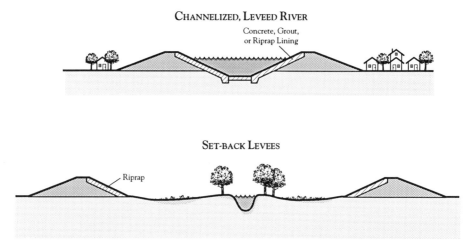

Fig. 15.9. Contrasting approaches to levee construction. Levees can be placed adjacent to channels, becoming part of the channel wall (top). This approach requires large and highly stable levees to accommodate flood flows. Levees that are set back from the channel allow the river to occupy the floodplain (bottom). These levees are smaller and tend to be less expensive.

river channel. Because the flow capacity of the floodplain is largely removed by this process, the levees must be built very high, usually at great expense. The other approach is to establish levees outside the meander belt of a river. This increases the overall capacity of the channel, requiring levees of lower total height and expense.

Levees are an engineering challenge. Like dams, they must be constructed to hold back a considerable mass of water. But unlike dams, water flows across the face of levees, subjecting them to intense scouring, which can cause oversteepening of levee banks and, eventually failure. For more than a century, Californians have been experimenting with different levee stabilization techniques. To date, the most popular is the use of rock revetments or riprap carpets that cover the water side of the levee, extending from a trench at the toe of the slope to the crest. The size of riprap material is usually chosen to be larger than the maximum size transported by anticipated flows in the channel. In many urban areas, the boulders are often grouted to increase bank stability, or, in extreme cases, the surface of the levee is covered in concrete.

IMPACTS OF CHANNELIZATION

There is a fundamental, underlying conflict inherent in channelization. Natural river systems achieve dynamic equilibrium, involving constant and occasionally dramatic change, to efficiently handle a watershed's supply of discharge and sediment. Yet it is the fervent hope of any flood control engineer that the structures designed to contain flooding remain static, predictably resisting all the unpredictable vagaries of a dynamic river system.

The commonly used blunt instrument approach to river engineering that tries to severely limit or constrain natural river behavior is expensive and, in many cases, simply not effective in the long run. The alteration of one or more of the independent hydraulic variables that govern the behavior of a river disrupts equilibrium. In many cases, since the basic influences of discharge and sediment supply remain unchanged, rivers will actively attempt to reestablish an equilibrium condition. This is often accomplished at the expense of the engineering solution that constrained the river in the first place. In addition, channelization inevitably involves wholesale disruption and, in many cases, permanent alteration of the preexisting aquatic and riparian communities.

Over the past few decades there has been a concerted effort to evaluate and limit the impacts of flood control projects that involve channelization. The nature of these impacts on California's rivers (and Californians) is reviewed here.

Impacts of Channel Modification

Since rivers meander or braid to balance their energy expenditures and transport their sediment load, channel straightening, dredging, and lining is a direct and significant contravention of natural river processes. The long-term consequences of river improvements, however, are highly variable and difficult to predict. Flow behavior and sediment transport characteristics of a modified river will usually attempt to restore a meandering or braided pattern and reestablish the original gradient.

A river's attempt to restore its original meandering or braided pattern usually stems from the development of flow separations and secondary circulation cells. As noted in chapter 4, secondary flow cells induce the formation of riffles and pools within rivers, while flow separations lead to localized deposition of material, usually in bars. Once established, the pools, riffles, and bars typical of any sediment-carrying river act to deflect flow, concentrating scour along banks. Once scour gets a toehold in bank materials, it is self-accelerating, creating meanders within formerly straight channel reaches. Where very high, coarse sediment loads occur, the formation and growth of midchannel bars during high discharge events can lead to lateral erosion of banks and, eventually, to the restoration of a braided pattern.

In attempting to reestablish its original pattern, a river will also attempt to restore its original gradient, often with unpredictable consequences.

Since a straightened river travels a shorter distance, the slope, velocity, and stream power of the river are increased. The break in slope at the upstream end of the straightened reach acts like a knickpoint. Increased competence and headward migration of this knickpoint can produce scouring upstream of the straightened channel; decline in competence that occurs at the downstream end of the straightened reach can lead to local deposition of material and aggradation of the channel, ultimately reducing its flow capacity.

Irrespective of changes in channel pattern or gradient, simply widening or deepening channel reaches to accommodate larger flows can also trigger numerous hydraulic changes that may ultimately undo the original alterations. Enlarged channels are usually designed to handle a specific, very large flow. During the design phase the impact of lower discharge flows is commonly ignored since they will clearly be contained by the channel. Yet the size and shape of a natural river channel is a product of the more frequent, intermediate flows associated with bankfull stage conditions, not the very large or extreme event. An increase in a channel's cross section through dredging produces a decline in the competence of these intermediate flows, because velocity and overall stream power are decreased. In this way, the channel is not capable of handling the sediment load that is delivered to it, resulting in localized deposition. In most cases, the channel size will be reduced utnil a cross section capable of handling the sediment load is restored.

The pitfalls of channel modification are illustrated in urban areas throughout California. The San Lorenzo River, which runs through downtown Santa Cruz, illustrates this problem well (fig. 15.10). Widespread flooding in downtown Santa Cruz in 1955 created a demand for extensive flood control projects in the area. The U.S. Army Corps of Engineers proposed a series of levees and channel alterations that would afford the downtown area protection from the 100-year flood. The design developed by the corps was the blunt instrument approach most popular at the time. The San Lorenzo River channel was straightened and, more important, deepened and widened. All riparian vegetation was removed from the riverbanks to reduce roughness; channel walls were lined with concrete and riprap to enhance stability. This "new and improved" river became a nearly straight concrete ditch—the pinnacle of river engineering efficiency.

Fig. 15.10. Problems associated with channel modification along the San Lorenzo ▶ River in Santa Cruz. *Top*: Channel was dredged, straightened, and lined by the U.S. Army Corps of Engineers to increase flood capacity. *Bottom*: Channel aggradation within improved reach of river led to significant reduction in flow capacity. Up until recently, the city spent millions of dollars yearly to dredge the channel, only to have it refill during winter floods. Photographs from Griggs 1982.

Less than 10 years after completion of the project, the San Lorenzo River had attempted to restore its profile by filling this ditch with more than 12 million cubic feet of sediment. In the end, it was calculated that the channel could only handle the 25- to 30-year flood. Millions of dollars and the complete destruction of the river had provided little to no real improvement in flood protection. To deal with this, Santa Cruz initiated a very expensive maintenance program. Up until recently, every year, like swallows returning to San Juan Capistrano, D9 tractors rumbled into the San Lorenzo ditch to push the sediment around into little piles, hoping that the next winter's flows would scour it and move it away. Not surprisingly, during very high discharge events, such as occurred during 1982 and 1983, a great deal of the sediment *is* scoured, temporarily increasing the channel capacity. However, the amount of scouring does not substantially increase the capacity of the channel to handle extreme floods.

Impact of Levees

According to the Army Corps of Engineers, there are over 5,000 miles of levees in California. In the Sacramento/San Joaquin Delta alone, there are more than 1,100 miles of levees. These levees have turned out to be both a blessing and a curse. On the positive side, many levee projects have saved local communities from regular inundation and the associated Draconian restrictions of the National Flood Insurance Program. In addition, the nation's most productive agricultural region, the Central Valley, would be flooded on a regular basis were it not for the extensive levee system. This is especially true of the delta. As a result of intense farming and associated oxidation of peat-rich soils, the elevation of large tracts of land in the delta has been declining steadily. Today, thousands of acres of farmland lie as much as 15 feet below sea level. If there were no levees, the constant interaction between freshwater flowing in from the Sacramento and San Joaquin rivers and marine waters pushed inland by wind and tides would keep much of the region underwater all year, making it impossible to farm. In addition, the massive pumping of freshwater out of the delta into the Central Valley and State Water projects would be impossible without the levee system. Agriculture and urban development have benefited greatly from the leveeing of the rivers.

On the negative side, the proliferation of levees along California's rivers has enhanced flooding hazards in some areas. Moreover, even those levees that are carefully engineered and maintained by the corps will eventually fail. The concentrated destruction associated with these failures and the inherent difficulty in predicting failures can make levees an untrustworthy partner in flood management.

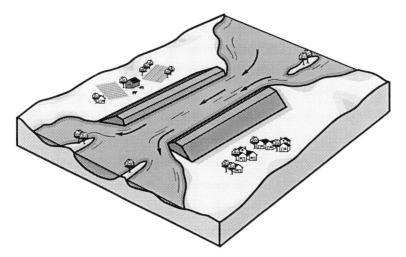

Fig. 15.11. Flow constriction during floods associated with levees. Constriction causes water to flow faster but deeper, which causes flooding upstream as well as downstream. See text for discussion.

Regional versus Local Flood Protection.   Because most levees are built either at the margins of a preexisting channel or on the floodplain some distance from the channel, the elimination of the floodplain limits the potential cross-sectional area for very high flows. This flow constriction, which produces higher flow velocities, is an integral part of a levee system's design. This constriction also increases flow depth, stream power, and stream competence, preventing the buildup of sediment within the channel (with notable exceptions like the San Lorenzo River). The high river competence in the area immediately downstream of the leveed section can produce localized bank scouring. Farther downstream, however, the expansion of the channel generates a decrease in stream power and competence, leading to local sedimentation in the river channel. This loss in channel capacity can, in turn, increase localized flooding. The areas upstream of a leveed reach tend to experience a different but related problem. Leveed channels are almost always much narrower than the natural channel system. This is especially true in urbanized areas like Sacramento where the land adjacent to the river channel has been developed. During rising flood stage, flow in the wide, natural channel is forced into these constrictions, causing the water to back up and lead to increased localized flooding upstream of the levees. (See fig. 15.11.)

The flooding that occurs upstream and downstream of the leveed portions of a river tend to initiate a vicious cycle of levee construction. Each flooded region inevitably has a town or farm in it which begins clamoring loudly for flood protection. Rather than simply telling these landowners to learn to live with the flooding or get out of the way, the usual solution is to build more levees. Each additional levee constructed along a river spreads the impact to another region, which, in turn, begins to plead for more flood protection.

If there is a lesson for California in the extraordinary Mississippi River floods of 1993, it is that overdependence on levees for flood protection is inherently dangerous. For more than 200 years the Mississippi has been progressively confined by levees built to protect each farming community or manufacturing center that grew along its edges and to enhance river transportation. During the spring and summer of 1993, the largest recorded flood in U.S. history struck the Mississippi River. Although peak discharges were not record-setting, the 90-day volume of water that passed through the system was unprecedented. Preliminary estimates by the Army Corps suggest a recurrence interval of approximately 500 years for these floods. When this large but predictable flood ran through the Mississippi basin, it encountered an altered plumbing system that had almost completely isolated North America's largest floodplain from its largest river.

As noted repeatedly, floodplains store water during major floods, attenuating the flood peak and spreading the discharge out over a longer period of time. As a river becomes progressively more leveed, an increasing percentage of the total discharge becomes confined to the channel. This moves discharge through the watershed at a faster rate, which translates to sharp increases in peak flows and a decrease in the lag time, exacerbating the very problem that levees were built to combat in the first place.

The aggregate effect of the thousands of miles of levees along the banks of the Mississippi was to produce a flow that greatly exceeded the capacity of the channels throughout the system, leading to levee failure and inundation of the floodplain. Fortunately for the larger communities like St. Louis, with its impressive floodwall protection, levee failures were numerous and the flooding was widespread. The Army Corps estimates that more than five hundred levee failures occurred within the 7,000-mile levee system. Each of these failures allowed the Mississippi to store discharge on the floodplain. This "natural" flood control system greatly reduced the impact of the floods. Had numerous levee failures not occurred, the city of St. Louis would have experienced extensive, damaging flooding, vastly increasing their toll.

Californians have depended heavily on the use of levees in conjunction with dams (chap. 16) for flood control protection. Although forward-looking projects like the Sacramento River Flood Control System have reduced the need for levees by allowing a river access to its floodplain, levees and channelization are still the first approach for dealing with flood control for most communities. Locally, levees may or may not prove beneficial; regionally, they often produce a negative effect.

Levee Failures

Intuitively, it might be assumed that levee overtopping is the biggest flooding hazard during floods. In reality, however, levee failure has caused most levee-related flooding and damage in California. Levees are usually constructed of mixtures of aggregate and local fill, often dredged from channels. To contain the mass of water within the channel, levees commonly have a relatively steep side that faces the water and a gentle slope that faces the dry-land side (see figs. 15.8, 15.9). For increased stability and resistance to waves and currents, the levees will commonly be lined with concrete, grout, or riprap.

The stablest levees that have been constructed in California are those built by the Army Corps of Engineers and the Soil Conservation Service. Although many of these levees have failed, causing intense local flooding, their overall durability is relatively high. Unfortunately, for the last 150 years, levee construction has primarily been performed by private landowners and some local flood control agencies, with little oversight from government engineers. Three-fourths of the over 1,100 miles of levees in the delta region are privately owned and maintained. Many of these levees were built in the last century, some by hand, almost all without proper engineering and maintenance. In this century alone there have been more than one hundred fifty levee failures in the delta. In recent years most of the costs of repairing a levee after failure have been picked up by the state and federal government, rather than by the private owners.

Levee failures typically occur when water under a strong hydraulic gradient seeps rapidly through a levee, discharging at its base on the landward side. The saturation of pores within the levee and increases in overall pore pressure cause cohesive material to lose shear strength, leading to failure (chap. 6). In addition, water moving through or even beneath a levee can achieve surprisingly high flow velocities. If flow rates are high enough, the water can dislodge and entrain the sediment that is used to construct the levee. This internal erosion, known as *piping*, is difficult to control once it has started. The process of piping within a levee can lead to widespread internal erosion, loss of shear strength, and eventual collapse.

Seismicity is a little-recognized but potentially widespread and sudden source of levee failure. Shaking during earthquakes increases the pressure within water-filled pores of the levee. The increased pressure causes the sedimentary grains that make up the levee to momentarily lose contact with adjoining grains, leading to a short-lived but sudden loss of all shear strength. When this happens the material that makes up the levees can flow like a liquid. This process, known as *liquefaction,* is particularly acute in older levees that were not properly engineered. When a large quake does finally strike the delta region (and it will), major portions of the levee system will undoubtedly collapse, flooding the innumerable islands and small communities that currently sit near or below sea level. Although the direct impact of this liquefaction will be local, the entire state will feel its effect since the water needs for two-thirds of the state's population passes through the complex delta plumbing system.

Urban planners throughout the state have encouraged development adjacent to or even on top of levee systems. In most disaster scenarios associated with levee failure, it is assumed that buildings and infrastructure will be inundated but not completely destroyed. This is not true for areas unlucky enough to be located adjacent to levee breaches. The velocity of flows that come through a levee break is so great that even large buildings and entire roadways are entrained, leading to increased damage costs and potentially great loss of life. Once an area is flooded from a levee breach, it remains inundated until the flood wave passes and river levels become low enough that floodwaters drain back into the river through the levee or until levee repair crews are able to plug the breach.

Biological and Water Quality Impacts of Channelization

Channelization represents an immediate and complete disruption of the riparian and aquatic communities that colonize rivers. In many cases communities will reestablish themselves within channelized reaches. However, maintenance of channels, including dredging, removal of vegetation along channel walls, and addition of riprap and concrete, can completely prevent the restoration of these communities, leading to long-term or even permanent disruption.

The overall effect of channelization and levee construction can be tied directly to a loss of habitat diversity and quality. Channelization inevitably involves a conversion of the river into a homogeneous system characterized by laminarlike flow over a smooth surface within a channel that is uniform in shape and size. The lack of spatial and textural diversity within the habitat eliminates numerous species dependent on a physically diverse substrate for shelter, reproduction, or food. This impact affects virtually all trophic levels, either directly or indirectly.

The removal of riparian vegetation that is associated with channelization directly affects both aquatic and terrestrial communities. Deciduous riparian vegetation is a local source of energy for aquatic systems. In addition, the removal of vegetation leads to increases in water temperature with associated decreases in dissolved oxygen. This can greatly affect fish, such as trout and salmon, which are dependent on cold, oxygenated water. The removal of riparian vegetation at numerous sites has a cumulative impact as well, increasing the water temperature through much of the river system.

A variety of water quality changes can be associated with channelization. During channelization, dredging and earthmoving suspends large amounts of silt and clay within the river, increasing turbidity downstream. In addition, dredging often suspends abundant nutrients and organics formerly buried within the sediment. Since most of this material resides in a highly reduced state while in the sediment, it can produce exceptionally high biological and chemical oxygen demands when mixed with river water. Materials that are often toxic, such as hydrogen sulfide, methane, and heavy metals, will also be suspended by dredging, greatly reducing water quality.

WORKING WITH A RIVER

Recently, many land use planning and river management experts have proposed that the traditional approach of channelization be abandoned for one that works *with* a river, rather than against it. This approach is elegantly summarized in a recent book by Andrew Brookes, *Channelized Rivers: Perspectives for Environmental Management.* Because of our increasingly sophisticated understanding of the biological and physical processes of rivers, we can generally predict the impacts of most land use alterations. Armed with this knowledge, engineers, planners, biologists, and geomorphologists can pursue the shared goal of minimizing the magnitude of alteration of the original river course while meeting the goals of flood control. This approach has been used widely in Europe and is beginning to become an integral part of some floodplain management and river restoration schemes in California.

As has been noted throughout this book, there is geomorphic diversity within any given river. The goal of urban flood control projects that work with, rather than against, rivers is to preserve as many aspects of this diversity as possible. This includes placing levees away from rivers so that channels have room to meander and develop riffles, pools, and riparian vegetation. Moving levees away from rivers has the added attraction of allowing rivers to store discharge on their floodplains, thereby reducing upstream and downstream flooding impacts.

Given the magnitude of land use changes in California, it is unlikely that the rivers are currently in a state of equilibrium. Rather, each river is probably adjusting to these changes in an effort to establish some new equilibrium. Any project involving flood control and river management cannot simply focus on current conditions. Instead, the project must be placed in the context of land use changes that are taking place throughout the watershed and how these changes might affect the behavior of the river and the project in the long term. Although basin-based approaches to river management have been the stated goal of the Army Corps and other public agencies, the dominant focus is still on developing incremental engineering solutions to local problems. The cumulative, long-term impacts are often ignored. By designing flood control and river management projects that work with the natural processes of a river, the overall impact on a watershed is greatly reduced—as are the overall costs.

SUMMARY

The urbanization of California during the twentieth century has led to a complete reconfiguration of many of the state's rivers and floodplains and a significant alteration of the runoff, sediment yield, and overall water quality of their watersheds.

The impermeable surfaces of urbanized areas contribute a wide variety of pollutants that degrade water quality. Accumulation of these pollutants in storm drains leads to shock pollution of local streams at the beginning of runoff from storms. The impermeable surfaces also significantly affect the hydrographs of watersheds. The reduced infiltration capacities of most urban areas and increases in drainage density and magnitude lead to sharp decreases in lag times and increases in peak discharge and runoff volume. Although sediment yields from urban areas undergoing construction are very high, they are sharply reduced in the long term.

The largest impact of urbanization is associated with channelization of rivers. Channelization can involve construction of levees and channel straightening, deepening, and lining. Almost all aspects of channelization disrupt the equilibrium of the river. Where a channel is straightened, the stream power will increase, often leading to channel and bank scouring as the river attempts to reestablish a meandering or braided pattern. Channel dredging and associated losses in stream power can lead to channel aggradation and loss of flow capacity, creating long-term channel maintenance problems. Levees create a number of upstream and downstream consequences. Declines in stream power downstream of leveed reaches lead to local deposition, loss of channel capacity, and increased flooding. Flow constriction within leveed reaches backs up water, leading to increased flooding upstream. Levee failure is a more common source of local flooding than levee overtopping. Failures are usually associated with piping, where water moves through a levee at such high velocities that internal erosion causes a loss in shear strength. Liquefaction of levees during earthquakes may be a source of future levee failures. There are regional or cumulative impacts associated with channel leveeing. Since levees deprive a river of access to its floodplain, peak discharges are increased and lag times are decreased, increasing the overall flooding hazard in the basin.

Levee construction and channelization have a number of water quality and biological impacts. The homogenization of the river substrate coupled with channel maintenance techniques leads to decreases in overall aquatic and riparian diversity. The loss of riparian vegetation increases water temperature, decreases dissolved oxygen, and reduces input of organic matter necessary for aquatic communities.

RELEVANT READINGS

Bollens, S. A. 1990. "Public Policy and Land Conversion: Lessening Urban Growth Pressure in River Corridors." *Growth and Change* 21: 40–58.

Brookes, A. 1988. *Channelized Rivers: Perspectives for Environmental Management.* Chichester, U.K.: John Wiley and Sons.

Chang, H. H. 1988. *Fluvial Processes in River Engineering.* New York: John Wiley and Sons.

Charbonneau, R., and G. M. Kondolf. "Land Use Change in California, U.S.A.: Nonpoint Source Water Quality Impacts." *Environmental Management* 17: 453–460.

DeVries, J. J., and S. Conard, eds. 1991. *California Watersheds at the Urban Interface.* Proceedings of the Third Biennial Watershed Management Conference, University of California Water Resources Center Report 75. University of California, Davis.

Evelyn, J. B. 1982. "Operation and Performance of the Corps of Engineers Flood Control Projects in Southern California and Arizona during 1978–1980." In *Storms, Floods, and Debris Flows in Southern California and Arizona 1978 and 1980,* ed. N. H. Brooks, 131–163. Washington, D.C.: National Academy Press.

Ferguson, B. K. 1991. "Urban Stream Reclamation." *Journal of Soil and Water Conservation* 46: 324–328.

Griggs, G. B. 1982. "Flooding and Slope Failure during the January 1982 Storm, Santa Cruz County, California." *California Geology* 35: 158–163.

Hupp, C. R. 1992. "Riparian Vegetation Recovery Patterns following Stream Channelization: A Geomorphic Perspective." *Ecology* 73: 1209–1226.

Kahrl, W. L. 1979. *The California Water Atlas.* Sacramento: Governor's Office of Planning and Research.

Kibler, D. F., ed. 1982. *Urban Stormwater Hydrology.* American Geophysical Union Water Resources Monograph no. 7.

Leopold, L. B. 1968. *Hydrology for Urban Land Planning: A Guidebook on the Hydrologic Effects of Urban Land Use.* U.S. Geological Survey Circular no. 554.

McPhee, J. A. 1989. *The Control of Nature.* New York: Noonday Press.

Miyabara, Y., J. Suzuki, and S. Suzuki. 1994. "Classification of Urban Rivers on the Basis of Water Pollution Indicators in River Sediment." *Bulletin of Environmental Contamination and Toxicology* 52: 1–8.

Nash, L. 1993. *Environment and Drought in California, 1987–1992: Impacts and Implications for Aquatic and Riparian Resources.* Oakland: Pacific Institute for Studies in Development, Environment, and Security.

Overton, D. E., and M. E. Meadows. 1976. *Stormwater Modelling.* New York: Academic Press.

Rantz, S. E. 1970. *Urban Sprawl and Flooding in Southern California.* U.S. Geological Survey Circular no. 601-B.

Rhoads, B. L. 1990. "The Impact of Stream Channelization on the Geomorphic Stability of an Arid-Region River." *National Geographic Research* 6: 157–177.

Shields, F. D. 1991. "Woody Vegetation and Riprap Stability along the Sacramento River Mile 84.5–119." *Water Resources Bulletin* 27: 527–536.

Simpson, P. W. 1982. *Manual of Stream Channelization Impacts on Fish and Wildlife.* Washington, D.C.: Office of Biological Services, Fish and Wildlife Service, U.S. Department of the Interior.

Waananen, A. O., J. T. Limeros, W. J. Kickelman, W. E. Spangle, and M. L. Blair. 1977. *Flood-prone Areas and Land-Use Planning: Selected Examples from San Francisco Bay Region, California.* U.S. Geological Survey Professional Paper no. 942.

Warner, R. E., and K. M. Hendrix. 1984. *California Riparian Systems: Ecology, Conservation, and Productive Management.* Berkeley, Los Angeles, and London: University of California Press.

SIXTEEN

The Damming
of California's Rivers

INTRODUCTION

California is loaded with water. An average of 71 million acre-feet (MAF) of water run off the surface of California each year. During droughts, this figure drops substantially; the all-time low of 15 MAF was recorded during the 1977 water year. In an ironic twist of climatic and demographic fate, 75 percent of California's runoff is located north of Sacramento while 80 percent of the demand for that water is located to the south. We like to live next to rivers, we routinely farm the floodplains, and, more important, we get all bent out of shape when rivers have the nerve to leave the confines of their channels and run through our houses. Moreover, given the current limits of solar energy, the kinetic energy of running water is the only truly clean and renewable source of energy available in a state whose burgeoning population gobbles up more than twice the energy it produces.

The response to California's water needs—and desires—has been the development of the largest water engineering program in the world (fig. 16.1). The statistics, summed up in the 1993 Department of Water Resources Draft California Water Plan Update, are mind-boggling. There are now more than 1,200 nonfederal dams under state supervision in California. These dams alone provide a reservoir capacity of roughly 20 MAF. There are 181 federal reservoirs in the state with a combined capacity of nearly 22 MAF. Taken together, these 1,400+ reservoirs hold about 42 MAF, or almost 60 percent of the average annual runoff in California. The water from these dams is routed through a complex network of surface delivery systems consisting of more than 140 different aqueducts and canals (and rivers that are made to act like canals) stretching for thousands of miles up and down the state. In addition, the potential energy of much

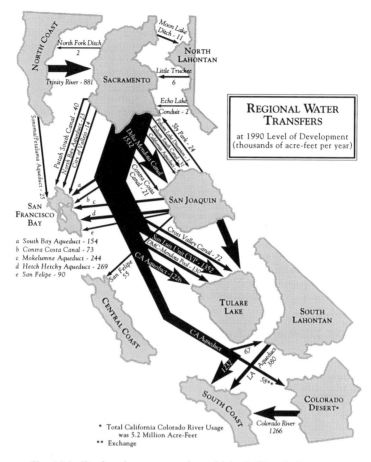

Fig. 16.1. Regional water transfers within California for 1990.
(Modified from 1993 Department of Water Resources Draft
California Water Plan Update.)

of this water is converted into electricity that supplies the needs of millions and supports the largest investor-owned utility in the United States.

Without question, these water projects and their related flood control
and hydroelectric benefits have allowed, if not fueled, the extraordinary
economic growth of California during the latter half of this century. Without these projects the main population centers of the state—Los Angeles
and San Francisco—could not have grown so large and prosperous. Without these projects California's highly profitable agricultural industry would
be a fraction of its present size. Whether viewed as public works projects

that bring benefit and wealth to all Californians or as pork-barrel environmental disasters that provide subsidized water for the benefit of a few, it is an inescapable fact that modern California is linked directly to water development.

The water that is captured and delivered by these projects is not passed around equally. Of the 71 MAF of runoff, agriculture uses around 30.9 MAF. Urban users consume about 7.8 MAF, with residential uses accounting for about half. This means that agriculture takes about 80 percent of the total amount of surface water that is consumed, while urban residential uses, such as watering lawns and filling swimming pools, takes only 10 percent.

The economics of water in California have not followed the traditional principles of supply and demand. Armed with the Reclamation Act of 1902, the Flood Control Act of 1936, the Reclamation Project Act of 1939, and the overriding mission of the New Deal, a beaver mentality permeated the U.S. Bureau of Reclamation, the U.S. Army Corps of Engineers, and the various state water agencies (chap. 10). Beginning in the late 1920s, water projects were initiated at a headlong pace. Spurious cost/benefit approaches were employed at all levels to justify spending tax dollars on the construction of dams and canals. Most of these projects were sold to the public based on their flood control and urban water benefits. In reality, the vast majority of the diverted water has been earmarked for irrigation.

Today, the availability of cheap, subsidized water has produced an artificial market in which the state's most valued resource is dedicated to some of the least valuable crops. An often-cited illustration of the market inconsistencies that permeate California's water economy is the amount of water that is used to grow the big four water users: alfalfa, irrigated pasture, cotton, and rice. These four crops receive between one-third and one-half of the total amount of water used by agriculture in California. These four crops also have the highest unit evapotranspiration rates in the state, which are a measure of the rate of water consumption. For example, an acre of alfalfa, the largest crop of the Imperial Valley, requires an average of 8 acre-feet of water per acre per year. Only irrigated pasture, the second-largest total water user, requires more. It is logical to assume that these four crops that consume so much irrigation water form a vital part of the state's economy. Rice is making inroads into Japanese and other foreign markets, and the cotton that is grown in the arid San Joaquin Valley is of particularly high quality. But these four crops, which consume nearly half of the irrigation water, make up less than 10 percent of the $20 billion total value of crops produced in California and less than 0.3 percent of the total value of all goods and services produced by the state.

How is it that so much water can be used with such little economic return? Irrigation water in most parts of California is cheap. In the San Joaquin and Sacramento region, Central Valley Project and State Water Project water costs as little as $12 per acre-foot. Compare this to urban water users in the south coast districts that pay between $455 and $875 per acre-foot or industrial users in Santa Barbara that pay as much as $2,782 per acre-foot (DWR statistics). Given the low costs, why not grow low-value crops in arid regions or areas with marginal soils? But this subsidized water, which provides irrigation for more than 9 million acres in California, is not cheap in a larger sense. The tax-supported network of dams, canals, and rivers used to collect runoff carries significant social, environmental, and political costs.

Dams and water diversions represent the most widespread and profound meddling with the natural processes of California's rivers. In this chapter, a few of the more obvious impacts are reviewed. In general, the response of the state's rivers to this near-complete rearrangement of surface runoff can be broken up into two groups: (1) channel, floodplain, and riparian responses to changes in sediment supply and discharge; and (2) water quality and wildlife impacts associated with water withdrawals and channel changes.

CONTROLLING THE VARIABLES
WITH DAMS AND DIVERSIONS

The trapping and rerouting of more than half of the surface runoff and much of the sediment supply from this state represents an unprecedented experiment in geomorphology. The factors that control equilibrium in the river systems, such as sediment supply and discharge, have been altered on a scale matched only by significant changes in climate in the past. Thus there ought to be dramatic adjustments in the profiles, patterns, and cross sections of the state's rivers. These adjustments *are* taking place, albeit in a highly variable manner and at disparate rates. However, all of these changes can be traced to the way dams and diversions alter discharge and form sediment-trapping knickpoints.

Dams as Knickpoints and Sediment Traps

A dam and the reservoir that is created behind it form the grandest of all knickpoints (fig. 16.2). Like natural knickpoints, dams represent a break in the longitudinal profile of a river. The response of most rivers will be to attempt to smooth this profile by depositing material upstream and downstream of the knickpoint, coupled with headward erosion at the knickpoint itself (chap. 7). Luckily for those of us who live downstream of ma-

Fig. 16.2. Dams of California form exceptionally large knickpoints in overall river profiles. In addition, dams create a local, highly variable base level. Monticello Dam, one of the smallest in California, is a gravity arch dam that backs Lake Berryessa. Photograph courtesy of Robert Matthews.

jor dams, these knickpoints are not often removed by headward erosion. Outside of the San Francisquito Dam disaster and the near-disaster at Baldwin Hills Dam, the state's engineers have done a fairly good job of preventing dam failures. In addition, the trapping of sediment behind the dam ensures that little to no deposition takes place immediately downstream. Thus the only "natural" smoothing of the profile comes from the deposition of material within and upstream of the reservoir.

The filling of a reservoir with water produces a new local base level for a river. For the Feather River where it meets Lake Oroville, it is as if there has been a dramatic, 600-foot rise in sea level. This rise has inundated thousands of acres of river channel and floodplain, effectively removing their contribution to the overall river system. This change in base level represents a major disruption in the shape of the equilibrium profile of the river. Throughout the state the larger rivers all have these new local base levels that alter the generally smooth concave-upward shape of their profiles. The rise in base level and readjustment of profiles *should* be causing aggradation of the river channels immediately upstream of most reservoirs. However, most rivers in the state contain multiple dams, each reducing the sediment supply to the next. Given the artificially low sediment yields, it is unlikely that we will be able to recognize significant upstream profile changes for most dams.

The local effects of profile disruption are evident to varying degrees in all of California's reservoirs. Rivers undergo a rapid decline in capacity and competence as they enter the relatively still waters of reservoirs. Stokes's law (eq. 3.1, chap. 3) tells us that the larger the diameter of the sediment, the higher the settling velocity. Differences in settling velocity lead to segregation of the deposits within the reservoir: coarse particles, which have high settling velocities and are typically transported as bedload, are deposited in the upper reaches of the reservoir while the slowly settling clays and silts form the muds that dominate the deeper portions of reservoirs. Depending on the reservoir, a portion of the very fine material can remain in suspension long enough to eventually be released to the river downstream through penstocks and pipes.

The deposition of sediment in California's reservoirs is complicated by seasonal and long-term fluctuations in reservoir levels. During droughts, most of the state's reservoirs are drawn down to very low levels. The lowering of base level rejuvenates the rivers, causing them to incise or erode material deposited when the lake level was high and to shift the sites of coarse-grained deposition toward the dam.

All the major dams of California are accumulating sediment within their reservoirs. Termed *trap efficiency*, most of the large dams capture between 90 and 100 percent of the load that is supplied to them. With the exception of very small dams, the load that does escape is dominated by the finest-grained (lowest settling velocity) material; virtually all of the bedload is trapped. When a reservoir is low, trap efficiency tends to decline as the river-reservoir transition shifts closer to the dam.

To put it simply, our reservoirs are filling up with sediment. With trap efficiencies between 90 and 100 percent, large volumes of sediment are accumulating in the reservoirs, displacing an ever-increasing volume of water and progressively limiting storage capacity. Hydroelectric and flood control operations can be significantly affected as sediment begins to encroach on penstocks and intake pipes. The nature and extent of the problem is highly variable, depending on the location and size of the dam and reservoir. In the north coast region, where naturally high sediment yields are exacerbated by logging and grazing practices, sedimentation has limited reservoir life expectancy considerably. The reservoir created by the Sweasy Dam on the Mad River has been completely filled. The Scott Dam, which creates Lake Pillsbury on the Eel River, is losing its capacity rapidly (about one-fourth has been lost so far) due to high sediment yields in heavily grazed and logged upstream drainages. There are numerous dams throughout southern California and the central Sierra Nevada that were designed to either capture coarse debris, attenuate flood flows, or supply hydroelectric power. Many of these dams are filling rapidly or have already filled with sediment, thereby reducing their effectiveness. Unfortunately, relatively little is known about the rate at which the state's reservoirs are filling. In most cases, estimates of reservoir life expectancy were made prior to dam construction. Land use changes and associated changes in sediment yield have occurred in all the watersheds that feed runoff into these reservoirs. In general, we have no idea what these changes are doing to the reservoirs and how soon they are likely to fill up.

Although there are ways to design reservoirs so that their overall trap efficiency is reduced somewhat, no one has discovered a cost-effective way to get most sediment past the dam. Some of the state's smaller hydroelectric and water storage dams have become so full of sediment that dam operators are attempting to sluice material out of the reservoir by opening the floodgates and drawing the reservoir down. This incises a channel through the stored reservoir sediment and increases the reservoir's capacity. If this operation is not conducted properly, the downstream consequences of the rapid introduction of sediment can be severe.

There is no easy engineering solution to reservoir sedimentation. The usual approach is to simply build more dams upstream to trap sediment and extend the life expectancy of the reservoir. However, for a variety of political, economic, social, and engineering reasons, there is a dearth of suitable new dam sites. Therefore, as every engineer knows, each reservoir in California is ultimately doomed.

Given that each reservoir, like a nuclear power plant, has a limited life expectancy, what is to be done when they fill with sediment? In southern California, some of the filled reservoirs are now called debris dams. They still trap coarse material, which is often mined as aggregate. Unfortunately, the larger reservoirs like Shasta and Oroville, which will not fill for many generations, will accumulate vast quantities of mud, which is unsuitable for mining as aggregate. What then? Do we dismantle the dams and allow the river to scour this vast reservoir of sediment? This would undoubtedly produce significant downstream results. In most large reservoirs a thick blanket of organic-rich mud covers what used to be canyon walls and river floodplains. What will be the regional and local impacts of suddenly adding this new "soil" to the watershed? Normally, these and other related questions would be left for the next generation to deal with. After all, our large reservoirs are far from full. However, past and present heads of the U.S. Department of Interior have proposed dismantling dams in some areas, including dams that have been around for more than 50 years and have accumulated a considerable volume of sediment. Before this option is even considered, a great deal of research on impacts needs to be done.

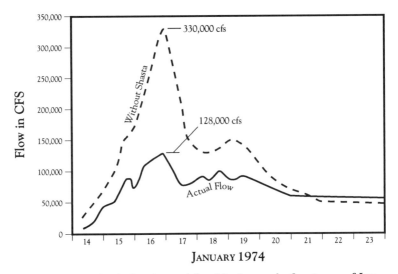

Fig. 16.3. Hypothetical and actual flood hydrographs for storms of January 1974 at Bend Bridge on the Sacramento River. Shasta Dam reduces peak flows significantly. (Modified from California Department of Water Resources 1980.)

Changes in Discharge

Dams and diversions intercept approximately 60 percent of California's surface runoff. This remarkably efficient system has reconfigured the hydrographs of all but a few rivers in the state. The nature and magnitude of the effects on hydrographs depend on the size of the impoundment and its primary function, including flood control, water supply, and interception of coarse debris.

Large- to intermediate-sized multipurpose reservoirs, like Shasta, Oroville, and Folsom, alter flood hydrographs the most. The large storage capacity of these dams allows dam operators to significantly increase the lag time and decrease the magnitude of peak discharges. In this way, all peak flood discharges, from those typically associated with bankfull stage to those with very low exceedance probabilities, are greatly reduced (figs. 16.3, 16.4). The smaller water storage, hydroelectric, and debris dams in California have a distinctly different effect on flood hydrographs. For small and intermediate runoff events, these structures produce the same reduction in peak discharge and increase in lag time seen in larger reservoirs. However, the smaller storage capacity of these reservoirs limits their impact during intense runoff events.

In addition to significantly altering the flood hydrographs of rivers, dams and diversions also change the magnitude and character of low flows

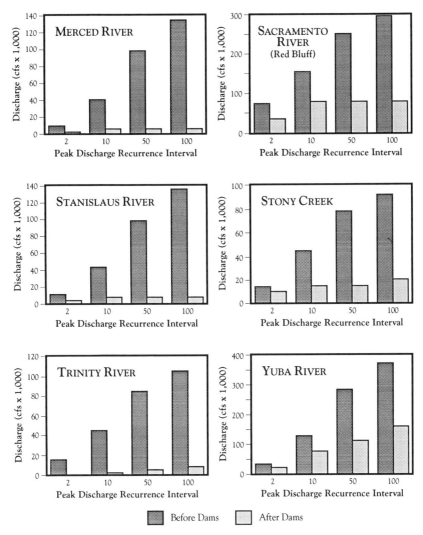

Fig. 16.4. Comparison of peak discharge/recurrence interval relationships prior to and after dam closure on selected rivers in California. (Based on data summarized in Kondolf and Matthews 1993.)

during the summer and fall. Smaller reservoirs and debris dams with no hydroelectric power-generating capability can divert perennial streams completely. Some hydroelectric and water supply projects divert so much water that large river channels become bare ditches during the summer. In contrast, dam releases for hydroelectric power generation, irrigation water, and wildlife needs on some major rivers can increase the amount of discharge severalfold over typical base flow levels. Since these summer releases are typically below the velocities necessary to entrain sediment, they have little direct effect on the river channel itself. An exception to this is the Colorado River, where daily fluctuations are exceptionally high.

GEOMORPHIC RESPONSE TO DAMS

As might be anticipated, the rivers of California have adjusted to the construction of dams and diversions in myriad ways. Differences in the magnitude and type of adjustments depend on initial conditions and the extent of changes in discharge and sediment supply. More important, for any given river, these changes are likely to be significantly different in space and time. Studies throughout the Southwest have shown that the impact of dams on the morphology of a river tends to diminish rapidly downstream due to discharge and sediment contributions from tributaries. In addition, the rate of channel adjustment to dam closure is highly variable. Most channel changes that can be ascribed to upstream dams appear to take place in the first few decades following dam construction. Regrettably, there is a dearth of data available on predam conditions downstream of most of California's major dams. During the planning stages for the state's many dams, most water engineers focused on what would come into a reservoir, not out. In addition, there is limited information about the long-term response of California's rivers to dams. Despite this, a number of generalizations can be made about the response of California's rivers to dam-controlled changes in profile, discharge, and sediment supply. For a more in-depth review of this topic, see the California Water Resources Center report by G. Mathias Kondolf and W. V. Graham Matthews and the U.S. Geological Survey Professional Paper by G. P. Williams and M. G. Wolman cited at the end of this chapter.

Changes in Channel Cross Section

The geometry of a channel is a direct consequence of sediment-discharge relationships and, more important, the magnitude of bankfull stage, Q_b (see chap. 4). For this reason, we might anticipate adjustment of channel cross sections in response to dam regulation of rivers. However, as noted above, no two rivers respond alike to construction of dams. *In general,* channel adjustments following dam closure will usually lead to a reduction in the width and capacity of the main channel, an increase in the hydraulic radius, and a coarsening of the bed.

Since dam closure decreases the magnitude of discharge, the river will seek a configuration that presumably reduces its overall energy expendi-

tures. To achieve this, river channels will modify their cross sections to reduce energy lost to friction. This is usually accomplished by increasing the
hydraulic radius of the channel through decreasing the wetted perimeter
(e.g., narrowing the channel). Where the original bed material is a sand-
gravel mixture and discharge peaks are still capable of entraining most
bed material, channel incision will often accompany channel narrowing.
Since peak discharges are usually significantly less than those that occurred
prior to dam construction, they will lack the competence to entrain the
coarsest bed material in the channel. By entraining only the finer material, the river will eventually armor its channel, preventing further scour
and changes in depth (see fig. 3.7).

Channel narrowing can create a channel-in-channel section within the
former river channel where new natural levees or berms are established
within the previous levees and a new, smaller channel is established whose
geometry is adjusted to the smaller bankfull discharge. Where sediment
supply and peak discharge are greatly reduced, channel incision isolates
the river from its former floodplain and prevents overbank flooding. This
essentially converts the floodplain into a terrace.

The change in discharge regime associated with dams is not the only
cause of changes in channel morphology. The loss of coarse sediment supply due to the high trap efficiency of most dams may ultimately play a
major role in channel adjustments. As noted above, the magnitude of the
impact of these changes is highly variable. Immediately below dams that
have relatively high discharge releases, the loss of coarse bedload and the
resultant excess stream power cause channel erosion. Where rivers traverse valleys with thin alluvial fills, rapid incision or lateral channel scouring will often remove this fill, exposing the local bedrock. Once these
rivers cut into bedrock, channel adjustments slow considerably. In channels established in broad alluvial valleys, the "hungry water" will also lead
to channel scouring and bank erosion. The magnitude of the scouring
depends on the composition of the bank material and the nature of discharge fluctuations. Channel erosion and selective entrainment of sediment below dams lead to an overall coarsening of the riverbed. The coarsening of the bed will commonly proceed until it is armored. At this stage,
channel adjustments will usually cease unless very large, rare flows erode
the armor and initiate channel erosion. The widening and/or deepening
of the channel can have dramatic local effects, including increased braiding of the river, lowering of groundwater tables, and destruction of riparian corridors.

Not all channels located below dams will undergo channel erosion.
Where dam releases substantially reduce peak discharges, the low overall
stream power may produce little to no transport of coarse sediment (see

discussion of the Trinity River below). In these settings, coarse sediment supplied to the river by local tributaries exceeds its competence and leads to channel aggradation. As a result, a narrower channel with a smaller capacity will commonly establish itself within the boundaries of the aggraded, older channel.

Downstream Channel Changes
and the Role of Riparian Vegetation

The physical processes of a river cannot be entirely separated from the biological. This is especially true for the response of river cross sections to the construction of dams. Plants in the riparian corridor have remarkable regenerative and reproductive capabilities, because they are inundated and often removed by relatively small or frequent floods. Scouring limits riparian growth to the margins of the active channel of most rivers during average runoff years. However, this does not appear to be for lack of trying on the part of the plants. During the summer the banks and exposed bars of most of the state's rivers are covered with seedlings or sprouts from willows, alders, and other riparian plants. Despite their best efforts, these seedlings cannot resist the bankfull stage flows that scour the rivers on average every 1.5 to 2 years.

One of the most visible but unstudied effects of extended drought in California is the impact that it has had on the relationship between riparian vegetation and channel dynamics. For those of us who raft California's rivers, the geomorphic effects of the 1986 floods in northern California were dramatic. Extensive migration of gravel bars, widespread destruction of riparian vegetation, and locally intense bank erosion were common. During the following six years of drought, few, if any, of these rivers achieved discharges equivalent to bankfull stage. As a result, the gravel bars and riverbanks were colonized by alders and willows. The wet winter of 1992–1993 interrupted the drought, and discharges with typical recurrence intervals of 5 years or more were recorded throughout the state. When the rafting season resumed that next spring, I anticipated seeing newly replenished gravel bars, scoured banks, and destroyed riparian vegetation, erasing the overgrowth produced by the drought. Instead, what I saw on numerous northern California rivers was a maintenance of the status quo, with virtually no significant changes. The reason, according to G. M. Kondolf of UC Berkeley, is that the fast-growing riparian species that populated the active channels and banks of these rivers were able to get a sufficient toehold to prevent erosion by the high flows. When bankfull stage or greater arrived, established vegetation stabilized the bars further by baffling flows and trapping sediment. It appears that because of the drought it is going to take exceptionally large flows to start the natural process of riparian destruction and regeneration over again. This may be the most tangible long-term impact of the drought on these rivers.

Dams mimic the effects of long-term droughts. The natural tendency of a river to reduce its channel cross section and narrow its width during periods of reduced discharge is reinforced by the rapid encroachment of the riparian vegetation. Within a few years after closure of a dam this vegetation can become fully established along the banks of the new channel. Once this vegetation becomes established, it can resist the natural tendency of the river to migrate laterally by inhibiting channel erosion. This can arrest the effects of bank scouring associated with excess stream power. However, where armoring of the channel does not take place, the increased erosional resistance of the banks can promote the deepening of the active channel through incision.

Closure of dams does not always lead to expansion or encroachment of the riparian corridor. The trees and shrubs that compose the riparian community are dependent on a shallow local groundwater table. Where incision occurs and steep, high riverbanks form, riparian vegetation cannot be easily supported and will not contribute to bank stabilization. In these settings, bank stability can be decreased by the loss of vegetation, leading to increased lateral scour and bank collapse.

Changes in Channel Pattern

The pattern of a river channel represents a least-work design that balances a river's energy expenditures while transporting the sediment and discharge supplied to it by its watershed (chap. 4). Where rivers traverse upland watersheds, the channel patterns are usually controlled by incision into bedrock. In these settings the erosional resistance of canyon walls restricts the river to a single channel. However, river channels often braid or meander in lowland areas where erodible riverbanks, declines in gradient, and increases in overall discharge require a river to expend more energy.

Depending on the size of the water impoundment and the nature of its discharge regime, the impact of dam closure on channel pattern can range from negligible to substantial. As noted in chapter 4, the meander amplitude and wavelength of a river are proportional to bankfull discharge. In the absence of channelization and levee building, single channel rivers like the San Joaquin which have had their flows greatly attenuated should show a reduction in meander wavelength and amplitude. However, since few of the larger single channel rivers in the state have been allowed to meander freely, it is difficult to determine if meander shortening has occurred.

For large dams, the muting of peak discharges (fig. 16.4) and the reduction of coarse load can promote the conversion of braided rivers to single channel meandering rivers. Stony Creek, which drains a 750-square-mile watershed along the eastern edge of the northern Coast Ranges, may offer the best illustration of this process. A large alluvial fan occurs where Stony Creek emerges from the Coast Ranges into the northern Sacramento Valley (fig. 16.5). Prior to construction of Black Butte Dam, Stony Creek was a high-gradient, bedload-dominated creek that exhibited sharp fluctuations in discharge regime. Where the creek flowed across the steeper, upper portions of its alluvial fan, erosive banks and highly fluctuating discharge promoted the development of a multichannel or braided pattern. The closure of Black Butte Dam in 1963 attenuated the flood peaks responsible for the development of the braided channel patterns (fig. 16.4). In addition, by storing storm runoff and releasing it slowly, the creek's storm flows were spread out over longer intervals of time. Most important, Black Butte Dam eliminated all bedload and 90 percent of the suspended load supplied by the upper Stony Creek watershed. Today, erosion of the channel banks and channel bed is the only source of coarse bedload below the dam.

Recent channel surveys of Stony Creek demonstrate that a significant realignment of the channel occurred following closure of Black Butte Dam (fig. 16.5). In the upper reaches immediately below the dam, the decrease in coarse bedload and the decline in peak flows have precipitated conversion from a braided, aggrading channel with a wide active channel area to a narrow, sinuous, single-thread channel. Although peak discharges are greatly reduced, the clear water being released from the dam maintains sufficient stream power to entrain material that currently lines the channel. For this reason, the channel is also undergoing incision and lateral erosion as meanders develop.

IMPACTS OF DAMS ON FISHERIES AND WATER QUALITY

Of course, the debate over the impact of dams is not centered on the downstream adjustment of river channels. Rather, most of the debate surrounding California's dams focuses on the decline of fisheries and water quality. According to studies conducted by Peter Moyle of UC Davis and others, over two-thirds of the state's native fishes have either become extinct or have declined to a level that evokes concern among fisheries biologists. Although the introduction of nonnative species has played an important role in this decline, habitat degradation and barriers to migration are the major causes. At the same time, overall water quality in the state appears to be diminishing. The primary causes of both problems are our increasing demand for water and the structures that we build to meet that demand. The complexity of these two issues is well beyond the scope of this book. However, a brief summary is offered here.

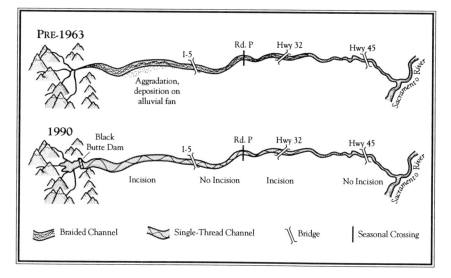

Fig. 16.5. Channel changes in lower Stony Creek following closure of Black Butte Dam. Note the conversion of a braided river to a single-channel, meandering river. (Modified from Kondolf and Swanson 1993.)

Impacts of Dams on Fisheries and Wildlife Habitat

The state's anadromous fishes have been hardest hit by dams and water diversions. Because these fish must occupy many different niches during their migration downriver to the ocean and upriver again to spawn, they are particularly susceptible to habitat degradation. Of all California's anadromous fishes, the Pacific salmon has become the center of debate. Their significant commercial value, their value as an index species for measuring habitat decline, and the precipitous decrease in their overall population have made the salmon the poster child of efforts to preserve and restore wildlife habitat in the state's rivers.

As noted in chapter 12, the decline in anadromous salmonids is associated primarily with the construction of dams, although logging, channelization, in-stream mining, and other land uses have contributed. Dams limit the ability of salmon to spawn by inhibiting their migration. Despite millions of dollars invested in the design and construction of fish ladders, salmon are simply unable to get around the state's large dams. In addition to acting as barriers to migration, dams severely degrade spawning habitat and water quality.

The spawning needs of the Pacific salmon are discussed in chapter 12. To review, adult female salmon lay eggs in the coarse, well-sorted gravels of riffles and gravel bars. Infiltration of the eggs into the interstices between gravels protects them from entrainment, while the fast-moving, cool, well-oxygenated water that moves across the gravels is ideal for their development. Changes in discharge and coarse sediment supply associated with dam closure can alter the number and quality of salmon nesting sites significantly.

As noted above, where dams with high trap efficiencies continue to release high peak discharges, excess stream power will lead to widespread channel scouring or incision. To build Shasta Dam on the Sacramento River, state engineers mined millions of cubic yards of gravel out of the Sacramento River bed. Following completion of the dam, hungry water cannibalized the remaining gravels, leaving little to no available spawning habitat. In addition, channel incision and channel scouring have led to the development of armored channels or, in many cases, exposure of erosionally resistant bedrock units. Because Shasta Dam continues to release highly competent discharges (fig. 16.4), the size of the sediment that makes up the channel armor is, in most areas, too coarse for spawning salmon.

To rectify this problem, the California Department of Fish and Game and the California Department of Water Resources have been attempting to restore spawning habitat by reintroducing gravel to the Sacramento River. This unusual program has met with variable success, primarily because large releases simply wash away most gravel that is put into the river. The source of the introduced gravel makes this a particularly nettlesome problem. Presently, much of this gravel is derived from in-stream mining operations on tributaries that feed into the Sacramento. Besides creating a number of direct aggregate mining-related impacts (chap. 11), this reduces an important supply of gravel from tributaries that feed into the Sacramento.

Not all dams cause loss of spawning gravels through erosion. Prior to the closure of the Trinity Dam in 1960, the Trinity River supported one of the richest salmonid stocks in northern California. Events related and unrelated to the Trinity Dam have severely altered the spawning habitats along the Trinity, leading to a sharp decline in salmonid populations.

Since dam closure, nearly 80 percent of the runoff in the upper Trinity River has been transferred to the Sacramento River via tunnels and aqueducts. The impact of the export of this water has been the virtual elimination of floods. To add to this, the watersheds of the Trinity's tributaries have been logged intensively using tractor yarding techniques (chap. 12). These watersheds are underlain by notoriously unstable soils that, when disturbed, produce exceptionally high sediment yields. Sediment produced by these high erosion rates usually is stored within tributaries. However, high runoff events, such as the storms of 1964, have moved much of it into the main stem of the Trinity.

The increase in available fine sediment and the decrease in peak flood flows have led to substantial readjustment of the Trinity River channel (fig. 16.6). Although the channel underwent initial aggradation and lateral scouring during the flood of 1964, it has narrowed substantially since then. Alders and other riparian plants have become well established along the edges of the base flow channel, stabilizing it and inhibiting lateral migration. Although still present, the gravels that would normally make up the key spawning habitats have been buried by the fine sediments that have filled the aggraded channels. Lack of "flushing flows" competent to remove the fine sediment has inhibited the exhumation of the gravels.

The loss of flushing flows and the reduction in availability of coarse gravels for spawning habitat are not the sole causes of habitat degradation. Many dams also affect the timing, magnitude, and temperature of flows. During the summer and fall, large reservoirs tend to develop stratified water masses, with cold, dense water sinking to the deeper portions of the reservoir and warm water covering the surface. For maximum hydroelectric power generation, dam operators like to tap the warm water near the top of the reservoir because, with its higher elevation, it has the highest hydraulic head and the most potential energy. However, salmon eggs and fry are highly susceptible to increases in water temperatures. The warm water released for hydroelectric power generation appears to produce high rates of mortality when it reaches spawning grounds downstream.

The timing of releases may also work against the migratory and spawning habits of anadromous fishes. Large releases during the incubation period, or immediately after the eggs hatch, can scour spawning gravels, removing the eggs. In addition, once the alevins become fingerlings, they are dependent on spring runoff and snowmelt to aid their movement to an estuary or the Pacific Ocean. Reductions in spring flows associated with dams reduce the ability of these fish to reach the ocean.

Sacramento/San Joaquin Delta: Declining Water Quality and Endangered Species

If the Pacific salmon has become the poster child of the movement to preserve or restore wildlife habitat in rivers, the Sacramento/San Joaquin Delta has become the battlefield. It is the centerpiece of California's water politics and policies. The delta receives run-off from 40 percent of the state's surface, annually channeling 27.8 MAF through almost 750,000 acres of wetlands, farms, tidal channels, floodplains, and river channels (figs. 16.7, 16.8). According to the Department of Water Resources, the delta is also the state's most diverse and productive ecosystem. Two-thirds of the state's Chinook salmon stocks migrate through it annually, more

Fig. 16.6. Aerial photograph of Trinity River below Lewiston Dam. *Top*: River prior to dam closure (1960) showing large, active channel area. *Bottom*: Photograph in 1977 following closure of dam. Note reduced channel size and evidence for encroachment of riparian vegetation. Photograph from Kondolf and Matthews 1993.

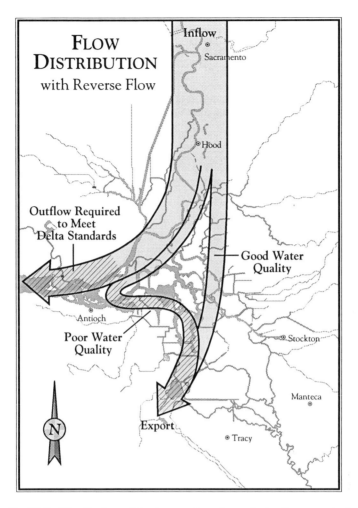

Fig. 16.7. Distribution of freshwater flow through the Sacramento/
San Joaquin Delta. During low-flow periods, pumping plants located
at the southern end draw high-salinity water from the mouth of the
delta, creating reverse flow conditions and declining delta water
quality. (Modified from 1993 Department of Water Resources Draft
California Water Plan Update.)

Fig. 16.8. 1987 USDA aerial photograph of the Sacramento/San Joaquin Delta illustrating intense channel modifications to accommodate farms. These channel modifications have significantly altered the plumbing system of the delta. See the text for discussion.

than three hundred species of animals colonize its waters and shores, and nearly half of the waterfowl of the Pacific Flyway winter in its marshes and sloughs.

Currently all or part of the water for two-thirds of the state's population and the irrigation water for nearly 5 million acres of farmland passes through the delta. The State Water Project extracts around 2.1 MAF per year from the delta at the Harvey O. Banks Pumping Plant, and the Central Valley Project extracts around 2.5 MAF at the Tracy Pumping Plant. Municipal water districts in the San Francisco Bay Area extract around 0.4 MAF per year, and local delta farms remove around 0.9 MAF per year

(Department of Water Resources statistics, 1993). Besides reducing the total outflow of the delta, these diversions contribute to significant losses in fisheries and wildlife. There are more than 1,800 unscreened diversions for agricultural use in the delta alone. In the prime growing season they divert roughly one-quarter of the freshwater flowing through the delta, sucking up large numbers of larval and juvenile fish stocks.

Although the amount of water extracted from the delta is large, a far greater amount of water is prevented from ever reaching it. Upstream agriculture and, to a lesser extent, urban water users remove 12.8 MAF of water, with 7.1 MAF removed from the Sacramento drainage and 5.7 MAF from the San Joaquin drainage. This represents a reduction of the unimpaired flow to the delta by more than one-third. In addition, not all of the water that is delivered to the delta by these rivers is of high quality (chap. 13). Spring pesticide pulses have been recorded in the lower Sacramento River; during the summer months and during droughts, most of the flow of the San Joaquin River water is made up of agricultural runoff. As this water enters the delta, it is "augmented" by hundreds of agricultural drains that pump excess water from the numerous farms on delta islands.

The conflicts between land use and wildlife in the delta are compounded by the highly altered internal plumbing network and the interaction between this plumbing system and the San Francisco Bay. In the lower reaches of the delta, there is a gradual gradient between the freshwater supplied by the rivers and the salt water of the Pacific Ocean. Twice a day, rising tides force salt water into the delta, pushing this transition zone eastward. The amount of water pumped in and out of the delta by these tidal forces is staggering. Incoming and outgoing average tidal discharges are approximately 170,000 cfs, with peak discharges exceeding 300,000 cfs. In comparison, the total delta freshwater outflow can be less than 3,000 cfs during low flow periods. The limited amount of freshwater outflow allows intense landward migration of the transition between freshwater and brackish or mixed saltwater and freshwater. During the 1929–1934 drought, irrigation withdrawals coupled with low runoff allowed saltwater intrusion in the delta to reach as far east as Stockton, seriously degrading water supplies for delta agricultural communities. Today, releases from CVP and SWP dams are used to help hold back some of the saltwater intrusion, although intrusion reached well into the delta during the 1976–1977 and 1987–1992 droughts.

That cruel twist of geographic and demographic fate that has placed the water of far northern California as far away as possible from water-hungry southern California operates in microcosm within the delta. Most of the water that flows into the delta comes from the Sacramento River to the north, while all of the demand for that water lies to the south (fig. 16.7). Upstream withdrawals have virtually eliminated the San Joaquin River as a major contributor to delta flows. The channel networks that develop in estuaries (remember, the delta is not a true delta but an estuary) evolve in a manner that most efficiently transmits freshwater out during high runoff events while absorbing tidal flows throughout the year. During much of the year, the CVP and SWP withdraw 11,000 cfs. This means that water entering the northern end of the delta through the Sacramento River must somehow make it across the existing channel network to the pumping plants located at its far southern end (fig. 16.7). This north-south flow of water is in direct conflict with a delta plumbing system "designed" to primarily move water in an east-west direction after it enters the delta. During high runoff years, the transfer of this water across the delta does not cause problems. Water that enters the delta in the north makes it to the export pumps via various canals and leveed river channels. However, in low runoff years, such as during the drought of 1987–1992, there is widespread development of *reverse flow* within the delta (fig. 16.5). This occurs when water demand for delta agriculture and the SWP and CVP pumps exceeds the through-flow of freshwater in local channels. This excess pumping causes the lower portions of the San Joaquin River and parts of the Old River and Middle River to defy natural laws and reverse, or actually begin flowing uphill. Many biologists have suggested that the reverse flows directly or indirectly attract fish, eggs, and larvae toward delta pumps. In addition to the high mortality rates caused by the pumps and screens themselves, biologists have found that populations drawn to the pumps tend to have lower overall productivity and increased losses from predation.

Reverse flow is a complex engineering and water quality problem. Since the tidal action of the delta dwarfs the amount of freshwater flow, tides accelerate reverse flow and exacerbate declining water quality. To counteract reverse flow conditions, releases from CVP and SWP reservoirs must be increased. Known as *carriage water,* these releases have to be timed for the optimum interaction with the tidal cycle and export pumps. Of course, it is rarely suggested that the pumps simply be turned off.

SUMMARY

The regional impacts of diversions and dams on California's rivers stem from the response of a river system to emplacement of a nonerodible knickpoint (a dam), reductions in size and quantity of sediment supply, decreases in peak and total discharge, and the timing and/or source of water released back into rivers. California's rivers are adjusting to these changes in a variety of ways. The upstream change in base level associated with closure of a dam causes rapid sedimentation and aggradation as a river enters the reservoir. The trap efficiencies of the state's reservoirs are high. For this reason, accumulation of sediment and the loss of storage capacity are likely to be long-term management problems. The downstream effects of dams are associated with modified releases of clear water with excess stream power.

Where discharge releases are high, competent flows scour riverbanks and incise channels. Erosion within sediment-starved rivers can armor channels and bars with cobble or boulder-sized material, reducing the long-term effects of scour. Where peak discharges are greatly reduced, channel aggradation can occur due to the lack of flows with sufficient stream power to scour material supplied by tributaries. Reductions in peak and average flows may also produce hydraulic readjustment of the geometry of channels. This often involves a reduction in the hydraulic radius of the active channel to accommodate the new bankfull stage. Where summer and fall releases are sufficient to support growth of riparian vegetation, encroachment has stabilized riverbanks, further confining adjusted channels. In other areas, channel incision has drained local water tables, leading to the complete elimination of riparian communities.

The decline in coarse bedload and the muting of peak discharge will have an impact on channel patterns. Some of the state's rivers have responded by converting from multichannel, braided patterns to single channel, meandering river patterns.

Wildlife habitat and water quality have been impacted by dams and water diversions. All major dams in California act as barriers to migration, eliminating some populations of Pacific salmon and greatly reducing others. Reduction in the supply of coarse gravels and the lack of flows sufficient to remove fines have limited spawning habitat for salmonids. In addition, the timing and temperature of releases from large dams have inhibited the development of their eggs and alevins.

The cumulative downstream effects of dams and diversions are best represented by events currently taking place in the Sacramento/San Joaquin Delta. Declining water quality is a result of too many diversions, both upstream and within the delta, coupled with a natural plumbing system that is poorly designed to transfer water north to south. Flow reversals, saltwater intrusion, unscreened water diversions, and a burgeoning population of introduced species have led to a speedy decline in the delta's native aquatic fauna.

RELEVANT READINGS

Andrews, E. D. 1986. "Downstream Effects of Flaming Gorge Reservoir on the Green River, Colorado and Utah." *Geological Society of America Bulletin* 97: 1021–1023.

Blodgett, J. C. 1989. *Assessment of Hydraulic Changes Associated with Removal of Cascade Dam, Merced River, Yosemite Valley, California.* U.S. Geological Survey Open-File Report no. 88-0733.

Brune, G. M. 1953. "The Trap Efficiency of Reservoirs." *Transactions of the American Geophysical Union* 34: 407–418.

California Department of Water Resources. 1980. *California Flood Management: An Evaluation of Flood Damage Prevention Programs.* Sacramento: Resources Agency.

Gregory, K. J. 1987. "River Channels." In *Human Activity and Environmental Processes*, ed. K. J. Gregory and D. E. Walling, 207–235. Chichester, U.K.: John Wiley and Sons.

Hunt, C. E., and V. Huser. 1988. *Down by the River: The Impact of Federal Water Projects and Policies on Biological Diversity.* Washington, D.C.: Island Press.

Kondolf, G. M., and W. V. G. Matthews. 1993. *Management of Coarse Sediment on Regulated Rivers.* California Water Resources Center Report no. 80.

Kondolf, G. M., and M. L. Swanson. 1993. "Channel Adjustments to Reservoir Construction and Gravel Extraction along Stony Creek, California." *Environmental Geology* 21: 256–269.

Lufkin, A., ed. 1991. *California's Salmon and Steelhead: The Struggle to Restore an Imperiled Resource.* Berkeley, Los Angeles, and Oxford: University of California Press.

Mahmood, K. 1987. *Reservoir Sedimentation: Impact, Extent and Mitigation.* World Bank Technical Paper no. 71. Washington, D.C.: World Bank.

McPhee, J. A. 1989. *The Control of Nature.* New York: Farrar, Straus, Giroux.

Moyle, P. B., and J. E. Williams. 1990. "Biodiversity Loss in the Temperate Zone: Decline of the Native Fish Fauna of California." *Conservation Biology* 4: 275–284.

National Research Council. 1992. *Restoration of Aquatic Ecosystems: Science, Technology, and Public Policy.* Washington, D.C.: National Academy Press.

Petts, G. E. 1984. *Impounded Rivers: Perspectives for Ecological Management.* Chichester, U.K.: John Wiley and Sons.

Simmons, P. 1993. *California Water: The Inland Surface Waters Plan Litigation, and Revisiting Basic Issues in Water Quality Regulation.* New York: Shepard/McGraw-Hill.

Stromberg, J. C., and D. T. Patten. 1990. "Riparian Vegetation Instream Flow Requirements: A Case Study from a Diverted Stream in the Eastern Sierra Nevada, California, USA." *Environmental Management* 14: 185–194.

van de Ven, F. H. M., ed. 1991. *Hydrology for the Water Management of Large River Basins.* Wallingford, U.K.: International Association of Hydrological Sciences.

Williams, G. P., and M. G. Wolman. 1984. *Downstream Effects of Dams on Alluvial Rivers.* U.S. Geological Survey Professional Paper no. 1286.

Xu, J. X. 1990. "An Experimental Study of Complex Response in River Channel Adjustment Downstream from a Reservoir." *Earth Surface Processes and Landforms* 15: 43–53.

SEVENTEEN

The Future

Changing Climate, Changing Rivers

INTRODUCTION

For those charged with the unwieldy task of managing the rivers and water resources of California, land use changes over the past 200 years have produced a complex and often intractable array of problems. All government agencies who have some jurisdiction over the rivers of California are faced with these problems and how to manage them in the most cost-effective manner. There are no simple answers, no silver bullets, no Best Management Practices that can resolve these problems overnight. Most important, solutions will inevitably involve political risk. Because of this, changes are likely to take place slowly and incrementally. At the time of this writing, new faces and new ideologies are appearing at the top of the major federal regulating agencies. The indication is that at least some of the important players are willing to take the political risks to try to solve these problems. Change has yet to filter down to the state level, but eventually change will be forced, either by the courts, or by an angry electorate, or by federal mandate.

Although the attention of most government agencies is absorbed with managing our current and near-term resource problems, there is a larger, long-term problem looming on the horizon: global climate change. Since climate is a dominant independent variable in geomorphic systems, even subtle changes in temperature and seasonal precipitation patterns may produce substantial readjustments in the state's rivers. Most of the billions of dollars' worth of infrastructure that captures runoff, prevents (some) floods, and transfers water was designed in the first half of this century. By all measures this was a relatively benign period in the state's climate history. If there is a substantial change in the climate of California, it is very likely that our present water supply and flood control system will prove inadequate to meet the needs of our growing state.

Fortunately, this problem is not being ignored. There are numerous researchers all over the world (with a healthy contingent in California) who are attempting to predict the nature of global climate change and the consequences for our water resources. This chapter provides a brief, generalized overview of the identified problems that we are likely to face as the earth's climate shifts.

CLIMATE CHANGE:
GLOBAL COOLING, GLOBAL WARMING

Global climate is hardly static. As discussed in chapter 8, climate is the product of the earth's effort to balance differential heating by the sun. This balancing system is frighteningly complex, involving the transfer of heat and moisture between the ocean, atmosphere, continental landmasses, and ice sheets—all in a system with a seemingly infinite array of feedbacks. It is these feedbacks, coupled with long-term changes in the distribution and intensity of solar radiation, that produce large fluctuations in the earth's climate.

Glacials versus Interglacials

For two centuries earth scientists have been pointing to evidence for dramatic prehistoric changes in climate as a predictor of our fate. During the past few million years, the earth has vacillated back and forth between glacial periods, when large continental ice sheets dominated the high and midlatitudes, and interglacial periods, when latitudinal temperature gradients were not as extreme and midlatitude and boreal regions were characterized by warmer, more equable climates. There have been no less than seventeen glacial-interglacial cycles over the past few million years, with even more numerous smaller-scale fluctuations. The mechanism(s) that trigger ice ages remain, to this day, in dispute. Sunspots and variations in intensity of solar radiation have been cited as a cause. Volcanic eruptions like that at Mount Pinatubo have been shown to greatly reduce solar radiation, which may lead to cooling that initiates ice ages. The eccentricity of the earth's orbit around the sun, along with the procession or "wobble" in the earth's axis of rotation, causes cyclic variations in intensity in solar heating as well as the duration and timing of the earth's seasons. These changes, known as Milankovitch cycles, have distinctive periodicities and have been widely linked to cyclic climatic changes of the past billion years. Interglacial dust, changes in continental configuration, Antarctic ice sheet surges,

positive feedback between albedo and surface temperatures in high latitudes, global rises and falls in atmospheric CO_2—all have been cited as
mechanisms that either trigger ice ages or bring them to an end. It is a
veritable candy store of choices, with each potential mechanism a reasonable cause. Regardless of how ice ages are initiated or terminated, they *are*
going to happen again, and their appearance will change the way rivers in
California work.

Since few of us will live for more than a century, it is difficult to get ex-
cited about the natural oscillation between glacial and interglacial periods.
It has long been assumed that the global changes associated with these os-
cillations are relatively gradual on a human scale (but abrupt by geologic
standards). After all, for the last ten thousand years or so the earth has
been in an interglacial period with generally stable or mildly fluctuating climatic conditions. Return to glacial domination of the earth will inevitably
occur, and with it will come dramatic dislocation of human populations and
a reconfiguration of innumerable plant and animal communities, especially in the high to midlatitudes. But most who study glacial periods have
pointed out that change will occur over centuries, allowing a gradual adjustment rather than catastrophic change—maybe.

In 1992 and 1993, American and European researchers began analyzing two separate two-mile-long cores taken from the Greenland ice sheet.
The light stable isotope geochemistry of the Greenland ice allowed the researchers to reconstruct temperature fluctuations. At the same time, dust
particles trapped in the ice allowed them to track periods when high winds,
typically associated with cold climates, blew dust off the world's deserts
and into the atmosphere. The results of this ongoing research are both surprising and disturbing. It has long been suspected that global temperatures fluctuate a great deal during ice ages but are relatively stable during interglacial periods. During ice ages, the large temperature gradients
that occur between the poles and the equator and the general refrigeration of the midlatitudes make for a very active atmosphere that is capable
of rapid, dramatic changes. The ice cores from Greenland have confirmed
these assumptions, showing wide swings in temperature during the last few
ice ages. However, the data belie the assumption of more stable climates
during interglacial periods. During the Eemian interglacial (known as the
Sangamon here in North America), which lasted from around 135,000 to
115,000 years ago, Greenland averaged several degrees Fahrenheit warmer
than at present. The high-resolution ice cores indicate that this greater
warmth was a remarkably transient, unstable phenomenon (fig. 17.1). Average temperatures whipsawed during the Eemian by as much as 25°F
(14°C), with lows roughly equal to temperatures recorded during ice ages.
More important, the change from warm to cold took place over a period

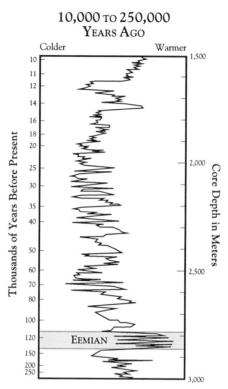

10,000 TO 250,000 YEARS AGO

Fig. 17.1. Episodes of cooling and warming over the past 10,000 to 250,000 years as recorded in the Greenland ice cores. Generally warm conditions of the Eemian gave way suddenly to cool conditions several times. (Modified from Johnsen et al. 1992.)

of as much as a few centuries to as little as a few decades. In one documented case, a 25°F (14°C) decline and recovery occurred within one *single* decade.

If the initial results of the Greenland ice core studies are borne out by further research, the implications for water resources and the rivers of California are, at best, unnerving. It is important to note that temperature shifts associated with climate change are usually much greater at high latitudes than at low latitudes. Therefore, California's climate probably changed substantially less than Greenland's during the Eemian. However, changes in average temperature of only a few degrees can have profound impacts on the amount and type of runoff that occurs (described below). Moreover, dramatic global shifts in weather patterns typically accompany cooling episodes. If the last ice age can be used as an analog, refrigeration of the North American landmass will probably lead to a southward shift in the northern jet stream, delivering more storms and more total precipitation to California. We will be a wetter, cooler place. This may, at first, seem like a real improvement, but since virtually all of the infrastructure that handles runoff in this state is adapted to our Mediterranean climate, such a change would produce some major difficulties.

Greenhouse Gases and Global Warming

Few scientists are predicting or even speculating that California—and the rest of the world—is going to cool dramatically over the next few decades. This is, in part, because it has only been recently discovered that such dramatic changes occur during interglacials. The impact of the Greenland research has yet to sink in. In addition, most scientists are convinced that, if anything, we are undergoing global warming, not cooling. Since the last Little Ice Age during the Middle Ages, the world has been warming steadily. Much of that initial warming reflects the apparent warming that follows cooling (any return to "normal" will appear as a warming event if it follows a cooling event). However, for fifteen years, legions of scientists have been loudly proclaiming that increases in anthropogenic gases like methane, nitrous oxide, and carbon dioxide are tied directly to the continuing rise in global temperature. These so-called greenhouse gases trap radiative heat that would normally escape the earth's atmosphere. Computer simulations of the greenhouse effect abound. Almost all of these general circulation models (GCMs) predict that continuing increases in greenhouse gases will raise global temperatures substantially over the next 50 to 60 years. The various models differ only in their estimates of the amount of warming.

The precise impact of global warming on California's climate is difficult to estimate. In all of these models, there are explicit and implicit assumptions and estimations that must be used in order to simplify complex natural systems enough to make them manageable. This becomes especially true for dealing with positive and negative feedbacks within these systems. Difficulties also arise because of the scale of the models. Because they are so computationally demanding, GCMs typically operate on a scale of thousands of square miles to tens of thousands of square miles. Their resolution is inadequate for most watershed planning and policy efforts.

The Greenland ice core results tend to muddy the global warming predictions as well. During the Eemian, temperatures were about 3.6°F (2°C) warmer than today. It is possible that the relatively high temperatures of the Eemian represented threshold conditions that triggered dramatic, unpredictable swings in global climate. Many of the GCMs predict that the earth will warm to the level of the Eemian during the next century. It could be that our relatively stable interglacial climate will be driven to this unstable threshold condition by our own greenhouse emissions. Or the climate may simply become unstable of its own accord. We just don't know.

THE RESPONSE OF CALIFORNIA'S RIVERS
TO CLIMATE CHANGE

Given the uncertainties built into GCMs and the results of the recent Greenland ice core studies, any precise estimations of the impact of global warming on the rivers of California should be greeted with healthy skepticism. What should be of greater concern is our ability to respond to these changes. It may be that change will occur slowly, involving a matter of a few degrees over many hundreds of years, allowing us the opportunity to plan and adapt in an orderly fashion. However, there is a distinct possibility that these changes will be abrupt and dramatic, requiring rapid responses. For this reason, it seems prudent for planners to consider all aspects of climate change and not focus solely on the consequences of increased warming.

The important hydrologic impacts of climate change are likely to be felt most strongly through changes in the state's snowpack. As shown in chapter 5, the snowpack that forms in the mountains of central and northern California acts as the state's largest single reservoir, storing winter precipitation for release throughout the late spring and early summer. Changes in the amount of water stored in the snowpack, along with shifts in the timing and amount of peak snowmelt, are likely to be the first noticeable effects of climate change. They are also likely to be the largest water management challenge.

Scientists from the U.S. Geological Survey and the University of California have been attempting to model the potential impacts of climate change on runoff conditions in California. The usual approach is to evaluate how historic seasonal differences in temperature and precipitation have translated into changes in the timing and magnitude of runoff.

As noted in chapter 8, it is the irregular distribution of precipitation that controls the character of runoff in California. Even in winter, precipitation is an unusual occurrence. According to researchers from Scripps Institute of Oceanography, measurable precipitation in the Sierra Nevada occurs on only 45 percent of winter days, and most of that precipitation is light. Infrequent heavy precipitation, which occurs less than 20 percent of the time, makes up almost two-thirds of the total amount of precipitation that is received by the state. In addition, the longer a storm lasts, the more intense the daily rainfall totals are likely to be. Any changes in climate that alter the frequency and duration of rare large storms even slightly may produce substantial changes in total precipitation.

Variations in the total amount of precipitation are not likely to be the sole cause of changes in California's runoff picture. The overall temperature of circulation patterns plays a key role. There are four general types of winter precipitation patterns in California: cool-wet, cool-dry, warm-wet, and warm-dry. Each pattern is associated with its own unique atmospheric circulation (chap. 8). There are a number of key differences between these patterns that control the timing and amount of runoff. In higher-elevation watersheds there is an unmistakable delay in the timing of runoff between cool years and warm years, regardless of the amount of precipitation. During cool-wet and cool-dry winters, peak runoff is delayed by as much as two months because of the slower ripening of the snowpack. Low-elevation watersheds, like those of the north coast, are less affected by this difference. The limited amount of snowfall in these watersheds means that peak runoff occurs primarily within the winter months, regardless of the type of winter circulation patterns.

Temperature not only controls the timing of peak runoff but also appears to influence the total yearly volume of runoff that occurs within a watershed. Studies cited at the end of this chapter have shown that changes in average annual temperature in the Sacramento–San Joaquin basin are likely to affect the total amount of runoff significantly. The reasoning behind this is based partially on the distribution of snowfall and rainfall and the impact of higher temperatures on winter soil-moisture contents and evapotranspiration rates. For example, regressive models of runoff in the American River watershed show that increases in average annual temperature of 2°C to 4°C (3.6°F to 7.2°F) would not only shift peak runoff to earlier in the season but would also lead to decreases in total runoff of 12 percent to 14 percent, respectively (fig. 17.2), even if the amount of precipitation remains unchanged. When these increases in temperature are coupled with a decrease in total precipitation (a scenario predicted by many), the effects are synergistic. A 25 percent decline in total precipitation and an increase in temperature of 2°C to 4°C (3.6° to 7.2°F) leads to a decline in total runoff of 51 percent and 54 percent, respectively.

Warming Up, Drying Out

The consequences of the warming up and drying out of California's climate cannot be accurately estimated until there are reasonably precise estimations of the magnitude of change. Although the necessary precision is still far off, it is useful to speculate about the nature of some of these changes. Declines in total runoff and shifts in peak runoff periods would

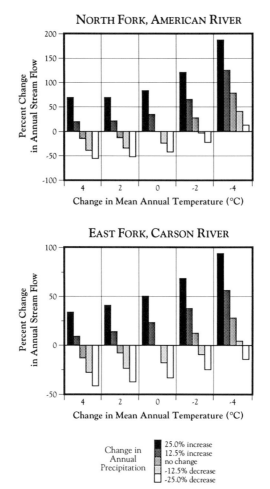

Fig. 17.2. Percentage change in mean stream flow for the East Fork of the Carson River and the North Fork of the American River from postulated changes in average annual temperature. Estimates are based on regression analysis of historical runoff and climatic data. (Plot based on data summarized in Duell 1992.)

undoubtedly have severe consequences for the state's water users as well as for fisheries and wildlife.

The state's larger reservoirs currently operate to control floods as well as store runoff. If there is a shift in the timing of peak runoff to the winter months, there is likely to be a substantial change in the recurrence intervals and magnitudes of flows. For example, 100-year floodplains will undoubtedly grow (chap. 14). To accommodate these larger flows, reservoirs will need to be drawn down farther during the winter. These flood storage requirements will ultimately limit the amount of water that can be stored by reservoirs for use in the dry months. This, in conjunction with an overall reduction in runoff, would translate to significant reductions in spring and summer flows and the total runoff available for the state's various water users.

The impacts of these flow reductions would be felt throughout the state as the various competing water users receive less total water with lower overall quality. Higher water temperatures are likely to accompany reduced releases from the state's reservoirs. These changes will accelerate current declines in water quality and adversely affect numerous aquatic species, especially those that are already endangered or threatened. In addition to reductions in the amount of water delivered to urban and agricultural users, there would logically be declines in water quality due to loss of diluting effects. This is likely to be felt most acutely in the delta, where almost all of the problems currently plaguing the region would be amplified. Substantial declines in freshwater inflow and increased demand for water from agricultural and urban users will presumably lead to increased landward migration of the freshwater-saltwater transition and a decline in overall delta water quality. If flows decline sufficiently, this intrusion may reach the large pumping plants in the southern delta, rendering two-thirds of the state's drinking water unusable.

One of the most significant impacts of global warming, regardless of whether or not it causes California to dry out and warm up, is likely to be its effect on sea level. Presently, sea level is rising, albeit very slowly. Global warming, which should ultimately lead to a reduction in polar ice caps and thermal expansion of the oceans, will presumably lead to a significant increase in the rate of sea level rise. For vast portions of California, a doubling or tripling of the rate of sea level rise is unlikely to make a significant difference in the near term. Rather, it is the wetlands, estuaries, and, most important, the delta that are likely to feel the brunt of sea level rise.

Currently, large portions of the delta lie well below sea level. Any rise in sea level is likely to increase pressure on the fragile delta levee system, increasing levee failures and disrupting the present plumbing system. In the lower delta, it is a virtual certainty that a number of tracts will become inundated and, in all likelihood, abandoned to the rising ocean. Increases in saltwater intrusion associated with declining freshwater inflows will be exacerbated by rising sea level. Given the combination of rising sea level and declining flows, it is not unreasonable to project a complete collapse of some ecosystems in the delta as it becomes increasingly saline.

Declining runoff associated with climate change is likely to impact a number of river-related industries. Geologic and historical records show that periods of warming are often accompanied by widespread forest fires.

Although this is most pronounced in boreal areas, the spectacular fires of the 1987–1992 drought show us that the same process would probably dominate California's forests. Increased frequency of severe fires would lead to conversion of forested areas to grassland and scrub. This conversion may decrease slope stability and increase sediment yields in many of the state's watersheds. The ability of the state's wildlands to supply feed for cow-calf and stocker operations would be reduced in most areas. Overall, there would be an increase in the amount of land that is sensitive to overgrazing, increasing sediment yields and impacts on already stressed riparian corridors.

The geomorphic response of the rivers of California to the warming and drying of the climate is difficult to predict. As shown in the previous chapters, the adjustment of rivers to dam-related changes in sediment supply and discharge is highly variable. There are likely to be fire-related increases in sediment yields in many watersheds. In upland watersheds the reduction in runoff and increase in sediment supply may overwhelm the rivers, leading to widespread aggradation and further reductions in storage capacities of reservoirs. Change is also likely to be associated with shifts in the discharge regime of major reservoirs. For larger reservoirs, increased winter peak discharge releases are likely to induce a cycle of channel and bank erosion. Where proportionally more water is held back in order to supply irrigation needs, the peak discharges may be significantly reduced, leading to channel narrowing and armoring. In the lower reaches of the state's river systems, sea level is likely to induce channel aggradation as rivers adjust to a new, higher base level.

Cooling Off, Getting Wet

Warming up and drying out is not the only possible scenario for the near-term future of California's rivers. The impacts of temperature and precipitation changes are even more dramatic during *cooling* events, such as those that might have occurred during the Eemian interglacial. For example, for the American River, decreases in annual average temperature of 2°C to 4°C (3.6°F to 7.2°F) would produce increases in runoff of 26 percent and 76 percent, even if precipitation totals are *unchanged* (fig. 17.2). All of these increases are accompanied by significant delays in the timing of peak runoff and general increases in runoff during the spring, summer, and fall months. If, as the Pleistocene history of California suggests, cooling is accompanied by increases in total precipitation, the runoff response is even more dramatic. A 25 percent increase in average precipitation coupled with decreases in temperature of 2°C to 4°C (3.6°F to 7.2°F) would produce whopping increases in runoff of 116 percent to 187 percent.

Imagine doubling or almost tripling the total amount of runoff from

Sierran watersheds and increasing the amount of runoff that occurs during the normally dry months of the year. In an "average" future year (remember, "normal precipitation" is an oxymoron; chap. 5), the system of dams and bypasses would probably be able to handle this, but in above-average years of runoff, our current system would be hard-pressed to prevent flooding. Although the impact of an increase in runoff would be muted by the increase in snowpack, many of the dams that were built primarily for water storage and diversion would probably become spring flood control structures. The increases in discharge released by these dams would, in all likelihood, lead to expansion of river channels through scouring. The sediment-starved water that is released will have excess stream power and, therefore, be capable of widespread erosion. The negative aspects will be increases in levee and bridge failures, bank erosion associated with increased rates of meander growth, and persistent flooding of low-lying areas like the delta. In the long term, the state's timber and grazing industries would probably benefit from a change to a cooler and wetter climate, although logging and grazing in the higher-altitude areas of the state would be greatly reduced by shorter growing seasons. The agricultural industry would also benefit from increased water supplies, although many of the crops that depend on long, hot, dry summers may need to be replaced by more suitable ones. The delta is likely to be affected most positively by declines in annual temperature and increases in total runoff. Presumably (although not certainly), global cooling would lead to an increase in the polar ice sheets and a fall in sea level. The lowering of base level and the seaward shift in the freshwater-saltwater transition are likely to cure many of the ills of the delta. Overall, it appears that the state and its rivers would be better able to adapt to global cooling rather than to global warming.

A FINAL NOTE

Regardless of which type of climatic change is in store for California, the magnitude of its impact will ultimately depend on how we, as a culture, respond. Like no other animal on earth, we possess the power to manipulate the physical and biological processes that control the behavior of rivers. For almost two centuries Californians have poured vast amounts of resources into controlling and exploiting their most precious resource. With few exceptions, these efforts have worked against, rather than in concert with, natural river processes. Today, land use planners, naturalists, bureaucrats, and even many of the engineers who have remade the rivers of the state are recognizing the economic, aesthetic, and environmental benefits of symbiotic blending of the designs of man and rivers. These changes bode well for the long-term future when a fluctuating climate will pose ever-greater challenges. Over the next few decades, the learning curve is likely to be steep and subject to the vagaries of political cowardice and expedience. But failure to learn from our failures will prove ultimately more costly. As Rudyard Kipling so aptly stated,

> For agony and spoil of nations beat to dust,
> For poisoned air and tortured soil
>   and cold, commanded lust,
> And every secret woe the shuddering water saw—
> Willed and fulfilled by high and low—
>   let them relearn the Law.

SUMMARY

At this point it is difficult, if not impossible, to predict the future of California's rivers in the near and long term. Global climate models, with all their inherent assumptions and errors, do not currently operate on a scale that is useful for planning purposes. Most predict that increases in anthropogenic greenhouse gases are causing global warming. Because of these global changes, California's overall climate will become more like that of southern California, reflecting a warming up and drying out of the state. The impacts of this type of climate change on the rivers of California and the industries that affect those rivers are likely to be severe. A shift in peak runoff to the winter months and a decline in the state's overall snowpack will require adjustments in the manner in which the state's reservoirs are managed, leading to significant reductions in spring, summer, and fall releases and a decrease in water available for urban, agricultural, and wildlife interests. The reductions in flow and a probable rise in sea level associated with global warming would have a devastating impact on the delta, leading to widespread flooding of delta tracts and a landward shift in the freshwater-saltwater transition.

Several recent studies of ice cores from the Greenland ice sheet indicate that large temperature fluctuations may occur during interglacials. In particular, these fluctuations, which may reach as much as $14\,°C$ ($25\,°F$) in high latitudes, may be triggered by global warming episodes similar to today's. During cooling events, California would presumably become cooler and much wetter. This would increase overall runoff and may, as in the warming scenario, require significant changes in the management of reservoirs. There would probably be an increase in downstream flooding associated with higher overall precipitation, although the impact of this is reduced by the tendency to form a larger and more persistent snowpack. Most industries that are dependent on surface runoff would benefit from this type of change, although there would be some dislocations in agriculture. The delta, which would experience increased freshwater flows resulting from a presumed drop in sea level, would clearly benefit greatly from this type of change.

RELEVANT READINGS

Berger, A., R. E. Dickinson, and J. W. Kidson. 1989. *Understanding Climate Change.* American Geophysical Union Geophysical Monograph no. 52.

Bull, W. B. 1991. *Geomorphic Responses to Climate Change.* New York: Oxford University Press.

Cayan, D. R., and D. H. Peterson. 1989. "The Influence of North Pacific Atmospheric Circulation on Streamflow in the West." In *Aspects of Climate Variability in the Pacific and Western Americas,* ed. D. Peterson. American Geophysical Union Geophysical Monograph no. 55, 375–397.

Charles, C. D., D. Rind, J. Jouzel, R. D. Koster, et al. 1994. "Glacial-Interglacial Changes in Moisture Sources for Greenland: Influences on the Ice Core Record of Climate." *Science* 263: 508–511.

Duell, L. F. W., Jr. 1992. "Use of Regression Models to Estimate Effects of Climate Change on Seasonal Streamflow in the American and Carson River Basins, California-Nevada." In *Managing Water Resources during Global Change,* 731–740. AWRA 28th Annual Conference and Symposium.

Hansen, J. E., et al. 1981. "Climate Impact of Increasing Atmospheric Carbon Dioxide." *Science* 213: 957–966.

Hanson, K., G. A. Maul, and T. R. Karl. 1989. "Are Atmospheric 'Greenhouse' Effects Apparent in the Climatic Record of the Contiguous U.S. (1895–1987)?" *Geophysical Research Letters* 16: 49–52.

Herrmann, R., ed. 1992. *Managing Water Resources during Global Change.* American Water Resources Association Technical Publication Series TPS, vol. 92–94.

Johnsen, S. J., H. B. Clausen, W. Dansgaard, K. Fuhrer, et al. 1992. "Irregular Glacial Interstadials Recorded in a New Greenland Ice Core." *Nature* 359: 311–313.

Knox, J. B., and A. F. Scheuring. 1991. *Global Climate Change and California: Potential Impacts and Responses.* Berkeley, Los Angeles, and Oxford: University of California Press.

Lettenmaier, D. P., and T. Y. Gan. 1990. "Hydrologic Sensitivities of the Sacramento–San Joaquin River Basin, California, to Global Warming." *Water Resources Research* 26: 69–86.

Lettenmaier, D. P., and D. P. Sheer. 1991. "Climatic Sensitivity of California Water Resources." *Journal of Water Resources Planning and Management* 117: 108–125.

Logan, S. H. 1990. "Simulating Costs of Flooding under Alternative Policies for the Sacramento–San Joaquin River Delta." *Water Resources Research* 26: 799–809.

Malanson, G. P., and W. E. Westman. 1991. "Modeling Interactive Effects of Climate Change, Air Pollution, and Fire on a California Shrubland." *Climatic Change* 18: 363–376.

Meko, D. M., and C. W. Stockton. 1984. "Secular Variation in Streamflow in the Western United States." *Journal of Climate and Applied Meteorology* 23: 889–897.

Meo, M. 1991. "Sea Level Rise and Policy Change: Land Use Management in the

Sacramento-San Joaquin and Mississippi River Deltas." *Policy Studies Journal* 19: 83–92.

Miller, J. R., and G. L. Russell. 1992. "The Impact of Global Warming on River Runoff." *Journal of Geophysical Research-Atmospheres* 97: 2757–2764.

Moss, M. E., and H. F. Lins. 1989. *Water Resources in the Twenty-first Century: A Study of the Implications of Climate Uncertainty.* U.S. Geological Survey Water Supply Paper no. 1804.

Roemmich, D. 1992. "Ocean Warming and Sea Level Rise along the Southwest United States Coast." *Science* 257: 373–375.

Schlesinger, M. E. 1986. "Equilibrium and Transient Climatic Warming Induced by Increased Atmospheric CO_2." *Climate Dynamics* 1: 35–51.

Solomon, S. I., M. Beran, and W. Hogg, eds. 1987. *The Influence of Climate Change and Climate Variability on the Hydrologic Regime and Water Resources.* International Association of Hydrological Sciences Publication no. 168.

Starkel, L., K. J. Gregory, and J. B. Thornes, eds. 1991. *Temperate Palaeohydrology: Fluvial Processes in the Temperate Zone during the Last 15,000 Years.* New York: John Wiley and Sons.

Washington, W. M., and C. L. Parkinson. 1986. *An Introduction to Three-Dimensional Climate Modeling.* Mill Valley, Calif.: University Science Books.

CONVERSIONS AND EQUIVALENTS

Author's Note: Throughout this book I have purposefully commingled English and metric units. Since the Reagan presidency, U.S. students have had to be multilingual when it comes to measurements. Here, in tribute to our former president, are English to metric conversions.

Length

1 in. = 2.54 cm
1 cm = 0.394 in.
1 ft. = 0.3048 m
1 m = 3.281 ft.
1 mi. = 1.609 km
1 km = 0.6241 mi.

Area

1 in.^{2} = 6.452 cm^2
1 cm^2 = 0.1550 in.^{2}
1 ft.^{2} = 929 cm^2
1 m^2 = 10.76 ft.^{2}
1 mi.^{2} = 2.590 km^2
    = 640 ac
1 km^2 = 247.1 ac
    = 0.3861 mi.^{2}

Volume

1 in.^{3} = 16.39 cm^3
1 cm^3 = 0.0610 in.^{3}
1 ft.^{3} = 7.480 U.S. gal.
    = 28317 cm^3
    = 28.32 l
1 m^3 = 35.31 ft.^{3}
    = 264.2 U.S. gal.
1 l = 61.02 in.^{3}
    = 0.2642 U.S. gal.

Weight

1 lb. = 0.4536 kg
1 kg = 2.205 lb.
1 ton = 1,000 kg
    = 2,205 lb.

Velocity

1 ft./sec. = 0.6818 mi./hr.
    1.097 km/hr.
1 m/sec. = 3.6 km/hr.
    2.237 mi./hr.
1 km/hr. = 0.2278 m/sec.
    0.9113 ft./sec.
1 mi./hr. = 1.4767 ft./sec.
    0.4470 m/sec.

Discharge

1 cfs = 0.0283 m^3/sec.
    28.32 l/sec.
    2447 m^3/day
1 cfs for 1 day = 1.98 ac-ft.
1 cms = 35.32 cfs

Other Hydrologic Information

g = 32.2 ft./sec.^{2} = 9.82 m/sec.^{2}
1 in./hr. of runoff from 1 acre = 1 cfs
1 ac-ft. = 325,851 gal.

INDEX

Designer: UC Press Staff
Compositor: Prestige Typography
Text: 10/12 Baskerville
Display: Baskerville
Printer: Malloy Lithographing, Inc.
Binder: Malloy Lithographing, Inc.